CU00747113

Practical Philosophy

ST ANDREWS STUDIES
IN PHILOSOPHY AND PUBLIC AFFAIRS

Founding and General Editor:
John Haldane, University of St Andrews

Practical Philosophy

Ethics, Society and Culture

John Haldane

St Andrews
Studies in
Philosophy and
Public Affairs

imprint-academic.com

Copyright © John Haldane, 2009

The moral rights of the author have been asserted.
No part of this publication may be reproduced in any form
without permission, except for the quotation of brief passages
in criticism and discussion.

Published in the UK by
Imprint Academic, PO Box 200, Exeter EX5 5YX, UK

Published in the USA by
Imprint Academic, Philosophy Documentation Center
PO Box 7147, Charlottesville, VA 22906-7147, USA

ISBN: 978 184540 181 8 (cloth)
ISBN: 978 184540 182 5 (paper)

A CIP catalogue record for this book is available from the
British Library and US Library of Congress

To the memory of the philosophers

Will Aiken (1947–2006)

Jim Child (1941–2005) and

Terry McLaughlin (1949–2006)

fellows and friends

[W]hat is the use of studying philosophy if all that it does for you is to enable you to talk with some plausibility about some abstruse questions of logic, etc., & if it does not improve your thinking about the important questions of everyday life.

Ludwig Wittgenstein

[O]ne may make a great progress in school ethics without ever being the wiser or better man for it, or knowing how to behave him self in the affairs of life more to the advantage of himself or his neighbours than he did before.

George Berkeley

The idea of being 'practical', standing all by itself, is all that remains of a Pragmatism that cannot stand at all. It is impossible to be practical without a Pragma. ... Philosophy is merely thought that has been thought out. It is often a great bore. But man has no alternative, except between being influenced by thought that has been thought out and being influenced by thought that has not been thought out.

G.K. Chesterton

Contents

Foreword

by Lord Sutherland of Houndwood

Even, or perhaps especially, in the time of Aristophanes the idea of connecting the terms 'philosophy' and 'practical' would have raised eyebrows and smiles if not guffaws.

Things have not changed a great deal since then, and as a term of scorn in politics, 'philosophical' ranks only after 'theological' and 'academic' in the hierarchy of dismissal. Yet in so many ways this is to show ignorance of facts and reality. For example, arguably England's most important philosopher, John Locke, wrote his most significant works later in life after many years of engagement in public affairs, and of course his search for foundations for knowledge and belief and their links to his work on toleration and government owed much to his experiences of private and political life in the second half of the seventeenth century. Then again we all know of the case of Spinoza who earned his living as a lens grinder!

An even more startling example of philosopher as man of action is Voltaire. Exiled in Switzerland, he showed the razor sharp opportunism of the entrepreneur in seizing business advantage. The extreme Calvinists then in charge of Geneva, adopted policies, including disenfranchisement of artisans, which drove most makers of pocket watches out of the city. Voltaire invested in creating geographically nearby working conditions which allowed him to build a significant and profitable business manufacturing pocket watches.

Admittedly there are counter examples: notably David Hume who managed to lose the sheep he was instructed to care for on the family farm — justifying his aunt's claim that 'our Davy's uncommon wake-minded'.

However, this book is not engaging in the discussion of that very basic form of 'the practical' and its relationship to philosophy. Nor is it a survey of those philosophers in the recent times who have engaged in the business of policy-making and policy advice although there have been many notable instances, for example A.D. Lindsay and Mary Warnock in England.

John Haldane explores a more significant relationship between practice and philosophy in a series of illuminating directions and contexts.

In essence, there are deep and significant lines of connection between our conception of what it is to act and our understanding of the nature of human beings. This is true in a variety of ways. For example, our view of whether or not human beings are in any sense capable of free or creative acts is fundamental to what it is for human beings to 'do' any of the things which make up the daily dross of experience. Equally, as Peter Strawson brought out in his seminal British Academy Lecture, 'Freedom and Resentment', concepts such as resentment, praise, blame, and so on do not function in a conceptual world devoid of the ideas of responsibility and freedom. The fragile, delicate, (and sometimes robust) relationships which make up so much of the stuff of human life are premised upon an understanding of the nature of human beings, which rules out, for example, accounts which are wholly deterministic.

There is equally a strong connection between our understanding of the nature of human society and the concepts of justice and equality with which we operate. Amartya Sen's recent book *The Idea of Justice*, challenging the dominant views of John Rawls, is set to re-ignite many basic philosophical disputes in this area. That will be interesting and arresting in itself, but beyond that the implications for the practical ways in which we order our society can hardly be overestimated.

The Scots and the Americans have both been aware of the importance of what they call 'useful knowledge' and indeed have built this into the founding documents of their respective Academies. Benjamin Franklin brought this expression with him in his visit to Edinburgh in the middle of the eighteenth century, and the term found its way into the founding document of the Royal Society of Edinburgh.

However, this was not a separation of the aims of philosophy and 'useful knowledge'. To the contrary it was a way of establishing the interconnections between what Hume and others came to describe as the Science of Human Nature, and the decisions of both individual and society about how to live. To this extent at least there is a resonance between the Aristotle and Aquinas on whose insights Haldane builds his discussion, and the empiricism of Hume and his Common Sense Philosophy contemporaries. Both groups shared the view that the practices and policies of life were essentially related to a proper understanding of the nature of human beings and human society.

Stewart Sutherland
December 2009

Preface

The present volume appears in the series St Andrews Studies in Philosophy and Public Affairs which originates in and derives its title from that of the University's Centre for Ethics, Philosophy and Public Affairs. This year (2009) marks a quarter century of the Centre's existence. The original decision in 1984 to create such a centre represented an aspect of the long-standing commitment of the University of St Andrews to teaching and research in moral philosophy: the subject having been part of the curriculum since teaching began here in 1411 under a charter issued by Bishop Wardlaw.

Over the six centuries of its existence not only has moral philosophy been taught, but there is probably no year during which this did not involve some reference to Aristotle's ethical and political writings. In these respects the present book is very much 'in the tradition'. Moreover, as the title and introduction indicate and then explain, the approach to matters of value, conduct and policy developed in these pages is Aristotelian in broad conception and perhaps also in some particulars. The title *Practical Philosophy* is deliberately chosen to emphasise the ultimate direction towards action, and also in opposition to the more recent, and I believe misconceived notions of 'applied philosophy' and 'applied ethics'. The reasons for this opposition are explained in the introduction. This also outlines something of the long history of practical philosophy from antiquity to the present, and addresses the presuppositions of the subsequent enquiries in respect of the objectivity of value and requirement, and of the freedom of human agency. The first matter is discussed only in brief and to distinguish between fact/value and is/ought 'gaps', which are then explored more extensively later. The second matter is considered in greater depth and then not subsequently discussed, though related issues about the nature of human agents as rational bodily animals are explored later on.

The Centre for Philosophy and Public Affairs (as it was first titled) was established with two principal aims. First, to encourage research in those areas of philosophy most pertinent to the discussion of topics of public importance, and secondly to facilitate discussion of those same topics between philosophers and other people (such as politicians, public servants, lawyers, educationalists, and health-care professionals) whose concern is more directly practical.

Among the means through which the first of these aims has been pursued is publications. For most of its history these were occasional small booklets, but in 2004 (following an earlier volume deriving from a Royal institute of Philosophy conference and entitled *Philosophy and Public Affairs*, published in 2000 with Cambridge University Press) the present series was launched with two collections of essays by a variety of authors, almost all professional philosophers: *Values, Education and the Human World*, and *Philosophy and its Public Role*. Since then some dozen or so further volumes have appeared, most by single authors.

Having directed the Centre for most of its history, and conceived the series and overseen its development as general editor, it seemed appropriate in the Centre's twenty-fifth anniversary year, and fifteen volumes in, to contribute a volume on my own account setting out a particular understanding of practical philosophy, and some illustrating its methods and its reach. In doing so I have drawn extensively on a range of essays and acknowledge these sources below. I also wish to take this opportunity to thank the hundred or so individuals who have come to the Centre as visiting fellows or special lecturers and who have enriched the philosophical environment at St Andrews and provided me with instruction, inspiration and correction. The book is dedicated to the memory of three former fellows, Will Aiken of Chatham College, Pittsburgh, Jim Child of Bowling Green State University, Ohio, and Terry McLaughlin of the Universities of Cambridge and London, who sadly have all passed on but who leave others with strong memories of their commitment to practical philosophy and their capacity for deep friendship.

I am grateful to Luis Tellez, to Jesse Tomalty, and especially to Anthony Freeman, who have each contributed in practical ways to the project of composing this volume. Final thanks are due to my wife Hilda and children Kirsty, James, Alice and John for their patience and encouragement.

John Haldane
Centre for Ethics, Philosophy and Public Affairs
University of St Andrews

Introduction

Historical introduction

The Greek historian Herodotus recounts that the great Athenian statesman, legislator and poet, Solon arrived in Sardis the capital of Lydia where he was engaged in conversation by King Croesus. The subject of the exchange was the nature of happiness, and in response to the king's proud assertion that he (Croesus) was the most fortunate and happiest man alive, Solon suggested rivals to the life of great wealth and power and offered the general caution 'Count no man happy until he be dead'. This maxim is later referred to by Aristotle in the course of his own investigation of the nature of happiness as the aim of human life (*Nicomachean Ethics* Bk I, Ch. 10). What is less often quoted from Herodotus are the terms in which Croesus first addresses Solon: 'Stranger of Athens, we have heard much of your wisdom *(sophie)* and of your travels through many lands, from love of knowledge *(hos philosopheon)* and a wish to see and examine the countries of the world' (*Histories*, I. 30).

The meeting was legendary but, had it occurred, the date would have been in the middle of the sixth century BCE and Herodotus did not write his account until over a hundred years later. Even so, his reference to Solon as being one of the sages of Greece, and his quotation of the expressions 'wisdom' and 'love of knowledge' come some fifty years before Plato's *Republic* and eighty or so before Aristotle's *Nicomachean Ethics*. Herodotus's account is, therefore, among the earliest uses of the term 'philosophy' *(philosophia)* to refer to the desire for a true understanding of human life.

Herodotus also tells us that prior to coming to Sardis, Solon had visited the court of Amasis in Egypt. Amasis is sometimes spoken of as the last of the great Egyptian pharaohs, but from Herodotus's account he was initially despised because he was not from a distinguished family, and it was only through his wisdom in judgement and action that he won the people over. Evidently practical wisdom was prized among the Egyptians as well as among the Greeks. In fact it is among the peoples of Egypt and Mesopotamia that the first 'wisdom literature' is to be found, and it later served as a model for both Hebrews and Greeks. Two brief quotations give a flavour of the style and substance of the Egyptian tradition. Both come from sets of guidance prepared by fathers for their sons.[1] The first is from *The Instruction of Ptahhotep* (2300–2150 BC):

> If you are a man who leads, who controls the affairs of the many, seek out every beneficent deed, that your conduct may be blameless. Great is justice, lasting in effect. … Baseness may seize riches, yet crime never lands its wares; in the end it is justice that lasts; for a man can say: 'It is my father's ground' [it was the property of his father before him].

The second is from a century or two later and comes from *The Instruction of Khety for Merikare* (c. 2150 BCE)

> Speak truth in your house, so that the officials of the country may respect you, for a sovereign's renown (lies in) straightforwardness; it is the front room of a house that inspires the back room with respect. … Do justice that you may live long. Calm the weeper, do not oppress the widow, do not oust a man from his father's property … Beware of punishing wrongfully.

There is a notable resemblance between these words, from a court official and a king respectively, and the Solomonic wisdom sayings gathered in the Hebrew Bible in the books of *Proverbs* [of Solomon] *Míshlê Shlomoh*, (1000–600BCE), and in *Ecclesiastes Kohelet* (950–350 BCE). Both the Egyptian and Hebrew authors are concerned

---

[1]   Miriam Lichtheim, *Ancient Egyptian Literature*, 3 volumes (Berkeley, CA: University of California Press, 1975).

with the business of social relations, and in particular the behaviour of those in positions of power, and both direct the intended readers to lives of virtue and practical wisdom. As these traditions develop so there is a noticeable shift from justifications that appeal to readers' self-interest, showing the utility of justice in promoting or protecting this, to reasoning that appeals to the intrinsic merit and beauty of virtue as an attribute of noble character. The Greeks too were aware of this duality of considerations favouring wisdom and virtue, and in the period of Solon and even more in that of Herodotus's account of his meeting with Croesus, it was recognized that in some circumstances these considerations might be in tension. Virtue and advantage in the conduct of life were already matters of serious reflection but they would soon become subjects of disciplined analytical enquiry.

The turning point from sage advice to critical investigation came with Socrates and his method of *elenchus* or dialectical enquiry. So whereas the Egyptians, the Hebrews and the earlier Greeks spoke of justice and listed some of its requirements, Socrates asked the question what is justice? and exposed the inadequacy of conventional responses, as for example in the *Republic* where Plato has him elicit a range of accounts only to demolish them. The technique of disambiguating proposed definitions and challenging them by means of counter examples is central to the Socratic method and its principal effects were negative. It exposed the inadequacy of a series of interlocutors' ideas, and since the characters were introduced as representatives of recurrent lines of thought, served to refute generally held views. It has often been concluded that Socrates' sole purpose was to reveal error and ignorance and not to offer any constructive account of his own. This accusation is put in the *Republic* by Thrasymachus when he is encouraged to offer his definition of justice: ' "Oh yes" he said; "so that Socrates may play the old game of questioning and refuting someone else, instead of giving an answer himself".'[2] Nevertheless he is persuaded to offer an initial definition – 'that 'just' or 'right' means nothing but what is to the interest of the stronger party' (338c) – which is duly refuted! More to the point, however, in the course of his challenge Socrates does advance positive claims as when he says 'I will make no secret of my own conviction, which is that injustice is not more profitable than justice, even when left free to work its will unchecked' (345a), and yet more positively 'any kind of authority, in the state or in private life, must, in its character of authority, consider solely what is best for those under its care' (345d). Arguably this is more a matter of formal analysis of the notion of authority but it points to the idea that justice on the part of the ruler involves directing the people towards some appropriate virtue or excellence.

Socrates marks the beginning of *practical philosophy*: *practical* in being concerned with questions of what one ought to do as an occupant of some social role, or more generally with how one ought to live as a human being; and *philosophy* as being engaged in analytically and dialectically with the aim of arriving at some true account of these matters. Plato carries on the same practice while also taking up issues in epistemology and metaphysics, and on that basis his disciple Xenocrates divided philosophical enquiry into three areas: *ethics*, *dialectic* and *physics* or philosophy of nature. It is only with Aristotle, however, that a systematic and reasoned scheme of the division of philosophy is introduced. Again the broad division is into three parts, this time the *theoretical* (*epistêmê*), the *practical* (*praxis*) and the *creative* (*poiêsis*) corresponding to speculative knowledge, conduct, and manufacture or production. These in turn are subdivided with practical philosophy being distributed between ethics, politics and economics – though these fields are not separated by well-defined boundaries. Because comparatively little of Aristotle was directly inherited in the West, the favoured scheme of division until the twelfth century

[2]   *The Republic of Plato* trans. F.M. Cornford (Oxford: Oxford University Press, 1945) p. 17 and other editions I. 337e.

was the Platonic one, but with the arrival of texts and commentaries from the Arabic world the Aristotelian scheme was reintroduced into medieval thought as in Thomas Aquinas's commentary on the *Nicomachean Ethics*. There he repeats the further Aristotelian point that the principal kinds of philosophical knowledge are specified by their proper objects: *the order of nature* which speculative reason discerns, *the order proper to voluntary actions* which practical reason deliberates, and *the order created through manufacture* which is the business of productive reasoning. Leaving the last to one side, though it is relevant to the subject of the final chapter where I consider the effects of misapplied philosophical thought upon art-making, we arrive at the distinction between speculative and practical philosophy. Distinguishing these with regard to their goals we may either say with Aristotle that speculative thinking (*theôrêtikê dianoia*) is concerned with truth and falsity regarding the orders of reality, while practical thinking (*praktikê dianoia*) is concerned with truth and falsity with respect to action; or else and more familiarly that speculative thinking is aimed at knowing the true, while practical thinking is aimed at achieveing the good.

Interestingly, although Aquinas adopts this theoretical/practical schematisation he rarely uses the expression 'practical philosophy' (*philosophia practica* or *practica philosophia*). In the *Ethics Commentary* when he remarks on Aristotle's threefold division of philosophy, he says that 'the order of voluntary actions pertains to the consideration of moral philosophy' (*Ordo autem actionum voluntariarum pertinet ad considerationem moralis philosophiae*). Indeed, I have only been able to discover one occurrence of the expression *philosophia practica* in the entire corpus of his writings. Aptly enough, it is to be found in the prologue of Thomas's commentary on Aristotle's *Politics* where he writes as follows:

> Since practical sciences are distinguished from the speculative in the respect that the speculative are ordained to the knowing of truth while the practical are ordained to a product, it is necessary that this science [politics] be comprised

under practical philosophy. (*Cum enim scientiae practicae a speculativis distinguantur in hoc quod speculativae ordinantur solum ad scientiam veritatis, practicae vero ad opus; necesse est hanc scientiam sub practica philosophia*).[3]

Perhaps because of its debt to Aristotle's analysis and its Latin origins, it is natural to think of the expression 'practical philosophy' as being common among medieval and scholastic philosophers; but although the general idea is familiar and generally presupposed the expression itself is rare. Indeed, it first comes to prominence not in the middle ages but in the German Enlightenment. In 1703 the philosopher Christian Wolff completed a doctoral dissertation at the University of Leipzig under the supervision of Ehrenfried Walther von Tschirnhaus. The latter was something of a polymath. For in addition to being a philosopher, he was an original mathematician and the inventor of European porcelain. Perhaps this practical orientation had an influence on his student, but at any rate the title of Wolff's dissertation was *Philosophia practica universalis, methodo mathematica conscripta* (*On Universal Practical Philosophy, Composed from the Mathematical Method*). He sent a copy of this to Leibniz who then also used the expression, as did Kant and subsequent German philosophers including Hegel. Evidently Wolff was enduringly concerned with the practical orientation of philosophy for in his work entitled *Logic, or Rational Thoughts on the Powers of the Human Understanding with their Use and Application in the Knowledge and Search of Truth* he writes that '… a person should learn philosophy …[not with] a view to perceive the vicious taste of the schools for idle disputation and wrangling, but in order to [enjoy its] usefulness in future life'.[4]

[3]   Aquinas, *Sententia libri Politicorum*, pr. 6. For a translation of the prologue (by P.H. Conway, O.P, and R.F. Larcher, O.P.) see Mary T. Clark ed. *An Aquinas Reader* (New York: Fordham University Press, 2000).

[4]   Christian Wolff, *Logic, or Rational Thoughts on the Powers of the Human Understanding with their Use and Application in the Knowledge and Search of Truth* (London: L. Hawes, W. Clarke, and R. Collins, 1770) Preface.

The idea that academic philosophy might be taught and practised in such a manner as to detach it from the business of life was also of concern to English language philosophers in the eighteenth century. Indeed Berkeley suggests that even the study of ethics might have become narrowly and impotently academic. In the same decade as Wolff completed his inaugural dissertation the equally young George Berkeley published *A Treatise Concerning the Principles of Human Knowledge* (1710) in the course of which he complains of the distorting effects of intellectual abstraction and adds the following observation in a footnote: 'One may make a great progress in school ethics, without ever being the wiser or better man for it, or knowing how to behave himself, in the affairs of life, more to the advantage of himself, or his neighbour, than he did before.'[5]

Recent influences

From the second half of the seventeenth century until the latter third of the twentieth, however, (and notable exceptions notwithstanding) academic philosophers generally preferred to operate within the narrower compass defined by purely abstract questions about the metaphysics and epistemology of morals. Although Wolff's encouragement and Berkeley's warning went long unheeded, the prejudice that in their professional writings philosophers should only concern themselves with the epistemology, logic and semantics of moral discourse, has largely been set aside. This is owing largely to two philosophers: in Britain Elizabeth Anscombe and in America John Rawls.

In 1939, while a second year undergraduate at Oxford, Anscombe together with a fellow undergraduate Norman Daniel co-authored and published with a pamphlet entitled *The War and the Moral Law*.[6] In the introduction to the third

[5]   G. Berkeley, *Principles of Human Knowledge* in *A New Theory of Vision and Other Writings* (London: Dent & Co., 1960) p.163, note 1.
[6]   In later years Daniel became something of a pioneer in the effort to achieve a sympathetic understanding of Islam. He worked for the British Council in Sudan and in Egypt and authored several works on

volume of her collected papers (*Ethics, Religion and Politics* (Oxford: Blackwell, 1981) in which the essay is reproduced, Anscombe explains that she and Daniel described the pamphlet as presenting 'a Catholic view'. This led to a demand from the Archbishop of Birmingham, communicated to Daniel by the Catholic University Chaplain, that the pamphlet be withdrawn on the grounds that not having sought or received an imprimatur the authors had no right to describe it as 'Catholic'. Anscombe, who was twenty at the time of writing the essay, explains that while they obeyed nevertheless they both thought the demand to be 'wrong and unreasonable'. She goes on to say that when, in 1956, she opposed the conferment of an honorary degree by Oxford on President Truman, the then Master of University College (A.L. Goodhart, an American and Professor of Jurisprudence) 'sneered at my 'hindsight' about the conduct of the war by the massacre of civilian populations: the pamphlet shows that this was already seen by us as what was going to happen, and as lying in the intention of our rulers, in 1939'. She adds, with characteristic honesty, 'My remarks about the 'injustice of the Treaty of Versailles were, I fear, a mere repetition of the common propaganda of the day'.

For the most part Anscombe's subsequent work as a professional philosopher was highly academic. Yet she continued from her student days the practice of discussing and writing about issues of moral and political significance. When in 1956 she protested Oxford University's plan to award President Truman a degree she charged that since he had commanded the murderous use of nuclear weapons against innocent Japanese civilians it was evident that he was an agent of great evil, and that to honour him would be to 'share in the guilt of a bad action by praise and flattery'. Perplexed by defenders of Truman she came to the conclusion that they failed to understand the nature of his actions, and it was this that led her to write *Intention* which is gener-

the subject including the much praised *Islam and the West: The Making of an Image* (1972; revised edition 1993).

ally acknowledged to be one of the most profound explorations of the subject of practical reason and action.

I discuss the work of John Rawls at some length, and largely critically, in chapters 8, 9 and 10; but here let me emphasise a point made more than once in later chapters, namely that the revival of practical philosophy in the American academy, and among those whom it influenced, owed more to Rawls than to any other figure. The origins and development of Rawls's academic interest in matters of ethics and politics is better known than that of Anscombe, save in one respect to which I will return in a moment. In 1950 Rawls completed a PhD thesis *A Study in the Grounds of Ethical Knowledge: Considered with Reference to Judgments on the Moral Worth of Character*, and the following year published 'Outline of a Decision Procedure for Ethics' *Philosophical Review* (April 1951). Four years later he published 'Two Concepts of Rules' *Philosophical Review* (January 1955) influenced by his study with H.L.A. Hart in Oxford, and in 1958 'Justice as Fairness' again in the *Philosophical Review* (April 1958). These were much reprinted in various anthologies and supplemented by a couple of more articles before the publication in 1971 of *A Theory of Justice*. The effect of this, coming at a point when the anti-Vietnam War movement had grown to its strongest, in the wake of a decade of race riots, of the Kent State shooting of four protesting students, and in the lead-up to the Roe vs Wade Supreme Court decision on Abortion, was considerable. It was evident that one could engage in serious, rigorous, complex philosophical argumentation to a practical end.

So put the point sounds formal, abstracted from moral substance and motivation. With regard to the former, Rawls's commitment to, and argument for welfare liberalism is explicit in *A Theory of Justice*, and as regards the latter there is now a new source to consider. In 1942 Rawls submitted his senior thesis to the philosophy department at Princeton. Its title was *A Brief Inquiry into Sin & Faith: An Interpretation Based on the Concept of Community*. At the time of writing Rawls was a believing Christian influenced by liberal protestantism. Quite what that amounted to is an uncertain matter save to the extent that it was marked by a strong ethical commitment. The parallelism between the shift within liberal Christianity from dogmatic to moral theology and Rawls's move from speculative to practical philosophy is worth exploring, and with the recent publication of Rawls's Princeton thesis such studies are likely to be pursued in the near future, not least in PhD theses at Princeton.[7]

Practical and 'applied' philosophy

To this point I have spoken exclusively of 'practical philosophy' and it might well be remarked that the turn from theory to practice has more often been described in terms of the rise of 'applied philosophy'. I have avoided this expression thus far for two reasons. First, so far as I am aware, it does not occur prior to 1970 with the publication of an article of the same title by Leslie Stevenson in the journal *Metaphilosophy*,[8] hence it is not part of any earlier self-description. Second, and more importantly, however, the idea represents a quite different conception of the relation of philosophical thought to action than was envisaged by the notion of practical philosophy. For the advocate of applied philosophy the relationship is as Stevenson describes it:

> [Just as there is] an academic subject of applied mathematics, not very clearly distinct from pure mathematics on one side and not sharply defined from industrial and commercial applications on the other; so why should their not be a somewhat loosely defined discipline of applied philosophy, with a fuzzy borderline with pure philosophy on one side, and branching out into multifarious everyday problems on the other? (p. 261).

In the earlier tradition, by contrast, the distinction is not between 'pure' and 'applied' philosophy but between two forms of philosophical thought directed respectively to the resolution of speculative and practical questions. The con-

[7]   See John Rawls, *A Brief Inquiry into the Meaning of Sin & Faith (with 'On My Religion')*, ed. Thomas Nagel (Cambridge, MA: Harvard University Press, 2009).

[8]   Leslie Stevenson, 'Applied Philosophy', *Metaphilosophy*, 1 (1970).

trast between 'pure' and 'applied' enquiries does not correspond to this older distinction, and if it is to be pressed upon it then it may well cut across the speculative/practical contrast. More importantly, however, the 'pure'/'applied' division is liable to prejudice thinking about practical questions by favouring a way of approaching them that envisages the essential philosophical work as engaged in *and* completed antecedently, and then simply brought to bear, in a more or less mechanical way, upon some practical issue. There is at least one style of moral philosophy that conforms to this model, namely utilitarianism in which the general theory is conceived and developed independently and is then brought in to process particular contingent issues. The problem with this, however, is that it is antecedently, and hence prejudicially committed to subsuming morally-relevant aspects of a question or issue in terms of some previously constructed evaluative category – in this case utility.

Practical philosophy, by contrast, harbours no such prejudices. It begins with questions posed by some area of human practice and has no prior interest in bringing these under some master concept. In consequence it is open to the idea that the relevant evaluative, normative and prescriptive notions may be subject-specific and not instances of more general notions. Thus in considering the ethics of warfare, for example, it has been customary for practical philosophy, going back at least as far as the Iberian scholastics of the sixteenth century, when considering the facts of the matter to draw a morally significant distinction between combatants and non-combatants. This, however, is informed 'from below', not derived 'from above'; in other words it is a philosophical response to a real distinction in the domain of practice, not a derivation of a philosophical concept from the sphere of abstract theorizing. Further examples may easily be arrived at. Some, besides those deriving from reflection upon the business of military defence, are identified and explored in the following chapters.

Two challenges to practical philosophy

Having said something about the history of practical philosophy, and distinguished it from the idea of applied philosophy, I now want to identify two objections to the possibility of such an undertaking. The first is rooted in ethical subjectivism, and more precisely in the idea that insofar as practical philosophy is thought to be an enquiry into practical truth or objective goodness it rests on the mistake of assuming that there are such things. For the subjectivist, thoughts about conduct can at most be reflections upon attitudes of approbation or sentiments of approval, be they individual, communal or universal. It is worth observing that even if that were so it would not rule out a form of enquiry into conduct and policy, but it would convert that into a psychological or sociological study, possibly supplemented by some elements drawn from decision theory.

Here though there is a dilemma for the subjectivist: either principles of rational choice are themselves expressions or reports of approbation, or else they are objectively true or correct. If the former then the supplement to psychology or sociology is just more of the same; and if the latter then why not allow objective truth or correctness with respect to the initial body of thought about value and conduct? This is not an argument against subjectivism but it is a challenge to the idea of mixing it with elements of objectivity. So far as the force of the former is concerned it tends to rest on arguments either deriving from or analogous to those of David Hume who argues against the possibility of moral truth and aginst the possibility of deriving statements of requirement from matters of fact. I discuss these issues in chapter 2 and at several places therafter but it may be helpful at this early stage to explain how I understand the Humean challenges to evaluative and prescriptive objectivity.

First, I regard them as distinct but closely related arguments. That is to say I read the fact/value and is/ought distinctions as these feature in Hume's philosophy as being different distinctions. Hume writes as follows:

Take any action allowed to be vicious: Wilful murder, for instance. Examine it in all lights, and see if you can find that matter of fact, or real existence, which you call vice. In whichever way you take it, you find only certain passions, motives, volitions and thoughts. There is no other matter of fact in the case. The vice entirely escapes you, as long as you consider the object. You never can find it, till you turn your reflection into your own breast, and find a sentiment of disapprobation, which arises in you, towards this action. Here is a matter of fact; but it is the object of feeling, not of reason. It lies in yourself, not in the object. So that when you pronounce any action or character to be vicious, you mean nothing, but that from the constitution of your nature you have a feeling or sentiment of blame from the contemplation of it.[9]

I cannot forbear adding to these reasonings an observation, which may, perhaps, be found of some importance. In every system of morality, which I have hitherto met with, I have always remarked, that the author proceeds for some time in the ordinary way of reasoning, and establishes the being of a God, or makes observations concerning human affairs; when of a sudden I am surprized to find, that instead of the usual copulations of propositions, is, and is not, I meet with no proposition that is not connected with an ought, or an ought not. This change is imperceptible; but is, however, of the last consequence. For as this ought, or ought not, expresses some new relation or affirmation, it is necessary that it should be observed and explained; and at the same time that a reason should be given, for what seems altogether inconceivable, how this new relation can be a deduction from others, which are entirely different from it. (*ibid.*)

As I read them, and as Hume's language suggests, these are distinct arguments to different conclusions. The first is part of an extended reflection on the idea of moral knowledge intended to show that insofar as this presumes moral truth there can be no such thing, since if there were to be moral truths they would either have to reside in 'relations of ideas' (and hence be a priori), or else correspond to 'matters of fact' (and be a posteriori). At this stage in the extended argu-

[9]   David Hume, *A Treatise of Human Nature*, ed. L. A. Selby-Bigge (Oxford: Clarendon Press, 1978) and other editions Bk III, Part I, section 1.

ment, having eliminated to his own satisfaction the former possibility, he is concerned to show that they neither consist in nor are implied by (non-evaluative) matters of fact. The second argument, by contrast, concerns the question as to whether it can ever be valid to derive a statement of requirement or prescription from a statement of fact. It is natural given the previous argument to think of this as equivalent to the fact/value distinction but Hume's is a logical point which if sound would equally well apply to the attempt to move from statements of value to prescriptions for action. As will emerge, I regard both of Hume's arguments as resistable, and I find the counter to them in a form of ethical naturalism akin to the 'natural law' approach, so called, of Aristotle and Aquinas. I shall not develop the points further at this stage but alert the reader to the fact that the reasoning that seeks to close the fact/value gap resides in a teleological understanding of the nature of the human animal, while the closing of the is/ought gap is achieved through an understanding of that animal's practical rationality.

Determinism and the problem of freedom

The second challenge to the possibility of practical philosophy derives not from an alternative account of the status of values and directives but from a view of the nature of human action. Practical philosophy seeks to arrive at conclusions about how one one ought to act, what we ought to do, what ought to be made, and so on. But deliberating about alternative courses and policies seems to presuppose the possibility that these are open to one, not as an issue of practical availability merely but more fundamentally as a matter of free choice. That is to say practical deliberation appears to presuppose that it is up to the agent(s) to decide how he, she or they may act. This presupposition may be defeated in particular circumstances but this possibility does not impugn the general assumption of liberty. It has often been thought, however, that the idea of ourselves as free agents is threatened by the claim that the course of events in which we participate is strictly and completely determined by prior events which are themselves the causal consequence of yet earlier episodes, and so on back beyond the time of our conception to the earliest stage of the universe. Contrary to modern compatibilist traditions that seek to reconcile the ideas of free action and of causal determinism I believe that this threat is real.

If universal causal determinism is true then we are not free. For example, if it were the case that the ascent of my arm from my side upwards, as I illustrate a movement, is entirely causally determined as the upshot of a series of events leading backwards from muscle contractions to nerve stimulations to brain events and so on, then although that movement may be characterized as an action, and I may be described as its agent, I am not freely responsible for it. All that has happened is that the course of world events has passed through my body.

As I mentioned, however, there are traditions of modern compatibilism which take issue with this view of the implications of determinism. Let me describe and comment on two of these traditions. First, following Hume, some philosophers have sought to provide an analysis of the idea of freedom purporting to show that what we mean by this (and all we could mean by it) is not in contradiction to the claim that our actions are causally determined. Thus we are told that to say that an action was *free*, and that the agent is thereby responsible for it, is to say that it was *unforced* and *unconstrained*. Take the case in which we say that I moved my arm. If it was not driven upwards by an external agent or thrown up in an involuntary spasm induced by a drug, etc., but arose as a causal consequence of a decision, then it was a free action, one exhibiting *liberty of spontaneity*. 'Free' means unconstrained: the agent could have done otherwise.

But suppose we respond to this by saying that if determinism is true and the action was caused by the decision then in reality I was not free. Here the compatibilist reply is that when it is said that I could have done otherwise what this meant is not that given this very same decision (as cause) some other event might have resulted, but rather that had my decision been different then so might have been the resulting action. In other words 'A could have done otherwise' is analysed as 'A would have done otherwise if the antecedent had been different in certain respects'. Well, of course, *that* is compatible with causal determinism. The problem, however, is that it leaves the prior antecedents themselves causally determined, and is incompatible with the claim that even had the immediate antecedents been the same I could have done otherwise than as I did. What I take the claim of free agency to amount to in such a circumstance is the idea that prior to acting it was not determined what would ensue. In the limiting case just the same antecedents might have obtained in conjunction with different consequences. The difference between the outcomes being ascribable to the agent's power of free choice; his *liberty of indifference*.

One rejoinder to this is to add to the empirical claim that all events are causally determined by prior events, the so-called 'logical paradox of freedom'. This is a dilemma purporting to force what would be free action into the category of random behaviour. Either actions are determined or they are not. But if what I do is *not* the causal consequence of my prior states, and different courses of action can follow upon (what is anyhow a fiction) the same antecedents, then this means that the direction of movement arises in a random and uncontrolled fashion. My arm might go up, it might stay down, it might wave around wildly and so on; but what it does is not influenced by prior events. Who would want to try and place an account of action within such a chaotic picture?

Two points need to be made in reply. First, the claim that an event is either *determined* or *random* (in the sense of unconditioned chance) remains an assertion which nowadays lacks even the support (apparently) once given it by physical theory. Clearly these are *contrary* predicates: something cannot be both determined and random; but it has to be shown that they are *contradictories*: that it is not possible that something may be neither, that there is no *tertium quid*. However, and quite independently of the issue of human action, physical theory no longer holds that all causation conforms to exceptionless laws, but now regards sequences of events at the microphysical level as conforming to patterns that are precisely instances of non-determined, non-random behaviour. This is because it views them as possessing indeterminate probabilities.

While the reflective advocate of free action will not want to identify the liberty of human choice with the indeterminacy of quantum systems, none the less he too claims that there is an alternative to determinacy and chance. Moreover, he may see a parallel between on the one hand the notion of objective probabilities rooted in the natures of physical systems, and on the other the idea of behavioural tendencies issuing from habitual rational agency. Physical events and human actions may both admit of a high degree of predictability without either resulting from deterministic causes. In the case of the former prediction is based on natural propensities, in the case of the latter upon rational inclinations and responses. Second and relatedly, the believer in freedom should reject the claim that the only influences there can be upon events are other prior events. It may be true to say that an action is not (wholly) influenced by these, yet also true that it is influenced by the agent whose action it is. This is an idea that needs further discussion and shortly I will consider more generally the nature of human agents.

Before that, however, I need to address the second kind of compatibilism that is familiar in analytical philosophy. This holds that even to think that there could be a threat to agency from causal determinism is to make a mistake. The suggestion is that causality is appropriate to physiological accounts of the dynamics of the human body, but that when one turns to the explanation of action then causal explanations are never or only rarely at issue. So we may ask how did my arm move upwards? and find an answer in the course of prior physiological events; but if we are concerned with my *action* then the relevant question is why did I move my arm? and the answer will specify my wants, intentions and purposes. Moreover, to specify these is not to identify *causes* of my action but to characterize it as intentional under some description, e.g., as illustrating a philosophical point. To do this, however, is not to go 'behind' the action; but to place it in a context which renders it intelligible. And whether it is intelligible or not, whether it makes sense as appropriate in the circumstances, is quite independent of the question of the causation of the movement.

I feel somewhat ambivalent about this view because while I do not believe that it resolves the question of free action, I think it is right to insist that the explanation of human action is only rarely, if ever, a matter of causal explanation in the sense of 'causal' standardly employed by analytical philosophers; that is, explanation by reference to a set of prior events which, among those occurring at the earlier time, were individually necessary and jointly sufficient for the later occurrence in question. I believe that action explanation is causal, but that it is so in a *variety* of ways corresponding to all of and more than Aristotle's four (be)causes.[10] One of these forms is that adverted to above, i.e., explanation by re-description. Whereas many Wittgensteineans would probably want to deny that this is a kind of causal explanation, I am happy, and indeed would prefer, to say that it is causal, but then to add that the causality is formal and not efficient. That is to say it specifies the behaviour by giving a principle of identity for it: *What is he doing?* is a question of the form: *What is it? (quid est?)* to which the answer might be: this is a case of illustrating a philosophical point.

So long as the terms are properly understood it may be that to speak of causation in this connection need not involve taking deep issue with the Wittgensteineans. Certainly it is not to subscribe to the anti-Wittgensteinean orthodoxy established by Donald Davidson's classic essay 'Actions, Reasons and Causes'.[11] But I do want to insist against many who have written in the anti-causal tradition that their interpretative or hermeneutic accounts of action

[10]   See John Haldane, 'Gravitas, Efficacy and Social Causes', *Analysis*, 68 (2008).

[11]   See D. Davidson, 'Actions, Reasons and Causes' in *Davidson, Essays on Actions and Events* (Oxford: Oxford University Press, 2001).

explanation do not in and of themselves resolve the issue of freedom and responsibility. For while it may be the case that my behaviour is describable in intentional terms, as doing this or that, if the dynamic history of my body is causally determined then I am *not* the agent of those sequences of movement described as actions. If determinism is true then it is simply not the case that what took place occurred because I wanted to illustrate a point. Rather it happened because of antecedent physiological events. The price of maintaining the two-explanations story in this form is a certain kind of anti-realism about action descriptions and explanations. The changing patterns of description-independent events and states are accounted for causally, but they are given certain other descriptions relative to a scheme of interpretation. It is as if one were to watch the movements of seeds blown around in the wind and view them as being like dancing — choreographically describable after the fact. But the movements themselves are not choreographed, and the fact of the matter is one of non-rational causation. The point to keep sight of is that in the familiar senses of 'do' or 'make happen' it just will not be true on this account that we do things or make them happen. Rather, things happen in and through us. To repeat my opening claim: if universal causal determinism is true then we are not free. What libertarianism requires, therefore, is at least an account of how it might be possible for human beings to be free agents. This I shall try to provide.

Human agency

Notwithstanding periodic announcements of the end of speculative and practical reasoning, philosophical problems neither die nor go away. They do, however, periodically undergo reformulation. The question of freedom of action provides one such example insofar as it relates to the general issue of the relationship between personhood, as this involves the possession of powers of cognition and intentional activity, and material constitution. For much of the period of modern philosophy this issue was discussed in terms which have invited the general description 'the mind/body problem'. More recently, however, there has been increasing attention given to the nature of action, and this, I suggest, should encourage us to consider the merits of reformulating the old issue of the relationship between personhood and embodiment as 'the agent/body problem'.[12] Cast as a question, the issue is this: what is the nature of the relation between human agents and the bodies with which they are associated? or again, what is the relationship between an action and the bodily movement, if there is one, with which it appears to be closely correlated?

I remarked that this way of raising the issue of the constitution of persons is different to its older formulation, i.e., as the 'mind/body problem'. This seems to be confirmed by general philosophical discussions which catalogue various theories of persons relating them to familiar views of the mind advanced by historical figures such as Descartes, Spinoza, Locke, Hume, etc. Setting aside certain fragmentary statements of some sorts of teleological physicalism, the first developed position on this issue appears to be that of Plato who is usually characterized as a clear advocate of mind/body dualism. There are difficulties with this characterization, but I am not concerned with these save to the extent of wanting to draw attention to the fact that even for Plato (whose interests so far as the metaphysics of personhood are concerned are more in the area of cognition than of action) there is none the less a philosophical issue as to how intelligent behaviour is related to bodily movements. The problem arises again in connection with the nature of different forms of explanation and is addressed in a philosophically powerful passage in the *Phaedo*. Complaining of the inadequacies of Anaxagoras's explanatory metaphysics Socrates remarks:

> I might compare him to a person who began by maintaining generally that mind is the cause of the actions of Socrates, but who, when he endeavoured to explain the causes of

[12] See, for example, the essays in J. Heil & A. Mele (eds.), *Mental Causation* (Oxford: Clarendon Press, 1993).

my several actions in detail, went on to show that I sit here because my body is made up of bones and muscles ... and as the bones swing in their sockets, through the contraction or relaxation of the muscles I am able to bend my limbs ... and he would have a similar explanation of my talking to you ... There is surely a strange confusion of causes and conditions in all this. It may be said, indeed, that without bones and muscles and the other parts of the body I cannot execute my purposes. But to say at the same time that I act from mind, and that I do as I do because of them and not from the choice of the best, is a very careless and idle mode of speaking. I wonder that they cannot distinguish the cause from the condition without which the cause would never be the cause; it is the latter, I think, which the many, feeling about in the dark, are always mistaking and mis-naming 'cause'.[13]

Plato, as we should expect, has discovered an important idea, namely, the difference between explanations of actions by reference to reasons and explanation by reference to prior material dispositions of, and events in, related bodies. However, Plato's manner of marking this distinction is liable to be confusing to those familiar only with the modern 'reasons and causes' literature. For one thing, the 'mind' whose role is adverted to in the report of Anaxagoras's view, and again that to which Plato is himself inclined to look in explanation of action, is not that of any given human agent whose behaviour is being made sense of. Rather, it is something quasi or wholly abstract such as a set of universal principles which orders all events in the *Kosmos* according to the requirements of reason, that is according to 'what is best'. Another, and conceptually more troublesome difference, is that whereas there is now a familiar, though controversial, tradition of distinguishing reasons and causes of behaviour, and of rejecting the latter as relevant only to the explanation of physiological events, Plato reserves the title of 'cause' for whatever rational principle, i.e., reason, directs human actions — through, as he puts it, choices for the best. The operative physiological events and processes Plato then consigns to the category of

[13] *Phaedo* trans. B. Jowett (Oxford: Clarendon Press, 1903) pp. 241-2, and other editions 98c-99c.

'conditions'. In other words, for Plato the cause of an action is a reason effective through a choice, the reason in question being that the action is for the best.

In classifying reasons as causes, then, Plato is apparently at odds with more recent writers who have denied both this and the related thesis that rationalization is a species of causal explanation. By the same token his view *seems* to place him on the side of those who follow Davidson in favouring a causal theory of action. In fact, however, Plato's position cannot so easily be mapped into the structure of modern discussions. None the less, it is worth returning to as a source for thinking about agency and reason, and later I shall suggest that one aspect in particular of Plato's position needs serious attention—that concerning universal principles directing action 'for the best'.

The explanation of action

At this point, however, I want to focus more clearly on what, due largely to the work and influence of Davidson, has become the orthodox contemporary view about the nature of action and its explanation, and for convenience I quote a concise statement of this orthodoxy:

> Our bodily actions are best understood as movements of our bodies or their parts caused by the beliefs and desires that explain those actions of which those bodily movements are manifestations; in bodily action, belief and desire cause, often via a decision, our bodies to move. The grounds for thinking that the relation between beliefs and desires, on the one hand, and bodily actions that they explain on the other, is causal are the same as the grounds for distinguishing a person's real reasons that are not good from good reasons that are not really his, that is, rationalisations of what he does, by saying that the first, but not the second, causes him to do what he does; no other way to make the distinction clear seems known.[14]

The argument given in the second half of this passage is widely favoured by causal theorists and as this passage sug-

---

[14] See W. D. Hart, *Engines of the Soul* (Cambridge: Cambridge University Press., 1988), p. 169.

gests it is usually thought to be conclusive. As I noted, my own view is that in the sense of 'cause' intended by these and other modern authors the causal theory is false. I also believe that the argument given above is, again on the relevant reading of 'cause', inconclusive. Suppose someone places a bowl of fruit in a patch of sunlight on a table by the window. We ask why did she do this? and a list of reasons suggests itself: she supposed it would add to the appeal of the room; she thought the fruit looked better in the sunlight; she wanted the heat to release the aroma of the oranges; she needed to ripen the fruit; she was trying to conceal a stain on the tablecloth, etc. All of these and more might serve to render the action intelligible, yet it seems reasonable to suppose that not all of them were actually relevant to her behaviour on this occasion. Now for Davidson and Hart the only way to single out *the* reason is by asking which of these possible rationalizations mentions something that was also the *cause* of her action, the antecedent condition sufficient for it.

But rather than providing an argument for the causal theory this way of approaching the matter already assumes that in order to explain what someone is doing it is necessary to identify something 'lying behind it', in a more or less literal interpretation of those words. I believe that this is a mistake and that it is related to an error in the theory of (cognitive) intentionality according to which the only way of saying what someone is thinking is to identify something else that is related to his mental activity. Here the picture is of thought as a kind of featureless medium through which one becomes related to objects, like a projection ray in reverse. Thus one would distinguish possible thoughts a subject might be having from the thought he is actually engaged in by looking to see what object both terminates the thinking and is its cause. There are many things wrong with this view. A very obvious one is that there may be no object, real or ideal, of which one is thinking, and *a fortiori* none to cause this. Instead, therefore, we should realize that we specify thoughts by their intentional content and that this is constituted by exercises of concept which serve as the formal principles of the thinking activity. Similarly, one may distinguish between an agent's possible and actual reasons by providing ever more specific and contextually related descriptions of what he or she is actually doing. In order to know why the subject placed the fruit where she did one does not need to look at something else — a causal ancestry, in the Davidsonian sense — but only to enquire further as to the circumstances (past, present and future) of the agent and her behaviour.[15]

What emerges from this alternative way of viewing matters is an account of thought and action as exercises of rational and appetitive powers. To understand how an agent may act freely on a given occasion one needs to ask how is it possible that a living thing should act at all. Stones are moved by external forces but, as the Aristotelian scholastics say, agents are moved 'from within' (*ab intrinseco*). What this means is something very different from the 'motions' suggested by present-day causal theorists. A compatibilist may very well say that the immediate causes of what he is willing to regard as free action are to be found inside the agent; indeed some compatibilists make the spatial location of the proximate causes (in or *outside* the body) the ultimate criterion of whether the resulting behaviour is the agent's. But this is clearly a desperate measure. 'Did he jump or was he pushed?' 'Well, he was sort of pushed by something inside, so I suppose he jumped.' There really is no prospect of finding a coherent account of agency along these lines, never mind of making good sense of liberty.

What is required instead is that the ideas of non-random indeterminacy, of rationality and of interior principles of movement be brought together in a more satisfactory fashion. The alternative method of reason-identification

[15] For further discussion of these and related issues see John Haldane 'Folk Psychology and the Explanation of Human Behaviour', *Proceedings of the Aristotelian Society*, Supp. Vol. 62 (1988) reprinted in S. Christensen & D. Turner (eds.), *Folk Psychology and the Philosophy of Mind* (Hillsdale, NJ: Erlbaum, 1993); and 'Theories, Concepts and Common Sense: A Reply to Paul Churchland', *Proceedings of the Aristotelian Society*, 93 (1993). In each case my essay is preceded by another by Paul Churchland who offers a very different view.

sketched above provides a clue as to how this might be done. But it also calls for a more general account of persons as embodied agents. We are rational animals; that is to say we are living things whose principles of organization and functioning are ordered towards a form of life that is responsive to reason, to what, borrowing Plato's words, 'is the best'.

One may allow that in attributing behaviour to an agent one is identifying its efficient cause while yet denying that the cause is anything other than the agent himself. That is to say, one need not suppose that what explains its happening is the occurrence of a prior event. Analyses of these forms of action description and explanation show that there is no entailment of such events, for in saying that *A* Φ*ed* we are only committed to two items: the occurrence of an event or process, the Φ*ing*, and a source of this, viz., *A*. Even if we add that *A* Φ*ed* 'because he wanted to' (or more awkwardly 'because he had a want to do so') this does not entail the existence of something distinct from the action and the agent: a mental state or event 'inside' him, a want. Rather, the natural way of describing this situation is to say that *A* Φ*ed voluntarily*, i.e., that the agent's behaviour issued from him in a certain way. Indeed it is perhaps more accurate to say that in being told that he wanted to do it, we are informed that the behaviour did *not* issue in any one of an indefinite number of ways that would have rendered it involuntary. The point here is that there is a presumption in favour of voluntariness.

Voluntary action is a capacity of rational agents, but the point about agency and behaviour requiring no intermediary is more general. Among the things that there are, are natural substances, i.e., unified subjects of predication that are not themselves predicated of anything else. Such substances have characteristic powers of action and reaction; and sometimes their names convey these powers directly. Thus if we hear that something is an *acid* we know that in certain sorts of circumstances (which we may not be able to specify) it will exert a corrosive effect. Similarly, we know that if something is an *animal* then it has organic powers, typically ones of metabolism, growth and reproduction. In explaining an occurrence by mentioning its agent we are adverting to the operation of such powers as providing a full and adequate account. It is a mistake to think that if a substance is cited as the cause of an event the latter *must* be due to some other event having taken place inside the agent. What it is to be an agent is to be possessed of certain powers which there are tendencies to exercise in appropriate circumstances. Certainly, if such a power is actualized one may well look for a prior event that was the occasion for this, but in doing so it will generally be more appropriate to look to the surrounding environment than to the substance itself, for the operation of the power will usually be in response to an external event.

In the case of intelligent agents the relevant power is that of rational willing. Doubtless, much needs to be said about the structure of motivation, but for present purposes I only want to emphasize that in trying to provide an analysis of the will one need not (and one should not) think of this in terms of a mechanism the various parts of which are brought into operation.in sequence, as one element begins to exert an influence on the next. Instead one should think of a structural description that relates aspects of agency to one another without assuming that these are distinct items. Thus when I mentioned 'rational willing' I meant to suggest a kind of power the understanding of which requires that one see it as expressed in intrinsically intelligible behaviour.

The picture then is this. When a human being acts there may be no event that is the cause of his or her behaviour, or if there is this event may be an external occurrence to which the behaviour is a rational response. But in the latter case, as in the former, there need be no event in the agent prior to the action and which is its immediate cause. This is not to deny that actions are caused, but merely to insist that the only cause they need have is the agent whose powers are exercised thereby. In a mature human being these powers are possessed continuously even when, as we would say, he or she is not doing anything 'in particular'. Consider how different this is to the 'constant kicking' picture of the standard causal theory. In that, agents are viewed as naturally inactive but as liable to undergo changes (mental events) which give rise to movements (actions). Movement then calls for an explanation, and since it is very frequent in the life of a complex creature such as man we get the idea of a constant series of events kicking the nerves and muscles into action.

Actions and the good

On the alternative picture of agency which I am recommending most action calls for no explanation. If one knows that one is dealing with a rational animal then there is no need to say why it is doing things, for animals are active by nature (even sitting quietly and sleeping are activities). The absence of a need to offer explanations arises from two facts: that activity is the norm, and that most activity is normal, i.e., it is what would be expected of a reasonable human being in familiar circumstances. The first point is a general one true of all agents, rational and otherwise; but the second point returns me to Plato's remark about 'acting from mind' and 'from the choice of the best'. If we say that a piece of behaviour is an action then we are committed to the claim that in doing it the agent was aiming at some end (even if this is just the performance of an action of that sort). Action differs from mere movement in being purposeful, in advancing an interest of the agent. This thought is what lies beyond the scholastic tag that all action is performed under the species of the good (*sub specie boni*), and I believe it provides a plausible interpretation of Aquinas's first principle of practical reason that good is to be done and evil avoided (*bonum est faciendum et prosequendum et malum vitandum*) and of the remarks from the *Phaedo*.

Rather more needs to be said about this and I shall return to it in later chapters, but the obvious point to raise is whether the claim is that every action is necessarily directed towards a real good (or in the case of Plato *the* good), or merely to what is believed by the agent to be a good. Clearly, the second interpretation is weaker and I believe it is what authors such as Anscombe had in mind when they spoke of actions being performed under some 'desirability characterization'.[16] Although the latter account may seem to be the more plausible I want to end by suggesting that the former deserves further consideration. In the case of non-rational agents it is reasonable, both philosophically and as part of biological science, to maintain that their powers and tendencies are ordered or adapted to objective natural goods. If the general pattern is to be maintained we should then say that the power of rational choice is similarly directed towards states objectively beneficial to the agent. But that claim seems to be refuted by the fact that agents are forever choosing objective evils. (Here I am content to speak of natural goods and evils, leaving to one side for now the question how moral values are related to these.) One might respond to this, however, by considering whether the 'evil' of what is chosen attaches to the time and place of its being chosen, or to the further end for which it is selected, or to its incompatibility with a higher good, etc. That is to say, it may be that every end of action is objectively good in some respect relevant to the agent's real interests as a being of a certain sort, but that this goodness is more or less partial and reduced by the sorts of features I have listed. I take it that this thought is part of what lies behind the idea that evil is a privation — to adapt words of Wittgenstein (regarding sensation), not a something but not strictly a nothing either.

My conclusion, then, is that rational agents act freely when they exercise a power of choice with respect to an end conceived of as good. The agent is the cause of his or her action not through causing mental events or necessarily as a result of prior events. Rather, acting follows upon being, upon being a substance of a certain kind; in the human case a rational substance. Substantial natures, causal powers and rational tendencies towards the good: these are some of the metaphysical aspects of human agency and the conditions of the possibility of practical philosophy in my conception of it.

[16] See G.E.M. Anscombe, *Intention* (Oxford: Blackwell, 1957).

Conclusion

As these last sections have indicated, practical philosophy may involve moving between matters of ethics and metaphysics. Equally it may involve weaving between (or combining) political philosophy and theory of persons, aesthetics and epistemology, and so on. These and other such movements will be observed in the following chapters which range across a number of fields and topics. What unites them is in part a common understanding of the nature of human value, in part an expanding movement from general to particular issues, but also the influence of two styles of philosophical thought: on the one hand that of Aristotelianism as developed by Aquinas and later thomists; and on the other that of contemporary analytical moral, social and political philosophy.

In other writings on issues in philosophy of mind, metaphysics and philosophy of religion I have used the expression 'analytical thomism' to characterise a synthesis of these styles of thought, and this has occasioned an amount of discussion.[17] This is not the place to explore the interesting question raised about the compatibility of these approaches but I hope that something of the fruitfulness of cross-pollination is evident in the discussions that follow.

[17] See John Haldane, *Faithful Reason* (London: Routledge, 2004) and *Reasonable Faith* (London: Routledge, 2010); also *Analytical Thomism: Traditions in Dilaogue* eds C. Paterson and M. Pugh (London: Ashgate, 2006).

1

Practical Ethics

Introduction

Practical ethics is a branch of moral philosophy involving the systematic use of philosophical thinking to identify and resolve questions of values and conduct as these arise in the various departments of human life.[1] A major development of practical ethics in recent years has been 'professional ethics'. This concerns conduct engaged in as part of the exercise of a form of work generally associated with training, expertise and accreditation. Wherever there is professional activity there is the possibility of ethical dilemmas involving conflicts of responsibilities, loyalties and goals. It is part of the vocation of practical philosophy to address these; but to do so it has to draw on broader considerations about the nature and source of values, and about the way in which these latter relate to recommendations and requirements.

Philosophers often bemoan the fact that they are not heeded by others who, they believe, should be interested in their reflections, for example scientists, theologians, sociologists, art and literary theorists and policy makers; and they occasionally add that the trouble lies with the fact that people are not philosophically minded. There is some truth in this. Philosophers are generally very good at detecting

---

[1] By way of illustration, and for useful introductions to some of the main issues as these have been viewed and developed over the last three decades, see Joseph DeMarco & Richard Fox, eds. *New Directions in Ethics: The Challenge of Applied Ethics* (London: Routledge & Kegan Paul, 1986); Earl Winkler & Jerrold Coombs, eds., *Applied Ethics: A Reader* (Oxford: Blackwell, 1993); Brenda Almond ed., *An Introduction to Applied Ethics* (Oxford: Blackwell, 1995); and Hugh LaFollette ed., *Ethics in Practice: An Anthology* (Oxford: Blackwell, 2006).

fallacies and marking relevant distinctions; whereas non-philosophers are liable to confuse important differences: for example, between grounding and motivating reasons, i.e. confusing what might be *evidence* for a claim with someone's personal *motivation* in making it.

But it is a mistake to infer from the fact that people may not be philosophically *minded* that they are not philosophically *informed*, or in many cases *mis-informed*. For example, although many intelligent and educated people will show themselves to be confused in their thinking about the human mind they are not without a philosophical view on this issue. On the contrary, they are generally possessed of one or other of two opposing views: *dualism* and *materialism*. Consistent with the liability to confusion, however, they will sometimes maintain one of these positions while citing as grounds for it phenomena which would seem, if anything, to be evidence for the contrary view. All the same educated people often have a viewpoint and it is usually a recognisably philosophical one. Moreover, the source of these opinions is often philosophy itself.

So if philosophy has a vocation to help people think their way to the truth about fundamental matters part of its task may not be to provide an education in new philosophical doctrines so much as a re-education out of old ones, or out of the versions of these that have taken shape as ideas have trickled down through the culture. It is certainly the case that current ways of thinking about morality, and about values more generally, are the products of philosophical ideas developed by writers in the eighteenth, nineteenth and twentieth centuries. The ideas in question are much older than this, going back in fact to the earliest stages of philosophy; but in the last two centuries they have become part and parcel of what now seems to many educated people to be a body of established truths. In what follows, then, I need to dismantle some of the main elements of this orthodoxy and to show how questions about values are connected with other aspects of our thought.

Some Preliminary Distinctions

What are the 'questions about values' and what is the modern orthodoxy? True to the methods of philosophy I shall begin by making some distinctions, in this case ones between different *perspectives* and between different *levels*. Some questions about values and conduct are psychological and sociological. For example, biographers and historians are often interested in the ideals that motivated people; and periodically there are surveys of social attitudes designed to keep track of changes in 'morality', i.e. in people's thoughts about certain kinds of behaviour and in the behaviour itself. These are *empirical* questions to be investigated and answered by various means including sophisticated social science methods. But however successful these means may be, all they can tell us about are people's attitudes and behaviour. They cannot settle the many particular questions that people ask about what is good and bad, right and wrong; and nor can they settle the more abstract question of what is it for something to be good or bad, right or wrong.

Leaving psychology and sociology behind, therefore, we now move into the area of values and principles, and this quickly gives rise to *moral philosophy*. First, however, a distinction of levels needs to be made. Consider the most elementary questions of values such as: is friendship good? is honesty always the best policy? is human life inviolable? is justice more important than liberty? These are *ground floor* questions. They are the sorts of issues that are often discussed in the press, on television, and on the internet, and they are ones that exercise the minds of most thoughtful people at least from time to time.

Some questions of these sorts are felt to be easily answered, but most are judged to be difficult. Indeed the ones to which the answers seem obvious are for that reason generally not even posed. For example, it sounds odd to ask if torturing animals for pleasure is permissible, because virtually everyone to whom this question might be posed would answer that it is not and would be repelled by the thought that anyone could believe otherwise. Still the question can be asked, and as soon as it is a further question suggests itself. If torturing animals is wrong why is it wrong? Attempts to answer this sort of question about the basis and content of value judgements moves us up from ground floor moralising to *first floor* theorising.

As we make this ascent, however, it is important to bear in mind that while the majority of people may not be moved to ask why something is good or bad, nonetheless they will certainly be concerned with what they judge to be of value. The last point needs to be understood correctly. It is not being claimed that people go around all the time, or even part of it, asking is this good or bad? is that worth doing? should this be avoided? and so on. Many do, of course, but the general claim is not about what people consciously think, but about what is presupposed by their behaviour.

Consider for a moment the question what is the difference between a mere bodily movement and an action? Whatever else may be said, action is *intentional*, i.e. it is aimed at some end. When someone acts there is something he or she is trying to achieve. One can always ask why they did it, with the assurance that some goal, however humble, was intended. This being so we can also say that from the point of view of the agent the end in question was conceived of as desirable. This is not to claim that he or she consciously thought 'this is a worthwhile goal'; and even less is it to suggest that the goal is question was objectively good. The point rather is that inasmuch as an agent has performed an *action* he or she has an attitude of approval to that which the action was intended to realise. Certainly we can do things that we regret, even as we are doing them; but to the extent that we are acting intentionally there is some respect in which the result is viewed as desirable. It is in this sense that everyone who acts is concerned with values.

Conscious of our own fallibility, and curious as we are, reflection normally leads to questioning about what others regard as good and bad; and further reflection raises the mind to the more abstract level of *first floor* theorising where we ask what, if anything, makes things good (or bad). Otherwise expressed the question is: what do good things have in common? Historically a wide range of answers has been proposed, but most of these can be fitted into three broad categories. First, the *theological*: something is good if God approves of it and bad if He disapproves of it, the limiting cases of His approval being a command and of His disapproval a prohibition. Obviously views of this sort rest upon claims even more controversial than those likely to be made about particular values and as we shall see there are problems with this approach to values even for the theist.

The second broad category is that of the *deontological* .Theories of this sort hold that certain characteristics, actions and states of affairs are good (or bad) in and of themselves. One way of expressing views of this kind is by saying that they 'value-classify' things at the level of *types*. For example deontological ethical theories sometimes hold that lying is always morally wrong. Here the emphasis is on the type of behaviour not on individual actions. Of course in condemning the type one is condemning its instances, but the essence of this view resides in the fact that what is wrong with an episode of lying is not features of the individual case but rather the fact that, whatever the particularities, it is an instance of a *kind* of action that is always wrong.

So far, however, nothing has been said about why lying is prohibited or more generally about what, for the deontologist, makes things good or bad, right or wrong. There is no universally agreed deontological theory. However since the eighteenth century, and mostly under the influence of Kant, deontologists have usually related values to the fundamental duty of *respect*. Kant writes: 'Act in such a way that you always treat humanity, whether in your own person or in the person of any other, never simply as a means but always at the same time as an end'.[2] Strictly for Kant respect was owing to rational beings only; indeed one might say that respect was owing principally to *rationality* as such and to human beings only in so far as they are repositories of it. Later thinkers, however, have sought to extend the constituency of value beyond rational beings to sentient

[2]   I. Kant, *Groundwork of the Metaphysic of Moral* trans. H.J. Paton as *The Moral Law* (London: Hutchinson, 1976) and other editions, 4:429.

creatures, and more recently (in the West at least) to all living things. Some go so far as to claim a fundamental 'existential' value that is possessed by each and every thing, from micro-physical particles to planets and galaxies, and which is deserving of respect.[3]

The third broad category of value theory (or 'axiology') is perhaps the most widely supported in advanced industrial societies and is certainly that which people tend to find least puzzling. This is *consequentialist* axiology, according to which something is good to the extent that it promotes or constitutes states of affairs held to be good on their own account. Relatedy an action is right insofar as it results in good consequences. Notice that on the issue of whether a *type* of action is right or wrong the consequentialist has to look first to the instances and on this basis try to construct an answer to the general question. Unlike the deontologist, he regards rightness and wrongness as properly speaking a property of individual actions relating to their actual or probable results. Any account of the value of types, therefore, can only be based on the pattern of individual consequences.

Having ascended to the level of theory the reflective mind is liable to be struck by a further question. Is anything *really* good, i.e. objectively so? We begin in innocence presupposing the desirability of this or that goal, then ask explicitly what things have value? This stimulates the appetite for generality provoking the question: what (if anything) links together the variety of worthwhile goals? Now there arises the issue of whether deontological and consequentionalist theories are merely accounts of the underlying patterns of our thoughts and attitudes about values, or whether they describe an independent order of objective goods and requirements.

In asking whether these are 'real' we move to the *second* and (highest) *floor* in the structure of thinking about values: the 'metatheory' of value and ethics. Since most interest is in

---

[3]   I shall return to the idea of existential or ontological value in chapter two 'Persons and Values', distinguishing it from qualitative or welfare value.

the area of morality and first floor ethical theory, it is more common to find writers discussing 'metaethics' than 'meta-aesthetics' or 'meta-politics'. Nonetheless similar issues arise in respect of fields such as art and social policy, and although it is important to bear in mind the possibility that different accounts may be appropriate for different areas there are clear similarities in the arguments for and against objectivism and subjectivism in respect of moral, political, aesthetic and other values.

Two Philosophical Perspectives

Having distinguished between *empirical* questions about people's attitudes, and *philosophical* questions about the content of those attitudes; and then distinguished within the latter three levels — those of (i) particular valuations, (ii) general structures of valuation and (iii) the metaphysical status of values, we arrive at the issue which most exercises the philosophical conscience: *are values objective?* Earlier I noted that at this level of thought about morality and other spheres of value and requirement there is an established opinion and that this is related to a more general view about the nature of reality. For want of a more engaging title let me just call this the 'empiricist orthodoxy'.

To understand the power of empiricism it is helpful to appreciate something of the history of ideas out of which it developed and to much of which it was a deliberate reaction. In his work subsequently titled the *Metaphysics*, Aristotle tells us that philosophy began with leisure. Only when they had established the conditions for secure and stable life did men have the opportunity to distance themselves from immediate practical concerns and reflect upon the nature of the world in the broad sense of the universe or cosmos (*kosmos*).[4]

Whatever about the social history of philosophy it is clear from the earliest presocratic fragments recording the ideas of philosophers prior to Socrates that their principle concern was with such questions as how the world can be

---

[4]   See Aristotle, *Metaphysics* Bk. I, Ch 1, 981b 20.

thought about in a systematic way. Here the concern was as much with the possible structure of the world as with the powers of human understanding. For in order that there might be general truths about the nature and behaviour of the cosmos it must have some order. This thought led in due course to an idea about the natures of things that is expressed in a Pythagorean formula: limit (*peras*) imposed upon the unlimited (*apeiron*) producing the limited (*peperasmenon*). Further refined this became the doctrine of hylomorphism (*hyle*) = matter; *morphe* (= shape): the principle that every thing can be analysed in terms of a medium and an organisational form. So a wooden ball is so much matter having spherical form; a horse, so much flesh and bones arranged in a certain living form; a galaxy, stars and planets in a certain configuration.[5]

Clearly this ancient philosophical analysis is a powerful one, and it remained the central doctrine of philosophical thought through the middle ages only beginning to weaken in the fifteenth century. The reasons for its demise, which accelerated in the sixteenth century and seemed complete by the end of the seventeenth, are complex but the central force in its displacement was the rise of new analytical schemes associated with a particular method of enquiry: metaphysically unburdened empirical investigation conducted through controlled experiment. In short, the rise of modern natural science.

It is, in fact, a moot point the extent to which the 'new' knowledge was metaphysics free. Its account of the fundamental structure of the world involved a version of an ideal propounded by some of the presocratic cosmologists, the claim that material objects are compounded out of imperceptibly small particles '*atomoi*'. The modern version of atomism *viz.* 'corpuscularism' was importantly different, however, inasmuch as it progressively dispensed with the idea of governing forms or natures and substituted for these geometrical arrangements and mechanical causation. This process, which the phenomenologist Husserl was later to

[5]   For Aristotle's account of the Pythagorean theories, and for his own hylomorphism see *Metaphysics*, Bk I, Ch. 5, and Bk VIII, Ch. 2.

describe as 'the mathematisation of nature',[6] effected a radical change in the way the world was seen. For Aristotle and his medieval followers the natural world is a hierarchical order of species. Each thing has a governing nature which makes it to be a thing of that kind and determines the characteristic patterns of its development and behaviour. Although plants and animals are composed out of matter it is not their matter but their organising specific forms that explain their distinctive natures. Certainly matter has properties of its own such as the liability to fall downwards, and for the Aristotelian that explains the universal behaviour of natural things in this respect, but it does not explain the different structure and properties which quantities of matter possess when they are informed by specific principles of organisation and activity.[7]

One important aspect of the difference between Aristotelian and modern science, consequent upon the substitution of mechanics for organic activity, is the way in which explanation and understanding no longer invoked purposes and functions. In the older view one understands the behaviour of organisms and of their parts in terms of teleologies or directed activities. These link together various sub-organic processes and the different stages in the history of an organism. A fruit is a seed carrier; a seed is in process of developing into a sapling which is on the way to becoming a tree; the tree puts out blossoms and in due course fruits which are for the sake of propagating the species. On it goes: the parts and functions of living things contributing to larger processes themselves regulated by governing forms or natures.

Now notice two features of this view of the natural order: first, it is *non-reductive*; and second, it is *normative*. It is non-reductive because it does not think that the structure and behaviour of whole entities is a function or 'upward-generated' consequence of its basic material elements. It is norma-

[6]   Edmund Husserl, *The Crisis of European Sciences and Transcendental Phenomenology*, trans. D. Carr (Evanston, IL: Northwestern University Press, 1970).

[7]   For a non-historical discussion of the adequacy of Aristotelian and present day accounts of causality see J. Haldane, 'Gravitas, Efficacy and Social Causes', *Analysis*, 68 (2008).

tive because it implies that certain states and processes are good or bad inasmuch as they contribute to or inhibit natural processes of developments. Given, for example, that the heart has the function of pumping blood, and that the circulation of the blood is necessary for the distribution of oxygen, minerals and other nutrients throughout the body, and for the clearing of other substances out of it, it follows that damage to the heart is *ipso facto* bad. This feature which may be called the 'normativity of nature' is quite general. If it makes sense to describe objects in terms of functions, and events in terms of processes then questions of efficiency, harm and benefit arise.

Ethics after Aristotle

In rejecting the teleological view of nature and replacing it with the idea that the ultimate reality is one of mechanically interacting particles and that all the rest is just a complication of this, a matter of quantitative not qualitative differences, the modern view created a problem of the relationship between *facts*, the domain of science, and *values*, the domain of who knows what? In an age of religious belief it seemed that theology might take care of the issue: the world provides the facts and God dictates the values. But there are two problems with this. First, the science that dispensed with purposes also seemed to remove one basis for belief in God, i.e. that He was the designer of nature and the inventor of purposes. Second, even if one believes in God there are problems with the idea that His commands are the sole basis of values.

The most familiar of these problems is usually presented in terms of the 'Euthyphro Dilemma', deriving from Plato's dialogue *Euthyphro* in which a version of it features.[8] Consider the question: is something valuable because God commands it or does God command it because it is valuable? To favour the first seems to make value inexplicable and arbi-

---

[8]   Socrates addresses Euthyphro as follows: 'The point which I should first wish to understand is whether the pious or holy is beloved by the gods because it is holy, or holy because it is beloved of the gods', *Euthyphro* trans. B. Jowett (Oxford: Clarendon Press, 1903) 10.

trary. If God were to have commanded the ritual torture of infants it would on this account thereby be valuable, but that strikes most people as absurd. However, if one favours the second option the implication is that things are valuable independently of God's commanding them.[9] Support for this view comes from a further consideration that undermines the claims of theology to provide a general account of values. All sorts of claims have been made by individuals and groups about what God commands. In trying to determine whether these are, or even could be, authentic revelations religious believers assess the content of the purportedly Divine commandments. If, as in some cases, the claim is that God orders the ritual slaughter of those who are not believers this is generally taken to be evidence against the authenticity of the 'revelation'; the grounds being that a good God would not command evil acts. But this, of course, suggests that there is some criterion of what constitutes good and evil independently of the claims of revelation. It might be replied that the source of this is prior revelation; but if one is willing to apply a non-revealed moral standard at some stage in history then one cannot claim that God's revealed will is the source of *all* values.[10]

Nature having been reconceived in atomistic-cum-mechanical-cum-mathematical terms and thereby no longer being seen as a repository of telological norms, and the effort to provide a theological basis for values seeming to be ineffective, some writers tried to work out accounts of objective value based on reason and/or conscience. Although these have their interest, however, they were con-

[9]   For an account and assessment of responses to the divine command dilemma among Christian philosopher/theologians see J. Haldane 'Voluntarism and Realism in Medieval Ethics', *Journal of Medical Ethics*, 15 (1989).

[10] This does not exclude the possibility that a religious revelation might include moral truths authoritatively proclaimed, but it rules out the idea of *per se* revealed moral truths, i.e. ones essentially such as could not be otherwise known. For a different, though related, argument to the same conclusion see Elizabeth Anscombe, 'Authority in Morals' in M. Geach & L. Gormally eds. *Faith in a Hard Ground: Essays on Religion, Philosophy and Ethics* by G.E.M. Anscombe (Exeter: ImprintAcademic, 2008).

fronted with a series of objections which, in the following two centuries, came to be widely regarded as destructive of the possibility of any kind of value objectivism.

The empiricist theory of knowledge is in the tradition associated with the modern scientific world view. As in the rest of nature, changes in us, such as the acquisition of new beliefs, are to be explained by reference to interactions within and between objects. So far as our knowledge of the world is concerned these originate in the impact of the environment on the sense organs. Generalising, therefore, the empiricist maintains that knowledge of how things are is a function of (and probably reduces to) the content of sensory experience. Combining this with an atomistic metaphysics the conclusion is arrived at that all we can be aware of are the motions of material objects, and study of these fails to show us any values: good, bad, right and wrong. Nothing in the world or in our experience of it provides grounds for belief in objective values.

This, in brief, is the basis of the oft proclaimed 'fact/value gap'. No observed facts reveal or entail any values. Additional to this claim is another one equally important in the empiricist argument against moral objectivity and suggestive of a subjectivist account of moral thinking. Hume observes that in his reading of theologians and moralists he found that they move from propositions about what *is* the case to claims about what *ought* or *ought not* to be done; but this he professes (ironically) to find surprising. He writes as follows:

> In every system of morality, which I have hitherto met with, I have always remark'd, that the author proceeds for some time in the ordinary ways of reasoning, and establishes the being of a God, or makes observations concerning human affairs; when all of a sudden I am surpriz'd to find, that instead of the usual copulations of propositions, *is*, and *is not*, I meet with no proposition that is not connected with an *ought*, or an *ought not*. This change is imperceptible; but is however, of the last consequence. For as this *ought*, or *ought not*, expresses some new relation or affirmation, 'tis necessary that it shou'd be observ'd and explain'd; and at the same time that a reason should be given; for what seems altogether inconceivable, how this new relation can

be a deduction from others, which are entirely different from it.[11]

On the basis of these remarks Hume is generally credited with having identified a further logical gap: that between *is* and *ought*. Of course, we may argue from observed facts, such as that a main *is* starving, to a prescriptive conclusion, e.g. that he *ought* to be fed. But of itself this is taken to be no refutation of the Humean thesis since it is observed that the conclusion only follows when a further premise is added, *viz.* that starving men *ought* to be fed. Once more, generalizing, the empiricist claim is that no 'ought' proposition follows from a set of premises unless this already includes an 'ought' statement.

Part of the interest and power of the empiricist view is that it suggests an alternative basis for moral values and requirements, a naturalistic and empirical account of the source of our thoughts that some things are good and others bad, some actions right and others wrong. Instead of looking to facts in the world around us we should attend to attitudes and sentiments within ourselves. In short, judgements of value and requirement are expressions or projections of our subjective desires and preferences. The approach has received a variety of refining treatments producing a range of 'emotivist' and 'projectivist' theories. But the subtle differences between these are of less significance than the unifying thesis that values are subjective.

Before responding to this empiricist orthodoxy it is necessary to observe two points about the subjectivist theory of values. First it need not hold that all values are simply expressions of *individual* preference. Rather it can allow that many values are socially constituted out of commonly held attitudes and preferences. The importance of this is that it provides a reply to one kind of objection to crude subjectivism, namely that we think that individuals can be in error in their evaluations. For example we simply do not suppose that it is a matter of personal attitude whether torturing ani-

[11] David Hume, *A Treatise of Human Nature*, ed. L. A. Selby-Bigge (Oxford: Clarendon Press, 1978) and other editions, Book III, Part I, section I.

mals is wrong, and we would regard anyone who approved such conduct as morally wicked. This might seem to constitute strong evidence against a subjectivist theory until one appreciates that it is open to such a theory to identify wrongness with general disapprobation. Thus while it may not be a matter of fact but of feeling that torture is wrong, someone who did not share this feeling, or possessed contrary ones, might still be held to be 'mistaken' inasmuch as his response is at variance with the social norm in such matters.

The second point to note is that subjectivism is a *metatheory*. Unlike consequentialist and deontological theories of value it is not concerned with the content or justification of moral and other valuations but with their 'metaphysical standing' i.e. as factual or not factual, truth-bearing or non truth-bearing. It is, in other words, an account appropriate to the *second floor* of our structure. That being so a question remains open for the subjectivist, namely which if any sort of first-floor moral theory should be or she adopt? Largely for reasons that are easy to work out the empiricist tradition has strongly favoured consequentialism. If values are just preferences then it is natural to think of moral theory, say, almost as a branch of social psychology. And asking the question 'what do we approve of?' writers in the empiricist tradition have responded in terms of such notions as utility and happiness. Happiness is what we want and approve of, unhappiness what we shun; and we approve and disapprove of other things to the extent that we judge them to be conducive to or to constitute such end states. This view is well expressed by one of the founders of utilitarianism, Jeremy Bentham, when he writes as follows:

> Nature has placed us under the governance of two sovereign masters, *pain* and *pleasure*. It is for them alone to point out what we ought to do, as well as to determine what we shall do. On the one hand the standard of right and wrong,

on the other hand the chain of causes and effects are fastened to their throne.[12]

Thus we trace the passage from a pre-modern view of nature as a system of formally structured living substances and of values as objective features pertaining to proper functioning and natural well-being, to a modern conception of reality as constituted of basic physical units and forces and of values as projections of the states of some objects (human beings) on to other objects and situations. 'Postmodern' ideas on these matters are more or less radical extensions of value-subjectivism but often combine this with similar views about every other domain of human thought and practice — including science itself.

Natures and Values

Where then does this leave us? Ironically one consequence of the intellectual development that led to the fact/value gap might be the adoption of forms of postmodern thought in which that gap is itself transcended. If everything is subjective then there are no 'hard' facts to be contrasted with 'soft' attitudes. At most one might find reasons (i.e. attitudes) to distinguish between 'harder' and 'softer' attitudes; less and more locally subjective phenomena. This way of responding to the problem of values certainly finds support among contemporary philosophers. However it rests on claims hardly less controversial than theological ones and is not likely to be found attractive by those whose concern is with whether a place for values can be found in an objectivist world view.

Clearly the question: 'are there objective principles and values?' will continue to stimulate controversy, and it would be absurd to assume that it could be conclusively resolved in the space of a book chapter. This said, however, those inclined to subjectivism need to consider very seriously whether it is consistent to hold this as the truth about

---

[12] Jeremy Bentham, *Introduction to the Principles of Morals and Legislation* eds. J.H. Burns & H.L.A. Hart (Oxford: Clarendon Press, 1996) and other editions. Ch I, Section I.

moral and other values while continuing to treat issues of
personal behaviour and social policy as if they concerned
objective matters of fact. Indeed this raises the question of
whether a general subjectivism about all values is not
self-undermining. In arguing about these issues parties on
both sides of the dispute tend to assume the objective validity of cognitive and rational values. That is to say, even
'subjectivists' tend to be objectivists about the values of
evidential weight, rational cogency, argumentative rigour,
coherence, intelligibility and truth. They do not suppose
that the determination to be guided in one's thought by
such values is no more than a matter of preferences. On the
contrary they share the objectivist assumption that we seek
cogency, coherence and intelligibility because they are
rational goods, and not that they are goods because we seek
them.[13]

If this line of thought proves unsettling for the subjectivist
it also prompts the question how can one be an objectivist
given the modern empiricist world view? The challenge is
appropriate; but rather than try to reconcile moral
objectivism with orthodox empiricism one should recon-
sider the opposition between the latter and the Aristotelian
world view. A very considerable merit of that view is that it
permits the objectivity of values without forcing them into a
mysterious realm. Otherwise expressed, it offers the prospect of combining an objectivist metatheory of values with a
naturalistic metaphysics. In saying this, however, it is
important to recall that the older naturalism insists upon the
non-reducibility of the forms and teleologies of living
things. Indeed it is precisely because it discerns holistic patterns of growth, development and flourishing that it sees
norms in nature.

The challenge of the new science was that these
hylomorphic and teleological ways of thinking are misconceived and fail to grasp the fundamental structure of reality

---

[13]   In this connection see Thomas Nagel, *The Last Word* (Oxford: Oxford
       University Press, 1997) Chs. 5 & 6; and Hilary Putnam, *The Collapse of
       the Fact/Value Dichotomy* (Cambridge, MA: Harvard University Press,
       2002) Chs. 1 & 2.

which strides below the level of living things, and has no place for organic functions and goal-related processes. Undoubtedly post-Aristotelian science has vastly extended our knowledge of the world and no-one could seriously doubt the physical basis of organic entities. But in urging the truth of the earlier view one need not deny these facts. Organic forms and natural teleologies are compatible with microphysical particles and electromagnetic radiation. The empiricist mistake has been to insist upon the exclusivity of the reality of entities of the latter sort and to require that all other descriptions be reduced or rejected. The truth of the matter is that not every truth is a truth about matter. There are forms, principles of organisation and activity, by which things live and in favourable circumstances flourish.

Fact, Value and Requirement

Hume's problem as it arises for anyone seeking to derive prescriptions for action from information about the human constitution comes in two stages. The first concerns the attempt to derive norms from facts of nature (the fact/value gap) and the second bears upon the task of proceeding from statements of value to ones of requirement (the 'is' [good]/ 'ought' [to be done] gap). Setting aside the issue of absolute obligations, which raise further issues, I think the second stage of Hume's problem is largely untroublesome. That Hume and Humeans think it a problem is due to their unduly narrow conception of reasoning.

As so often, Hume first presents a restrictive account of some central concept, in this case of rationality — as 'abstract reasoning concerning quantity or number' and 'experimental reasoning concerning matter of fact and existence',[14] and then challenges his readers to see how this concept could possibly have the breadth of application they ordinarily ascribe to it.

---

[14] David Hume, *Enquiry Concerning Human Understanding*, ed. L. A. Selby-Bigge (Oxford: Clarendon Press, 1978) and other editions, Section XII, Part III.

However, the idea that there can be reasoning about how one ought to act, i.e. practical rationality, is an ancient and evidently coherent one. According to the type of view I am propounding the relevant subject matter of such reasoning is the good for a human being. And the connection between judging something to be good and concluding that, other things being equal, one ought to act so as to achieve it is an internal one. That is to say, in the domain of practical reasoning to assent to a value judgement is, among other things, to be disposed to act upon it. This is not an empirical psychological thesis but a philosophical one about the very nature of practical valuation and action.

In Aquinas' writings this point about the inseparability of evaluation and prescriptivity is demonstrated by reference to the notion of *synderesis*. This is an innate practical disposition directed towards the achievement of natural well-being. It is characterizable in the form of the first principle of practical reason (*primum principium in ratione practica*) which Aquinas a states as follows: 'Good is to be done and pursued and evil avoided' (*Bonum est faciendum et prosequendum et malum vitandum*).[15] It is especially important to recall that 'good' (and 'evil') is not restricted in this use to moral contexts. The point is simply that conceiving of something under a 'desirability chracterization' (*ratio boni*) is a necessary, though not sufficient, condition of being engaged in action. Purposeful behaviour, as opposed to mere bodily movement (or inertia), is specified by its object which stands as a goal to be realised. Thus, Aquinas's *synderesis* principle is not a piece of moral advice. Rather, it states a constitutive element of the domain of practice. As such it may be compared with the principle: truth is to be believed and investigated and falsehood disbelieved; subscription to which is presupposed in the chracterization of something as a theoretical judgement.

[15] Aquinas, *Summa Theologiae*, Ia. IIae, q. 94, a. 2c, here and in subsequent references to the *Summa Theologiae* see *The 'Summa Theologica' of St Thomas Aquinas* literally translated by Fathers of the English Dominican Province, second and revised edition (London: R. & T. Washbourne, 1920) or St Thomas Aquinas *Summa Theologiae* (London: Eyre & Spottiswode, 1964-1981).

The second stage of Hume's problem, the supposed gap between evaluation and prescription (is good/ought to be done) aims to make trouble for teleological ethics by claiming that there is no logical or rational connection between judging that something is a potential object of satisfaction of a need and judging that it ought to be sought after. But this fails to recognize that in the practical domain there is an intrinsic connection between holding something to be desirable (i.e. worthwhile) and being rationally disposed to secure it. For, from the point of view of the agent or practical deliberator, to conceive of X as desirable is to conceive of it as something to be obtained, again other things being equal. Of course, the agent may be mistaken. It may be (given the naturalistic account of value) that what he desires is not in fact desirable (worthwhile). But if he comes to recognize this he will, ipso facto, and assuming rationality, cease to be disposed towards it. Since, to repeat, in the domain of practical reasoning evaluation is intrinsically related to prescription. In short, there is no general 'is' / 'ought' gap.

Returning at this point to the account of value and virtue as relating to the promotion of human well-being, an explanation emerges of the special prescriptive force of moral judgements. In his catalogue of practical principles Kant first distinguishes between hypothetical and categorical imperatives and then draws a distinction within the former class between those which are assertoric and others which are problematic.[16] The second sort are what are usually referred to in discussions of whether morality is a system of hypothetical imperatives. These ascribe value to actions conditionally upon an agent's having a purpose which he may equally lack. Assertoric hypotheticals, by contrast, are concerned with actual purposes not merely possible ones.

Accordingly, one class of assertoric imperatives might have the general form: necessarily you seek what is good therefore you ought to do such and such. But this is just what a teleological theory of the kind discussed would yield, with the particular contents being determined by ref-

[16] I. Kant, *Groundwork of the Metaphysic of Moral* op. cit, Ch II. Classification of imperatives. 415.

erence to factors constitutive of human well-being. The prescriptive authority of morality is, therefore, no more or less than that of the facts. But it is unsurprising that their presentation in ethical judgements engages our interests and emotions in ways not paralleled in theoretical enquiry. First, because they feature in a practical context; one in which the question: What ought I to do? is presupposed. Second, because they concern our well-being as rational human animals.

MacIntyre and Modernity

In saying this it is also important to recognise that human existence is both more complex and different in kind from that of non-sentient organisms or non-rational animals. In particular human life is shaped by social forces in ways that complicate the appeal to nature. One of the most interesting attempts to deal with the philosophical issues raised by the plurality of forms of social existence and the attendant diversity of moral perspectives is that presented by Alasdair MacIntyre. Since the publication in 1981 of his book *After Virtue*, MacIntyre has come to be regarded as one of the most significant critics of the morality and moral philosophy of modernity.[17] For a long while prior to its publication he had argued that any attempt to understand moral concepts and moral reasoning without locating them in their social and historical contexts is bound to fail, and what is worse is likely to lead to scepticism about the very possibility of moral justification, for as he then claimed: 'Moral concepts are embodied in and are partially constitutive of forms of social life'.[18]

At that stage MacIntyre's insistence upon the contextuality of moral thought was offered primarily as a methodological corrective to the style of history of ethics then dominant within English-language philosophy. By the time of *After Virtue* and in the works published since then, how-

---

[17]   Alasdair MacIntyre, *After Virtue* (London, Duckworth, 1985).
[18]   Alasdair MacIntyre, *A Short History of Ethics* (London, Routledge & Kegan Paul, 1967, 2002) p.1.

ever, the claim that moral concepts are interwoven with cultural traditions has become part of a general critique of modern moral and political philosophy and has served in the development and defence of his own version of value objectivism.

In her famous essay 'Modern Moral Philosophy' of 1958, which inaugurated a period of neo-Aristotelianism in analytical ethical theory, Elizabeth Anscombe argued that the basic moral vocabulary of requirement and prohibition — 'ought' / 'ought not', 'must' / 'must not', etc — is a remainder from earlier religious ways of thinking about conduct.[19] The deontic or juridical character of this vocabulary derives from a law conception of ethics in which styles of action are prescribed by a Divine legislator. With the subsequent detachment of morality from religion this vocabulary lost its source of authentic meaning but retained its commandatory force, this latter then seeming to be unwarranted and at best explicable in subjectivist or emotivist terms as descriptive or expressive of certain commitments or attitudes of approval and disapproval.

In *After Virtue* MacIntyre adopted this analysis as part of his own diagnosis of the irresolubility of moral disputes in contemporary life; but he also enlarged and complicated the 'lost meaning' account according to which ethical language has become an incoherent assemblage of disordered fragments from earlier moral systems. One complication, for example, is that whereas Anscombe proposed the abandonment of the ethics of quasi-legal requirement in favour of an Aristotelian approach built around concepts of virtue, MacIntyre discerns the vocabulary of virtue ethics itself amidst the babble of competing moral claims, and argues that secular liberal consciousness is no better placed to make sense of this than it is of the strongly prescriptive vocabulary of the Judaeo-Christian moral law. In both cases what we lack are the historical and cultural contexts that

---

[19] Elizabeth Anscombe, 'Modern moral philosophy', *Philosophy*, 53 (1958); also in M. Geach and L. Gormally eds. *Human Life, Action and Ethics: Essays by G.E.M. Anscombe* (Exeter: Imprint Academic, 2005)

give meaning to these ways of evaluating and commending character and conduct.

A further point of contrast between Anscombe and MacIntyre is that whereas she believed that we might reconstruct the philosophical anthropology by which Aristotle was able to prescribe a natural end or *telos* for human kind, realisation of which constitutes *eudaimonia*, MacIntyre originally regarded this anthropology as being committed to a form of ahistorical, acultural 'metaphysical biology' which philosophy and the natural and social sciences have shown to be no longer tenable. However, while such a difference with respect to the philosophical foundations of ethics is potentially significant, in later writings MacIntyre explicitly draws back from his criticism, writing that:

> In *After Virtue* I had attempted to give an account of the place of the virtues, understood as Aristotle had understood them, within social practices, the lives of individuals and the lives of communities, while making that account independent of what I called Aristotle's 'metaphysical biology.' Although there is indeed good reason to repudiate important elements in Aristotle's biology, I now judge that I was in error in supposing an ethics independent of biology to be possible ... [20]

He goes on to explain that animal nature bears upon his account of ethics in two ways: first, inasmuch as that any account of the elements that constitute our moral life must show how such a life is possible for beings with our biological nature; and second, unless we understand our animal nature we will fail to comprehend the development of moral life in us. Here then it is more important to stress MacIntyre's agreement with the general character of Aristotelian moral psychology. For in keeping with this he argues that the value, and indeed the moral meaning of actions derives not, as in *utilitarianism*, from their efficacy in producing outcomes (e.g., happiness), whose worth is antecedent to moral values, nor, as in *Kantianism*, from conforming to some abstract principle of pure practical reason, but

---

[20] Alasdair MacIntyre, *Dependent Rational Animals: Why Human Beings need the Virtues* (London: Duckworth, 1999) p. x.

flows instead from habits of action and avoidance whose standing as virtues derives from their orientation towards ends constitutive of good human lives.

Like Anscombe and other neo-Aristotelians, therefore, MacIntyre hopes to restore coherence to morality by relating it to an account of life as teleologically ordered, but in part because of conclusions drawn and retained from his earlier studies in Marxism and sociology, he views that order more in terms of social practices than of culturally invariant natural functions. Central to this neo-Aristotelian scheme is the idea that in asking the question 'what ought I to do?' one is, in effect, asking a question about the kind of person one should be, or equivalently, about the kind of life one should lead. The unit of moral assessment is not, strictly speaking, individual actions but the form of life from which they issue and the agent's overall character. Furthermore, this moral character is formed and developed in a social context, out of participation (originally unchosen and not reflected upon) in practices whose meaning is given by their traditional goals. On this account moral maturation involves reflection upon the kind of life one finds oneself living, and the construction of a personal narrative in terms of which actions, habits, episodes, trends, commitments and aversions etc., can be judged as failings or achievements, vices and virtues.

In summary, to understand the moral identity and value of individual actions one has to relate then to the agent's life and through this to traditional practices and to social forms of his or her culture. The problem of modernity through to the present day, however, is that there is no single unifying culture and hence no shared set of values and virtues by reference to which actions may be interpreted and judged. As MacIntyre observes:

> The rhetoric of shared values is of great ideological importance, but it disguises the truth about how action is guided and directed. For what we genuinely share in the way of moral maxims, precepts and principles is insufficiently

determinate to guide action and what is sufficiently determinate to guide action is not shared.[21]

For example, and superficial appearances to the contrary,
modern societies lack substantial agreement on such basic
questions as whether or why lying is bad. In traditional
societies, by contrast, actions are subject to sets of norms
appropriate to various roles (though these norms are not
always codified or codifiable); and these prescribe what is
honourable and dishonourable, vicious and virtuous.

The interest of MacIntyre's explorations of these issues is
testified to by the considerable attention his work has
attracted[22] but it raises a problematic question. If the standards of moral assessment are not given by extra-moral and
uncontested values, or by ahistorical principles of practical
reason, but are immanent within the particular social traditions and practices in which agents are situated, then how is
relativism to be avoided? If what is right is determined by
virtues whose form and content is specific to a tradition
how can it even make sense to raise questions about the
morality of conduct from an evaluative perspective outside
that tradition? and since the diagnosis of modernity is that
there is no single moral order then the threat of relativism is
not merely speculative, it is real.

MacIntyre's concern with this question is reflected in the
title of the book that followed *After Virtue*, namely, *Whose
Justice? Which Rationality?* In this and in a sequel, *viz. Three
Rival Versions of Moral Enquiry*, he develops a dialectical
account of how one tradition of reflection can establish its
rational superiority over another. The argument is subtle
and draws upon a variety of historical sources, in particular

---

[21] Alasdair MacIntyre, 'The Privatization of Good', *Review of Politics*,
1990, p. 349.

[22] See, for example, Peter McMylor, *Alasdair MacIntyre: Critic of
Modernity* (London: Routledge, 1993; John Horton & Susan Mendus
eds., *After MacIntyre:* (Cambridge: Polity Press, 1994); Mark Murphy
ed., *Alasdair MacIntyre* (Cambridge: Cambridge University Press,
2003); Christopher Lutz, *Tradition in the Ethics of Alasdair MacIntyre*
(Lanham, MD: Lexington Books, 2004); and Thomas D'Andrea,
Tradition, Rationality and Virtue: The Thought of Alasdair MacIntyre
(London: Ashgate, 2006).

Greek, medieval and Scottish enlightenment thought; but in broad outline it maintains that while norms of reason are immanent within and particular to traditions of enquiry, a tradition may run into philosophical difficulties and recognise this fact without having the resources to solve these problems. It might yet, however, be able to appreciate that another, rival tradition does possess the means to diagnose and to resolve these difficulties. Acknowledgement of these facts therefore amounts to recognition of the superiority of the rival. Additionally, MacIntyre maintains, in Aristotelian fashion, that the defining goal of enquiry is truth and that the only adequate conception of this is a realist one which regards it as an objective relation of conformity between mind and world. As he observes, 'claims to truth, thus conceived, are claims to have transcended the limitations of any merely local standpoint'.[23] Thus, while styles and principles of enquiry may be tradition-specific, the ultimate goals of enquiry — truth for theory, goodness for action — are tradition-transcendent.

So much for the general objectivity of norms and the sometimes complex routes by which we may come to know them and be guided by them. This leaves a great deal to be done in developing a detailed account of the variety of human values. But the aims of this opening chapter have been to argue that philosophy does not exclude the possibility of an objectivist perspective of these and to suggest the general character of such an approach. As in the case of other natural beings we have natures by which our lives are structured and directed. But, of course, human natures are not only very complex they also include aspects which are certainly rare in nature and may be unique — such as rational psychologies.

---

[23] MacIntyre, 'Moral relativism, Truth and Justification', in L. Gormally ed. *Moral Truth and Moral Tradition:* (Dublin: Four Courts Press, 1994). In this connection see also MacIntyre, *First Principles, Final Ends and Contemporary Philosophical Issues,* Milwaukee: Marquette University Press, 1990) and John Haldane, 'MacIntyre's Thomist Revival: What Next?' together with MacIntyre's reply in Horton and Mendus, *After MacIntyre.*

Furthermore, while our natures may prescribe the general course of our lives they do not exhaustively determine it. It is part of the human form of life to deliberate and act in accord with reasons. In other words our rationality extends the possible range of directions in which we might develop. The task of moral thinking is to show how reflection can provide reasons for choosing some routes and not others. Practical philosophy may then employ this style of reflection in thinking about issues arising in the consulting room, the hospital ward, the laboratory, the military command centre, the court room or wherever else professional activities are pursued. I shall be concerned with issues from some of these fields in subsequent chapters where I will also explore further aspects of ethical and value theory more generally, and the derivation of recommendations and requirements, i.e. practical directives, from values and other facts. As will emerge, a central focus of my attention is the value of human life itself and the requirements, positive and negative, that follow from this.

2

Persons and Values

Introduction

This chapter falls into two markedly contrasting parts. The common theme is the value of persons, and in both parts a distinction is introduced between the (existential) value *of* life and the (qualitative) value that is realised *in* lives. Part one reflects upon discussions of an issue that was already known to earlier utilitarians in the form of questions about the qualitative and quantitative dimensions of hedonic value,[1] and about the utility of population growth.[2] These have become more prominent in recent value theory, however, as a result of Derek Parfit's influential work on the comparative value of contrasting situations involving different levels of wellbeing and numbers of people.[3] Here I am not directly concerned with Parfit's own thoughts but draw from a symposium involving two authors—John Broome and Adam Morton—whose work shares something of the 'moral mathematics' approach to value theory developed by Parfit, and whose exchange takes off from an

[1]   J.S. Mill, *Utilitarianism* (London: Dent, 1910) p. 6: 'It is quite compatible with the principle of utility to recognize the fact, that some kinds of pleasure are more desirable and more valuable than others. It would be absurd that while, in estimating all other things, quality is considered as well as quantity, the estimation of pleasures should be supposed to depend on quantity alone'.

[2]   Henry Sidgwick, *The Methods of Ethics*, seventh edition (Indianapolis, IN: Hackett, 1981) pp. 415-6: 'strictly conceived, the point up to which, on Utilitarian principle, population ought to be encouraged to increase, is not that at which average happiness is the greatest possible ... but that at which the product formed by multiplying the number of persons living into the amount of average happiness reaches its maximum'.

[3]   Derek Parfit, *Reasons and Persons* (Oxford: Clarendon Press, 1984).

issue posed by his writings, namely that of the 'repugnant conclusion'.

This manner of formulating and dealing with topics in moral philosophy tends to divide readers. Some welcome it as bringing rigour and precision to a subject that has often seemed to be little more than a melee of claims and counter claims, often invoking a confusing diversity of virtues, values and obligations. Others, however, see it as driven by a dominating desire for simplicity and unity that are entirely unsuited to the subject of human experience and conduct, and which forces reductionism with regard to it.

I do not propose to enter into that large and intractable debate; but having in the first part presented something of the methods and concerns of the moral mathematicians I shall then approach the issue of the value *of*, and the value *in* life through a contrasting method of case study. This involves exploring aspects of the circumstances and responses of imagined individuals with a view to answering a specific question about the nature of the responsibilities that persons may have for one another. In this second part issues are addressed not by using any kind of logic of value, but by imagining different kinds of descriptions, interpretations and assessments of a particular situation, examining what is most deeply at issue within it.

PART ONE

The Method of Intuition

As they are treated within formal social choice theory, population and reproduction ethics are notoriously difficult and not just because of their technicality. Some of the deepest problems concern the nature of the fundamental assumptions upon which formal techniques are deployed. It is difficult to know where to begin, with what premises to start. A widely-favoured approach aims to identify commonly held intuitions about the sources and forms of value. It does so either by cataloguing explicit expressions of such intuitions, or by seeking to show that they are presupposed to pre-theoretical judgements about what is prohibited, permitted, desirable, or required.

So, for example, it is sometimes held that *ceteris paribus*, the existence of a worthwhile human life is good, and that (yet other things being equal) situations in which there are more such lives are better than ones in which there are fewer. A problem arising from this purported intuition, however, is that it seems (on both total and average welfare-maximising theories) to lead, directly or indirectly, to Derek Parfit's 'Repugnant Conclusion' — the favouring of large populations suffering low welfare levels over smaller populations enjoying higher ones. As Parfit formulates it:

> *The Repugnant Conclusion*: For any possible population P, all with a very high quality of life, there must be some much larger imaginable population P+N whose existence, if other things are equal, would be better, even though its members have lives that are barely worth living'[4]

The appeal to intuitions and the concern to avoid paradoxes and other troublesome implications form a large part of the background to an exchange between John Broome and Adam Morton.[5] Both authors are concerned with the coherence of attempts to give precise expression to an idea that they term 'the basic intuition'. While Broome says that he is not engaged in its defence he describes this intuition as 'common and attractive' and explores arguments for it. Morton writes with similar sympathy; and along with others such as Jan Narveson,[6] both feel the draw of the 'intuition'. This common inclination gives added interest to their search after adequate formulations of it.

The initial imprecise expression of the basic idea is that a person's existence is ethically neutral, not *as such* a good thing. In the context of procreation this emerges in the thought that adding a person to the world has no intrinsic

[4]   Derek Parfit, (1984) *Reasons and Persons* ch. 17: 'The Repugnant Conclusion'.

[5]   John Broome, and Adam Morton, 'The Value of a Person', *Proceedings of the Aristotelian Society, Supplementary Volume*, 68, 1994.

[6]   Jan Narveson,' Moral problems of Population', *Monist*, 57 (1973); see also *Moral Matters* (Peterborough, Ontario: Broadview Press, 1993) Ch. 8.

value. It is allowed that the effects upon the welfare of others of such an additional life bear upon the question of whether to originate it, and that its own quality is also relevant, at least if it were bad; but the *fact* of a life's existence, even of the existence of a happy life, is not reason to create it. Such, at least, is the claim of the basic intuition.

John Broome is exercised not by the question of why some people think in this way, nor, directly with whether they are right to do so; but rather with what precisely the content of the thought is. To this end, and in Parfitian manner, he explores various possible formulations such as that the ethical neutrality of existence can be expressed in terms of comparative judgements about the value of states of affairs in which the person exists and those from which he or she is absent. Thus a state of affairs S^1 is equally good as another S^2 if and only if it is equally as good for the common population or constitutency C. The presence of an arbitrary individual x in S^2, even if x's life is a happy one, makes no intrinsic contribution to the value of that state of affairs. *Adding people is not, as such, adding value.*

It might seem that this formulation is so near to the original that there could be no objection to it that was not a direct objection to the intuition itself. Broome may concede this; but he is prepared to consider the possibility that difficulties with constitutency principles might not refute the basic intuition.[7] At any rate what he offers by way of objection to such principles seems pretty decisive. To take the simplest case involving equal goodness and strict betterness, consider the following sequence of states of affairs:

	1	2	3	...	N	N+1
S^1	$(p_1,$	$p_2,$	$p_3,$	...	p_n	$\Omega)$
S^2	$(p_1,$	$p_2,$	$p_3,$	...	p_n	x,1)
S^3	$(p_1,$	$p_2,$	$p_3,$	...	p_n	x,2)

---

[7]   He defines several such principles for different comparatives: intransitive betterness, conditional betterness and relative betterness.

In S^1 x does not exist; in S^2 x does exist and his lifetime wellbeing has the value 1; in S^3 again x exists, this time with a wellbeing value of 2. If we compare S^1 and S^2 according to the constituency principle the relevant population is the p_n number of people and, since the two states are as good for them, S^1 and S^2 emerge as equally good. If we next compare S^1 and S^3 the principle yields a corresponding evaluative equivalence, and for the same reason. However, comparing S^2 and S^3 involves a different constituency – the p_{n+1} people (i.e. x included) and what we find is that because of the greater well-being of x in S^3, it transpires that S^3 is better than S^2. Thus, where

$$\overset{g}{=} \quad \text{indicates} \quad \text{'equally good'}$$

and

$$\overset{g}{>} \quad \text{indicates} \quad \text{'better than'}$$

we have

(1) $\quad (S^1 \overset{g}{=} S^2)$

(2) $\quad (S^1 \overset{g}{=} S^3)$

(3) $\quad (S^3 \overset{g}{>} S^2) \quad$ i.e. $\neg (S^2 \overset{g}{=} S^3)$

(4) $\quad (S^2 \overset{g}{=} S^3) \qquad\qquad$ from (1 & 2) by transitivity

(5) $\quad (S^2 \overset{g}{=} S^3) \quad \& \neg (S^2 \overset{g}{=} S^3) \quad$ from (3 & 4). Contradiction!

Broome goes on to consider various cases involving different evaluative relations between possible states of affairs with varying constituencies and derives similar contradictory conclusions. I find these results decisive (and notwithstanding a technical suggestion of his own so too does Morton). The question, however, is what exactly it is that these results refute.

The arguments certainly show that one cannot hold on to *both* the constituency principle and the transitivity of evaluative comparatives, in particular that of strict betterness. So one or other or *both* must go. The following range of possibilities opens up.

(1)   Abandon the principle and the intuition.

(2)   Retain the principle and the intuition, expressing the former in terms that avoid betterness (perhaps deontically, in terms of obligations).

(3)   Retain the principle and the intuition but deny that betterness is transitive.

(4)   Abandon the principle and retain the intuition, formulating it in terms of relativised or vague betterness.

Broome and Morton examine several of the possibilities that involve retaining the intuition and find difficulties with them, yet neither seems inclined to worry about the proper object of the intuition itself.[8] However, there are reasons to do so. To begin with, consider the following purportedly pre-theoretical formulations:

> *[A]dding a person to the world is not valuable in itself* [9]

> *[N]o reason [to have a child] arises from the person's own interest* [10]

> *The existence of a person is ethically neutral in itself* [11]

> *We are ... neutral about making happy people* [12]

---

[8]   Subsequently, however, Broome returned to the 'intuition' of the ethical neutrality of existence in *Weighing Lives* (Oxford: Oxford University Press, 2004), and rejects it, accepting the repugnant conclusion in the form that a large enough population, each of whose member's well-being is slightly above the neutral level (that at which it is neither better nor worse to bring someone at that level of well-being into existence) will always be better than a small population whose members have better lives. All of this, however, is discussed in terms of the worth of states of affairs *in* lives, and does not the address the issue of the value *of* lives, where this might be independent of the former.

[9]   See Broome, p. 167; Morton, p. 190.

[10]   Broome, p. 167.

[11]   Broome, p. 167.

[12]   Narveson cited by Broome, p. 167.

It is not in a person's interest to be created [13]

These are not equivalent claims. At one point Morton wonders whether the intuition concerns value or requirement but that relates to what might be termed the moral modality of the claim—whether it is a matter of goodness or oughtness—and not its substantive content, in particular its point of focus.[14] In the formulations above, and elsewhere in their papers, there is a tendency to move between two thoughts:

1. *The existence of a person is, as such, evaluatively neutral;*

2. *A would-be person's positive interests give no reason to bring her or him into existence.*

This oscillation raises a question concerning the main underlying assumption about the locus of value, namely, that what has value is the actual or determined *wellbeing* of individuals. One might ask, however, why one should assume this and the intuition that expresses it? One reason might be that both are obvious; another could be a concern that different assumptions about the value *of* life (not only the value *in* it) lead to Parfit's repugnant conclusion. So that if we say that a life is, as such, intrinsically valuable and that it is therefore good to create it, we may end up committed to the view that larger populations are better than smaller ones even though their members are worse off. So we should only be concerned with improving the welfare of *actual* people; the prospect of good lives gives no intrinsic reason for creating them. This, however, risks blocking the way to what are certainly intelligible, and may also seem intuitively compelling policies of improvement—such as making a better world by raising the condition of mankind through creating people whose lives are foreseeably better than those of the present generation.

---

[13] Broome, p. 183.
[14] Morton, p. 190.

Challenging Intuitions

This latter worry touches upon the supposed asymmetry between creating bad and good lives, but it is also worth challenging the intuition directly. First, then, distinguish between two sorts of value: *existential* or ontological value, and *qualitative* or welfare value. Now consider the suggestion that, *ceteris paribus*, it is good to bring a life into being for reasons other than ones of wellbeing, either that of the created individual or that of others. What of the claim that life has intrinsic existential value? This might be put by saying that the actualisation of a living nature through the coming to be of an instance of it is good in and of itself, and that its perishing is *pro tanto* bad. Is *that* intuitively plausible? It is certainly a familiar idea and might be thought to be presupposed by various judgements, including comparative ones concerning smaller and greater populations. Something like it also features in environmentalist claims about the value of species diversity and the disvalue of species extinction. Of course, it is not as such a welfarist concern but to object to it on that ground alone is evidently question-begging.

What though of the repugnant conclusion? First, if I think it would be good to create a life because of its intrinsic value am I committed to the optimizing principle that it would be better to create two lives rather than just one, three rather than two, and so on? Not obviously. Apart from questioning the assumed requirement of maximising there is the point that if I do not operate within welfarist consequentialism it is not clear that I must accept the characterisations in virtue of which the repugnant conclusion is taken to be repugnant.

Furthermore, I might have a combined intuition to the effect that existence is a value and so is wellbeing; but that they are incommensurable. So suppose I agree that, *ceteris paribus*, more people is (*existentially*) better. This may stand alongside the claim that, *ceteris paribus*, higher wellbeing levels are (*qualitatively*) better. The latter provides an anchor against the pull towards the repugnant conclusion, but assuming incommensurability it also resists the attempt at a systematic and continuous ordering in terms of some common value.

Perhaps going this way may be thought to leave behind the means of substantiating other intuitions. Adam Morton discusses the asymmetry between creating and destroying life using his preferred incomparability formulation to explain this.[15] But the asymmetry is not weakened and indeed it is considerably strengthened if we say that creating a life has value, or even, deontically, that it is some sort of requirement — an imperfect duty, say, relativised to certain classes of agent. For the asymmetry to be preserved we need only recognise that it is a weaker requirement than that of protecting life, both of which are weaker than a requirement not to destroy it. All of this is just as one would expect if life itself is not ethically neutral.

Morton ends by saying that: 'the basic intuition that creating people is morally neutral would not be an interesting one unless people's well-being were not morally neutral. People are valuable but creating them is not'.[16] The rationale for the first idea is clear enough: if the well-being of people were neutral one would expect that the creation of them would be so too. Perhaps, but it is the second idea that puzzles me. If people are so valuable why is this not, *ceteris paribus*, reason to create them, or at least reason to regard their coming into existence as *a* good? I think I have an intuition that this is so; but I also have a hunch that intuitions *per se* are often best taken *cum grano salis* — with a pinch of salt. What need to be brought into the discussion are first, a phenomenology of human value giving an account of the objects of our experiential recognition of it, and second, a metaphysics of persons relating practical requirement to the realisation and protection of personal value, showing how such value attaches to rational sentient natures. By themselves, however, intuitions are blind. With that thought in mind let me now proceed to part two.

---

[15] Morton, pp. 193-4.
[16] Morton, p. 197.

PART TWO

The Method of Case Study

Within the fields of practical ethics there has been a growing trend over the last decade or so to use the method of case study. This involves framing reflections around consideration (often from more than one perspective) of real or imagined examples where relevant values or requirements are at issue. Although the historical origins of this lie in the field of casuistry, which I discussed in the introduction, recent deployments originated in bio- and health-care ethics.[17] By way of example, about twenty years ago the *Journal of Medical Ethics* invited its readers to consider an imagined, but entirely realistic case history involving a married couple Phillip and Patricia Green. Readers were then challenged to answer the question: what are Patricia Green's responsibilities to Phillip: are they those of a wife to a husband or those of a woman to a stranger?[18]

First, I present the case history. The problems presented in this narrative are clearly tragic. What is recounted is a not unfamiliar pattern of events involving a transition from a life of interest, activity and satisfaction to one of apathy, passivity and irritation. Often these changes bring great unhappiness to others, in particular to immediate relatives; and as in the imagined example, this unhappiness may be so great as to threaten the continuity of family life (the good of which I discuss in chapter seven 'Families and why they Matter'). Next, I consider the particular problems from three perspectives: those of the main characters Phillip and Patricia Green, and that of a philosopher interested in the nature of persons and personal values (these characters are not represented as being in dialogue).

---

[17] See A.R. Jonsen, 'Casuistry' in J. Sugarman and D. Sulmasy eds. *Methods in Medical Ethics* (Washington, DC: Georgetown University Press, 2001); and A. Lonsen & S. Toulmin, *The Abuse of Casuistry: A History of Moral Reasoning* (Cambridge: Cambridge University Press, 1988).

[18] *Journal of Medical Ethics* 14 (1988), p. 38. The following section originates in my response to the challenge 'Persons and Values' pp. 39-41.

Case History

Phillip Green is a 62-year-old car-manufacturing worker who takes early retirement. He enjoys his retirement, is active and helpful in the home, considerate to his wife and on good terms with his large family. His main hobby is gardening, and over the years he has won many prizes for his dahlias. In the year after retiring he does particularly well and wins more prizes than ever before. Phillip and his wife are also keen dancers. On Friday and Saturday nights they go down to the local club, dance and chat. Mr Green is a popular and sociable man and the couple are well liked.

On Sunday Mr Green and his wife go to morning service at their local Anglican church. For Sunday lunch they usually visit one of their three children, and particularly like playing with their grandchildren whom they are inclined to spoil. A year after retiring he has a stroke which leaves him with a mild left-sided hemiplegia (half-body paralysis). He is able to hobble around indoors. His speech is normal. Following the stroke his character is markedly different. He is morose and introspective. His only activity is to sit and think about the past. He is demanding of his wife, treating her like a servant. He loses interest in his gardening and no longer goes down to the club. When his friends call on him he usually shows little interest in them although occasionally he enjoys talking with them about the past.

He finds his grandchildren irritating, and the weekly visits for Sunday lunch have ceased to be a pleasure either for his wife or for his children. All are glad when the time comes for them to depart. He is unaware of the change either in his role or his character. His wife, Patricia Green, tells the social worker that she no longer wishes to look after her husband. She says: 'It is like being married to a stranger; it would have been better had he died'.

The Philosopher

Patricia's concluding remark about her husband is suggestive: 'It is like being married to a stranger; it would have been better had he died'. We can regard this as an anguished outcry, which it is; but to treat it as no more than that risks dismissing what may also be the expression of a moral view.

Patricia's remarks suggest two ideas that have long interested philosophers. First, that personal identity is a matter of psychological continuity,[19] and thus that if changes in personality (understood in these terms) are sufficiently radical one is no longer dealing with the same *person*, notwithstanding that one may be faced with the same *human being*. This psychological view of personal identity has specific implications for the present case.

The second idea that may be implicit in Patricia's words concerns the value of life. Here we need to distinguish two views which it will be convenient to term 'intrinsicalist' and 'extrinsicalist' and which correspond broadly to the earlier distinction between existential (ontological) and qualitative (welfare) values. According to the extrinsicalist, the value of an individual life is given by the value of the contingent states that occur within it and by the difference it makes to the world through its achievements and its effects upon others. In the extrinsicalist view, life itself has no value; mere existence is worthless and if that existence should suffer or produce bad effects (without countervailing positive ones) the life may be judged to have disvalue. By contrast, the intrinsicalist argues that whatever value attaches to human beings through their contingent conditions or accomplishments, they also have a basic intrinsic (existential) value which is immune to the effects of failure or misfortune. Whatever one achieves or fails to achieve, however one affects others or is affected by them, one's life retains (without increase or diminution) its basic intrinsic value.

---

[19] In Parfit's view such continuity is further explained in terms of connectedness thus: 'psychological connectedness is the holding of particular direct psychological connections [and] psychological continuity is the holding of overlapping chains of strong connectedness' *Reasons and Persons*, p. 206.

The relevance of this distinction in the present context is that if one regards the value of life as given by the values realised by and in it, and if these should reduce, or be replaced by negative values, then it makes sense to suppose that it would be better if an individual so affected were to die. For the intrinsicalist, however, while a life turned sour has lost much that gave it point and qualitative worth, nonetheless it retains its basic 'existential' value. To say this, however, is not to say that life should always be prolonged, nor even that it may not be intentionally ended. The question of whether one is required to refrain from or to pursue these ends is a further matter.

Patricia Green

My strongest feeling is of despair. I don't know what to do for the best. Phillip and I were very lucky. We built our lives together; we made a family in which we were all close and we created a happy home. We both worked hard and looked forward to enjoying the fruits of our efforts. When Phillip retired it seemed we could hope for many years of happiness. Things even became better. Phillip had his friends and his hobbies; he didn't pine after his old work but enjoyed the freedom to develop his gardening and was happy to have more time for me and the family. I was also happier than ever before. We could relax and share things together in a way that hadn't been possible before. We had a good marriage and were becoming even closer. Then Phillip had his stroke. At first I thought he was going to die and I prayed and begged God to spare him—I couldn't imagine living without him.

Then he was saved and seemed to be recovering. He was able to get out of bed and walk around. His speech was alright and although he was irritable and distracted I put this down to the stroke and the shock it gave him. Of course, I didn't think he would be exactly as before. I knew for instance that there wouldn't be any more dancing, and that his gardening wouldn't be the same. But I supposed that there was enough in our life together for us to be happy again. Now I can see that the stroke wasn't like a broken leg that would simply stop him getting around as well as before. It was more like the death of the man I had married and lived with all these years, followed by his replacement by someone that I don't like or want to be with, but who makes demands on me which everyone thinks I should obey.

I know it sounds cruel and selfish but I want to be free of this hell. The man I loved was destroyed by the stroke; the one who sits at home ordering me about, who has none of the interests of Phillip and has little time for friends or family, is a stranger. Surely it isn't right that I should be forced to be with this man until the end of his or my days? I am sorry for him but I cannot say I love him. It would be better for him and all concerned if he were dead. It would be better for me if I were free.

Philip Green

Some time ago I had a stroke. It left me partly disabled and so I can't do all the things I used to; but that apart little has changed for me since my retirement. It seems these days, though, that Patricia isn't so concerned about me as I think she should be. She wants too much and bothers me by going on about friends and family. I like to see people, but she can't understand that I also want peace and quiet. I worked hard for over forty years and brought home the money that bought this home, supported the family, paid for holidays, and so on. Now I'm entitled to spend my days in rest. Patricia should be more considerate and attentive. Especially since the stroke I need looking after, but these days she doesn't seem to be bothered or else vexes me for not doing what she wants. I think she should be grateful for what she has got and give me the attention I need.

The Philosopher

Perhaps the central feature of this case is the way in which Phillip and Patricia have changed their perceptions of one another. The stroke wrought havoc in their settled life together; but as important as the objective circumstances are the ways in which they now regard one another. Patricia oscillates between a view of her husband as the same person as before though changed for the worse, and a view of him as so altered as, in effect, to be a different person. Phillip unknowingly sees himself quite differently from in the past but supposes that Patricia's behaviour is an indication both of her inability to make the transition to a life of retirement and of her lack of sympathy for his condition.

We know what Patricia says she would like to do, and it is within the bounds of practical possibility that she could be relieved of the task of living with and caring for Phillip. The moral question to be considered, however, is that of what ought to be thought and done. A good deal could be said on behalf of both parties about the difficulties created by this tragedy but philosophically it will be most useful to return to the issues of the nature and value of persons.

In a familiar sense of the expression Phillip is undeniably a 'different character'. His personality has altered and this affects the way he acts and the ways in which he thinks about himself and others. Yet the changes in his psychology are not so radical as even to suggest the possibility that he should be considered a different person. What is essential to persons is not that they retain the personality they have developed but that they continue to exhibit characteristics constitutive of personhood. These include psychological and physical features, but it is not necessary that the same features should be preserved.

A man whose body has been destroyed ceases to exist; one who has been badly injured and had limbs and organs replaced is radically changed yet remains the same individual as before. Likewise, had all indications of personality vanished from Phillip perhaps we might say that he had ceased to be a person,[20] but this is not the case and for all the differences in him he is largely psychologically continuous with his former self.

---

[20] We might also say, however, that though he remains a person by nature he is no longer able to engage in personal life, he is a 'disabled' person.

The person from whom Patricia wishes to be free is undoubtedly one and the same person as that whom she married and with whom she was happy to make her life. She cannot legitimately claim, therefore, that her duties and other moral attachments to Phillip do not extend to the man with whom she still shares part of her life.

Patricia says that given the loss of so much that was of value about Phillip prior to his stroke (his abilities, interests, affections etc), it would now be better if he were dead. Though emotionally intelligible this betrays a view of persons that is both logically and morally confused. Patricia's problem is partly a failure of imagination. She cannot see things from Phillip's new perspective and is unable to appreciate that his life has as much reality now as it had before, or as has her own. Whatever may have befallen him he is still a person—a subject of consciousness and agency—and as such is deserving of equal respect. In point of personhood he is no less real than anyone else. This fact is independent of his merits and of the benefits and losses he brings to himself and to others. It is the basis of the respect owing to him, just as Patricia's personhood is the ground of her basic rights. In affirming these entitlements on her own behalf she cannot coherently deny them to Phillip.

Not all moral features are similarly basic and impartial. Some obligations hold in virtue of special relationships between persons both as individuals and as the occupants of social roles. While there may be some duties that we owe to all persons, and from which we are not discharged by changes in our relationships with them, there are others that only attach to specific relationships, such as the special duties of a teacher, of a doctor, of a friend, and of a parent.

Patricia has responsibilities towards Phillip of both these impartial and partial kinds. Firstly, she owes him the respect due to a person, and this prohibits the attitude that it would be better for all concerned had he died as a result of his stroke. Whatever losses are incurred by his change of circumstances his life has a reality and a value that demand respect. He should not now be thought of simply as an impediment to the happiness of others, any more than he should previously have been regarded simply as a means to the end of general welfare. When all was well Patricia may have thought of Phillip as someone whose life had intrinsic value or regarded his life in ways that presupposed this, and since nothing has changed in regard to his status as an autonomous person it would be wrong of her to regard him any differently now.

Secondly, Patricia owes Phillip the respect due to a husband, and this is at odds with her view of their present relationship as being akin to one between strangers. For all that Phillip's character has changed he is the same person whom she married and their connection as husband and wife remains as before. Over time personalities develop slowly in various intelligible ways which we usually find it relatively easy to accommodate in our relationships. Phillip and Patricia are unfortunate in that his character has changed in a manner and at a rate that would not normally be expected or prepared for. This presents deep and difficult psychological problems of adjustment and may impose burdens which their marriage cannot bear. But so far as concerns the moral relationship between them this is unchanged. Patricia Green's responsibilities to Phillip are those of a wife to a husband.[21]

Indeed, their difficult circumstances may be seen as disclosing how far marital responsibilities extend. Vows taken in a wedding ceremony commit the parties to a shared life together and are not contingent upon that life proceeding in a single direction towards the attainment of ever more and greater benefits. The extent of the commitment may never reveal itself yet it is implicit in the marriage. Patricia cannot consistently be grateful for her marital relationship with Phillip and now seek to be free of its implications. Either she must

---

[21] What these responsibilities are depends in part on the parties conception of the nature of those roles as they voluntarily and intentionally entered in to them, but also and essentially on the nature of the roles themselves as they are determined by the institution(s) of marriage. Compare the related case of responsibilities acquired through the making of mutual promises.

disavow her marriage, regarding their past lives together as a co-operative endeavour justified only by mutual advantage; or else she must affirm it, in which case she now faces the difficult task of caring for him and of finding new ways of their taking pleasure in one another's company. It is also important to emphasise that Patricia's duties are accompanied by entitlements. For although Phillip's faculties are diminished he retains moral responsibilities to his wife. Of course, reciprocity is easier to describe than to realise in practice, even in favoured circumstances, but it is necessary to note that while Phillip remains a fitting object of respect, he is also a proper subject of claims to be respected made of him by his friends and family.

These philosophical ideas also have practical implications: first, in the sense that they prescribe a norm for Patricia's conduct with regard to Phillip: she is to treat him as one deserving of respect as a person and of loving as a husband; and second, in the respect that they suggest a course of action which may serve to improve the situation. Each of the parties is inclined to view matters from the perspective of his or her own concerns. In the case of Phillip this is obvious enough from the case history and from his description of the situation. In the case of Patricia it is implicit in her remarks to the social worker and in her observations presented above. The unacceptability of moral solipsism and of a concern only with the extrinsic values of lives have been discussed from a philosophical point of view, but practically these tendencies are best overcome by attempting to achieve in turn both impartial and partial viewpoints.

One needs to see others and oneself as being equally real and equally deserving of respect and this is achieved by adopting the impartial viewpoint: thereby seeing oneself as being but one among many persons. Equally, though, if one is to care for others one must feel a sympathy towards them and this requires the ability to enter imaginatively into their perspective: to share for some while their partial viewpoint. Patricia's difficult task might be made easier and Phillip's outlook might be improved if each could be encouraged to make greater efforts to see things from the other's point of view and from the impartial perspective sought for by the philosopher. In that way some kind of limited solution to their problem might be forthcoming.

Conclusion

The approach and methods of Broome and Morton are less concerned with the question of what constitutes human wellbeing than with the issue of how various goods, of whatever sort, contribute to the overall goodness of a situation. It is entirely compatible with their approach — and both, I think, accept this — that there are factors other than wellbeing which determine the goodness of states of affairs; and also that the question of what should be done cannot in general be resolved simply by reference to situational goodness.

This suggests that the discussions of parts one and two above might be complementary: that the style of exploration illustrated in the latter is relevant to determining some of the non-welfare values that might stand alongside the comparative measures of goods illustrated in the former. Or again, that while the second is concerned with the specific content of judgements of wellbeing, the first addresses their formal features.

There is truth in both these 'ecumenical' suggestions but they miss more obvious contrasts. For while utility calculations and comparisons are most naturally concerned with abstract representations and measures of constituent and overall aggregated value, the case-study method explores the structure of situations in terms of human experiences and responses, and it is therefore sensitive to the particular, specific concepts participants themselves apply in interpreting situations. The importance of this is multi-faceted; but one obvious aspect is the fact that how agents conceive their actions is relevant to the question of what it is that they have done or failed to do, and consequently to whether their behaviour is reasonable or even intelligible.

While comparative formal measures abstract from detailed assessments they presuppose them as sources of valuation; and it at this earlier stage that concepts of value and as well as those of virtue and of requirement are formed and refined. Unless this has been achieved at least to some degree, then moral mathematics has nothing to work with. Talk of 'wellbeing', and the use of formal techniques can conceal this dependence. There is also the idea introduced in part one and deployed in part two that there may be value in the lives of human beings apart from the value of their experiences or effects, and this is in danger of being excluded as not amenable to quantitative measure or comparative weighting.

Yet arguably the deepest source of ethical experience lies in the recognition of the peculiar value of human beings as subjects and fellow persons, and as bearers of various kinds of mutual normative relations. Some of the latter may plausibly be regarded as contractual, such as marriage, but others, such as parenthood are culturally transformed relations rooted in our animal nature. It is in terms of such values and relations that we can best make sense of sentiments of solidarity. In the next chapter I shall be considering something further of these issues as they bear on conditions and stages of human existence. Later I will return to other aspects of the value of special relationships, more specifically family ones, and later still will take up the matter of solidarity as it relates to wider social relationships and serves to ground public responsibilities.

The dimensions of personal value extend beyond wellbeing to include existential and relational values, the first of which is logically antecedent to qualitative value, and the second of which is a condition of the possibility of certain elements of wellbeing, as well as a determinant of them. In order for welfare value to be realized many other things need to be in place, and these others are often the focus of our deepest moral experiences and are central to our sense of what it is to be a human person in community with others. That state or condition is itself misrepresented in utilitarian accounts of personal and social responsibilities as ultimately justified in relation to the promotion of some independent notion of wellbeing. It is misrepresented also by social contractarian accounts that look to the benefits of cooperation pursued for the sake of mutual advantage. For one thing the latter neglect, and are inadequate to deal with circumstances in which there are significant asymmetries of capacity and power between parties, or in which purported reasons for entering into a contract are strained or lapse but where parties remain under obligations of justice or charity (in the sense of *caritas* as altruistic concern).[22] As will become clear in the next chapter these considerations have application beyond the sphere of immediate personal relations.

---

[22] In this connection and in relation to the matter of the following chapter see Martha Nussbaum, *Frontiers of Justice: Disability, Nationality, Species Membership* (Cambridge, MA: Harvard University Press, 2006) Ch. 3.

3

Recognising Humanity

Introduction

Talk of 'persons' in moral philosophy often indicates an approach that looks to formal features of individuals such as the capacity for practical reason and autonomous agency. 'Humanity', by contrast, intimates a distinctive kind of animal nature, and although it typically introduces notions of moral status it does not carry resonances of a high competency requirement. It also has connotations of affectivity: for humanity is also what is cognised and expressed through forms of feeling.

In her book *Hiding From Humanity: Disgust, Shame, and the Law*[1] Martha Nussbaum addresses the place of emotions, and their objects in the justification of law and punishment, and in the ethical foundation of political liberalism. She brings to the task an unusual combination of philosophical reflections and psychological insights, controlled and applied by an unmistakably humane sensibility. In this chapter I discuss various issues raised by her treatment of these subjects, touching on four matters.

First, there is the extent to which Nussbaum's approach parallels that of Alasdair MacIntyre in *Dependent Rational Animals*.[2] Their interests are convergent and complementary, and it may be that a systematic synthesis of ideas

---

[1] Martha Nussbaum, *Hiding From Humanity: Disgust, Shame, and the Law* (Princeton, NJ: Princeton University Press, 2004).

[2] Alasdair MacIntyre, *Dependent Rational Animals* (London: Duckworth, 1999).

advanced by each would serve to strengthen the general case for reorienting moral, social and political philosophy so as to take greater account of universal human limitation and specific human disability. I shall not attempt that here but will begin by outlining a broad standpoint on the human condition within which the insights of both philosophers can be placed, noting towards the end of the section an apparent difficulty for the explicit structure of Nussbaum's own argument.

Second, there is the issue of the nature of disability and its relation to conditions such as handicap and impairment. I find reason to disagree with Nussbaum in respect of some conceptual claims but not, I think, in broad approach.

Third, there is the specific case discussed by Nussbaum of mentally disabled children. I would like to introduce the related, though in respects quite different, matter of mental disorder and the stigma attaching to that.

Fourth, acknowledging the strong case Nussbaum's makes for recognising and respecting humanity in its weakness and dependency, as well as in its strength and (relative) independence, there is the question of what bearing this might have on the issues of abortion as this is justified by reference to the diagnosis of embryonic abnormality and anticipated handicap, and euthanasia as the latter is argued for by reference to incapacity, loss of autonomy and the approach of death.

Dependent Humanity

From conception, through gestation, in birth and in infancy, through our inclining and in our declining years, we depend on others: materially, educationally, intellectually and morally. We are, to borrow MacIntyre's phrase, 'dependent rational animals'. Furthermore, our rationality is developed in dependence on others, and it is part of our animal nature, aspects of which we share with other species. Recognition of this latter fact is important for shaping an accurate understanding of and respect for the lives of other non-human animals but also, and more importantly, for keeping in view our own bodily character and needs.

For some while, moral philosophers have been asking us to consider and understand what human beings have in common with other animal species, but in modern times it is only quite recently that they have urged us to attend to human dependency, vulnerability and disability. *Hiding from Humanity* is an important contribution of this latter sort.[3] Whereas MacIntyre's main focus is the range and rationale of human virtue, Nussbaum is concerned with politics and law, and with the roles (good and bad) of emotions in relation to these. Both agree, however, that philosophers have given insufficient attention to our animal nature and to the extent of our dependence upon one another.

There is certainly something apt about this criticism, for advocates of virtue ethics have typically emphasised the role of habits of choice and avoidance in promoting a positively good, bright-eyed and bushy tailed kind of life. Admittedly, writing thirty years ago in answer to the question 'Why do men need virtues?' Peter Geach observed that 'we need courage in order to persevere in face of setbacks, weariness, difficulties, and dangers'[4] and went on to say that 'Men need virtues as bees need stings' suggesting their protective role; and others of the same generation of neo-Aristotelians, such as Philippa Foot and Geoffrey Warnock pointed out that virtue is made necessary by the fact that life is threatened with dangers. Even so, the dominant image has been of intelligent, educated, healthy and mobile adults, fashioning rewarding lives consisting of largely unimpeded activities. The mentally retarded, the physically disabled, the deformed, the senile, and others of similar conditions hardly feature in mainstream philosophical thinking about how to live. They or their proxies might well suppose that this is because contemporary moral philosophers conceive of virtue and the ends it serves in terms

---

[3]   See also Nussbaum, *Frontiers of Justice: Disability, Nationality, Species Membership*.

[4]   Peter Geach, *The Virtues* (Cambridge: Cambridge University Press, 1977), pp. 16-17.

that necessarily exclude them. To judge from much of the 'virtue ethics' literature it seems the good life is one only lived by the able and independent.

Of course, even on that assumption it does not follow that the virtuous should have no concern for unfortunates, but such concern will typically be conceived of as external to the benevolent's own formation as a rational agent, and far removed from his or her well being. On this account interaction with the dis- and un-abled may be of value as expressing a sympathetic and generous spirit, but it is inessential to the business of coming to live and of continuing to enjoy a good life. Relevant in this connection, since I will later return to the issue of life in the womb, is Rosalind Hursthouse's discussion of 'Virtue Theory and Abortion'.[5] Her principle concern is to respond to the charge that a virtues-based approach to ethics fails to provide a basis for decision, and she tries to meet that challenge by considering how the issue of ending a pregnancy looks from the perspective of virtue, rather than from those of duty or rights or utility. There is much of interest in the essay but for present purposes I want to identify a way in which the foetus is largely left out of consideration, or only enters indirectly.

The point I am concerned with has to be distinguished from another that Hursthouse herself makes. At one point she writes, with deliberate boldness: 'the status of the foetus — that issue over which so much ink has been spilt — is, according to virtue theory, simply not relevant to the rightness or wrongness of abortion (within, that is, a secular society)'.[6] Her claim here is that while the virtuous person should certainly be concerned with the familiar facts of human reproduction: conception, pregnancy and birth, they should not look for guidance to some special metaphysical facts about the moral status of embryos. The seriousness of aborting a pregnancy is, or should be known to anyone of ordinary experience and sound mind,: 'the fact that the premature termination of pregnancy is in some

[5]   Rosalind Hursthouse, 'Virtue Theory and Abortion', *Philosophy and Public Affairs*, 20 (1991).
[6]   Hursthouse, p. 236.

sense, the cutting off of a new human life, and thereby, like the procreation of new human life, connects with all our thoughts about human life and death, parenthood, and family relationships, must make it a serious matter'.[7]

Hursthouse certainly recognises that if there is an abortion then a human being ends up dead and that 'some evil has probably been brought about';[8] but the focus of her attention is on the attitudes, thoughts and feelings of the mother and what these say about the kind of person she is. The situation appears analogous to that in which philosophers have argued that the main objection to cruelty to animals is the harm done to human beings by allowing themselves to be vicious. What does not get much attention is the fact that the foetus is a vulnerable human being in process of biological development and existing in unique dependence on the mother, and that part of what it is to be a pregnant woman is to be formed by such dependence. In other words the moral relationship of the foetus to the mother is, like the physical one, internal and partly constitutive. A pregnant mother is not just a woman with a baby lodged inside her womb (which is one reason to resist Judith Jarvis Thompson's conjoined body analogy).[9] So to abort is to cut oneself free from an intrinsic intimate, existing in non-voluntary dependence upon one. Setting aside the issue of whether this is ever morally permissible the fact remains that virtue in this area should not be thought of as secondary to the agent's own formation, and removed from her well being.

MacIntyre observes that according to Aristotle 'since the recipient is inferior to the giver ... magnanimous men find pleasure in hearing of the good they do, and none in hearing what they receive'.[10] MacIntyre draws attention to this not only to reveal that the attitude Aristotle avows now seems distasteful, and to indicate that his account of the virtues

---

[7]   Hursthouse, p. 237.
[8]   Hursthouse, p. 242.
[9]   See Judith Jarvis Thompson, 'A Defense of Abortion', *Philosophy and Public Affairs*, 1 (1971).
[10]   Aristotle, *Nicomachean Ethics* IV 1124b 15.

should be corrected so as to replace it with something such
as humble generosity or, following Aquinas, *misericordia et
beneficentia* (taking pity and doing good),[11] but more com-
prehensively to suggest that in this respect Aristotle's view,
and a major strand in the tradition deriving from it go
wrong in failing to recognise the intrinsic vulnerability and
dependence of human lives. The virtuous man must needs
be disposed graciously to receive and is already indebted to
others for his formation and for the social dimension of his
life.

This provides part of a reply to the self-centredness challenge to virtue theory. As formulated by David Solomon in
the context of discussing internal objections to ethics of virtue, this appears as the claim that even if virtues such as justice, charity or amiability restrict the attention an agent may
give to his own interests, and require him to attend to the
needs and wants of others, an asymmetry remains between
a virtuous agent's regard for his own character and his attitude to the state of character of others. Solomon writes 'if I
am suitably concerned about others, shouldn't my concern
for them extend beyond a mere concerns that their wants,
needs and desires be satisfied, and encompass a concern
for *their* character?'.[12] His response is to acknowledge
some such asymmetry but to argue that it also occurs
ineliminably within deontological and utilitarian theories.
The relevance of MacIntyre's reminder of the modes of original and ongoing dependence is that it suggests that a
proper concern for virtuous character, with regard to both
doing and undergoing, will distribute itself across the
self/other distinction. Character formation, and reforma-
tion, are social activities already expressing various kinds of

---

[11] For Aquinas's account see *Summa Theologiae* IIa, IIae, qq. 30-32. Citing
Augustine's *City of God* Aquinas observes that ' mercy is heartfelt
sympathy for another's distress, impelling us to succour him if we
can. For mercy takes its name 'misericordia' from denoting a man's
compassionate heart [*miserum cor*] for another's unhappiness'. IIa,
IIae, q. 30, a. 1, *responsio*.
[12] David Solomon, 'Internal Objections to Virtue Ethics', *Midwest
Studies in Philosophy*, 13 (1988), reprinted in D. Statman, ed., *Virtue
Ethics* (Edinburgh: Edinburgh University Press, 1997), p. 172.

dependency and concern, and in choosing to act to benefit another it may be that my concern with their needs is partly focussed on their character as something important for them and important for me. Some asymmetries of agent/patient regard certainly remain ineliminable (and general to all theories) given (a) the distinctness of persons; (b) the requirement of personal responsibility; and (c) and, relatedly, respect for autonomy; but MacIntyre's reminder of the extent, variety and depth of human inter-dependence diminishes the contrast between self- and other-regarding concerns, and provides a better context to accommodate the facts of human vulnerability and the virtues of receiving and as well as of giving.

Martha Nussbaum is similarly mindful of the long-standing tendency of philosophers to work with an essentially positive, full-capacity, fully-functioning image of the human agent. Since her concerns are focussed on law and politics her attention is directed to discerning this sort of image in various picturings of the citizen. She writes first of the 'emphasis on perfection — self-sufficiency, competence, and (the fiction of) invulnerability' and links this to a second 'fiction', 'which has had and continues to have a profound influence on our very theories of social justice ... the myth of the citizen as a competent independent adult'.[13] And just as in the Aristotelean scheme the concern for unfortunates will generally be thought of as secondary and optional, so for recent contractarian political theorists 'provisions for people who aren't part of the bargain will be an afterthought, not part of the basic institutional structure to which they agree' (op. cit.). Nussbaum's point is well illustrated by the following from Rawls' *Political Liberalism* — and is heightened by the fact that the observation comes in a footnote:

> ... since the fundamental problem of justice concerns the relations among those who are full and active participants in society, and directly or indirectly associated together over the course of a whole life, it is reasonable to assume that everyone has physical needs and psychological capacities within some normal range. Thus the problem of spe-

[13] Nussbaum, p. 311.

cial care and how to teat the mentally defective are aside. If we can work out a viable theory for the normal range, we can attempt to handle these other cases later.[14]

Earlier Nussbaum characterises her own preferred 'imperfectionist' vision for society as follows:

> What I am calling for, in effect, is something that I do not expect we shall ever fully achieve: a society that acknowledges its own humanity, and neither hides us from it nor it from us; a society of citizens who admit that they are needy and vulnerable, and who discard the grandiose demands for omnipotence and completeness that have been at the heat of so much human misery, both public and private.[15]

One issue to which MacIntyre gives some attention, but on which Nussabum is surprisingly silent, is the way in which vulnerable people and groups are disadvantaged not by direct stigmatisation (which she does discuss in relation to dominant groups subordinating and stigmatising others by projecting onto them features found to be disgusting or shameful), but instead by being made the objects of forms of interest, concern or pity that entrench inequalities while putting them beyond the reach of challenge. MacIntyre mentions Foucault as one who 'reminds us that institutionalised networks of giving and receiving are also structures of unequal distributions of power, structures well-designed both to mask and to protect those same distributions'.[16] Nussbaum might find it helpful to consider analogous possibilities in relation to the ways in which pity is often directed towards the groups she selects for attention, in particular the economically disadvantaged, ethnic and racial minorities and the disabled.

Yet while this would be useful in analysing the mutual influence of emotions and political attitudes, it would also highlight the fact that not only pity but the emotions that she identifies and partitions into politically good and bad categories are all Janus faced. This fact cuts deep into the structure of Nussbaum's argument; for while disgust and shame

---

[14] John Rawls, *Political Liberalism* (New York: Columbia University Press, 1993) fn. 10. p. 272.

[15] Nussbaum, p. 17.

[16] MacIntyre, p. 102.

may be expressions of irrational disquiet about being human (weak, vulnerable, helpless against death, and so on), they may also be deployed in defence of that very status and in true recognition of its imperfection, and natural imperfectability. Likewise, anger, indignity, fear, grief and compassion, which are identified as particularly important in 'a political-liberal society, based on ideas of capability and functioning'[17] may, like pity, be expressions of irrationality and vice, and instruments of oppression.

Finally in this section in which I have been concerned to identify points of resemblance and complementarity between Nussbaum and MacIntyre it is worth introducing, in only briefly, a third contemporary philosopher who like these others registers a debt to Aristotelian thought and sees in it a better resource for an understanding of justice between persons than is provided for in liberal contractarian or utilitarian theories. In his recent book *Ethics*, David Wiggins develops a series of 'Neo-Aristotelean reflections on justice' out of which emerges a challenge to the Rawslian construction of various moral-political ideals.[18] Here, however, I am concerned with the background to these in what he describes as 'a first-order ethic of solidarity and reciprocity'.

Again like Nussbaum and MacIntyre, Wiggins emphasises against consequentialists and Kantians, the diversity of sources of morality, *pace* the unifying and reductionist impulses mentioned in the previous chapter. There is no single ultimate value or principle from which others may be derived or to which they contribute as parts. Yet there is a core to human morality, namely, the recognition of the common lot of human kind and the felt need to act out of solidarity, protecting one another from, and certainly not inflicting, 'menaces'. In connection with this idea which he also associates with Philippa Foot[19] he writes: 'In confrontation with the human form, we immediately entertain a

[17] Nussbaum, p. 345.
[18] David Wiggins, *Ethics: Twelve Lectures on the Philosophy of Morality* (Cambridge, MA: Harvard University Press, 2006) ch. 10.
[19] See Philippa Foot, 'Morality, Action and Outcome' in Honderich, T. ed. *Morality and Objectivity* (London: Routledge, 1985).

multitude of however tentative expectations, relating to the possibility that presents itself there of converse or colloquy, of interaction, or of treating with a personal being'.[20] The context suggests that Wiggins is here writing of the normal case, but allowing for an unfolding of the ideas of interaction and of treating with, the point can be generalised to embrace all states and stages of human life.

Certainly the dependent and the disabled are no less possessed of 'personal being' as Wiggins, I think, intends us to understand this expression. On the same page as the sentence I have cited he quotes Simone Weil writing of the 'indefinable influence that the presence of another human being has upon us'. In the place from which that quoted sentence comes Weil writes in terms well suited to Nussbaum's concerns:

> He who does not realize to what extent shifting fortune and necessity hold in subjection every human spirit, cannot regard as fellow-creatures nor love as he loves himself those whom chance separated from him by an abyss. The variety of constraints pressing upon man give rise to the illusion of several distinct species that cannot communicate.[21]

Like Wiggins, Weil also takes no space to identify different phases, categories or conditions of mankind, though she registers how that influence lapses in the circumstance in which one is preparing to inflict death or injury on another human being. This insight reveals that the phenomenology of encountering the human other, is subject also to the influence of one's attitudes, in particular one's moral dispositions, which in turn suggests a role for education in preserving and refining benign sensibilities (and of curbing malign ones). The idea of ethical solidarity and that of natural responses to the human form provide welcome supple-

---

[20] Wiggins, p. 243.
[21] Simone Weil, 'The Iliad, or the Poem of Force', as translated by Mary McCarthy in *Pendle Hill Pamphlet* no 91 (Wallingford, PA.: Pendle Hill Press, 1956) p. 7. For elaboration of Weil's manner of connecting moral phenomenology with issues in political philosophy see Peter Winch, *Simone Weil: 'The Just Balance'* (Cambridge: Cambridge University Press, 1989).

ments to the position already converged on, but they also pose challenges to policies of ending lives acknowledged to be human. Put another way, and one that has suitably Aristotelian resonance, the moral force of the appeal to recognising humanity derives, and cannot be willed away from recognising the human form in all its stages and conditions. I shall return to this shortly.

The Nature of Disability

In the penultimate chapter of her book, Nussbaum discusses the need of the institutions of society to go beyond the avoidance of stigmatising vulnerable people and groups, and protecting the dignity of citizens against shame and stigma. The agencies and mechanisms in question are those of law, but as becomes clear in the final chapter she is concerned also with political structures, and more broadly with social justice. Nussbaum observes that: 'no group in society has been so painfully stigmatised as people with physical and mental disabilities' and in the course of the following three pages writes the following:

> The first point to be made in confronting the pervasive effect of shame and stigma is a familiar one, and yet it evidently needs repeating, since one hears so many arguments that ignore it. This is, that a handicap does not exist simply 'by nature' if that means independently of human action. We might say that an impairment in some area or areas of human functioning may exist without human intervention, but it only becomes a handicap when society treats it in certain ways. Human beings are in general disabled: mortal weak-eyed, weak-kneed, with terrible backs and necks, short memories and so forth. But when a majority (or the most powerful group) has such disabilities, society will adjust itself to cater for them. ...
>   The problem for many people in our society is that their disabilities have not been catered for because their impairments are atypical and perceived as 'abnormal'. There is no intrinsic 'natural' difference between a person who uses a wheelchair to move at the same speed as a person walking or running and a person who uses a car to accomplish something of which her own legs are incapable. In each case, human ingenuity is supplying something that the body of the individual does not. The difference is that cars

are typical and wheelchairs are atypical. ...

    ... We may grant that some central functional capabilities are not just typical, but also very useful — good things to have in pursuing a variety of different human plans of life. In so judging, we need take no stand on the contested question of whether these abilities are 'natural' in any value free sense. Without any such controversial claim, we may say that seeing, hearing, locomotion of the limbs, et cetera, are valuable instruments of human functioning, and thus reasonable things to shoot for in thinking about what a system of health care should promote. They are thus political goods, whether or not they have any particular metaphysical or 'natural' status.[22]

Here it is possible to separate the normative, social and political conclusion from the reasoning preceding it, and it is important to do so, since that reasoning is, I believe, faulty and of such misdirection that it could be invoked in opposition to the conclusions Nussbaum wishes to advance and for which I have sympathy. In the discussion from which I have extracted this extended quotation a number of notions are brought into play: handicap, impairment, ability, disability, capability, typicality, atypicality, normality, abnormality, the intrinsic, and the natural. Individually separating and then exhaustively connecting these is the sort of task once beloved of conceptual mapmakers. My interest is more limited and so therefore may be my analysis.

    In one familiar use of the term a 'handicap' does refer to relative advantage or disadvantage in a competitive context; but in another equally familiar use it refers to a physical or mental disability. In that second sense an impairment of a natural capacity is a handicap in the effort to perform an activity quite independently of how society treats it, or of whether the activity occurs in a competitive context. Someone born without legs suffers the handicap of being unable to walk. That is a handicap because human life involves walking as a natural element of it.

    Human beings are not in general disabled. Mortality is not a disability; it is a state of being. If it were a disability

---

[22] Nussbaum, pp. 305-8.

there would be an implied counterpart ability immortality, which, being possessed of it, one could exercise, or refrain from exercising; but there is no literal verbal form 'immortalising' (or indeed 'failing to immortalise'). Admittedly there is the poet or songster sense of immortalising in verse or lyric but that relates to rendering unforgotten; likewise the ambition of attaining immortality is a hoped for state not an achievable task. Like being mortal, 'being immortal' is again a condition. The familiar premise 'All men are mortal' expresses common knowledge about the human condition; it is not believed that some men are immortal or indeed that any living species is. Being weak-eyed, weak-kneed and so on are not evidence of any general human disability. They mark sections on a series of spectra, or ranges of abilities or structural properties. Evidently they are contrastive notions which presume dimensions along which individual capacities are or could be distributed. Some people have strong eyesight, some weak; some are strong across the normal range of sight, some are short- others long-sighted. Deterioration of eyesight conforms to a familiar and explicable pattern with exceptions lying to either side of the main distribution. Even if a disability is widespread it is not evidence that humans are generally disabled. There is no relevant sense in which human beings are in general disabled; for that would require a standard of general ability which human beings in general failed to meet.

There is an intrinsic natural difference between a person who uses a wheel chair to move at the same speed as a person walking or running, and a person who uses a car to accomplish something of which her own legs are incapable. Assuming the latter is understood in the natural reading it refers to moving at speeds greater than those which human beings per se, are capable of achieving and maintaining by walking or running. In that regard the use of a car is not a substitute for a naturally accomplishable human activity; whereas the use of a wheelchair to move at the same speed as a person walking or running is precisely that. In other words while it may be true that 'in each case, human ingenuity is supplying something that the body of the individual does not', it is false that the cases are analogous in the relevant respect: one accomplishes by artifice what can normally be achieved by natural performance, the other achieves by artifice what it is impossible to accomplish by natural performance. The typicality or otherwise of cars and wheelchairs is quite beside the point.

Apart from getting clear about the facts and the ways in which they are represented by the concepts of nature and ability, all of this matters because Martha Nussbaum wants to invoke the idea of human capabilities to ground an account of justice in the distribution of goods, and in particular to argue that disabilities should be compensated for because they are impediments to human functioning, and hence to well-being. But if it were the case that the very idea of handicap or disability were socially relative, in the relevant sense, then it would be open to someone to say that there is no independent measure against which it could be shown that some set of people are inappropriately disadvantaged. Both the measure of disability and the question of whether it should be compensated for would be 'up to society'. It is not in the interest of the kind of approach to ethics and politics that Nussbaum favours, and to which I am sympathetic, to abandon the idea that sight, hearing, locomotion, and other functions are natural goods.

Fortunately, however, the fact that society may ease or not the impact of a disability goes no way to show that handicap is a socially relative concept. What is the case is that most of the concepts in the area are not simple empirical ones, but have normative aspects in virtue of relating to functions. Nussbaum shares Rawls concern to avoid controversial metaphysical assumptions in fashioning a liberal political theory, but a recognition of the functional character of descriptions of human activities and organs need not embroil one in controversial metaphysics—even if there may be some deeply metaphysical accounts of the teleological character of human activity.

The Burdens of Mental Disorder

Nussbaum offers an interesting and welcome discussion of the education of children with severe mental disabilities. I should like to call attention to a related group: people with mental disorders. Concepts of normality are particularly pertinent in this connection and the stigma associated with adult psychopathologies is particularly powerful and often crueller than that directed against mentally disabled children. In approaching the matter I begin with some brief general observations.

The current state of philosophical thinking about the nature of the psychological is broadly anti-reductionist. That is to say, while probably most philosophers believe in the physical basis of the mind, they do not suppose that psychological categories are reducible to physical ones. Thus, the identification and explanation of mental states is taken to proceed by reference to criteria that are ineliminably psychological. There are several arguments for this conclusion.[23] Here is one.

Any concept or predicate has associated with it conditions for its correct application. In the ideal case these amount to a strict definition but often things are hazier: the predicate ' is a triangle' has fairly straightforward application conditions (those that define triangularity); the predicate 'is a poem' is much less determinate. Reflecting on different classes of predicates leads to the thought that there are certain framework conditions for their application. For example, 'is red' presupposes actual or possible visibility; 'is divisible by 2' does not. In general we can define physical predicates as those the application of which presupposes

[23] In this connection see the following which offer different but congruent considerations against the reducibililty of psychology to a physical science: Donald Davidson, 'Mental Events' in *Davidson, Essays on Actions and Events* (Oxford: Oxford University Press, 2001); J. Fodor, 'Special Sciences and the Disunity of Science' in Fodor, *Representations: Philosophical Essays on the Foundations of Cognitive Science* (Brighton: Harvester, 1981); Anthony Kenny, 'Psychology' Ch. 10 of Kenny, *The Metaphysics of Mind* (Oxford: Clarendon Press, 1989); and John McDowell, 'Functionalism and Anomalous Monism' in McDowell, *Mind, Value and Reality* (Cambridge, MA: Harvard University Press, 1998).

certain framework conditions such as being spatially located, having mass, and so on including (perhaps) being subject to deterministic causal laws.

Next, notice that many and perhaps all mental predicates do not presuppose such physical conditions, e.g. 'is thinking about logic' does not seem to presuppose being spatially located. What psychological terms do imply, however, are certain holistic and rational conditions. Thus it makes no sense to say 'X fears Y' unless we suppose that X has certain beliefs, including ones about Y, and relevant desires. Beliefs, desires, and so on exist as parts of networks of such states. Further this holism of the psychological involves relations of coherence and intelligibility. In applying psychological descriptions we have implicit recourse to a psychological profile of the subject (and of social types and of human beings more generally) in which these descriptions are required to cohere with others. As with the earlier case of disability presuming its counterpart, abnormality is conceivable within this but only against the background of a 'normal' psychology.

The upshot is that any attempt to identify the physical and the psychological so as to give explanatory priority to the former is liable to refutation by imagining circumstances in which according to the neurophysiology a person 'should' be mentally impaired or in a state of depression, but his or her behaviour interpreted holistically in accord with psychological criteria shows them to be competent or untroubled. At the end of the day, one might say, 'disabled or troubled is as disabled or troubled does (or fails to do)', and no amount of non-psychological data can refute this. As well as the theoretical interest of this conclusion it provides an obstacle to scientistic approaches to human psychology and psychopathology.[24]

Can an individual human being come to personhood outside a social context? The question sounds an empirical one the answer to which may well be 'yes'. There has, however, been a long-developing consensus within philosophy that

[24] For further exploration of the 'mind/body' question see the following chapter 'Ethics and the Human Body'.

the question is not in fact empirical and that the answer is 'no'. The reasoning broadly is that personhood is a necessary product of interaction with others. For example, it is widely accepted that language is intimately connected with thought and that while human beings may have a natural potential for language this requires to be triggered by a linguistic environment. In brief, babies do not and cannot teach themselves English or any other language. Relatedly, it is generally supposed that the notion 'I' can only be applied by a being that has the idea of others ('you' 'him' 'her') and the capacity to view him or herself as an object of attention and interest to others. In short my ability to think of myself as a psychological subject is linked to my ability to think of others as subjects, and to think of them as regarding me as one. No other, no self; no linguistic community, no language development; no language, no thought; no society, no person. These appear to emerge as necessities of constitution not mere empirical generalisations.

We saw that in applying psychological predicates there are certain presuppositions about coherence and intelligibility. That is to say we make assumptions about what someone *ought* to think or feel in various circumstances. If someone says 'I am afraid of health' and their behaviour is otherwise ordinary — they don't make efforts to become sick, or refuse treatment when ill, etc. — then we will treat the claim as ironic, or insincere, or as confused. Likewise, if someone were to say 'I believe it is absolutely impossible to fly unaided but I am going to do my best to achieve this' we would suspect that they did not understand what they were saying or did not really mean it. This is because there are constitutive norms relating belief, intention and action.

Less logically rigid, but no less important, are the general society-specific expectations of normal psychology. Social historians interested in changing views of behaviour have speculated about the sources of these views and the causes of change. A favourite example is sexual behaviour and associated claims of insanity, pathological deviation and so on. At one point incomprehension, disbelief or utter revulsion at the suggestion of certain practices would have been criteria of psychological normality; at another point the very same reactions might themselves be taken as sure evidence of psychopathology. Notwithstanding what I argued earlier about the concepts of natural ability, and invoked in opposition to a general thesis of the social construction of nature and normality, it is clear that what counts as reasonable or unreasonable, regular or deviant, healthy or morbid, and so on, may differ across societies and across times. Additionally, rates of change and the departments of life in which change occurs may themselves vary. Plausibly the period since the second world war has been one of the most active so far as changes in assumptions about normality are concerned. It is as well to remember this when thinking about 'mental disorders'. Certainly one needs to be mindful of the possibility that conditions now regarded as involuntary pathologies may come to be viewed as legitimate lifestyles.

The implication of these comments is first that the idea of mental disorder can be made good sense of at the level of humanistic interpretation, but second, to a greater degree than those of physical handicap, disability or abnormality, its application may be subject to social influences. Drawing the lesson that Nussbaum offers regarding the ways in which general anxieties about human vulnerabilities (in this case to mental incapacity and disorder) may be projected on to vulnerable group who are then made objects of transferred disgust and socially stigmatised, we should be particularly attentive to the harms liable to be borne by and inflicted on those identified as mentally disordered.

Historically 'stigma' denotes a mark or brand impressed on the skin by a stick usually to identify a slave or criminal. On that account it carries the connotation of disgrace and shamefulness, and thus reason to avoid association with those bearing it. In discussing stigma Nussbaum makes use of a study by Erving Goffman [25] but there is more recent and methodologically more robust material to hand on the effects of stigmatisation of the mentally ill and incapaci-

[25] E. Goffman, *Stigma: Notes on the Management of Spoiled Identity* (Englewood Cliffs, NJ: Prentice-Hall, 1963).

tated.[26] Encounters with the mentally disordered are often described as frightening or disturbing and that encourages avoidance and alienation, but for the most part stigma results not from direct experience of difficult behaviour but from misconceptions about mental disorder, including most prominently the belief that it is associated with violence. One US study showed that while about 2.5% of mentally ill patients might be categorised as dangerous, prime time television depictions of the mentally ill represented over 75% as being violent, particularly towards strangers.[27] Meanwhile among persons convicted in the US for homicide those with no identified mental illness were more likely to have killed a stranger than those with symptoms of mental disorder.

Citing Goffman, Nussbaum writes in relation to attitudes to children with Down syndrome that 'the entire interaction with such a person is articulated in terms of the stigmatized trait, which means that the person's full humanity cannot come into focus'.[28] Stigmatising mental disorders adds further injury to marginalisation: on the one hand such people are represented in ways that demean and debase them, thereby damaging both their reputation and their sense of self and of self-worth, and on the other they are harmed through unfair treatment in respect of such goods as employment, housing and health care. In short, stigma both *constitutes* and *causes* injury. Furthermore, consequent upon marginalisation and these other effects, sufferers are less likely to seek treatment and so are liable to deteriorate producing a further and deeper cycle of stigmatisation and suffering. I entirely applaud Nussbaum's selection of the issue of disability as an example of unjust shaming and encourage her and others now to consider also the circumstance of the mentally ill.

---

[26] See, for example, the chapters by various authors in P. Fink and A. Tasmai, eds, *Stigma and Mental Illness* (Arlington, VA: American Psychiatric Press, 1992).

[27] See Fink and Tasmai, op. cit., ch 1

[28] Nussbaum, p. 305.

Recognising Humanity at All Stages
and in All Conditions

In other works to which she makes reference (*Sex and Social Justice* and *Women and Human Development*)[29] Nussbaum relates the needs and capabilities associated with sex to concerns about privacy, autonomy, reproductive and other civil rights. In *Hiding from Humanity* the focus of discussion of sexuality is the marginalisation and shaming of homosexuals and lesbians, but elsewhere she addresses the interests of heterosexual women in relation to the practice of sex-selective abortion that has been encouraged and even enforced in parts of the world where sons are deemed more desirable than daughters. On this account females suffer twice over: once as mothers pressured to undergo medically unwarranted terminations; and then as foetuses being made the targets of abortion. Evidently the cultural pressures in countries such as India are so strong that women themselves are generally reluctant to witness to the extent of forced abortion, even though parliament had prohibited sex-selecting abortion.

Seen in this perspective such abortions constitute a violation of women's reproductive rights and bodily integrity. But of course there is also the perspective of the aborted foetus whose destruction is one and the same loss whatever the reason given for the killing of it. In *Hiding from Humanity* Nussbaum does much to bring into view those whom illusory ideals of maturity and perfection would push to the margins of interest. She does not, however, discuss those who may still remain beyond the margin of sight: the unborn. In calling for

> a society that acknowledges its own humanity, and neither hides us from it nor it from us ... and in which — at least in crafting the institutions that shape our common life together — we admit that we are all children ... [and base society] on a recognition of the equal dignity of each indi-

---

[29] Martha Nussbaum, *Sex and Social Justice* (Oxford: Oxford University Press, 1999) and *Women and Human Development* (Cambridge: Cambridge University Press, 2000).

vidual, and the vulnerabilities inherent in a common humanity,[30]

Nussbaum invites her readers, whether or not she intended to, to wonder what in this framework can be the scope for abortion.

Certainly it cannot now be justified by any argument to the effect that on account of being undeveloped and out of sight humanity in the womb is less deserving of regard; or by one that ties human dignity to competent, independent adulthood. Of course in the developed world abortion is now commonly practised in response to ante-natal diagnoses of embryonic abnormality and anticipated handicap, just as euthanasia is argued for by reference to incapacity, loss of autonomy and the approach of death. But the message of Nussbaum's book would seem to be that as they stand these sorts of justifications are unsatisfactory. And if they need to be looked at again then it should be with the same suspicion that Nussbaum brings to bear upon the treatment of other vulnerable groups. The 'indefinable influence of the presence of another human being' of which Simone Weil wrote insightfully and compellingly, acquires a further and very special connotation in the case of pregnancy; and even when born life is diminished by disability, disease or degeneration, there is the sense that so long as it has not been extinguished, the human form is present and exerting its moral influence upon us.[31]

Conclusion

The recognition of humanity goes all the way to its points of origin and of cessation, and, returning to the theme of the previous chapter, it reveals to us forms of value other than qualitative wellbeing. Central to this is the idea that human persons are embodied subjects intimately associated with an animal nature. Quite what that involves and how it relates to matters of value and in particular respect for humanity is the subject of the following chapter.

---

[30] Nussbaum, *Hiding from Humanity*, pp. 17-18.
[31] Martha Nussbaum responds to some of the points made in the foregoing in 'Hiding From Humanity: Replies to Charlton, Haldane, Archard, and Brooks', *Journal of Applied Philosophy* 25 (2008).

4

Ethics and the Human Body

Introduction

As medical science develops, more and more possibilities are put before us. Some of these are versions of familiar circumstances, but others are genuinely novel. Such developments often bring benefits; but not infrequently they raise ethical problems, concerning, for example, the distribution of goods, and the legitimacy of transgressing boundaries hitherto uncrossed. In trying to deal with these problems we need to have a sure grasp of relevant values and principles. Yet it is one of the pronounced features of the modern era that as ethical problems have multiplied, so our common ethical resources have diminished. Oddly we seem able to recognise that human embryo research, gene manipulation, and xenotransplantation all raise difficult questions, but we are largely at sea when it comes to finding an agreed basis for answering them, let alone to agreeing particular answers.

Several factors underlie the inability to achieve consensus. Some are attributable to cultural pluralism. Modern societies are made up of different ethnic, religious, and ideological groupings, and while each may hold to a definite set of principles (though it is an idealisation to suppose so), there is no significant common set adhered to by all. There is, however, a more general problem which is the lack of confidence in the very existence of any secure basis for ethical deliberation. For obvious reasons (independent of the philosophical ones discussed in chapter one 'Practical

Ethics') appeals to the will of God are held to be problematic, and the idea that a special faculty of moral intuition or the exercise of pure practical reason might yield incontestable values and principles is difficult to take seriously given the failure of either to do so.

There is, however, one approach that seems to have flourished notwithstanding that philosophers have generally been critical of it, namely utilitarianism, or as it still sometimes referred to the 'maximisation of happiness principle'. Its success is due, I think, to the following.

First, it is easy to confuse the particular and restricted utilitarian doctrine that one has a duty to promote the greatest happiness of the greatest number, with a general principle of beneficence common to most moral systems, namely, where it is appropriate and where one can, and other things being equal, one should act so as to produce good. The fact that the latter is not equivalent to utilitarianism emerges when one notices the *ceteris paribus* clause and the non-identification of goodness and happiness. Unlike the utilitarian, the advocate of beneficence may say that in a given circumstance it is not permitted to bring about some good because the only way of doing so would be by doing something which was unjust, say. Nevertheless, utilitarianism may seem unexceptionable for being confused with beneficence.

Second, and following from what was said above, those who argue that happiness is not everything and that some values and principles may be more important generally have difficulty justifying those other ethical features.

Third, when it comes to practical ethics utilitarianism enjoys the apparent advantage of ease of application. While it may often be challenging to gauge the likely utilities of conflicting options, this problem is taken to be of a quite different and more tractable sort than faces the application of distinct and often incommensurable values, such as justice, liberty and the protection of the innocent.

Philosophers' qualms about utilitarianism have generally been ineffective in halting its adoption, in part because of its apparent advantages, in part because of the failure of critics to provide a compelling alternative, and in part because the philosophical criticisms of it tend to be rather abstract. For example, it is sometimes said that utilitarianism aggregates happiness and thereby fails to respect the distinctness of persons.[1] It is also objected that it undermines agency by denying moral actors any legitimate motive other than the maximisation of happiness.[2] Again it is argued that the very idea of double comparatives (in this case superlatives) such as 'the greatest happiness of the greatest number' fails to specify any unique state of affairs to be aimed at.[3] While one situation may involve *the greater happiness of the people* than another situation, the second may involve *more people being happy*; and for any given combination of people and happiness it is possible to imagine acting in a way that results in either more people or more happiness, with neither option uniquely satisfying the description 'the greatest happiness of the greatest number'. Finally, and for any theory that holds that the right course of action is that which among the alternatives available has the best possible consequences, there is the general problem that no unique exclusive and exhaustive set of alternatives can be specified for a given agent at a given time.[4]

Given these several considerations and others touched upon in earlier chapters I shall assume that for these or other reasons readers are open to rejecting utilitarianism, and I will direct my efforts to the task of providing a better philosophical basis for thinking about ethical issues concerning the care and treatment of human beings. As previously indicated, the approach I favour is a version of ethical naturalism. However, since this term is used in different and contrasting ways a word of clarification is appropriate. As it refers to positions of the sort I am concerned to advance,

---

[1]   This is John Rawls main objection to utilitarianism in *A Theory of Justice* (Oxford: Oxford University Press, 1971).

[2]   This line of objection originates in Bernard Williams 'A Critique of Utilitarianism' in J. J. C. Smart and B. Williams, *Utilitarianism: For and Against* (Cambridge: Cambridge University Press, 1973), pp. 108-18.

[3]   See P. Geach, *The Virtues* (Cambridge: Cambridge University Press, 1977) pp. 91-3.

[4]   For a detailed presentation of this last line of argument see Lars Bergström, 'Utilitarianism and Alternative Actions', *Nous*, 5 (1971).

ethical naturalism indicates that claims of value, virtue, or requirement, are to be justified by appeal to what befits the nature of human beings. On this account, an action is right if, other things being equal, it promotes or contributes to human well being as this is implied by human nature. So conceived, 'naturalism' is a form of moral objectivism and is related to 'natural law theory'.

The other main use, by contrast, associates 'naturalism' with forms of subjectivism. The most prominent example is David Hume's view discussed in chapter one according to which ethical claims are to be understood not as describing states of affairs independent of the state of mind of the claimant but precisely as reporting or expressing his or her sentiments of approval or disapproval. Why this second view is also termed 'naturalism' is that it reduces the ethical to something that might be the subject of natural study namely the psychological states of human beings. Having already responded to Hume's challenges to moral objectivism I shall not attempt to refute the second kind of naturalism beyond making and emphasising the point that it is one thing to ask if something is good and quite another to ask if it is approved of. The first concerns the thing itself, the second does not. This difference also comes out in the fact that we can ask of the sentiments of approval whether they are themselves good. For the subjectivist this question will be analysed as asking whether those sentiments should be the subject of second order sentiments of approbation. Yet we can ask the same question of these: is it good to approve of (approving of) such and such? At each turn the subjectivist can appeal to yet higher order sentiments or social norms, but the question of *their* value awaits an answer, and reference to what is felt by a subject is an answer of the wrong logical sort. Either common morality has an objective foundation or it rests on a mistake. The reason most commonly advanced for drawing the second conclusion is the belief that no objective foundation is available. I have argued that this itself is an error and I will return to the issue in the conclusion of this chapter.

Persons and Bodies

Since the naturalism I favour roots ethical value in human nature it is necessary that I develop a philosophical account of human beings, and this involves understanding the relationship between a person and his or her body — hence the title of this chapter. Although this is an ancient topic of philosophical reflection the work of Wittgenstein casts doubt upon the assumption that there is a philosophical issue to be resolved. Wittgenstein was much exercised by the fact that the central problems of philosophy involve matters with which we are, in an everyday sense, quite familiar. We are perfectly at ease with words, know how to use them and are generally understood in our use by others. Yet when we ask such questions as 'what is language?' or 'what does reference consist in?', the whole thing spins out of focus and we feel lost for answers. This is not new, of course. In the *Confessions* Augustine asks 'what is time?' and observes 'if no one asks me I know; if I want to explain it to a questioner I do not know'.[5] One diagnosis of this gap between everyday competence and philosophical understanding is that offered by Wittgenstein himself. This involves the remarkable suggestion that philosophical perplexity is a kind of psychic illness induced by the misuse of thought. His claim is that we take ideas out of their natural setting and then ask questions about them which really do not make any sense.

By way of analogy consider driving along in a car and asking a companion-cum-navigator questions about directions and likely times of arrival; and contrast this with a situation in which the car is sitting in the garage and one asks similar questions: where should it be going? when should it turn off? how far is there still to go? what time will it get there? These were perfectly sensible things to ask in the first context; in the second they make no sense. Going one step beyond this, imagine someone asking where cars as such are going and how long that journey will take. Madness has

---

[5] Saint Augustine, *Confessions*, trans. H. Chadwick (Oxford: Oxford University Press, 1998) Bk XI, Ch. xiv.

descended. Wittgenstein's treatment for the parallel condition that constitutes philosophical perplexity is a form of intellectual therapy involving repeated reminders of how language works in its proper use. The intended effect is that the patient will stop asking the misplaced questions and all will then be well. He or she, like the car, will be back on the road.

The relevance of this in the present context is that it may seem that there is something peculiar about the idea of the need for philosophical reflection on the human body. After all, there would be something peculiar in the suggestion that there is a philosophical problem about 'the snake body', say. There are snakes. They have bodies. Indeed, they *are* — living — bodies. What is puzzling about this? If the answer is 'nothing' that invites the thought that either the same response is appropriate so far as the human body is concerned, or else there is a significant disanalogy between the cases. The latter, of course, is what many suppose. One kind of disanalogy is expressed by saying that humans have souls and that snakes do not. Consequently, while the whole truth about snakes may be exhausted by telling the appropriate biological story about their bodies the same is not the case so far as human beings are concerned: 'John Brown's *body* lies a mouldering in the grave, but his *soul* goes marching on'.

Wittgenstein was not averse to talk of the human soul, in fact he uses the term approvingly; but he thought that this should be understood as expressively characterising aspects of living human beings (bodies) not immaterial spirits that inhabit them in life and depart them at death. Brilliant as he was, however, I think that Wittgenstein had too restricted a sense of the range of possible views of human beings, and underestimated the need for philosophical justification of one or other of them — including his own preferred 'ordinary' account. He thought that there was *materialism* (including *behaviourism*) which holds that everything true about human beings is reducible to descriptions of their bodies; *dualism* which supposes that the most important things about human persons are attributable to something other than their bodies (their immaterial souls); and his own view, let me just term it *Wittgensteineanism*, which is that while human persons *are* their (living) bodies, not everything that is true and important about them is reducible to descriptions of matter in motion. 'She was sad and cried' is not the same as 'her body was in such and such a state and a saline solution flowed from her eyes'. In addition to (living) human bodies, says Wittgenstein, there is the human form of life and this is affective, cognitive, artistic, and so on; it is of the nature of human beings that they have feelings, that they think and that they engage in creative practices.

The last is, of course, a philosophical view but it differs from the others in denying that in order to understand the human one has to see it in terms of something more fundamental: the material or the immaterial. What Wittgenstein missed out, I believe, is the possibility suggested by Aristotle and developed by Aquinas, which is that human beings are not immaterial selves plus material bodies but irreducibly psychophysical substances, that is to say beings to whose essence belong activities some of which are evidently physical (such as motion) and some of which are demonstrably non-physical (such as thought). The irreducibility of the human person to the human body is not due to the ineliminability of social modes of description but to the fact that what makes human social life possible is that human beings transcend the mechanico-physical powers of their bodies.[6] In disagreeing with Wittgenstein, however, I think it remains the case that much of what he says fits very well with the metaphysical view I will be defending. His error, if I may presume to put it that way, was to confuse bad metaphysics with metaphysics as such. Everyday competence may not require a theoretical underpinning but there remains the question of what must be the case if what we ordinarily suppose to be so is as we suppose it to be. Identifying and answering such questions is the proper task of philosophy.

[6]   See John Haldane, 'Rational Animals' in A. O'Hear ed. *Verstehen and Humane Understanding* (Cambridge: Cambridge University Press, 1996).

A Short History of the Philosophy of Mind

Western thinking about the human body has various sources of inspiration and influence. The first centuries of the Christian era were shaped by two important forces: one an understanding of the religion of Holy Scripture, bequeathed by Judaism; the other, the progressive incorporation of Graeco-Roman thought and the development of Christian philosophies. Figures such as St Augustine and Boethius are tremendously important in this connection, because they convey the influence of Neoplatonic thought into the developing Western tradition. Each was concerned with the nature and identity of persons; and each offers a relevant definition. According to Augustine a soul is 'a rational substance suited to ruling a body';[7] and for Boethius a person is 'an individual substance of rational nature'.[8] From the viewpoint of historical interpretation Boethius's definition is in the tradition of the dualism espoused by Augustine. For while a divine or an angelic person need not be thought suited to ruling a body, human persons, conceived of as Augustinian souls, would be such. Happily, however, the words of Boethius are more generally adaptable. That is to say one may accept the definition without thereby endorsing dualism; for one need not suppose that the rational substance that is the person is related to a living body as a driver is to a vehicle. Instead, for example, one might consider that the individual substance of rational nature is nothing other than a living human being, a rational animal.

In antiquity, Aristotle had already turned away from dualism of the Platonic sort, and something of his movement was to be re-enacted in the later medieval period. The thirteenth century saw the translation for the first time into Latin of most of the works of Aristotle including his great

---

[7] Augustine *De Quantitate Animae*, 13, translated by J.J. McMahon, *Fathers of the Church*, Vol. 4 (Washington: Catholic University of America Press, 1947).

[8] Boethius, *Contra Eutychen*, 13, in H.F. Stewart, E.K. Rand and S.J. Tester (eds. and trans.) *Theological Tractates* (Cambridge, MA: Harvard University Press, 1973).

text on the nature of living substances, the *De Anima*. This corpus had been preserved in the Arab world where it had also been the subject of a number of significant commentaries among the most influential of which were those in the Averroistic tradition. Averroes himself and those who followed him were very interested in Aristotelian natural philosophy, and they had much to say about human nature and the sense in which we are 'besouled bodies'.[9]

Unsurprisingly, the reception of Arabic-cum-Greek philosophy into the medieval Latin West raised questions about its compatibility with traditional Christian teachings, and for a significant period the new philosophy met with more opposition than support. Among those who saw merit in it, however, was the greatest figure of the period, *viz.* Thomas Aquinas, and in his commentary on the *De Anima* of Aristotle, and in his own writings on the soul, Aquinas goes as far as anyone yet has to reconcile the anti-Platonic character of Aristotle's view with the anti-materialist and spiritual teachings of Christianity.[10] I shall say more about the prospects for this project in due course, but for the present let me just extract two elements from it. First, on this account a human being is to be thought of as an animated substance and as a single unified entity. This draws from general Aristotelian natural philosophy according to which substances (things) are to be understood in terms of their organisation and powers. Accordingly, if you wish to know what a thing is, look at what it does; and if you want to understand what a human being is, look at how a human being acts and consider what is distinctive of its activities as a being of that sort. A second Aristotelian element is the idea that natural bodies can be analysed in terms of two aspects:

[9]   For a scholarly treatment of aspects of the Arabic tradition see Herbert Davidson, *Alfarabi, Avicenna, and Averroes, on Intellect* (Oxford: Oxford University Press, 1992).

[10]   See *Aristotle's De Anima in the version of William of Moerbeke and the Commentary of St Thomas Aquinas* translated by K. Foster and S. Humphries (London: Routledge and Kegan Paul, 1951); *The Soul: A Translation of St Thomas Aquinas' De Anima* by John Patrick Rowan (London: Herder, 1949); and *Summa Theologiae* Ia, 75-83 translated by Timothy Suttor (London: Eyre & Spottiswoode, 1970).

their *form* (or organisation) and their *matter* (that in which the organisation is realised). In the case of animate bodies, living things, the principle of organisation (form) is the soul.

In the century and a half following the death of Thomas Aquinas there was a strong revival of the more dualistically and Platonistically inclined Augustinian tradition which thought of a human being as, in effect, a conjunction of two substances: a natural, material substance, the human *body*, and a transcendent, immaterial substance, the human *soul*.[11] At the same time, however, another more 'naturalistic' trend was developing particularly among empirically-minded renaissance humanists. This movement might be termed 'Averroes's revenge' because it reasserted the interpretation of Aristotle with which he was associated, and because some of its advocates looked back upon this the Averroistic tradition with approval.[12]

In the seventeenth century, two great figures came upon the stage, Descartes and Hobbes. Descartes famously gives expression to a view very like Augustine's, in which he separates out mind and body. Hobbes, by contrast, looks to be, and is often characterised as, the first materialist of the modern age. It is a tribute to the power of these thinkers, and evidence of a tendency of opinion on the metaphysics of human nature to polarise along immaterialist/materialist lines, that Hobbes in one way and Descartes in another really defined the terms in which people currently think about human persons, human beings and human bodies. The inheritors of the Hobbesian tradition are ones who presume that thought and consciousness can be understood as 'motions in the brain' – to use a rather antique way of characterising materialism. Meanwhile the followers of Descartes think that there is something naturalistically inexplicable about human beings and that is their capacity for consciousness, thought and action.

[11] For further discussion of mediaeval accounts see John Haldane, 'Soul and Body' in R. Pasnau ed. *The Cambridge History of Medieval Philosophy*.
[12] For an outline of the history of this period see John Haldane, 'Medieval and Renaissance Philosophy of Mind' in S. Guttenplan (ed.) *A Companion to Philosophy of Mind* (Oxford: Blackwell, 1994).

Contemporary philosophical thinking about these matters is complex and extremely diverse at the level of detail. Those unfamiliar with it might suppose that there is now a consensus around reductive materialism. In fact, however, most philosophers are very unsure about how to characterise the nature of human persons, and it is far from being the case that they are deeply confident that the physicalist story is right.[13] They know that there are difficulties with materialism, on the other hand there is significant, and I think not inappropriate, hostility to the kind of dualism that is associated with Descartes.

Despairing of the possibility of reconciling the existence of ineliminably psychological states with universal materialism some have gone so far as to try and eliminate the mental descriptions in favour of neurophysiology. A different response to the same difficulty is to throw up one's hands and say that the whole thing is an unsolvable mystery; not only do we not have a clue as to how the personal could be explained in terms of the physical but we cannot even see what it would be to have a physical explanation. Somehow mind and body are conjoined, but we are never going to know what the nature of that connection is. Interestingly there are Cartesian and Augustinian echoes in this. At one point Descartes writes 'It does not seem to me that the human mind is capable of conceiving, quite distinctly and at the same time, both the distinction between mind and body and their union.'[14] And Augustine gave voice to similar puzzlement some centuries earlier when he wrote that, 'the manner in which spirits are united to bodies is altogether wonderful and transcends the understanding of men'.[15]

---

[13] For a representative sample of current opinion see the chapters in R. Warner and T. Szubka (eds.) *The Mind-Body Problem: A Guide to the Current Debate* (Oxford: Blackwell, 1994). The view advocated in the present essay is further described and defended in J. Haldane, 'A Return to Form in the Philosophy of Mind' in D. Oderberg (ed.) *Form and Matter* (Oxford: Blackwell, 1999).

[14] See A. Kenny (ed.) *Descartes Philosophical Letters* (Oxford: Clarendon Press, 1970) p. 142.

[15] Augustine, *De Civitate Dei*, XXI, 10.

Eliminativism and 'mysterianism' are responses to the difficulty of trying to give a coherent and plausible account of human beings, one that recognises that they are bodily creatures but also that they are possessed of minds. These are, however, minority positions and most prominent Anglo-American philosophers retain the ambition of harmonising the two elements within a broadly naturalistic framework. The most ingenious attempt to do so is that associated with Donald Davidson whose influence has been such that the expression he coined to describe his own account, *viz.* '*anomalous monism*', is often used as a general term to describe reconciliationist projects of the same broad sort.[16] It is worth taking a few lines to characterise Davidson's position, first of all because it has been, without question, the most influential approach in the philosophy of mind and philosophy of the person in the last four decades, second, because it is a fine example of philosophical imagination, but third because it is a solution that is itself dissolving.

Davidson starts off with the thought that there obviously are mental states. It clearly is the case that human beings are moved by their thoughts, and that their thoughts are often induced by the world. In other words there is some causal interplay between persons and their environment. Yet Davidson accepts the claim of hermeneuticists, personalists, Wittgensteinians and other non-reductionists that there are no scientific or any other strict laws governing mental/physical interactions. However, since he also supposes that all interactions are law-like he concludes that any 'mental-physical' interaction has in fact to be a physical-physical interaction. If there is interaction it has to be between two physical things or physical events.

Without denying mentality, therefore, we are forced to assert physicality. This amounts to the thesis that human beings are physical substances with physical attributes, but which also have mental attributes. The latter characteristics

[16] For Davidson's influential writings on this subject see *Essays on Actions and Events* (Oxford: Clarendon Press, 1982) especially essays 11-13.

are not identical to the former ones but they do depend upon them. If you want to explain what human beings are doing, you have to bring together these two kinds of attributes. You have to see human action as involving both the physical and the mental attributes or characteristics of physical objects. Davidson's theory is physicalist for the obvious reason that it takes human beings to be purely physical objects; yet it is non-reductive since it rejects the possibility of explaining the mental attributes physicalistically.

Throughout the 1970s and into the 80s this had the appearance of a happy and harmonious resolution, but more recently it has come to be thought of as discordant. The problem is simple. Anybody who really thinks that bodily movement is something wholly physical, something that has a complete physical explanation, is going to be in difficulty if they also want to say that it has a mental explanation; for this conjunction implies causal over-determination. It is equivalent to saying that a deliberate movement of my arm has two fully sufficient causes, a phys(iologi)ical cause and also a mental cause. But two completely sufficient causes seem one cause too many, and it looks as if one must make a choice as to which is the 'real' cause. This is liable to provoke one of two reactions: either a lapse back into some kind of dualism which holds that what *really* moved my arm were my thoughts, my mental states and so on, or a return to a version of materialism according to which what really moved my arm were motions in the brain. What seems impossible to fashion is an account that accords reality to both aspects.

This problem arises not just in respect of the mental and physical. It arises wherever there is an apparent rival to a purely physical explanation. Supposing we say that as well as the physical there is the chemical, that as well as the chemical there is the biological, as well as the biological there is the psychological, and that each of these makes its contribution to the activity of the relevant kind of substance — a human being, say. Then we are going to have multiple causal over-determination, because physics will completely explain the movement of the object at the level of the physical; chemistry ought to explain it at the level of the chemical, biology at the level of the biological, and psychology at the rational level. But now it seems as if we have four competing stories of why the object moved: a mechanico-physical one, a chemical one, a biological one, a psychological one; and these are now *three* stories too many.

The upshot is to force a single answer to the question of where the real causality lies. If one favours the physical, what you end up with is the idea that the psychological explanations are either merely a convenient way of speaking without realist implications, or else, if you think that the psychological has some reality it is reduced to an epiphenomenon. On the latter account his having a mind is not in any way responsible for a human being's movements; and since the idea of a rational substance is in part that of a substance whose activity is due to thought, this option leads to the denial that human beings really are rational substances or persons.

Perhaps it should have been clear from the outset that the attempt to combine physicalism with opposition to physical reductionism was an impossible one. At any rate there is now a growing consensus that anomalous monism suffers internal contradictions. And as this consensus grows so there is a return to versions of the Cartesian or Hobbesian positions. If one thinks that Davidson was right about the non-reducibility of the mental, and about its ineliminability from the explanation of action, then dualism may seem attractive, On the other hand, if one judges that Davidson's true insight was his insistence upon the physicality of substances and of causation, then reductive materialism beckons. I wrote earlier of 'the revenge of Averroes'; one might speak now of 'the revenge of Descartes and Hobbes'. For all these centuries later we appear to have returned to the situation of trying, like Hobbes, to explain everything about human beings materialistically; or else like Descartes, of having to say that there are really two substances involved, and then confessing puzzlement as to their nature and that of the compositional and causal relations between them.

In light of this, Wittgenstein's rejection of any metaphysics of human persons is likely to have renewed appeal. In the *Philosophical Investigations* he writes that 'the best picture of the human soul is the human body', and elsewhere he comments that, 'the best picture of the human souls is the human being'. Taken out of context these can seem somewhat puzzling aphorisms. It will be helpful, therefore, to quote at somewhat greater length. First from the *Philosophical Investigations* (Part I):

> It comes to this: only of a living human being and what resembles (behaves like) a living human being can one say: it has sensations; it sees; is blind; hears; is deaf; is conscious or unconscious. ...
>
> Look at a stone and imagine it having sensation. One says to oneself, 'How could one so much as get the idea of ascribing a *sensation* to a *thing*?' One might as well try to ascribe it to a number. — And now look at a wriggling fly and at once these difficulties vanish and pain seems able to get a foothold here, where before everything was, so to speak, too smooth for it.
>
> And so, too, a corpse seems to us quite inaccessible to pain. — Our attitude to what is alive and what is dead is not the same.[17]

Later (in Part II) we are given the following

> 'I believe that he is suffering'. Do I also believe that he isn't an automaton?
>
> It would go against the grain to use the word in both connections. ...
>
> 'I believe that he's not an automaton', just like that, so far makes no sense.
>
> My attitude towards him is an attitude towards a soul. I am not of the *opinion* that he has a soul. ...
>
> The human body is the best picture of the human soul.[18]

Part of Wittgenstein's aim in these passages is to remind the reader (as he often sought to do) of the unconcealed facts of the matter. We are so exhausted with the familiar that it is difficult for us to see things as they are, and theory rushes in where intuition has gone out the door. Wittgenstein is intent

---

[17] L. Wittgenstein, *Philosophical Investigations* (trans.) G.E.M. Anscombe (Oxford: Blackwell, 1953) 281 and 284, pp. 96 and 98.

[18] *Philosophical Investigations*, Part II, Sec iv, p. 178.

on trying to get us to see what lies before us, and in this case the most obvious thing is that human beings are animated human bodies. They are living things possessed of various sorts of characteristics, and these characteristics are regularly on display. When I see somebody talking, or watch them writing, or indeed just watch them walk across a room, I am in the presence of, and a witness to the activities of a rational animal. I see their rationality in action. I do not infer it, or conjecture it as part of a theoretical explanation.

The shared error of the dualist and the materialist is to assume that what I really see is only a physical object in movement, concerning which the question arises of what is making it move. That assumption leads immediately to a theory of the inner causes of observed effects. At which point one might either adopt a Cartesian theory: the inner causes are thoughts (in an immaterial medium) that somehow interact through some part of the brain so as to make muscles move; or a Hobbesian theory: the inner causes are motions in the brain that are communicated through the nerves, and so on. Wittgenstein's opposition is to any theory of the mind as something distinct from, and lying behind, the behaviour of living human bodies. He is certainly not denying that there is knowledge of human psychology to be had, but this comes from looking at what is happening. Watch somebody walk and you can see psychology in action. A human being is a rational animal whose nature is expressed in the activities that constitute its life. That is why Wittgenstein says that the human body is the 'best picture' of the human soul. He does not mean that the human body is something whose operations invite us to infer the existence of something else, a soul, that is the cause of its behaviour. Rather, the soul is the very principle of organisation of the body and of its activities.

Returning to the problem faced by Davidson and others concerning non-reducibility and epiphenomenalism, the difficulty arises from assuming a notion of the physical as that of the universal underlying nature of things. In this way of thinking reality is ultimately composed of microphysical objects. In order to explain the diversity of things it is then assumed that aggregates of these have various additional characteristics layered upon them. The problem is then one of allowing these subsequent features to play any role without thereby abandoning the assumption of the complete sufficiency of the physical. The fact that this problem has arisen and appears unsolvable has encouraged many philosophers to revisit the assumptions of Davidson's position; but few have been willing to give up physicalism; hence the recent revival of reductionist varieties of it.[19]

The adherence to physicalism in these circumstances suggests a form of intellectual prejudice, and once free of it other possibilities come into view. That which I am recommending is, in effect, a combination of Wittgensteinian common sense and neo-Aristotelian metaphysics. Observation tells us that there are very many different kinds of substances, of which human beings are one sort, cats are another, and sulphuric acid is a third. By looking at things of these sorts, watching their actions and their reactions, and thinking about the significance of these we build up a picture of their defining characteristics and thus of their natures. When we do this with regard to ourselves and our fellow human beings what we discover is that we are rational animals, and that our rationality is expressed in bodily activities such as drawing and talking, as well as in abstract thought. The human body is the medium of our personal existence. Aquinas recognises this when he says in his commentary on St Paul's first letter to the Corinthians that the hope for future life depends upon bodily resurrection. A pure intellect may survive death but a pure intellect is not a human person.[20] A person does not so much *have* a body as *be* one. On this account, however, the body should not be thought of in the terms favoured by philosophical physicalism. Certainly a human body has physical proper-

[19] In this connection see the essays in Jaegwon Kim, *Supervenience and Mind* (Cambridge: Cambridge University Press, 1993).

[20] See the extract from Aquinas's *Super Epistolam Pauli Apostoli* appearing under the title 'My Soul is not Me' in T. McDermott (ed. and trans.) *Thomas Aquinas: Selected Philosophical Writings* (Oxford: Oxford University Press, 1993).

ties such as spatial location, mass and so on, but it also has chemical, biological and psychological properties and these are in no way secondary or tertiary to the physical. As the principle of organisation and activity of a human being, a human soul is responsible for the shape of the body and for the activities of sub-personal biological systems as much as it is for emotions and thoughts.

Conclusion

Finally I turn to the bearing of this conception of the person/body relationship upon the consideration of bio-ethical questions. Here I may be brief for I am only concerned with the general framework of bioethics and not with particular issues located within it (in the following chapter I shall be exploring further aspects of this frame-work while also engaging a particular issue, viz. that of human cloning). An implication of the neo-Aristotelian view is that in important respects human life is continuous with other forms of animate existence. Equally, however, there is a dimension of human life that distinguishes us from fellow animals, namely our capacity for abstract thought and practical deliberation. In its speculative form reason aims at truth, in its practical form it is directed towards goodness. Both modes of rationality find expres-sion in bodily activities and this gives them a significance and a value that transcends the activities of other animals. Art-making and scientific experimentation are just two examples of this. Accordingly, while there are good reasons not to mistreat non-human animals the human body enjoys a privileged position by virtue of being the medium of rational life.

In order to understand any form of animal existence it is necessary to identify various activities whose occurrence serves the needs of the organism. The vital powers are ordered towards certain ends, and their exercise is subject to implied norms of efficiency and effectiveness. An anatomist who recognises a part of an animal's body as being a heart is well-placed to determine whether the organ is operating as it should. Likewise for other bodily parts and functions. So too, the activity of the organism as a whole is open to evaluation by reference to a notion of well-being appropriate to the species in question. As with plants and non-rational animals so with human kind. Our activities may be judged good or bad depending on their relationship to a norm of human flourishing whose content is given by our nature. There is goodness and badness in posture and in diet, as well as in language use and in economic activity. It is the work of the human sciences and of moral philosophy to say what the relevant standards are but the general question of their objectivity should not be in doubt. The human body is a locus of value inasmuch as it is the location of human life. This is the basis of the ethical naturalism that I characterised earlier as holding that claims of value, virtue or requirement are to be justified by appeal to what befits the nature of human beings.[21]

Goodness is not an occult property like a neo-Platonic emanation or a mystical aura. It is a state or condition of natural fulfilment (and theologically speaking, of supernatural completion). However complex bioethical issues may be, the starting point for investigating them must be the recognition that human well-being is rooted in our nature as rational animals. Utilitarians regard preferences as the basis for requirement; Aristotelians focus instead on human needs and interests. Not only may these criteria fail to coincide they may actually conflict. At that point the Aristotelian has the advantage of being able to show how value is rooted in the very nature of the human animal: in its body as well as in its mind. Having arrived at this conclusion regarding the nature of human persons I next return to the structure of morality, more specifically to its multidimensionality. Again I shall approach the issue from the perspective of issues in bioethics, but as will become clear the central points are general ones.

---

[21] For a theologically and philosophically informed presentations of this sort of naturalism see P.T. Geach, *The Virtues* (1977).

5

Science, Knowledge and Virtue

Introduction

In February 1997, following the announcement that the Roslin Institute in Scotland had successfully cloned a sheep ('Dolly') by means of cell-nuclear transfer, the then US President Clinton requested the National Bioethics Advisory Commission to review legal and ethical issues of cloning and to recommend federal actions to prevent abuse. In the meantime he directed the heads of executive departments and agencies not to allocate federal funds for 'cloning human beings'. The Commission consulted with members of relevant academic disciplines and other professions, representatives of interest groups and members of the general public, and received written submissions. Unsurprisingly, given the prospect of human cloning and the sensational announcement in January 1998 by the American physicist-cum-embryologist Richard Seed that he would aim to clone himself (subsequently he has decided that his wife would be a better subject), public debate in the US became fairly voluble.

In Britain a similar consultation exercise was engaged in by a joint working party of the Human Fertilisation and Embryology Authority and the Human Genetics Advisory Commission, established (in the same month as the US President's request to the NBAC) to advise government on human cloning issues. This reported in December 1998 and like the National Bioethics Advisory Commission cautioned against the non-therapeutic (reproductive) cloning of human beings. Howard Shapiro, Chairman of the NBAC recommended to President Clinton a three to five year period of study and reflection before the preparation of a code of ethics on human cloning. The HFEA/HGAC group proposed permitting therapeutic cloning but banning cloning for reproduction.

In subsequent years the US and the UK have seen further commissions and statutory agencies, with the UK also legislating to permit the cloning of human embryos for experimentation, and the US now set to liberalise stem-cell research. Even so reproductive cloning remains prohibited. These various legal measures, statutory authorities and policy recommendations are not likely, however, to resolve the issues or even to be particularly effective in controlling practice. Determined individuals are able to pursue the project of human cloning in secret and in parts of the world in which there is no relevant legal regulation and in which ethical considerations play little role in public policy. In addition, the issue of therapeutic cloning in which human embryos are created — in this case in order that stem cells can be harvested for genetic transfer — is also open to familiar anti-abortion objections. In British laboratories alone about 100,000 embryos are experimented upon or destroyed per annum.

There has been much written from ethical, political and scientific perspectives on the details of these matters, and here I wish instead to consider the broad philosophical context within which the issues are discussed. Along the way, however, I shall present a case against reproductive human cloning that also has implications for other procedures, though I shall not explore these.

Traditions, Customs, Principles and More Besides

In the course of its review of legal and ethical issues the US National Bioethics Advisory Commission made a point of stating its awareness that:

> ... the formation of appropriate public policy with respect to cloning human beings in this manner depends on more than the potential benefits and harms of reproductive clon-

> ing itself. It also depends on the traditions, customs and
> principles of constitutional law that guide public policy
> making in the United States.[1]

This is a very interesting observation and one to be
applauded for its sensitivity to the wider normative context
within which public policy must be formulated. Benefits
and harms are hard enough to assess and calculate; taking
account of traditions, customs and legal principles is a more
difficult task given the number, range and generally
uncodifiable character of these. Yet for reasons that will
soon emerge I think this broadening of the ethical and philosophical setting does not itself go far enough. It is a very
good beginning, but there is an even broader context to be
comprehended, that created by the question what is it to live
a good human life?

Of course, in the United States the relevant traditions and
customs include ones in which individual liberty is given
prominence and often priority, and this fact is liable to be
seized upon by those such as Richard Seed who advance a
free-market, libertarian agenda. European culture is less
individualistic and more communitarian in orientation,
and more accepting of social regulation; and these facts
should be taken account of in the fashioning of policy. It is
also worth noting, however, that in the US (as in the UK)
there is more than one such tradition or custom. This plurality is reflected in the sorts of discussions that go on nowadays and it is not something that we can expect to pass
away. At the same time, it would be premature to identify it
with relativism or even to suppose that it provides a good
case for this, for apart from the fact that some traditions bear
little rational scrutiny there is the fact that the plurality has
arisen out of the common condition of human animals.

From Clarification to Ethical Theory

So much has already been said and written about cloning,
reproductive technologies and genetic engineering that one

---

[1] *Cloning Human Beings* (Washington: National Bioethics Advisory
Commission, 1997).

might wonder what could now be added, in particular, what a *philosopher* could hope to add. Clearly it is not the business of philosophy to determine what scientific enquiry may achieve; nor is it the task of philosophy to predict social trends. So far as these matters are concerned anything a philosopher might say would just be amateur speculation. It does not follow, however, that philosophy has nothing practically useful to offer. Not every fact is a scientific one, and not every question about public policy concerns what people would do. There are facts about human life that are not reducible to any physical (or social) science; and there are issues about what we should do, not just about what we could do or would do in certain circumstances.

The study of human life and the regulation of action and emotion by norms and values is very much the business of philosophy — as indeed is the preliminary task of conceptual clarification. The phrase 'clarity is not enough' has been used in criticism of an exclusively analytical style of working fashionable among Oxford-trained philosophers for a short period in the 1960s. The criticism is apt, but of course it presumes (correctly) that clarity is a necessary condition for progress in philosophy. And clarification is usually called for. In the present case, as soon as mention was made of gene-based cloning commentators and others began to discuss the implications of replicating adult humans and contemplated the prospect of several 'identical individuals'. This reveals scientific ignorance and intellectual confusion. As a matter of logic individuals must be numerically distinct and hence cannot be one and the same person. As a matter of fact a clone would be a biological twin rather less similar to its partner than has hitherto been the case — for the clone of an adult would begin as a baby and lag behind its 'parent' thereafter. In addition, genetically identical twins often differ physically and psychologically and only the crudest determinism would support an expectation of extensive qualitative similarity in these respects.

On the other hand it is a confusion to suppose that whereas reproductive cloning involves the creation of a human embryo, therapeutic cloning does not. The difference lies not in what is created but in what is done to or with it. Reproductive cloning plans to preserve the embryo, therapeutic cloning plans to dismember and then destroy it. Of themselves, without supplementary premises, these observations do not constitute an argument in favour or against any policy but they are made necessary by the obscurities surrounding the very idea of human cloning.

Moving to the policy questions, my general concern, which applies equally well to other reprogenetic matters and to almost all morally charged issues – is that discussions (and I include ethical discussions) are conducted in at most two and more often just one dimension(s). One dimension produces a line, two constitute a plane; essential as these elements are in the constitution of something solid they are not themselves sufficient for it. For that we need to achieve depth.

The one-dimensional discussion is conducted in terms of welfare, more precisely in terms of harm and benefit. The second dimension added to this, often by professional ethicists, concerns rights (and corresponding social duties). Sometimes these two dimensions are collapsed back into one, as when it is argued that rights and responsibilities ultimately concern what is of benefit to an individual or perhaps to society. Even when they are kept distinct, however, there is a tendency to suppose first, that these features exhaust the range of relevant 'ethical' and 'philosophical' considerations; and second, that they can be weighed against one another in some more or less precise way – by some kind of moral mathematics such as was considered in chapter two 'Persons and Values' – bringing together utility summing, and rights vectors.

So far as the second supposition is concerned, while no-one really believes in the possibility of precise calculation there is a sense that there are broad bands and thresholds within and between which credit and deficit transfers can be made. So, for example, it will be said, in noble opposition to utilitarianism, that it would not be permissible to violate the *right* of one for the *welfare* of some small number. However, things change as the scale of potential benefit rises.

This way of thinking is intelligible but it suggests a fundamental commitment to consequentialism. Whereas the idea
of the right of the innocent, for example, was originally
conceived of as something inviolable, i.e. as something that
could not be infringed or transgressed *whatever the consequences.*

Those who still try to uphold the idea of inviolability are
sometimes seen as indifferent to human welfare, for it is
clear enough that if one denies oneself the very possibility
of certain courses of action, then it will happen that there are
circumstances in which one will refuse to countenance an
option even though performing it might produce great
benefits. In an effort to show that they are not indifferent to
welfare, advocates of inviolability appeal to the idea that
one may sometimes act (or refrain from acting) for the sake
of some good (or the avoidance of some evil) even though in
doing so one may cause harm. They then point out that in
determining the permissibility of this the relative impact on
human welfare is a factor to be taken into consideration.

This appeal to 'the principle of double effect' is sometimes said to be casuistical (by which, contrary to the original meaning of the term, is meant devious or deceptive).
More subtly it is sometimes held to show that advocates of
inviolability are themselves ultimately consequentialists.
Neither charge is warranted so far as the logic of double
effect is concerned. In essence the principle concerns the
scope of morally permissible action. It maintains that while
it is always wrong intentionally to bring about a bad effect
or an evil end—the death of an innocent, for example—it is
sometimes permissible to act in a way that one foresees will
have bad side effects. In brief, one may not directly intend
harm but one may countenance it as an unintended effect of
doing good. The historical source of the principle lies in a
passage in Aquinas where, in discussing whether it is
lawful to kill a man in self-defence, he writes as follows:

> Nothing hinders one act from having two effects, only one
> of which is intended, while the other is outside or beyond
> the intention (*praeter intentionem*). Now moral acts get their
> identity (*recipiunt speciem*) according to what is intended,

and not according to what is outside or beyond the intention, since this is accidental as explained above (43, 3; I-II,
12, 1). Accordingly the act of self-defense may have two
effects, one is the saving of one's life, the other is the slaying
of the aggressor. Therefore this act, since one's intention is
to save one's own life, is not unlawful, seeing that it is natural to everything to keep itself in existence as far as possible. And yet, though proceeding from a good intention, an
act may be rendered unlawful, if it be out of proportion to
the end.[2]

It would indeed be devious (and thus in the pejorative
sense 'casuistical') to redescribe an intended and primary
effect as a secondary and unintended one; and unscrupu-
lous persons have certainly sought to pervert double-effect
thinking along these lines. For example, if it is wrong intentionally to kill the innocent, then it will not do for a terrorist
who plants a bomb beneath the car of an innocent driver to
redescribe matters by saying that his intention is to advance
his political cause by causing an explosion, and that any
injury to the occupant of the car is a merely foreseen and
unintended effect. This will not do because it is false. The
terrorist does not hope to achieve his political goal by
destroying cars but rather by injuring and killing people.
This latter is therefore an *intended* means to a further end.
Admittedly, unlike the intention of a homicidal psycho-
path, the harm caused to innocent occupants may not be the
terrorist's only intended aim, but deployed as a means it is
certainly intended and not merely foreseen. Accordingly, it
is wholly excluded by the principle of double effect.

The charge of concealed consequentialism is no more
convincing. Consider what is precluded: one may not aim at
a bad effect as a goal, nor use one as a means to a good end.
What one may do in pursuing a good end is to deploy

[2]   Aquinas, *Summa Theologiae*, IIa IIae q. 64, a.7, *responsio*. For both
      supportive and critical discussions of the appeal to double-effect
      principles see P.A. Woodward ed. *The Doctrine of Double Effect:
      Philosophers debate a Controversial Principle* (Southbend, IN:
      University of Notre Dame Press, 2001); and for a full-length study
      (from a supportive standpoint) see T.A. Cavanaugh, *Double-Effect
      Reasoning: Doing Good and Avoiding Evil* (Oxford: Oxford University
      Press, 2006).

means which though not in themselves bad are foreseen to have additional and bad effects. This does not at all say that the end justifies the means, since it insists that some means are never justifiable (killing the innocent, for example). Moreover, elaboration of the principle involves the requirement that where unintended bad effects are foreseen they must be proportionate to the goods achieved. In other words in eschewing both evil ends and evil means one does not yet have a morally free hand. One will still have done wrong if in pursuing a small good one causes — be it unintentionally — a great harm. This element of weighing outcomes does not constitute consequentialism; indeed it only enters in *after* non-consequential values have been taken account of; which is to say once they have been respected.

The relevance of this style of reasoning to the argument of those opposed to therapeutic cloning on anti-abortion grounds is worth pointing out since it is not always understood. Suppose, what is admittedly controversial, that it is wrong intentionally to kill or to injure an embryo. If that is so then it is plausible to suppose that it is worse still intentionally to create an embryo in the knowledge that one will then intentionally kill or injure it. This is what therapeutic cloning involves. An embryo is created by nuclear replacement in order that cells may be taken from it. Thereby it suffers injury. Indeed, further development would be impossible or at best abnormal. Accordingly, it is destroyed in, or subsequent to the process of cell removal.

I assume that even advocates of this procedure would allow that to create embryos *just* for the sake of dismembering them would be wrong. Their claim, of course, is that the creation of embryos for experimentation and therapy is justified by the end it serves. Perhaps that is so, but we should now be able to see that if it is wrong it cannot be saved by appeal to double effect. For just as the terrorist intends and not merely foresees the harm to the car occupant, so the medical scientist intends and does not merely foresee injury to the embryo. In each case this has been chosen as a necessary means to an end; and to the extent that these ends are taken to justify causing harm the moralities in question are consequentialist.

Moral Limits

The opposing position that certain policies remain excluded, especially those that would challenge inviolable values, is an absolutist one. There is now a general avoidance of such ideas. This is probably because it is supposed that absolutes are only intelligible within a religious framework. There is some irony in this given the marked tendency in the latter half of the twentieth century for moral theologians to abandon absolutist ethics in favour of forms of consequentialism, *viz.* 'situation ethics' and 'proportionalism'.[3] In any case the supposition that absolutism only makes sense on religious grounds has to contend with the fact that arguably the three greatest moral philosophers, *viz.* Plato, Aristotle and Kant, *all* maintained that rational reflection unaided by any kind of religious revelation establishes that there are unconditional norms and absolute values, and that these set inviolable boundaries to prudential calculation.

Whatever the abstract theories of these particular philosophers it is a recurrent conclusion of serious reflection that beyond the realm of individual and collective advantage lie considerations about what is permissible, impermissible, or required, and that these set limits to consequential calculation. The sense of this, if not the philosophical language and argumentation, is in fact quite common. People will spontaneously exclaim that something would not be right, or that it would be unjust, or cruel or cowardly, and so on. These verdicts are quite independent of any thought of whether the proposed policy would be advantageous or disadvanta-

---

[3]   The principal advocate of the first is the Protestant moral theologian Joseph Fletcher who sets out his position in *Situation Ethics: The New Morality* (London: SCM Press, 1966). Perhaps the best known proponent of proportionalism are the Catholic writers Charles Curran and Richard McCormick; see, for example, R. McCormick and C. Curran (eds.) *Moral Norms and the Catholic Tradition* (New York: Paulist Press, 1979).

geous, and they are not always liable to be withdrawn when it is claimed that, whatever about the action itself, great benefits would flow from it.

It may be said that this sense of moral limit is what is captured by the ethics of rights and duties, and therefore that these ethical concepts are enough to guide the pursuit of welfare and the causing of harm. So, for example, welfare is to be maximised up to the point where no rights are violated. As I remarked, however, most of those who talk of rights do not think that they are absolute, and they generally allow that things may be done to an individual if the benefit to others is very great (or the others are very many) which it would be wrong to do if the benefits were less (or the beneficiaries fewer).

Notice, the difference lies not in the condition or circumstance of the victim but in the condition and circumstance of others. Not only is the status of the innocent not absolute, it is not, at least on most versions of this approach, something possessed independently of the interests of others. In this connection some readers may recall the counsel attributed to the chief priest Caiphas in one of the accounts of the trial of Jesus: 'it is expedient that one man should die for the sake of the people' *John* 18. 14.

Moreover, and this is the point I want to emphasise, the ethics of rights fails to explain the sense we have that to act in a certain way would not just injure others materially or morally, but would undermine the person who acted in that way. The best way to develop this thought is by reflecting on two different perspectives represented in the history of moral philosophy and to be found deep in most reflective people's moral thinking. First, there is a conception of morality which sees it as consisting in a system of principles and rules (mostly negative or proscriptive ones). The Judaic 'Decalogue' in its non-theological commands is an important and enduring example of this: 'Thou shalt not kill. Thou shalt not commit adultery. Thou shalt not steal. Thou shalt not bear false witness against thy neighbour. Thou shalt not covet thy neighbour's house … nor anything that is thy neighbour's' (*Exodus* 20).

As in the biblical example of Moses and the 'children of Israel', the natural context for this conception is that of a community or society in which co-operation and the avoidance of conflict are very important for the achievement and maintenance and certain goods. Unsurprisingly, therefore, two ideas are associated with it. First, that of a social contract involving mutually binding obligations agreed to explicitly or implicitly—and most likely tacitly. Second, that of agent/patient reciprocity. By this latter I mean the assumption that anyone who can and should be a beneficiary of moral consideration must themselves be capable of according it to other beneficiaries. In other words every moral patient must be a moral agent and vice versa.

This social (or, better, societal) focus is intelligible and in terms of the conceived function of morality important and defensible; but today we are perhaps better placed than in the past to see that it omits certain classes of individuals who there are reasons to suppose deserve of moral consideration and respect. First, there are those who as a matter of circumstance lie outside the contract, for example members of other and distant societies, and isolated individuals outwith the bounds of our or any other society. Second, there are those incapable of moral deliberation and thus who cannot satisfy the condition of patient/agent reciprocity. Among these might be included human beings who for one reason or another lack competence. This would cover both those who have lost the relevant abilities such as the senile, and those who have not developed them, such as retarded adults, children, and foetuses. As well as incompetent humans there are non-competent animals to be considered. Focus on the latter has been a common feature of recent writings by Peter Singer who has described the enlargement of the domain of beings worthy of consideration, beyond the field of those capable of according it, in terms of an 'expanding circle' of moral concern. Other writers have insisted that animals and even plants and primitive organisms possess moral rights and to that extent enjoy moral standing analogous to that of persons.

Besides straining a moral vocabulary developed to describe the position of participating members of human societies this way of thinking is not necessary in order to accord respect to non-humans and to nature. Interestingly, Roger Scruton — an agnostic philosopher working within the broadly Kantian tradition that defines moral worth in terms of the potential for reciprocity, and one not known for progressive moral sentiment — has found it appropriate to invoke the idea of a 'natural piety' felt in the presence of something other than oneself, and to cite this response as a ground for acting respectfully towards its objects.[4]

Given the limitations of the conception of morality as a system of principles and rules governing human interaction, and the possibility of grounding conduct in a sense of what is felt reflectively to be appropriate, one may turn to the other main perspective on value and action, that which locates morality *within* a broad structure of rational sentiments, motives and behaviour — as that part of the whole of a person's normative outlook that is sometimes termed 'the moral psychology of virtue'. Unlike the rules-based approach this ('aretaic') philosophy of virtue is concerned not just with setting requirements and limits to action (responsibilities and duties) but with introducing values that might inform the general direction of one's life — not just drawing an outline but filling in the shape. It also has a wider concern and serves to link questions of conduct with a view of the world and of the human way of being; in short, with metaphysics and with philosophical anthropology.

In fairness it should be noted that in recent years advocates of utilitarianism and of the ethics of rights have acknowledged the need to address the role of virtue in morality, but they have thought of it as something secondary to the value of good outcomes or the requirements of principle, viewing it as a disposition to promote the former or to discharge the latter. This is both question-begging in its assumption that virtue is secondary, and restrictive in confining its operation to the sphere of morality as those

[4]   See Roger Scruton, *Animal Rights and Wrongs* (London: Demos, 1996).

other theories conceive of it. In contrast, proponents of virtue argue either that it (virtue) is what has priority over welfare or rights, or that if not prior to these other factors it is equally fundamental; and to this they add that the perspective of virtue is broader than that of ethics. Virtue consists in the possession of values that shape and animate one's entire range of sentiments, reactions and conduct. Put broadly, to be virtuous is to be disposed towards human goods and to be inclined away from human evils.

The ancients and the medievals saw clearly that virtue is called upon quite generally in the effort to live a good life. While bearing on one's relations with other competent, adult members of society it also touches upon a far wider constituency of concern and is also necessary for the management of affairs in which others have no place. The obstacles to human fulfilment are many and various. Some are local and avoidable such as social inconveniences, but others are global and inescapable such as illness and death. These various factors, the coming to terms with which is a part of living well, set the conditions for the project of being human.

Virtue and Demeanour

Thoreau observed that 'the mass of men lead lives of quiet desperation'.[5] It is clear enough what he meant by this, and the popularity of self-help literature suggests that anxiety, disappointment and frustration remain features of modern life. Indeed, notwithstanding material affluence the sense of insecurity would appear to be more widespread. One analysis sees this concern in terms of the feared loss of preferred goods. For example, having worked to secure a good job, or having acquired or inherited the means to sustain a leisured lifestyle, or nature having bestowed a good physique, a man or woman might then come to see that these goods are vulnerable to fortune, and might become increasingly desperate as they contemplate the prospect of their loss.

---

[5]   Henry David Thoreau, *Walden* (London: Dent, 1974) p. 5. He went on to add that 'what is called resignation is but confirmed desperation'.

Significant as this is, however, it does not reach the desperation felt by those whose reflections go deeper. Their concern would not be assuaged by the assurance that what they have valued will be protected, *per impossible*, against the tides of misfortune and the ravages of time. For part of what they (and here I must say 'we') doubt is whether the preferences one has, and for the sake of which one has struggled, *ought* to be satisfied. And a reason for doubting that they ought to be is that commonly their satisfaction does not bring contentment. Not infrequently, the educated, liberal, middle-class think that this is an anxiety that others less cultured than themselves ought to feel. I agree that those who have pursued material goods at the expense of the cultivation of the aesthetic or the cultural have chosen the lesser part, but I also note that among those whose feel this superiority many have abandoned spouses and partners (not being 'obsessively faithful'), encouraged abortions for reasons of convenience (not being 'fanatically pro-life'), and cultivated appetites far removed from human needs (not being 'obsessively puritanical'); and further note that not everyone feels at ease with the pursuit of these preferences. In particular, women are more likely to be used and abused in these 'non-material' respects and to feel that fact as the years advance.

There is more to a good life than observance of moral responsibility, and more to moral value than welfare and rights. There is the question of virtue: the cultivation of habits of action and reaction directed towards human well-being, which is to say — conceiving of this good as something dynamic and maintained by activity — towards *being-human well*. Hitherto I have been speaking of the life of individuals, but the same holds good at the level of society. Hard enough as it may be to shape policy in accord with welfare assessed impartially, and with rights accorded universally, there is also the need to consider social virtue. It takes a good deal of dialectical ingenuity — though somewhat less rhetoric — to induce the conviction that questions about collective virtue are incoherent.

The attitudes developed in the course of cultivating virtue constitute a form of *demeanour*. This is a way of being, formed and held constant in the face of such facts as that we grow old, that we are more or less talented, that we have varying personalities, that we are vulnerable to abandonment, betrayal, loss, sickness and death. Virtue, and the happiness it brings, lie in proper concern and appropriate indifference to these realities; attitudes that should be informed by a wise assessment of the conditions of life and an ennobling sense of the possibility of living well under conditions given and not chosen. We will not develop this outlook if we see nature always as something to be overcome, or if we always give priority to the satisfaction of antecedent preferences — preferences held prior to the discovery of natural obstacles or, assuming those to have been identified at an early stage, counterfactual ones. Additionally, recalling that a great part of what it is to be human is to teach others what this should involve, we cannot help them cultivate a demeanour of reasonable acceptance if we do not have it ourselves and show it in our own dealings with given circumstances.

The good life is necessarily one achieved under limits — that is what makes it good and makes the living of it something that merits praise. Put another way the virtues are capacities forged in the face of adversity: courage in the face of danger, justice in the circumstance of shortage or in that of wrong-doing; fortitude in the face of difficulty; perseverance in the context of enduring opposition and so on.

Conclusion

The relevance of these reflections to aspects of the issue of reproductive cloning should be clear. According to non-consequentialist moralities the creation of human beings exclusively for the client's benefit is a violation of the ethical requirement not to use others only as a means. That is true even where the embryo is cultivated to term. So much the worse where embryos are created, for client's benefit, in the expectation of being destroyed as is the case in both therapeutic and non-therapeutic cloning. According to the wider perspective of virtue, reproductive cloning is also a breach of the philosophical responsibly to live within human limits according to norms of openness to the being of others. I recognise that of itself this latter consideration may be held to be inconclusive, but I hope nevertheless that its significance may yet be felt and taken account of.

Some of the ethical objections to cloning concern contingent matters of safety, such as the risk of transferring mutations in the somatic cells of donors. In the course of time, due to ultraviolet radiation and chemical contamination, body cells are liable to be damaged. In itself this may not matter if the process of replacement proceeds normally. However, cloning from adult body cells carries the risk of creating an embryo out of mutant genetic material. The resulting clone would then have a greater chance of developing cancer and could also be expected to have below average life-expectancy. Additionally, as the efforts involved in the production of Dolly the sheep showed, embryos created by cloning are likely to suffer developmental abnormalities. The reason for this is not yet established but it seems likely that the 'reprogramming' of transferred body cells is often incomplete.

The risks of malformation and early death provide a good reason not to clone. However, they are contingent and consequential factors which one can easily imagine being overcome through further scientific research; though that research will itself involve creating embryos for experimentation and destruction. Turning from physical dangers there are other harms to be contemplated. The process leading to the production of Dolly required the surgical removal of more than 400 unfertilised eggs from donor ewes. Current practice concerning human in vitro fertilisation (IVF) involves on average the recovery of 10 eggs per woman donor. Sheep are more highly reproductive than humans: a fertile ewe has over ninety per cent chance of becoming pregnant through a single mating; a fertile woman has about a 33% chance of pregnancy through intercourse, and rates drop to 10-20%. under IVF. These figures suggest that any clinic seeking to clone a human being will require well over a 1,000 eggs gathered from over 100 women (or fewer women and more harvestings). The potential for exploitation of donors and of clients is evident and need not be elaborated.

I return, however, to the broader issues of virtue and demeanour. Bringing another human being into existence is one of the fundamentals of life and should be regarded as such. It involves opening oneself to physical, emotional and moral challenges so various and considerable that some decline the option, preferring instead to develop their own projects. Yet for most people the challenges are felt to be worthwhile and are accepted as the corollary of creating another human being. The sense of otherness which is felt at the sight of a new born child registers a combination of continuity and difference that contributes in part to the value of conceiving and having children, and also underlies many of the common difficulties in parent-child relationships. By contrast, the deployment of genetic science in the service of reproductive cloning suggests a wish to assert one's own being, extending it into space hitherto occupied by uncertain otherness. In this respect the wish to clone also marks a failure to have cultivated the sort of respect towards human existence that is now widely encouraged as a proper response towards the lesser being of non-human nature.

In reply it may be said that the development of selective cloning offers the prospect of bringing children into being whose initial condition and subsequent development are likely to be better than those of natural offspring; and who, because they are possessed of characteristics chosen by their 'parents' are more likely to be loved and cherished. But that very reply illustrates the perspective I have been concerned to oppose. A good human life is not one that tries to overcome human contingencies, but is one that is developed within the context of them. In having children we carry forward the human enterprise not as a form of self-advancement or as a method of increasing wellbeing, but as a way of enabling others to realise the value of shaping a life in circumstances which are given rather than chosen.

Reproductive cloning aims to overcome that limitation but thereby threatens the very possibility of a meaningful life.

If this style of thinking seems less clear and determinate than that represented in the appeal to rights and welfare, then I suggest readers consider the possibility that the latter fails to represent the complexity of human values, and that in this of all matters it is dangerous to sacrifice accuracy for simplicity. Discussions of the ethics of human cloning and of other contemporary moral problems generally lack a dimension that I believe to be essential, namely, a phenomenology of human value, that is to say, a descriptive account of the meaning and value of living a human life. Progress in this regard would be an important contribution to moral philosophy and, given the policy implications of cloning and related bioethical issues, to the conduct of public affairs.

6

Defence, Deterrence and the Taking of Life

Introduction

In previous chapters I have been concerned with providing a general philosophical and ethical framework within which to place thinking about particular issues, and in the last of these 'Science, Knowledge and Virtue' turned to the matter of the creation and manipulation of human life. In the present chapter the ethics of life is again under discussion but the particular issue is that of killing: on the battlefield, against non-combatants, and in the womb.

It is now quite common for philosophers to address matters of practical concern by beginning with established opinions and then attempting to confirm or refute them. This pattern of argument is in fact very old. It originates in the *quaestio disputata* technique developed in the thirteenth century and can be seen employed to great effect by Aquinas, such as in his examination of the morality of war in the *secunda secundae partis* (the second part of the second part) of the *Summa Theologiae*. The topic of war is addressed in question 40 which is further divided into four parts. Two of these (articles 2 and 4) concern specifically religious constraints: whether clerics may fight in war, and whether it is permissible to fight on holy days. Aquinas answers 'no' and 'yes' respectively. The other two parts (articles 1 and 3) concern the general moral permissibility of war, and the permissibility of laying ambushes. Regarding the latter he provides a qualified 'yes'; what is excluded is anything involving direct lying or promise breaking. Unsurprisingly, articles 2, 3 and 4 have attracted little attention outside of specialist moral theology; but Aquinas's response to the issue of the legitimacy of warfare soon became and remains a classic source for just war theory. His position is set out very briefly but it clearly emphasizes the requirements of political authority, just cause, and rightful intention.

Unlike modern philosophers, moral theologians have never felt restrained by the theoretical aspects of their subject from engaging in debate about questions of conduct. Yet the separation of philosophy and theology in the twentieth century has meant that the theologians' contributions to contemporary debates often lack rigour. In this respect modern moral theology compares badly with its medieval and scholastic counterparts. Recently however, there have been signs of a resurgence of systematic, moral thinking among theologians of different denominations. Several names come to mind in this connection including those of John Finnis, Germain Grisez, Stanley Hauerwas, Gerard J. Hughes, and Oliver O'Donovan. Significantly, each draws to a greater or lesser degree upon the traditions of medieval natural-law theory and analytic philosophy, and passes to and fro without discomfort between meta-ethical and first-order issues. Of more particular interest here is the fact that they all have addressed themselves to the question of the morality of nuclear deterrence, though they come to rather different conclusions concerning it.[1]

---

[1]   See J. Finnis, J.M. Boyle, Jr. & G. Grisez, *Nuclear Deterrence, Morality and Realism* (Oxford: Clarendon Press, 1987); Stanley Hauerwas *Against the Nations: War and Survival in a Liberal Society* (Southbend, IN: University of Notre Dame Press, 1992); G.J. Hughes, 'The Intention to Deter', in F. Bridges (ed.) *The Cross and the Bomb* (London: Mowbrays, 1983); and Oliver O'Donovan, *The Just War Revisited* (Cambridge: Cambridge University Press, 2003). Although much has been published since, *Nuclear Deterrence, Morality and Realism* remains the best and most comprehensive ethical treatment of the issues so far produced. For an interesting discussion of it see G.J. Hughes 'Philosophical Debate on Nuclear Disarmament', *Heythrop Journal*, 29 (2), 1988. Another excellent treatment of the issues informed by a career in the UK Ministry of Defence is provided by Sir Michael Quinlan in *Thinking about Nuclear Weapons: Principles, Problems, Prospects* (Oxford: Oxford University Press, 2009).

In what follows I present a line of argument regarding killing in war, and the threat of such. This too draws its inspiration from Aquinas and scholastic moral thinking but does not invoke any theological premises or religious modes of knowledge. I then return to the matter of abortion, having previously introduced it when considering Martha Nussbaum's insistence on the need to recognize humanity, especially in its most hidden and vulnerable conditions.

Counterforce and the Just War

The nuclear weapons policies of France, Great Britain, NATO and the US, as of the former Soviet Union and now of Russia, have traditionally been based upon the assumption that the aims of a response would be to destroy the enemy's capacity and willingness to wage war by attacking his nuclear and conventional forces and his centres of command, control and logistic support. This strategy is echoed in statements by the three Western nuclear powers: France, the United Kingdom, and the United States; and by China. The position of the remaining nuclear states (currently India, Israel, North Korea and Pakistan) remains uncertain. As described, this policy is properly speaking a 'counterforce' one and as such its employment *may* satisfy the long-established conditions of Just War, *viz*:

(1)   The war must be made by a lawful authority.

(2)   The war must be waged for a morally just cause, e.g. self defence.

(3)   The warring state must have a rightful intention, i.e. to pursue the just cause;

(4)   The war must be the only means of achieving the just end.

(5)   There must be a reasonable prospect of victory.

(6)   The goods to be achieved must be greater than the probable evil effects of waging war.

(7)   The means of war must not themselves be evil: either by being such as to cause gratuitous injuries or deaths,

or by involving the intentional killing of innocent civilians.[2]

Of course a counterforce response might be unjust and it is clear enough where the threat of its being so is most likely to arise. For while any of the above conditions could be breached the destructive power of nuclear weapons is such that even a well-intentioned, lawful authority waging war in pursuit of a just cause may easily violate conditions (5, 6 and 7).

It should be obvious that the liability to injustice is a function of the targeting policy and the destructive power of the weapons involved and is not a matter of their physical constitution as such. However, in the long-running debate about the morality of nuclear defence policy there has been a tendency for all parties, but in particular for opponents of such policies, to become obsessed with the *nuclear* aspect of the matter and thereby to lose sight of the central philosophical arguments which are instances of quite general ones concerning the ethics of violence. Principal among these is the following:

(1)   It is always wrong intentionally to kill innocent human beings.

(2)   A nuclear weapons strategy involves intentionally killing innocent human beings, either directly or indirectly.

(3)   Therefore, a nuclear weapons strategy is always wrong.

Assuming the truth of (1), the conclusion (3) can yet be avoided by denying premise (2). And indeed, as a universal claim (2) is surely false. For example, the counterforce use of tactical weapons at sea and even on land may pose no threat to innocent parties. Accordingly, the blanket condemnation

---

[2]   Conditions (1)–(3) correspond to those elaborated by Aquinas in *Summa Theologiae*, IIa, IIae, q. 40, a1. The others also originate in scholastic moral theology. For a useful discussion of the tradition of the Just War see J. Teichman, *Pacifism and the Just War* (Oxford: Blackwell, 1986). This includes extracts from several historically influential texts.

of nuclear defence policy based on Just War principles is contentious given the (probable) non-moral, empirical facts about the power of certain weapons and about the targeting strategies involving them.[3]

Furthermore, the nuclear obsession blinds many (on both sides of current debates about the ethics of modern warfare) to the important fact that not all unjust defence policies are nuclear ones. For, as before, a lawful authority engaged in war as a means of last resort and in pursuit of a just cause may yet act wrongly by employing evil means; for example, by using weapons of mass destruction against civilian populations.[4] Injustices of this sort are familiar from recent history and include, most shamefully for the former Allied forces and in particular for Great Britain, the deliberate area bombing of German centres of population during World War II.

Countervalue and Morality

In short and in general therefore, the use of nuclear weapons is neither sufficient nor necessary for violation of the conditions of Just War. There are, however, certain nuclear strategies which if employed would be unjust. Among these are some counterforce policies, e.g. first strike without declaration of war, acts of aggression, use of disproportionate force, etc; and all countervalue strategies. The latter cannot

---

[3]   This said, any use of nuclear weapons may put non-combatant lives at risk either by prompting retaliatory countervalue attacks, or by virtue of the collateral effects of even counterforce exchanges. The dangers of escalation are authoritatively discussed by M. Bundy, G. Kennan, R. McNamara and G. Smith, 'Nuclear Weapons and the Atlantic Alliance', *Foreign Affairs*, 60 (4), 1982. On the various effects of nuclear attacks see *The Effects of Nuclear War* (Washington, DC: Office of Technology Assessment, 1979); C. Sagan 'Nuclear War and Climate Catastrophe: Some Policy Implications', *Foreign Affairs*, 62 (2), 1983; and M.A. Harwell *et al.*, *Environmental Consequences of Nuclear War* (New York: Wiley, 1989). These matters are interestingly examined and set within a moral context by J. Child, *Nuclear War: The Moral Dimension* (London: Transaction Books & Social Philosophy and Policy Center, 1986). This latter is a clear, well-informed and well-argued defence of deterrence as a legitimate policy option.

[4]   For further discussion of this see J. Haldane, 'Ethics and Biological Warfare', *Arms Control*, 8 (1), 1987

ever be just since they violate (at least) condition (7) of those listed and are condemned by the argument set out above.

Addressing the question 'What if the deterrent fails?' General Sir Hugh Beach focuses on the issue of proportionality, i.e. the requirement that the costs of war (of individual operations and of the whole campaign) be proportionate to the goods achieved by it. But this focus gives insufficient attention to other essential factors. Considering the prospect of a strategic interchange involving an allied retaliatory strike on Minsk, the effects of which are 'many times worse' than those suffered by Birmingham in the initial (then presumed to be Soviet) attack, he comments:

> Most people would have no difficulty in determining the moral propriety of this action. The allied nuclear strike though undoubtedly indiscriminate is redeemed by being proportionate both in the sense of tit for tat but in the much more important sense that the good achieved (of stopping the war) far exceeds the damage inflicted horrifying though that is.[5]

Setting aside questions about the greater violence of the retaliation and about 'tit for tat' justification, it is important to note that failure to satisfy one condition of *jus in bello* is not something that can be 'redeemed' by satisfying another. Satisfaction of each requirement is individually necessary and only jointly sufficient for Just War. Thus, the admission that a prospective attack is 'undoubtedly indiscriminate' is enough to condemn it. The matter is perhaps obscured by confusing a scenario of the type depicted with one in which an attack directed upon a military target causes non-combatant deaths. Since the latter are foreseen but not intended one might justify such an attack by appeal to the principle of double effect (see below). Here proportionality is relevant as it serves to restrict the scope of the principle. Collateral damage must be proportionate to the good secured. In the envisaged strategic interchange however, both strikes are directed against non-combatants and thus are knowingly

---

[5]   Hugh Beach, 'What if the Deterrent Fails?' in Richard Bauckham and John Elford eds., *The Nuclear Weapons Debate: Theological and Ethical Issues* (London: SCM, 1989), p. 208.

and intentionally indiscriminate. This renders them immoral. The contrary verdict, which Sir Hugh considers would be the judgment of most people and which he endorses, employs the idea of proportionality in a consequentialist fashion alien to its role in Just War theory.

Since 1945 the defence policies of Western nuclear powers as individual nations and in association with NATO have drifted from the tradition of counterforce, with which I began, to countervalue. And from the late 1950s onwards, talk of 'mass destruction of Soviet cities' and of 'annihilating an enemy society' has featured in official policy reports and in research analyses of national and NATO targeting strategies.[6] The clear implication of the foregoing therefore, is that, inasmuch as it includes a countervalue component, current Western defence policy is immoral.

In reply, advocates of such policies have tended to argue in one of two ways: claiming either that the ethics of violence and warfare have been changed by the development of weapons of mass destruction and that the Just War doctrine in particular is anachronistic; or else, that while the enactment of currently held strategies would certainly be immoral it is not wrong to threaten to enact them with the intention of thereby deterring hostility from potential aggressors.

The first line of reply can itself be interpreted in one or other of two ways. Either it is being asserted that the moral claim set out as premise (1) in the earlier argument, and those others implicit in the conditions of Just War, are false; or alternatively the suggestion is that somehow a countervalue attack is not at odds with them. The historical drift from counterforce to countervalue defence strategies does, I believe, mark a movement away from general acceptance of these moral claims. But this is no argument against their truth, and it is difficult even to conceive of a plausible

---

[6] For an examination of Western retaliatory threats see Finnis *et al.*, *Nuclear Deterrence, Morality and Realism*, op.cit., Part One; and for an interesting discussion of the British dimension see L. Freedman, 'British Nuclear Targeting', *Defense Analysis*, 1 (2) 1985. For a more recent, and well-informed account see Michael Quinlan, *op.cit.*

moral view according to which it is permissible intentionally to kill innocent human beings. The prohibition against doing so is a familiar and prominent tenet of the Judaeo-Christian ethical tradition and persists in secular moral theories. Certainly adherents of this tradition and of its non-theological rivals have not always practised as their theories preached but the prohibition has never been thought to be less than absolute for being violated. Even offenders pay tribute to it by attempting to represent the victims of their killings as being in some way culpable, or otherwise legitimate targets.

In the Judaeo-Christian tradition murder is an absolute evil, a course of action that can never be justified by weighing the taking of innocent life against the achievement of some material or social benefit. As St. Paul cautioned the Romans, it would be slanderous to say that what Christians believe is that one can do evil if good may come of it. (*Romans* 3. 5-21). And it is clear that he takes the rejection of this consequentialist view to be obligatory for all who are 'under the law' (*torah*).

The inviolability of human life can be argued for in different ways. One line of thought connects the idea of rational agency with that of universality. The potential killer requires that his own life not be threatened by others in order that he may pursue his goals. But if these goals include causing the death of another person then he is simultaneously affirming and denying the requirement that an agent should not have his life threatened. The pattern of argument can be reworked in a variety of ways but the basic idea remains the same, i.e. that murder involves inconsistency and is thus irrational.

A second, related approach involves the notion of reciprocity in claiming that one ought not to act towards an individual in a way that you would not want them to act towards you. This, a version of the 'golden rule', is more restricted in scope than the previous reasoning. It cannot rationally bind those who are prepared to be 'done unto as they would do unto others'. However, it is not likely that any sane person would assent to being killed so as to legitimize his killing another. Certainly, it has been known for murderers to seek execution as retribution for their actions and this is intelligible, but not because it is thought to make the first killing acceptable. On the contrary, it is because the murderer sees the enormity of what he has done, and the impossibility of nullifying it, that he volunteers his own life. One may perhaps question the coherence of his attitude inasmuch as it seems to compound the evil of taking life. But it is crucially important to note that this is the direction in which our thoughts move in search of consistency, and not towards the view that murder is acceptable so long as the murderer is willing to be killed in turn.

A third line of argument in favour of respect for human life rests not on appeals to general rationality but instead focuses attention on the particular value of our lives. The sort of worth in question is obviously meant to be intrinsic to human beings as such. As discussed in chapters two and three, this kind of value does not attach to them in virtue of capacities or other valuable features which may be possessed to a greater or lesser degree by different individuals. Within the moral theology in which the Just War theory originates, the notion of an inalienable right to life is derived from the claim that we are all alike in being children of a loving god. However, even accepting general religious doctrines there are challenges in giving sense to this metaphor and then of showing how particular moral claims can be derived from it. It is not obvious (even it if is true) that the fact that two men are related as brothers makes the killing of one by the other wicked; as if it otherwise would not be. Certainly, we do think that fratricide is evil but this is in part because we already think that homicide is bad.

Challenges to the theological approach notwithstanding, it is not implausible to argue that the instrinsic value of human life is a fundamental, underived fact such that to destroy human life intentionally is always bad no matter what goods are achieved by doing so. This would serve to explain the phenomenology of moral experience. For the idea of innocent life presents itself as that of something to be respected whether or not the sorts of arguments against murder outlined previously are found compelling. Of course, the moral nihilist is not likely to be troubled by this or any other response since he denies that any moral claim can be true. Nonetheless, national governments, international military codes and the thought and practice of most people presuppose morality, and more precisely acknowledge such claims as that one may not deliberately slaughter the innocent—which is what countervalue attacks intend. Even if murder could not be shown to be irrational, blasphemous or contrary to the natural order, its being anathema according to common judgment and positive national and international law is sufficient ground to discount the denial of the moral claim set out as premise (1). Furthermore, the belief that one may intentionally kill the innocent, for whatever reason, is not only repugnant but also self-defeating with respect to whatever other value or end is given priority. Anyone who urges that it is acceptable to act in this way in order, for example, to advance a political ideal, is unlikely to live to see the kind of society he wants. Nor could such a society be expected to survive, since from the very moment of its conception it would be vulnerable to the activities of those who, like its architects, adhere to a doctrine of justified murder.

The second interpretation of the first reply to the charge that current Western defence policy is immoral implies that, contrary to initial appearances, such attacks escape moral condemnation. This follows, it is said, because the Just War doctrine and the earlier argument both presuppose a distinction between the innocent and the non-innocent which is no longer applicable in the modern context. Thus, countervalue would be evil *if* the target populations were innocent; but they are not.

This line of thought has gained support, particularly in the United States following the attacks of 2001 and the identification of regimes as sponsors of terrorism and advocates of the destruction of western societies. Yet, as before, and leaving aside the veracity of these claims, acceptance is no argument in its favour. All it betokens is woeful ignorance or neglect of the moral dimension of war. From the middle-ages onwards the principle of the immunity of the innocent has been the primary rule governing the conduct of hostilities and it is no objection to it that it has been neglected in recent times any more than that it was often ignored in the medieval and intervening periods. Certainly the scale of likely hostilities has increased and this encourages the idea that we now face 'total war' in which the distinction can no longer be made. The latter claim, however, though familiar is either false or question-begging. If it means that every member of the community wages war it is clearly incorrect. And if it is interpreted as saying that modern warfare is often (and henceforth always will be) directed against entire populations then while this may be true it remains to be determined whether such a practice is acceptable. That it is done is no proof of the claim that it is legitimate to do it. There can be no serious doubt that there is a difference between those who are engaged in threatening one (either as combatants or as suppliers to them of the means of waging war) and those who are not. Indeed, the strategists' language of 'counterforce and countervalue policies' and of 'hard and soft targets' is intended in large part to mark just this distinction.

Threats and Bluff

It is principally in recognition of the collapse of the previous response to the moral arguments that other defenders of current nuclear policy have adopted the second line of reply, arguing that although it would be immoral to attack centres or population it is not wrong to threaten to do so. Moreover, the reply continues, the manufacture and deployment of strategic weapons is justified because it is a way of avoiding nuclear warfare. Thus, not only is it not evil to threaten with sincere intention an action which it would be evil to perform, but where the formation and expression of this conditional intention (to retaliate if attacked) is designed to serve the purpose of ensuring that one never has to act upon it such a policy may actually be morally virtuous and perhaps even obligatory

Before turning to consider something of the ethics of intention it is appropriate to address the issue of a deterrence policy based upon the mere threat of retaliation in circumstances in which there is no actual intention by government to do so—either because the authorities are committed never to use nuclear weapons, or else because they do not possess them. Policies of these sorts obviously involve deception and it might be argued that this fact alone is sufficient to condemn them. To mislead a person into holding false ideas and planning his life on the basis of them is to deprive him doubly of the truth: once as the proper object of belief and again as the correct foundation for practical reasoning. This consideration does show that lying (or otherwise deliberately misleading someone) is bad, and if all one knew about an action was that it was a case of deception this would be reason to refrain from doing it.

However the matter is not so simple. Actions can be described in (indefinitely) many different ways. For example, my moving my hand is also an instance of writing, a case of making a philosophical point and a contribution to earning my living as an academic. To determine the moral value of a particular piece of behaviour therefore, one has to bring it under a relevant description. Sometimes this can be difficult but the real problems for moral assessment arise when an action instantiates two or more act-types which merit conflicting evaluations, e.g. to withhold the truth from someone about their partner's infidelity may be bad because dishonest, yet good because compassionate. Fortunately, not all moral conflicts of this sort are intractable. It may be that one of the types which the behaviour instantiates is such as ought never to be performed whatever other values it realizes.[7] The infliction of gratuitous suffering on a child against its will is a clear case of an

---

[7]   This thought is as ancient as Aristotle, as is the general framework of action theory employed in this section. In the *Nicomachean Ethics*, 1107a10-25, Aristotle writes: '[some actions and affections] imply by their names that they are themselves bad ... It is not possible, therefore, ever to be right with regard to them; but only to go wrong.' See *Nicomachean Ethics* trans. C. Rowe, and commentary by S. Broadie (Oxford: Oxford University Press, 2002).

action-type every instance of which is prohibited. No matter that some of them may also be cases of gaining pleasure or relieving frustration, which considered in themselves are valuable activities.

A less obvious resolution of conflict in practical deliberation can be achieved even when none of the action-types to which the proposed behaviour belongs is morally prohibited though one or more of them is nonetheless bad. Intentionally depriving someone of his property without his consent, for example, is a bad sort of action but in some circumstances it may be that this is the only available way of maintaining one's life. Here then a single piece of behaviour is bad *qua* theft, yet good *qua* act of self-preservation. However, assuming what will generally be the case in such circumstances that the good to be achieved is greater than the likely bad effects, it will be permissible to steal. Indeed, it may even be that in a particular case one has a duty to do so.

It is important to note that the moral view invoked above is not a version of utilitarianism or of consequentialism more generally. The difference emerges in two ways. First, unlike the latter which claims that the moral value of an action derives entirely from its consequences, and which therefore cannot reconcile the idea that a type of action is bad though an instance of it may be morally right, the former view allows that the bad aspects of an act are not nullified by its valuable ones. Hence it requires that, where possible, subsequent recompense should be made. Secondly, and relatedly, this view makes sense of feelings of regret and even of remorse generally experienced in such circumstances. For again it does not deny that the right thing to have done may have been bad in some other respect.

I have elaborated this line of thought because it has often been too quickly assumed by opponents of deterrence policy that the deception involved in a strategy of bluff is clearly morally wrong — and also assumed by the defenders of deception that so long as it delivers the goods there is nothing whatsoever wrong about it. Both assumptions rest on a shallow conception of the structure of morality. The fact that a threat to retaliate if attacked is insincere is reason to judge it bad, but this alone is not sufficient to condemn it. For it may be that the threat succeeds in deterring an otherwise certain lethal onslaught in which case it also instantiates a good sort of action — one which may even be obligatory; *viz*: saving life.

If current or likely future defence policies were of this form I should not oppose them. However, various aspects of the strategy of bluff imply that it is either practically impossible or else morally unacceptable. To this point the supposition has been that the powers issuing the threat lack the will or the means of executing it. But without both it is not clear how an aggressor is to be deterred. Certainly for a threat to be effective it may be enough that an opponent believes in one's willingness and ability to carry it out, and this belief may be false. However, he is hardly likely to hold it without very good evidence and in the modern world it is impossible to succeed in pretending that one has an effective, nuclear, counterstrike capacity if in fact one does not. Without this ability therefore, there can be no successful policy of bluff.

Similarly, an enemy will not be deterred unless the threat appears to be backed by sincere intentions to carry it out. Of course it is logically compatible with creating this appearance that the authors of defence policy and those at the top of the ladder of command lack such intentions but the vast majority of those in government, in the civil and military services, and in the population at large must be deceived into believing that their nation is willing to retaliate. The problem this presents is not simply that of justifying large-scale deception for the sake of a greater good, which I allowed may be done.

The moral difficulty arises from the practical policies which this deception requires. For in addition to commissioning the design, manufacture and deployment of adequate weaponry, government must also secure that those charged with those tasks are willing to have the weapons used and, in the case of the military, intend to use them if commanded to do so.[8]

In this context, therefore, there can be no deception without corruption. The weapons must be deployed and the services must maintain them with the intention of retaliating if attacked. Such retaliation is likely to be murderous because directed against soft targets or because of collateral environmental effects, or through initiating countervalue exchanges. The only practical form of dissuasion by bluff thus involves murderous dispositions. In this respect it does not differ from direct deterrence policies incorporating sincere intentions on the part of government to order retaliatory strikes. Only real military power can deter and a nuclear arsenal only constitutes real power if it is in the hands of persons trained and willing to use it.

This state of affairs directly raises issues concerning the ethics of deterrent intentions. Before turning to consider these, however, it should be noted that, aims and attitudes apart, practical policies of bluff may already be morally culpable inasmuch as the production of the weapons required to sustain them creates risks of accidental and deliberate exchanges. Given the destructive power of these devices, therefore, policies which depend upon them can be challenged by appeal to principles of just defence modelled on the conditions necessary for just war. In particular the following are of immediate relevance:

(1)   The weapons must be deployed for a morally just cause;

(2)   Their deployment must be the only means of deterring aggression;

(3)   There must be a reasonable prospect of success of the policy;

(4)   The goods to be achieved must be greater than the probably evil effects of deployment.

(5)   The means of deterrence must not themselves be evil.

---

[8]   See General Sir Hugh Beach, 'What if the Deterrent Fails?' *op. cit.* for a clear elaboration of this point.

It is not obvious whether the mere possession of nuclear weapons without the intention to use them must, or is likely to, offend against these conditions. The issue seems to be an *a posteriori* one and to depend upon contingent facts of deployment. Nonetheless, in present circumstances even if it were the case that NATO and Russian policies did not involve countervalue retaliatory intentions, the contingencies of deployment would seem to bring them into opposition to the idea of just defence as defined by principles (1)–(5).

The question of the possession of nuclear weapons in circumstances where the power to which they belong disavows any intention of ever using them, even in retaliation, raises a number of interesting and important issues. The idea that the mere retention of weapons may be morally justfied if it is accompanied by the active pursuit of multilateral disarmament, in which process the weapons are discarded only as and when others also disarm, has found favour among philosophers and theologians who are otherwise opposed to nuclear defence policies on grounds similar to those presented above.[9] So far as concerns the morality of 'possession without intention' it is liable to objection on grounds additional to the broadly consequentialist ones indicated above. The advocate of mere retention hopes to evade the charge of immorality by disavowing even conditional intentions of use while still securing the deterrent benefits of possession. For potential aggressors are likely to continue to be dissuaded from risking an attack since, notwithstanding all one's declarations and sincere intentions, it remains a possibility that the weapons may yet be used – either because of a change of heart, or because of a change of leadership.

Certainly weapons retained after public disavowals of intentions of use may continue to deter but this casts doubts upon the scope of such declarations. To remain an effective

---

[9] See, for example, Anthony Kenny, 'The Logic and Ethics of Nuclear Deterrence', in A. Ellis, (ed) *Ethics and International Relations* (Manchester: Manchester University Press, 1986) pp. 92–105. For responses to Kenny by Sir Arthur Hockaday and others see the following pages 105–12.

threat a nuclear arsenal needs to be maintained and updated. Instruction in its possible use must also continue. Thus to preserve the threat by which deterrence is secured a power must go on threatening potential aggressors by continuing to operate a system designed to destroy centres of population. Given this, countenancing anything but the very briefest period of retention following disavowal undermines the claim to have abandoned completely any intention of ever using the system and thereby renders a practitioner of this policy liable to the charge of persisting in his murderous intent.

The Intention to Deter

Attempts to provide a morally acceptable deterrent strategy by securing the benefits of threats while not relying upon sincere intentions fail because without effective weapons and a genuine willingness of the part of the military and many others to use them such threats are not credible. If the conditions for credibility are supplied however, the resulting strategy is open to the objection that it involves evil intentions.

The latter objection is the one replied to by the counter-claim that while it may be wrong to use certain weapons it is not thereby wrong to intend to use them if attacked. Furthermore, if the purpose of forming this conditional intention is to deter an aggressor, and therefore to ensure that the circumstances for which retaliation is designed never actually occur, the policy is morally virtuous.

This argument is subtle and admits of further refinements which there is not the space to detail and examine here.[10] Nonetheless, I believe they, and it, can be shown to rest upon several false assumptions. The first of these is the

[10] A clear presentation of this line of argument is given by G.J. Hughes in 'The Intention to Deter' op.cit. For a short discussion of this and of an attempt to defend the possibility of deterrence by mere bluff see J. Haldane, 'The Morality of Deterrence', *Heythrop Journal*, 26 (1) 1985. My criticisms of the latter are themselves challenged in J. Thomas, 'A Comment on John J. Haldane's Article', same issue of *Heythrop Journal*. On the ethics of intention with regard to defence see G.

belief that intentions are not in themselves liable for moral assessment. The intuitive idea supporting this claim is the thought that right and wrong, permissible and obligatory etc., are properties of *behaviour* and that while there is a conceptual connection between intention and action it is not such as to allow the transmission of moral properties from the latter to the former. No piece of behaviour is an action unless it embodies an intention but not every intention is acted upon. Given this direction of independence the moral character of actions does not extend to prior intentions. Hence, whatever may be true of an act of violence the mere intention to perform it is not liable to assessment, and *a fortiori* it cannot be morally wrong.

Certainly merely intending to kill someone but never actually doing so lacks the evil of carrying out this policy. However, it is not on this account immune to criticism. Intentions are psychological states whose content is given by a description of the circumstances they aim to produce and therefore they cannot be divorced entirely from the moral assessment of their intended states of affairs.

One who countenances the evil acts of others or prepares himself to perform such acts, reflects in his moral character the quality of that behaviour. The intensity of this reflected image is perhaps less than that of the state of affairs it mirrors but nonetheless it shares its moral quality. Thus, intentions to do evil are themselves bad. Independent evidence for this conclusion is provided by the familiar fact that we regard someone who harbours evil intentions as being of bad character no matter that for whatever reasons he never succeeds in achieving his ends. Correspondingly, we regard him as morally improved if he comes to recognise the evil of his intentions and disavows them. Virtue and vice are essentially traits of character relating not only to what one does but to what one intends to do, or is willing to do, or is prepared to countenance in others.

Following from the recognition that intentions involve dispositions to action it becomes clear that even in advance

Kavka, 'The Paradoxes of Deterrence', *Journal of Philosophy*, 75 (6), 1978.

of their enactment mental attitudes of this sort make a practical difference to the state of the world. To have a genuine intention to act in a particular fashion in certain circumstances one must believe that it is possible for one to act in the prescribed way and often this will involve making preparations in advance. In the context of seeking deterrence through sincere threats to retaliate this means establishing a counterstrike capacity and appropriate command structure with the implication, considered above, of creating some probability of an actual exchange initiated either by accident or design. In this case, because of the general presence of sincere intentions, the probability is greater than that attaching to the mere possession of nuclear weapons.

To this point, then, it has been argued that threats and bluff will either be ineffective or else must involve genuine violent intentions and that these latter are liable to moral assessment in respect of both their intrinsic character and their likely consequences. The final reply to be considered acknowledges both conclusions but insists that nonetheless a policy of nuclear deterrence may be morally acceptable. The core of this response is the claim that the complex of intentions involved is not evil.

Complex Intentions and Double Effect

One version of this reply returns us to the principle of double effect discussed in the preceding chapter ('Science, Knowledge and Virtue') claiming that while an agent is always morally responsible for the foreseen and intended consequences of his voluntary actions he is not always morally responsible for those effects which though foreseen are not intended. Thus, while it may be the case that a disposition to wage-nuclear-war-if-attacked is bad, the content of the agent's intention is not this but rather the avoidance of war. This will not do however, for it misconstrues the circumstances of deterrence. The disposition to retaliate is not a merely foreseen consequence of the policy. It is an essential constituent of it. Relatedly the intention to deter war is more fully described as the intention to avoid-it-by-intending-to-wage-it-if-attacked. The concept of deterrence by sincere threat simply does not admit of the separation of means and end in the manner required by the principle of double effect. One may speak intelligibly of 'primary' and 'secondary' intentions in this context, but then the waging of war in relevant circumstances is both a foreseen and intended component of the policy. Accordingly, the latter cannot escape from the challenge that it involves a murderous intention and as such may not be justified by the (valuable) end it is employed to serve. As was seen earlier, an action or intention may be good and bad in different respects. If, however, it instantiates a type which it is absolutely wrong to realise, then regardless of whatever may be good about it or its consequences, one is morally prohibited from employing it. Put simply and familiarly: one may not be or do evil in order to achieve good.

The last twist in the attempt to justify the policy of nuclear deterrence again begins with a concession. It allows that the policy involves both war-making and war-preventing intentions but observes that the former is a conditional intention and secondary to the unconditional aim of avoiding war. Accordingly the agent in these circumstances is importantly different from an aggressor. For, unlike the latter, he does not have a categorical intention to commit mass murder but rather is unconditionally intending to prevent war, albeit by making preparations to wage it and intending to do so if attacked. The proper object of moral evaluation in these circumstances therefore, is not the latter conditional intention in isolation but the complex of which it is a part, *viz*: the intention to-deter-war-by-intending-to-wage-it-if-attacked. And this, it is claimed, is morally acceptable and perhaps even obligatory.[11]

Once more, however, the defence of deterrence is vulnerable to the objection that it involves murderous intentions. In the circumstances described the agent has a complex intention including a genuine one to use weapons of mass destruction. Certainly he is not merely and unconditionally

---

[11]   See G.J. Hughes, 'The Intention to Deter', pp. 32–34.

intending to make war but aims to wage it in the belief that by having this intention war is less likely to break out. Clearly the structure of this complex psychological state is central to the argument and what matters most at this point therefore, are the agent's understanding and intention.

In leaving behind the bluff interpretation of deterrence we must take it that the subject believes that if attacked he will retaliate. Otherwise we cannot ascribe to him a sincere intention to wage war. Certainly should the day arrive when the enemy launch an attack he may correctly say: 'I did not believe that this would happen. I thought that my intention to counterstrike would prevent it and I would not have formed that intention unless I hoped and sincerely believed that I would never be brought to act upon it.' At that point he may even change his mind and disavow retaliation. The intention to perform a certain action in given circumstances does not logically commit one to acting in that way should the circumstances come to pass.

All of this allowed, however, it remains the case that the pre-war policy in question involves a genuine intention to wage nuclear war. To form this intention — not just to go around saying 'I intend to retaliate', or to build bombs — it is necessary to believe that in some circumstances one would launch an attack. Otherwise, whatever one's mental state it is not that of intending to retaliate. On the most charitable interpretation of his policy the agent believes that only by being able, willing and disposed to strike back if attacked can he prevent aggression and for this reason brings himself to intend to counterstrike. But this last move goes morally wrong. It is the formation of a murderous intention.

Unjust Defence

The argument of the preceding section can be put in the form of a dilemma to the defender of deterrence. Does the agent have a genuine intention to wage war be it that he hopes that thereby war is made less likely? or is it that he has absolutely no war-waging intentions but seeks to deceive the enemy and in this way to deter him? If the latter, then the objections to bluff present themselves. If the former, then he is countenancing evil and thereby is himself corrupted. The final response was to claim that the genuine war-waging intention is embedded in an intention to prevent hostilities. But once one considers the relation between a) intending to perform an action, and b) believing that one would do so, it becomes clear that any attempt to disconnect the intention to wage war from the belief that one really would, has the effect that the former ceases to be a genuine intention. And it thus fails to meet the condition which the defender of deterrence takes to be necessary for avoiding war.

None of this is to claim that if an agent intends to act in a certain manner then he will. The point is simply that if a military power believes that intending to wage war against civilians is the only way of preventing it, and so makes whatever preparations are necessary, then *ipso facto* it believes that in a given circumstance it would retaliate. These states of mind are morally bad ones and the states of the world they bring about involve danger and further corruption.

A power thus condemned may ask: what else are we to do? For, in the circumstances we face, this policy is the only means of avoiding war or nuclear blackmail. Two replies now suggest themselves. The first is, as previously given, that some means are such as may not be employed and hence some goods may be denied us if the only route to them is an evil one. The second concerns not morality but empirical fact. What good reason is there to believe that unless they are deterred the great world powers will attack or invade other nations? And even if the image of them as waiting to pounce were accurate, what good reason is there for supposing that the only deterrent is a nuclear one? Some current Western and Eastern defence strategies are immoral. They probably also rest upon faulty empirical assumptions. These suggestions can hardly be matters of indifference to those concerned with strategy, design and enactment. Or if they are then our problems are even greater. No less should they concern theorists and analysts of defence policy, for if the arguments presented above are correct it follows that the most significant feature of the policies of the world's greatest military powers is that they must be abandoned and replaced with just forms of defence.

Killing in the Womb

Considerations such as those set out above have been effective in persuading many Christians of the unacceptability of nuclear weapons and now they find themselves aligned with progressive sentiment in denouncing current policies. This alliance is of considerable interest. Not least because it raises the question: what underlies the secular opposition to nuclear forces? The development in the churches results from the application of ancient teaching to the contemporary context, and it seems plausible to suppose that it is a shared belief in the inviolability of innocent human life that motivates all advocates of disarmament.

While doubtless some non-religious supporters of the peace movement urge this cause on these grounds, it seems that this can hardly be the case generally. For many who are wholly opposed to the means of modern warfare also maintain that procuring an abortion is an acceptable course of action for a woman who for some reason does not wish to give birth to the child that grows within her. It is a quite striking feature of contemporary liberal morality that the clamour against policies countenancing the use of weapons of mass destruction ('WMDs') has reached a peak at a time when abortion is rife, since there is a strong *prima facie* case for maintaining that the two are instances of just the same evil. Indeed, the argument against terminating the life of an individual in the womb is a further application of the general principle invoked earlier. Thus:

(1) It is always wrong intentionally to kill innocent human beings.

(2) A foetus in the womb is an innocent human being.

(3) Therefore, it is always wrong intentionally to kill a foetus in the womb.

Since the reasoning involved in this argument (as in the parallel one concerning the use of nuclear weapons) is valid the conclusion can only be rejected by denying one or other, or both, of the premises. As regards (1) however, the cost of denying it is a lessening of respect for life and thereby a weakening of the argument for disarmament. After all, the case against nuclear and other WMD warfare directed against non-combatants is not merely one of quantity, as if killing a thousand people was wrong though killing one or two was not. If it were, then the staggering total of procured abortions (over 40 million per annum worldwide[12]) rivals the 'Megadeath' figures calculated by military strategists and rightly made much of by peace campaigners and other opponents of current nuclear policies. The other more popular option for the defender of abortion is to deny (2).

Very often such a denial is supported by the claim that human beings exhibit certain species-specific characteristics such as thought, deliberation and language use, and that since a foetus lacks these capacities it therefore cannot be classed as a human being. Such reasoning is fallacious, for it rests on an equivocation over the meaning of 'capability'. To be capable may mean either: currently able to do a thing, or potentially able to do it, i.e., to be the sort of creature that can engage in a certain activity. While a foetus may be incapable of thought, say, in the first sense it may yet belong to a species of thinking animals. And incapacity in its former meaning no more disqualifies it from being a human subject than does senility or imbecility remove an individual from the human race. A human is not as such a foetus, an infant, a young man or an old man. Rather these are proper stages in the development of life. Thus there is no good reason to deny that a foetus is a human being that is not also a reason for denying that an infant or an adult is.[13]

As before, it will be as well to anticipate and respond to objections to my argument. The first will come from those who argue that anti-abortion legislation forces women to

---

[12] See *Facts on Induced Abortion Worldwide* (New York: Guttmacher Institute, 2008).

[13] For further discussion of these matters see John Haldane & Patrick Lee, 'Aquinas on Ensoulment, Abortion and the Value of Life', *Philosophy*, 78 (2003), also in Haldane, *Reasonable Faith* (2010).

procure miscarriages in circumstances and by means which are likely to lead to more deaths not less. This concern to eliminate the 'back-street abortion' is quite proper, but it fails to touch the present issue. If, as I maintain, intentionally procured abortion is unjustfied killing then it is irrelevant in moral terms whether it is legal or illegal, and it is also beside the point whether the context is or is not that of a medically safe operation. Certainly unqualified terminations are dangerous and ought to be avoided for the sake of the mother, but all abortion is lethal and ought to be avoided for the sake of the innocent foetus. Let me add, however, that the adoption of this position obliges the defender of life to do what he or she can to enable women to bear unwanted pregnancies by removing stigmas attached to illegitimacy and handicaps, and by campaigning for proper assistance for those in need.[14]

A different form of objection is that brought forward under the banner 'A Woman's Right to Choose'. This charges that the question whether or not to have an abortion falls within the scope of a person's prerogative to decide how their body may be used. This need not be (though, I suspect it sometimes is) the trivial, because generally undisputed, claim that each person has the right to choose how to act. Though arguably true, this principle is quite independent of issues of rightness or wrongness regarding behaviour. For in the sense in which it is there employed, a person has the 'right' to choose to do wrong. The substantial claim relevant to the issue of abortion is rather that an unwanted

[14] There is a parallel obligation on those who oppose current Western defence policices to indicate how military aggression might be responsed to. Here I simply note that nothing argued above is intended to suggest that we should disavow retaliation or even that, on pain of immorality, this may not involve any use of nuclear weapons, e.g. of underwater torpedoes or depth charges directed against low-lying submarines. Modern political and technological circumstances complicate matters in ways not conceived of in traditional Just War theory. However the resources of this tradition are, I believe, sufficient to develop a contemporary military ethic which like its scholastic predecessor conceives of virtue as both warranting and constraining the use of lethal violence in defence of one's country.

pregnancy is an infringement of a property right, and that the woman's entitlement to determine the use of her body overrides the right of the foetus not to be killed.

This argument has several aspects but given the limits of space it will be sufficient here to note two points. First, suppose we allow the (contentious) claim that an unwanted pregnancy constitutes the violation of a property right. It is surely an error to believe that this proprietorial claim licences the killing of an innocent human being. To suppose otherwise is to fall in with those challenged earlier who elevate some other feature above the right to life and who in consequence put at risk their preferred value. Secondly and relatedly, property rights are conditional upon the maintenance of life. Without full respect for the latter the former are reduced to a set of accidental facts of possession lacking any substantial moral justification. In short, the right of the innocent not to be killed is fundamental to any coherent conception of human rights and is the basis for further claims to entitlements.

As regards the nature of the embryonic individual, it has been suggested that while the arguments against killing extend to the early human embryo they may not extend to the immediate product of conception, the zygote. Given that the latter may split to form twins or other multiple embryos (which may also re-fuse) it has been argued by some — including pro-life philosophers — that while being human, the zygote is not an individual human being.[15] This, however, seems to rest ultimately on a confusion between identity and individuality. Given the transitivity of identity it cannot be that twins B and C developing by fission out of a zygote A are identical with it; but that only establishes the

[15] See Elizabeth Anscombe, 'Were you a Zygote?' and 'The Early Embryo: Theoretical Doubts and Practical Certainties' in, respectively, M. Geach and L. Gormally eds. *Human Life, Action and Ethics: Essays by G.E.M. Anscombe* (Exeter: Imprint Academic, 2005) and M. Geach and L. Gormally eds, *Faith in a Hard Ground: Essays on Religion, Philosophy and Ethics* by G.E.M. Anscombe (Exeter: Imprint Academic, 2008). See also Anthony Kenny, 'The Beginning of Individual Human Life' in M. Baur ed., *Intelligence and the Philosophy of Mind*, Proceedings of the American Catholic Philosophical Association, 80, 2006.

non-identity of a resultant embryo with the original conceptus: it does not show that the original zygote was not itself an individual human being.

What emerges from this overall discussion, I suggest, is that the strongest moral argument for WMD disarmament is one that rests on the same principle as yields the rejection of intentional abortion. If this is right then there is a curious parallel between the former position of many Christian churches with respect to the bomb and the present condition of the liberal secular consensus, in as much as both appear to have neglected areas of application of the principle that innocent life must be respected. However, whereas the churches have generally overcome their hesitation in condemning modern defence policies,[16] progressive sentiment seems for the most part not to have recognised the possible inconsistency in its position. It is to be hoped then, that reflection upon these issues may promote convergence from all sides upon the principle that it is always and everywhere wrong intentionally to take the life of an innocent human being whether the latter be a non-combatant in time of war or a foetus lodged within its mother's womb.

For most people, however, consideration of the rights and wrongs of killing does not involve intricate argumentation or the analysis of central ethical and philosophical concepts. Nor is it a matter of consulting special moral intuitions. What lies at the heart of such moral judgements is most often an unarticulated sense of the special value of human life as a form of animate existence. This sense is related to what I earlier described as 'recognising humanity', and which I later connected to the idea that human persons are embodied subjects. Central to the formation of a capacity for recognizing humanity is the introduction to the reality itself that comes with living alongside others. It is appropriate, therefore, that in moving now to a section in

---

[16] See, for example, *The Church and the Bomb: Nuclear Weapons and Christian Conscience* (London: Hodder & Stoughton, 1982), *Peace and Disarmament: Documents of the World Council of Churches and the Roman Catholic Church* (Geneva and Rome: 1982); *The Challenge of Peace: God's Promise and Our Response* (London: CTS/SPCK, 1983.

which I consider aspects of society and politics I begin with
the primary mode of social existence and turn to consider
the nature and value of family life.

7

Families and Why they Matter

Introduction

As a social unit, the family continues to be lauded, though in rather general terms as in a report by Kofi Annan, the former Secretary General of the UN, regarding preparations for the tenth anniversary of the 1994 International year of the family. He writes:

> The family has a continuing and crucial role in social and human development as well as in provision of care and support to individuals. Strong family bonds have always been part of most societies, and families in most places continue to make important contributions to social and economic well-being. ... Yet the contribution of families in achieving these objectives has generally been overlooked. Part of the reason for this may be that families themselves are experiencing tremendous change. ... The tendency has been to have smaller families with fewer children, with a weakening of extended family relationships based on mutual obligation and shared responsibility. These changes have sometimes led to social problems as families have become less able—or willing—to provide for the needs of all their members.[1]

Two important contributions of the family are the rearing of children and the care of the elderly. These activities are connected in a variety of ways. In an essay whose main points are to show the 'weirdness' of the question posed in its title

[1] *Report of the Director General of the UN* (23 July 2004) regarding preparations for and observance of the tenth anniversary of the International year of the family in 2004 (New York: United Nations, 2004) p. 4.

'Why Have Children?' and the problems associated with its no longer seeming odd to ask it, Elizabeth Anscombe allows that extrinsic reasons can nevertheless be given for resisting efforts to control the having of children. Writing of an Indian woman reproached for having babies in the face of her government's population control policy,[2] Anscombe reports the woman as saying 'Will the government take care of me when I am old?'[3] Recent concerns about the sustainability of health- and elderly-care in Western Europe suggest that this is not just a question for the third world. The working populations of Austria, Germany, Greece, Italy, Japan, Spain, and Sweden, are already contracting; by 2050 the current Eurozone is set to lose 27 million workers while gaining about 37 million pensioners, and the number of people over 80 will treble. The current European ratio of people of pensionable age to those of working age is 0.35 to 1; by 2050 it will be 0.75 to 1, and in Italy and Spain it may reach 1 to 1.

Nor will the problems of European demographic change only affect the old (and the young as providers for them). To maintain the level of a population it requires an average fertility (live birth) rate of 2.1 children per woman. The current average fertility rates in Europe estimated for 2009 stands as follows (with 2000 figures in brackets): *Ireland* 1.85 (1.88), *France* 1.98 (1.89), *Norway* 1.78 (1.85), *Denmark* 1.74 (1.77), *Finland* 1.73 (1.73), *Netherlands* 1.66 (1.72), *Sweden* 1.67 (1.54), UK 1.66 (1.65), *Belgium* 1.65 (1.66), *Portugal* 1.49 (1.55), *Swit-*

[2]   As noted in chapter three ('Recognising Humanity') Martha Nussbaum has emphasized the wrong done to women in India and elsewhere by policies of populaton control and sex-selection by abortion. She reports a finding by the Indian Association of Women's Studies (from *India Abroad*, July 10, 1998) that 10,000 female fetuses are aborted in India every year, see Nussbaum, *Women and Human Development* (2000) p. 27. This practice is also widespread in Pakistan, China, Taiwan, Korea, Vietnam and elsewhere in S.E. Asia, even where it is not state sanctioned.

[3]   G.E.M. Anscombe, 'Why Have Children?' in L. P. Schrenk (ed.) *The Ethics of Having Children* (Washington, D.C.: ACPA, 1990) p. 51. In relation to the intrinsic values involved in having children see also her essay 'The Dignity of Human Beings' in M. Geach and L. Gormally (eds) *Human Life, Action and Ethics: Essays by G.E.M. Anscombe* (Exeter: Imprint Academic, 2005).

zerland 1.45 (1.50), *Austria* 1.39 (1.34), *Germany* 1.41 (1.30), *Italy* 1.31 (1.24) and *Spain* 1.31 (1.24). By contrast rates for the *USA* are 2.05 (2.06), and for *Israel* 2.75 (2.95).[4]

More generally, the ratio of fertility rate to 50% reduction of population gives the following: at 1.5 the population is halved over 65 years, at 1.3 over 44 years, and at 1.1 over 32 years. Less abstractly, current trends suggest that by 2050, 60% of Italian and Spanish children will have no brother, sister, aunt, uncle or first cousin.

The situation in the UK is less extreme, but the decline in fertility since 1970 has been from 2.49 to 1.9 (1980) to 1.8 (1990) to 1.66, with rates of delayed pregnancy, abortion, sexually transmitted diseases, early divorce and separation increasing during the same period with consequences for those already alive as well as for future generations. Around 10% of women born in the UK in the mid-1940s are childless; the corresponding figure for women now reaching the end of their natural fertile lives (i.e. in their late 40s) is 20%, and it rises for younger generations.[5] In the spring of 2006 the UK government revised its national building plans. Drawing on the 2001 national census it recalculated upwards its estimate of house building needs, and of single occupancy housing. In England, by 2026 there will be a 25% increase in the number of homes, and almost 10 million people will be living alone. The solitary dweller estimate represents a 50% increase on the most recent figure and most of these home-aloners will be over 35.

---

[4]   The current estimates come from the CIA *World Fact Book* (Washington, DC: US Government, August 2009). The electronic text is updated as new information becomes available for fertility rates calculated as the average number of children that would be born per woman if all women lived to the end of their childbearing years and bore children according to a given fertility rate at each age, see https://www.cia.gov/library/publications/the-world-factbook/fields/print_2127.html.

[5]   Figures drawn from information gathered by UK Office for National Statistics, General Register Office for Scotland and Northern Ireland Statistics and Research Agency.

It is shallow to say in reply that anyone who has children with the thought in mind that this may bring support and comfort in later life is 'instrumentalising' their offspring; just as it is shallow to suggest that a hope for support and companionship 'instrumentalises' marriage or domestic partnership. What binds personal relationships together is primarily community of feeling rather than commonality of purpose, but feelings detached from shared practices of mutual support and dependence are uncertain for want of operative criteria; and, whether in a spirit of idealism or of sentimentalism, separating the value of expressive practices from any benefits they may provide is liable to lead to less, not more fulfilling and respectful relationships.

So far as the rearing of children is concerned, particularly as this connects with issues that fall within the scope of contemporary political interests, the family is subject to increasing criticism, often combined with suggestions for state intervention, as in the following recent UK report on children and family policy:

> The absence of a rights approach guiding the relationship between the interests of children and families is significantly in evidence around concessions to that ill-defined attribution parental autonomy, which in some circumstances one sees perversely preserved at the expense of children's rights.
>
> In education, for example, parental choice of school and religious education for their child has been questioned as undermining children's rights. ... Overall in education, the Government's role in the parent-child-State axis is to support children's individuation and opportunity for self-determination and fulfilment. But the relationship is seriously undefined and needs principled clarification.[6]

In the course of an essay addressing the provocative question 'Does Oxford Moral Philosophy Corrupt Youth?' Elizabeth Anscombe writes as follows:

> Everybody knows that we have long since discarded the hideous conception of parental authority ... The disservice

---

[6] Clem Henricson and Andrew Bainham, *The Child and Family Policy Divide: Tensions, Convergence and Rights* (London: Joseph Rowntree Foundation, 2005) pp. 105-6).

> of [parents] imposing their own standards, which may
> become outmoded, is evident. ... Clearly all we can do is to
> equip our children as thinking human beings, capable of
> forming and indefinitely improving their own standards of
> action without impediment.[7]

The article is a spirited piece of sustained irony. Much of it,
including this passage, should be read as lying within the
scope of an emphatic negation operator. In that respect it is
rather like an ecclesial denunciation in which the body of
the text is prefaced by the phrase 'If anyone holds that ...
anathema sit' (let him be anathema) — and this literary form
may well have been her inspiration. Remarkably,
Anscombe delivered the piece as a BBC radio talk half a century ago. It must have been a challenge then, but now it
could almost be read unironically, for there is (in hindsight)
a prophetic quality about the essay, as is evidenced by the
passage just quoted from the Rowntree Report concerning
children's rights. That someone should come to speak of
'concessions to that ill-defined attribution parental autonomy' and of a need for 'principled clarification' of 'the Government's role in the parent-child-state axis' would not
have surprised Anscombe. Certainly it expresses a challenge to traditional understandings of the relationship
between parents and children. Evidently such understandings can no longer be taken for granted, and there is, therefore, scope for some consideration of the basic value of
families and the respect due to them.

Families and Human Nature

It is equally evident that families matter. One can say this
confidently without any appeal to philosophical, political
or theological theories or analogies. Families are where
things start for the mass of human beings — so far at least.
Children are conceived by couples who generally know one
another and live in close proximity. They are themselves
members of families, and the newborn child is received into

---

[7]   Elizabeth Anscombe, 'Does Oxford Moral Philosophy Corrupt
      Youth?' in M. Geach and L. Gormally (eds) *Human Life, Action and
      Ethics: Essays by G.E.M. Anscombe*, pp. 166–7.

one or other of these: either indirectly through the relationships of the primary family comprised of the parents, and any other children of their union; or directly where no such union exists and the child is taken in by one or other of the parents' families. There are other classes of cases, of course, but their normal characterisation is given in terms of how they approximate to or deviate from these primary forms. This pattern may be changing, but it is still both the cultural and the statistical norm in Western and Central Europe, Africa, North and South America, Asia and Australasia.

In the context of the family, small or large, the child is trained in ways of eating, sleeping, washing, dressing and so on, and learns a language by which is acquired and developed the primary human mode of relating intelligently to the world. Because as a matter of practical necessity food, drink, shelter and hygiene have to be provided by others, and because as a matter of natural necessity initial language learning has to be social, a child takes shape, well or badly, under the influence of other persons. Where a family is concerned, however, this influence is not just originating but continuing, and is also, or ought also to be, unconditional. The observation that it 'ought to be' such is not a piece of moralising, but recognition of the fact that unless it were unconditional then the process could not get going, since a parent is generally not in a position to know whether an infant will satisfy any requirement that the parent might set for it as a condition of care and upbringing. (One important class of parent-child pathologies resides in according attention and interest only in exchange for behaviour conforming to ends specified by the adult; in effect treating children according to a pattern of animal training.[8])

The fact of the dependency of children upon immediate providers is part of human natural history so deeply rooted

---

[8] For relevant findings and discussion see R.A. Thompson, 'The Development of the Person: Social Understanding, Relationships, Conscience, Self' in N. Eisenberg ed. *Handbook of Child Psychology*, Volume 3, 6th edition *Social, Emotional and Personality Development* (Hoboken, NJ: John Wiley, 2006).

as to be proximate to, if not part of, the human essence. Family relations are inalienable and cannot be annihilated though they may be strained and even sundered. Conversely, they naturally strengthen under conditions of respect, care and affection. It is for these reasons that children lacking the natural norm are variously and often evidently, ill-formed and ill-equipped; while those provided with it are more naturally inclined to flourish. I add 'evidently' not as a further point but as a reminder that it is usually easy to tell when things have not been right. This is because the malformation is not something external to the child as a feature of its environment, rather it resides in the child and is expressed in its behaviour rather as a disfigured limb is not so much a *cause of*, as a condition *expressed in* a limp. Of course, it happens that children provided with the natural norm of family formation both fail to flourish and even suffer, but when this happens we rightly look to see where the normal process has gone wrong, rather than wonder whether the family as such is the right context for child rearing.

It matters that children be raised in a family context and that this context be a normal one in which there is the complement of father and mother, supplemented ideally by male and female of prior generations and also by siblings. Uncomfortable as it may now be to confront this fact, a single parent home, or one in which there is only one sex, is in those respects, at least, less favourable than a two (male/female) parent household in which the partners are joined in marriage. The social scientific research on these issues is extensive and there is a high degree of convergence on the conclusion that every major pathology that can afflict children occurs more frequently when there is only one parent or the parents are not married.[9] Single parents and others can, of course, produce happy and well-adjusted

[9] See, for example, S. McLanahan and G. Sandefur, *Growing up with a Single Parent: What Hurts, What Helps* (Cambridge, MA: Harvard University Press, 1994); P. Amato and A. Booth, *A Generation at Risk: Growing Up in an Era of Family Upheaval* (Cambridge, MA: Harvard University Press, 1997); L. Waite and M. Gallagher, *The Case for Marriage: Why Married People are Happier, Healthier and Better-Off*

children, but to quote the summary of a research brief on family structure from the (non-profit, non-partisan) Child Trends research centre:

> Research clearly demonstrates that family structure matters for children, and the family structure that helps the most is a family headed by two biological parents in a low-conflict marriage. Children in single-parent families, children born to unmarried mothers, and children in stepfamilies or cohabiting relationships face higher risks of poor outcomes ... There is thus value for children in promoting strong, stable marriages between biological parents.[10]

The State and the Family

It is a significant transition from these facts about the relationship of children and families to any conclusion about what ought to be the state's family policy with regard, say, to birth rates or education. Knowing nothing but these facts, and the further point that the relevant causes being present natural processes occur unless inhibited, one might be inclined to begin with something negative, namely that, other things being equal, the state ought not to interfere with these structures and processes. One might next think that if this is so because there is a presumption in their favour, then it may also be true that the state has a responsibility to promote the family. Apart from other assumptions, however, this supposes that the state has directly constructive responsibilities; whereas it could be that all that can be justified are defensive policies: the protection of the boundaries of the state from external threat and the maintenance of civic order. It is worth noting in this regard that Anglo-American culture tends to be wary of the idea that the state has extensive positive responsibilities (and hence permissions to act) whereas Continental Europeans tend to take

---

Financially (New York: Doubleday, 2000); and W. J. Doherty *et al.*, *Why Marriage Matters: Twenty-One Conclusions from the Social Sciences* (New York: Institute for American Vales, 2002).

[10] Kirsten A. Moore *et al.*, 'Marriage from a Child's Perspective: How Does Family Structure Affect Children and What Can we Do About it?' *Child Trends Research Brief* (Washington, DC: Child Trends, 2002).

the positive role of the state for granted. I add as a comment that if the former pay a price in having a thin idea of political community, the latter may be liable to have only a thin idea of personal responsibility.

It has long been a matter of debate what defines a state. Cicero wrote of a 'multitude formed into a partnership by common agreement on law and a sharing of benefits' (*coetus multitudinis iuris consensus et ultilitas communione sociatus*). [11] Augustine modified this, speaking of a society as a multitude of rational beings united by agreement as to the objects of their love (*populus est coetus multitudinis rationalis, rerum quae diligit concordi communione sociatus*). [12] His intention was to move from an account that would invite disputes about whether Rome or Babylon counted as polities (since, being purportedly unjust their regulations might not really be 'laws', properly speaking) to a less demanding definition.

The same trend is dominant in recent thought and is represented by a well-known and influential style of definition owing largely to Max Weber that links the idea of the state to that of special coercion. By this account the state is the sole agent within a territory that claims a monopoly on the legitimate use of force, or threat of force, to conform the behaviour of people to its mandates. [13]

In Weber's own account the idea of legitimacy enters in only as what is claimed or bestowed upon itself by a pervasive social agent, and to that extend it is simply a kind of power. But while wanting to avoid the consequence that all states (let alone all state acts) are necessarily legitimate, some normative element is called for in the definition so as to make sense of the idea that the state is, defeasibly, a proper arbiter and protector of at least some social rights and obligations. Accordingly, we may say that the difference between the control of a region and population by a

---

[11] Cicero, *De re publica*, 1.39.

[12] Augustine, *De civitate Dei*, 19, 24.

[13] In Weber's original formulation 'a state is a human community that (successfully) claims the monopoly of the legitimate use of physical force within a given territory'. See 'Politics as a Vocation' *From Max Weber: Essays in Sociology* trans. and ed. H.H. Gerth and C. Wright Mills (New York: Oxford University Press, 1946), p 77.

gang of bandits and by an authoritative government is that the latter administers a system of justice answering to the need for laws, trials and punishments, a requirement itself geared to the social need for systematic protection.

This is a familiar and plausible idea. It is compatible with, but neither presupposes nor requires the contractualist assumption that members of the state voluntarily hand over prior rights to self-protection in exchange for just and effective governments. Contracts, covenants and democratic control are further features additional to the core fact that a political state is, or proclaims itself to be, an organised, authoritatively governed community.[14]

Even this much, however, is liable to discomfort libertarian individualists who tend to identify a state's exercise of legal power to regulate the behaviour of its members with the idea that it seeks to control people. The identification certainly is not a logical one, since for one thing it is conceivable that the regulative laws of a society might all be enabling ones, constituting a system of permissions. Someone might reply to this that permissions require protection and that this necessitates coercive laws: thus if a law is passed allowing some activity, then this will involve complementary legislation prohibiting interference with it (subject to the usual sorts of defeating circumstances). Certainly it is easy to see how such complementary legislation, whether specific to the entitlement or more general, might come to be passed; but permissions do not logically entail restrictions and they may not even require them in practice.

Where law turns in the direction of control, the question to ask is what is the purpose of this? And very often the answer will be that it is to protect the right of the individual or the family, or some civic grouping, to act in ways that are

---

[14]   For an account of how contractualism may play a role in justifying authority, though it does not create it, see P. Winch, 'How is Political Authority Possible?' *Philosophical Investigations*, 25, 2002. He writes 'The question is not whether some notion of consent is central to our understanding of political authority; I do not believe *that* should be in doubt. The question is rather whether political authority can be thought of as *derived from*, or as *originating in*, the consent of those over whom it is exercised' p. 26.

either expressly permitted by or lie outwith the scope of law. Regulation, in the sense of a rule or law, is simply not the same as control in the sense of direction and restraint. On this account libertarians are wrong to suppose that 'family law' must necessarily be intrusive into family life. Certainly some states do seek such control, but if they do so that is not simply in virtue of them being states.

There is also the question of whether when a state does have a family policy allowing it to control the lives of family members against the disposition of the family as a whole this is necessarily a bad thing. Enabling law might be supported by specific or general prohibitions. Those who think that autonomy is a good thing thereby have reason to think that it is sometimes proper for governments to protect it from threat of interference. Indeed, one may wonder whether, if autonomy is as great a good as it is now commonly said to be, the state thereby has a right, if not a responsibility to promote it, and for the courts to uphold this.

And where there is reason to protect or promote something may there not be reason to protect or promote that which is an immediate necessary condition of it? So the good of autonomy provides grounds for protecting a young child, say, from influences that would destroy or severely undermine the possibility of its attainting autonomy.

If this puts pressure on the libertarian individualist it also needs to be noted what does *not* follow from this kind of argument. For example, if acting against one's best interests for entirely irrational reasons constitutes a failure of self-determination, and hence is something protection from which constitutes a valid social policy, then one might also suppose that family policy should allow a child seeking treatment at variance with her parents assessment of her best interest to receive it as a matter of self-determination. Or again that it should favour a child's view of what sort of education it should or should not have whatever the view of the parents. But even setting aside parental rights of influence and control with respect to their children — which is evidently no small matter — there is also the question of the state's duty to enable parents to discharge their duties of care and formation. Failure to take note of this may lead one to into a position in which all judgements of disqualifying ignorance, and resulting restrictions on conduct, are reserved to the state. That in turn threatens the integrity of family life — and indeed that of any form of sub-civic association in which authority is exercised by some for the sake of the good of others.

Autonomy

This leads to the general theme of law and the family, and requires that something be said about autonomy in the context of family life, since this is one of the main areas of conflict between traditional and recent understandings of the relative claims of individual, family and state. In some sense we are 'all liberals now' and for the same reason we are all believers in autonomy. Although each idea admits of a range of interpretations it is simply not credible to speak and act (as do some social conservatives) as if these were not widespread commitments. Indeed, given the connections between action, intention, deliberation and responsibility it would be difficult to construct an account of reflective agency in which some notion of self-determination did not feature. But that leaves much still to be said and there is certainly room for contrasting views. An obvious dimension along which these might be ranged is one in terms of conditions that are entirely self-originating and internally validated, and of alternatives that are other derived and externally confirmed.

Liberal philosophy as contributed to in different ways by Nietzsche and Mill, and by Rawls and Dworkin, tends to regard autonomy as originating and residing in the individual. Even in Rawls's later writings, where his focus is on liberal polities and doctrinal rather than personal autonomy, the idea of citizens as free and equal persons preserves a strong element of individualism.[15] Discussing, late in his

---

[15] For further discussion of this issue see chapter nine below, 'The Individual, the State and the Common Good'.

life, the issue of the relationship between liberal justice and the family he writes:

> Political principles do not apply directly to its internal life, but they do impose essential constraints on the family as an institution and so guarantee the basic rights and liberties, and the freedom and opportunities, of all its members. This they do, as I have said, by specifying the basic rights of equal citizens who are the members of families. The family as part of the basic structure cannot violate these freedoms.
> …
>
> To put the point another way we distinguish between the point of view of people as citizens and their point of view as members of families and of other associations.[16]

This strongly agent-centred view is methodologically solipsistic inasmuch as it regards the social context in which an agent's political as well as moral autonomy develops as extrinsic to them *per se*. At most, the relation will be one of partial and contingent dependence. Set against this is the view of the Hegelians in which what we think of as an individual's autonomy is in reality a non-localised collective condition of deliberative maturity — or some moralised or politicised version of this. The communtarian nature of the Hegelian approach is evident in what Hegel himself writes about family:

> The family, as the immediate substantiality of mind, is particularly characterised by love, which is mind's feeling of its own unity. Hence in a family, one's frame of mind is to have self-consciousness of one's individuality within this unity as the absolute essence of oneself, with the result that one is not in it as an independent person but as a member.
> The right which the individual enjoys on the strength of the family unity and which is in the first place simply the individual's life within this unity, takes on the form of right (as the abstract moment of determinate individuality) only when the family begins to dissolve.[17]

---

[16] See John Rawls, 'The Idea of Public Reason Revisited' in *The Law of Peoples* (Cambridge, MA: Harvard University Press, 1999) p. 147.
[17] G.W.F. Hegel, *Philosophy of Right* trans. T.M. Knox, (Oxford: Clarendon Press, 1977), pp. 158–9.

It is an accomplishment of philosophy to recognise the existence and character of these opposing poles of thought, but the real task is to locate a stable position between them. If one thinks of autonomy as deriving from one's development in a normative social environment, and as involving reflective evaluations the standards of whose correctness are at least in part externally located, then one will be more inclined to see in the judgements of parents and of surrounding family, and of courts in supporting these, expressions of legitimate constraint on a young person's decisions.

If autonomy is an acquired attribute many of the sustaining roots of which lie outside the individual, then the reference to these sources and respect for their inclinations will be more appropriate than the libertarian allows. Relatedly, decisions which he thinks of as being the proper business of the individual alone will be seen as having to defer to the authority of more mature minds to which that individual is indebted for its evolving autonomy. For reasons given earlier the normal immediate source of this is the family.

The implication of the present line of thought, then, is that in considering the question of policies directed towards the wellbeing of children it is not enough to ask whether they consent to being treated or formed in various ways (in respect say of medical and educational matters). Rather there are two forms of family involvement to be taken account of. First, there is the dependence of the reflective agent upon the immediate 'moral' environment; and second there is the family considered now not as a source of moral consciousness and formation but as a community whose wellbeing is partly constitutive of the child's own interests.

The most important relation is the *internal* one: a child or indeed another family member needs to see that its identity (at least in important aspects) is not separable from that of the family as a whole, and that effects on it are generally effects on it *qua* family member. Put another way, a child who seeks to act in opposition to the deepest convictions of his parents does damage to that family, and thereby to him- or her-self. Save in the most extreme cases that is something to be avoided, and is something which the state, if it is to respect the integrity of the family, will not wish to bring about. Here the situation is in some respects analogous to that of the imagined couple Philip and Patricia Green in chapter two above ('Persons and Values') inasmuch as Patricia's response to Philip's personality changes and to a lesser degree his physical disablement involved a weakening of the sense of the solidarity and mutual existence associated with a familiar conception of marriage. Further, as in the case of the relations between children and parents so in that of spouses, the state should be wary of encouraging the idea that these relationships are like contracts for the competent exchange of goods and services.

The Family and Marriage

I have not discussed particular examples but it is evident how what I have suggested might apply to the sort of cases that are now quite common in which advocates of children's rights appeal beyond the interest of the home to those of individuals as grounds for policies that subvert the claims of the family.

Modern liberalism has difficulty finding a place for the common good of family because of its commitment to neutrality between life-shaping values. At most it can register and even celebrate convergence in evaluations, seeing in this happy coincidence possibilities for establishing and extending a social consensus. However, the liberal idea of social members as free and equal persons remains individualistic: the good of persons that results from their participation in social orders regulated by the political conception of justice is a private one. This fact is sometimes overlooked on account of the regulated order being a public good; but therein lies a lesson: public good does not equal common good.

In later chapters I shall have more to say about the idea of citizens as free and equal individuals and about the concept of the common good and its place in political philosophy. Before concluding this discussion of the value of family life, however, I want to say something about the issue of marriage mindful of the facts that this form of association is changing and that it has become a subject of much public discussion and some significant dispute. Of course, not all marriages lead to or involve the having and rearing of children or the care of parents, and not all families are joined by bonds of matrimony. Nonetheless there are strong connections between marriage and family life. Earlier I argued that it matters that children be raised in a family context, and added that it is best for a child if this consists of a mother and father, ideally supplemented by male and female of older generations and by siblings. Evidently this bears on the issue of same-sex and polygamous and polyamorous households and so connects with current debates about the legal recognition of sexual partnerships.

Sex and Marriage

In the 1980s and 1990s the policy issues that seemed most pressing upon family life were ones concerning divorce and children's rights (also, perhaps, certain economic measures to do with welfare benefits). More recently the strongest challenge is that posed by 'alternative sexual lifestyles'. Along with abortion, sexuality has become one of the main issues of contention between traditional morality and politics, and the moral and social philosophy of 'liberal pluralism'. Although a range of matters are in contention the most prominent is the issue of homosexual practice and its legitimation by the state. It is only relatively recently that homosexual relations have been decriminalised in many societies, and in some they are still illegal. Yet in many of the states where homosexual activity was once prohibited legal rights are now bestowed on homosexual partners and there are calls to extend the institution of marriage to them.

For those liberals who uphold the moral neutrality of the state this latter prospect can be perplexing. For on the one hand while they do not believe that it is for the state to proscribe sexual practice on moral grounds, nor do they believe that it should endorse, let alone prescribe, forms of sexual union as expressions of moral values. Yet this latter is precisely the basis on which some gay, lesbian and transgendered activists seek the extension of marriage to homosexual and transgendered partners. In this respect at least they share with the traditional defenders of heterosexual marriage a common belief in the value of publicly recognised partnerships.

What the advocate of traditional natural law ethics as developed by Aristotle, Cicero, Aquinas, Suarez, Hobbes, Locke and on to Jacques Maritain, Elizabeth Anscombe, John Finnis and Alasdair MacIntyre in the present day, has to say about this matter will depend on what he or she believes about human nature and the goods that perfect it. What is generally and unsurprisingly the case, however, is that most proponents of natural law reasoning take a socially conservative position. According to traditional natural law ethics, judgements as to the moral acceptability of sexual practices must be keyed to an understanding of the proper role of sex in human life. Sexual activity is defined by function and its (primary) function is that of reproduction. What follows is that the definitive use of sexual organs is inter-sexual, i.e. between male and female, and for the sake of procreation.

This is not to say, however, that the only function of sex or of the sexual organs is to reproduce. Sex obviously gives pleasure and serves to express and deepen emotional bonds as well as to effect an uniquely intimate union between distinct but complementary psychophysical natures; but these features are located within the framework of its primary, reproductive function. Something of this plurality is invoked by Anthony Kenny in arguing that homosexuality is a form of disability or handicap.

> A person who is incapable of enjoying heterosexual activity suffers a double disability: he or she is incapable of combining sexual pleasure with procreative function, and he or she is deprived of the possibility of combining intimate personal union with the diversity of experience distinguishing the different sexes. ... Because an incapacity for normal heterosexual congress is, for the reasons given a disability, I believe that any homosexual proselytising, or

the creation of a homosexual culture is not to be encouraged. Nor do I welcome proposals for homosexual marriage. However much its original purpose has been downgraded in contemporary culture, marriage still remains an institution whose primary purpose is to provide a stable context for the procreation and education of children.[18]

Suppose, then, that a natural law theorist or ethical naturalist believes homosexual practice to be contrary to the proper natural functions of sex, and thus at odds with right reason. What should follow so far as policy is concerned given the fact that this opinion is now widely contested? Here it may be useful to recall a real case in which moral and political views on just these issues have been in heated conflict. In 1988 under the Conservative administration of Margaret Thatcher a piece of legislation was enacted in the United Kingdom regulating local government. This contained within it the following clause, known universally as 'Section 28' (2A in Scottish legislation):

A local authority shall not (a) intentionally promote homosexuality or publish material with the intention of promoting homosexuality; or (b) promote the teaching of homosexuality as a pretended family relationship.[19]

This was introduced in legislation designed to curb what were represented as 'doctrinaire' policies then being advanced, and sometimes implemented, by political activists particularly in London. The general legislation was contested by the parliamentary opposition, and the clause was viewed with some disquiet by others, but it was presented as part of a general restraint on policies for which the public appeared to have little if any sympathy. In fact, the dominant feeling, then as now, was probably one of wishing not to know what people do in private so long as it is not contrary to the well-being or interests of others.

Following the removal from power of the Conservative government in 1997 by the election of New Labour, several

---

[18] Anthony Kenny, 'Sex' in *What I Believe* (London: Continuum, 2006) pp. 144 & 145.
[19] *Local Government Act*, London: Her Majesty's Stationary Office, 1988, Section 28.

moves were made to repeal Section 28. While they were ultimately successful (new legislation omitting the clause was
passed in Parliament in September 2003), along the way
they met with considerable opposition from various quar-
ters including many leaders of Christian, Jewish and
Islamic faiths — all traditions in which natural law ethics has
had an influence. On the other side of the debate the proponents of repeal divided into three broad groups. First, liberals of the sort who do not believe that it is the business of law
either to promote or to prohibit behaviour on moral
grounds. Second, advocates of alternative sexualities who
insist that the state has a responsibility to encourage attitudes and actions favourable to these sexualities; not in the
sense of teaching people to adopt them, but of teaching
them to affirm or even to celebrate them. Third, moral conservatives who, while not favouring the neutral state, were
unhappy about the way in which matters of sexual morality
are now dealt with.

There was certainly ground for complaint that the clause
was discriminatory in singling out one particular sexual
group. So far as public opinion is concerned it is hard to suppose that those who maintain the moral superiority of heterosexual over homosexual activity would be happy to
have local authorities promote heterosexual sadomasoch-
ism or fetishism or 'heteropolyamory'. And if that is not the
case then the charge of unfairness commonly levelled
against opponents of the repeal of Section 28 begins to look
justified.

What is in fact the case, however, is that most people do
not want local authorities or schools to promote, recommend or celebrate *any* particular form of sexual activity
though they would, I suspect, be happy and indeed wish to
see heterosexual marriage, or at least stable, domestic heterosexual family life presented as a desirable norm. Clearly,
though, this would be unacceptable to sexual radicals.
Moreover, they are likely to regard mere social toleration of
homosexuality, or of other alternatives, as insufficient, noting (correctly) that toleration is compatible with moral disapproval. But approval cannot be coerced, and it is evident

that the majority do not regard all forms of sexual activity as 'equally valid'. If pressed as to why, they will usually speak in terms of what is 'normal' or 'natural', ie. according to design or proper function. Of course, such reasoning is unlikely to persuade those who maintain the moral equivalence of all non-coercive forms of sexual lifestyle. And against this background of fundamental moral disagreement the liberal idea of state neutrality may have some appeal. But it is neither practical, nor consistent with non-neutralist views of the state. For advocates of natural law, nineteenth-century liberal, and perfectionist theories of political society, morality does and should constrain the public sphere in so far as policies bear upon basic rights and interests. The state exists in part to promote the common good, and more fundamentally to protect its members interests from harm or injury arising from the actions of others. On this at least social conservatives and radicals are likely to agree.

How then to proceed? On the one hand, discrimination in law on the basis of private, consensual sexual practice is hard to justify. On the other hand, society has a right to expect its commonly shared interests to be protected, and these include the norm of heterosexual marriage, particularly as that bears upon the needs and formation of children. Reasoning about what policies it is rational for an individual or a government to pursue has to be related to the question of what burdens and harms arise from the effort to encourage or to enforce any given option. Here it may be useful to make the distinction between value-promoting and value-protecting policies. Natural law based legislation will seek to protect the good of heterosexual union open to procreation and it will not *promote* forms of union other than this. Equally, however, where there is strong demand for alternatives it will consider the cost of opposing this, and where that seems too great in its impact upon civil order and the common good it may elect to *tolerate* what it cannot endorse. As I mentioned, however, issues of marriage and the family are subject to social change and it is hard to say where matters now stand. Accordingly the philosophy of these subjects needs to look hard at sociological as well as anthropological data and resist the temptation to resolve matters on a wholly *a priori* basis.

Conclusion

In a now familiar sentence from the preface to his *Philosophy of Right*, Hegel observes that 'when philosophy paints its grey on grey, then has a form of life grown old, and with grey on grey it cannot be rejuvenated, but only known'.[20] Though enduringly enigmatic, this aphorism seems to give priority to actual practice over philosophical evaluation but it does so within a context of presumed historical progress. But there is another tradition of thought represented in different ways by Augustine, Burke and Wittgenstein which gives due place to practice while yet being alive to the possibility that things may get worse as well as better.

Considering that prospect one should look to what is most extensively and most enduringly valued, and hold fast to it as very likely to be good. Adopting that procedure one could hardly fail to see that the family is a preferred mode of human association, and in consequence one should look to the state to protect and to promote it. In these as in so many other practical matters what people freely choose to pursue, and to avoid, is often a more reliable guide than abstract theory. The best advice that philosophers and sociologists might offer to policy makers is to make it possible for families to flourish in the ways they themselves recognise are best. This policy, however, is compatible with the idea that it is appropriate for the state to favour single-spouse, heterosexual marriage over other forms of household, whether single parent or two (or more) partnered; and with the idea that in exceptional circumstances it may be necessary for the state, operating at one or more levels, to intervene to protect children from their families, however the latter may be composed.

Individual, family and even *society* are not as such political concepts or categories for they do not logically imply nor

[20]   G.W.F. Hegel, *Philosophy of Right* preface.

materially require the existence of state or government. Nowadays, however, they are most commonly thought of in relation to political structures and forces, and at this point, therefore, it is necessary to examine some of the central issues for the dominant political philosophy of contemporary western societies, *viz. liberalism*.

8

Political Theory and the Nature of Persons

Introduction

It has been argued that liberalism is an individualistic political theory in that it constructs a conception of society, and of the conduct of social life, which assumes a view of its participants as being in important respects prior to it. More precisely, the view is taken to be a metaphysical-cum-moral one according to which persons are autonomous centres of consciousness and agency capable of formulating, and acting in the light of, self-generated conceptions of the good. Individuals are basic, society is derived and political institutions are instruments through which its members pursue their objectives. Collectivity and even community, understood as political notions, are thus abstractions constructed out of the contingent facts of association.

In the nineteenth century the British Idealist philosopher F.H. Bradley attacked social theories of this sort arguing that their idea of persons is a more or less exact inversion of the truth:

> ... the 'individual' apart from the community is an abstraction ... the assertion that communities have been manufactured by exclusive units is ... a mere fable ... man is a social being; he is real only because he is social.[1]

More recently liberalism has again been subject to the challenge that it presupposes a false view of the relation of

---

[1] F.H. Bradley, 'My Station and its Duties', in Bradley, *Ethical Studies* (Second Edition) (Oxford: Clarendon, 1927) pp. 173-4.

priority between persons and the societies to which they belong. The main target of current anti-individualist criticism is the derivation of a political conception of justice attempted by John Rawls.[2] Like Bradley, these critics argue that political liberalism incorporates an untenable moral psychology which rests upon a false and possibly even incoherent metaphysical account of the self.[3] As Michael Sandel interprets it, the central device employed by Rawls for deriving an idea of political justice from social conditions — the *original position* — implies a dispossession of persons of their empirical nature, their social attachments and their acquired values and affections. Thereby, it presupposes a concept of the self as essentially independent of these features.

> ... the self, shorn of all contingently-given attributes, assumes a kind of supra-empirical status, essentially unencumbered, bounded in advance and given prior to its ends, a pure subject of agency and possession, ultimately thin.[4]

Again like Bradley, the new critics of liberalism are also communitarians arguing that principles of justice and other moral values are antecedently given to persons by the relations in which they stand to other members of the 'social organism'. On this account political theory does indeed presuppose a philosophical anthropology but the correct metaphysics of the person is anti-individualist. Employing various considerations bearing upon the criteria of identification and individuation of persons, such as that many of our ways of dealing with and thinking about people involve characterising them as the bearers of social properties and, in particular, as the occupants of roles, Sandel and others argue for a concept of persons as socially constituted.

---

[2]   Most notably in *A Theory of Justice* (Oxford: Clarendon, 1971).
[3]   See especially Alasdair MacIntyre, *After Virtue* (London: Duckworth, 1981); Charles Taylor, 'The Diversity of Goods', in Amartya Sen & Bernard Williams (eds), *Utilitarianism and Beyond* (Cambridge: Cambridge University Press, 1982); and Michael Sandel, *Liberalism and the Limits of Justice* (Cambridge: Cambridge University Press, 1982), hereafter referred to as *Liberalism*.
[4]   Sandel, *Liberalism, op. cit.*, p. 94.

The Anti-individualist Challenge

Elsewhere I have claimed that Sandel's attack on metaphysical individualism and his positive case for a broader constitution both fail.[5] The former collapses because it wrongly assumes that the only available individualist accounts of persons are either as *'metaphysical selves'* in the Cartesian or Kantian versions of this view, or else as *'radically situated subjects'* — very roughly the bundle-of-psychological-properties theory suggested by Hume and developed by others;[6] and so, given the familiar problems facing these accounts, fallaciously concludes that individualism must be false.

Sandel's positive case fails because it confounds epistemological and ontological interpretations of the notion of criteria of identity and individuation. That we often characterise others and ourselves by means of social concepts, and that the acquisition (and perhaps even the regular employment) of all concepts *may* require a social context, do not entail that persons are socially constituted. Indeed, the correct application of such person related notions as those of 'shared assets' and 'common purposes' implies the contrary: assets are only 'shared', and purposes are only 'common', if they attach to bearers who, at base, are numerically diverse.[7]

This is not to deny, however, that challenges to individualist doctrines are ever successful or that any thesis of social holism is correct. For example, much recent work on the individuation of psychological attitudes (which takes them to be extension-involving) when applied to members of a linguistic community supports the epistemological claim

[5] John Haldane, 'Individuals and the Theory of Justice', *Ratio*, 27 (1985).

[6] David Hume, *A Treatise of Human Nature*, Bk I, Part IV, section vi 'Of Personal Identity'. Hume writes '[selves] are nothing but a bundle or collection of different perceptions, which succeed each other with an inconceivable rapidity, and are in a perpetual flux or movement'. For recent developments of this Humean idea see S. Shoemaker, *Identity, Cause and Mind* (Cambridge: Cambridge University Press, 1984) Ch 2; and, most famously, Derek Parfit *Reasons and Persons*, Part 3.

[7] See 'Individualism and the Theory of Justice', pp. 193–6.

that part of the content of our thoughts is essentially social.[8] This and other considerations concerning, for example, the division of epistemic labour within the community; the genesis of self-consciousness as being in mutual dependence with the development of awareness of others; and, less intentionalistically, the extent to which we are innately sociable creatures, suggest a view of the relationship of persons to their society which, while not endorsing the neo-Hegelian collectivism of Sandel and Taylor, is at odds with radical individualism and almost certainly has important implications for the conduct of social life.[9]

The Disavowal of Metaphysical Foundations

In later writings subsequently brought together in 1993 in *Political Liberalism* Rawls was concerned to emphasise both the pragmatic aspect of political philosophy and the context-relativity of its aims, and in this connection he responded to criticisms by Sandel and other communitarians.[10] The reply which he offers to the challenge that his theory has a faulty metaphysical foundation is not, as outlined above, that the objections to individualism fail or that the case for a collectivist ontology is flawed (or that both). Rather, he argues that the challenge is entirely misconceived: the theory of justice which he has constructed makes no controversial philosophical assumptions. More specifically, it does not rest upon any particular metaphysical view of the self—or

[8]   For a useful, largely expository, discussion of this claim which connects it with social morality see Philip Pettit, 'Social Holism and Moral Theory: A Defence of Bradley's Thesis', *Proceedings of the Aristotelian Society*, 86 (1985) pp. 173–97. However, Pettit is (I think) unreasonably sanguine about the prospects for the defeat of methodological solipsism.

[9]   For some discussion of this issue in relation to education, see John Haldane, 'Religious Education in a Pluralist Society: A Philosophical Examination', *British Journal of Educational Studies*, Vol 34, 1986.

[10] Rawls, 'Justice as Fairness: Political not Metaphysical', *Philosophy and Public Affairs*, 14 (1985) (hereafter, 'Justice as Fairness'). See also, 'The Idea of an Overlapping Consensus', *Oxford Journal of Legal Studies*, 7 (1987) (hereafter,'Overlapping Consensus') especially sections II & IV. The corresponding parts in *Political Liberalism* are Lecture I, sections 2, 3 and 5, and Lecture III, sections 2, 3 and 4; then Lecture I, section 6 and Lecture IV, sections 3, 4 and &. 7.

at least it always was and remains his intention that it should not. For, as he allows, 'it is not enough simply to disavow reliance on metaphysical doctrines, for despite one's intent they may still be involved'.[11] Given the widely shared assumption of Sandel's attack, *viz.*, that political theories do presuppose philosophical accounts of the nature of persons — though, of course, these presuppositions may not be explicit — it is clear that the resolution of this issue is important for the success of Rawls' project. Here I wish to consider the adequacy of his reply.

Once one sets out the structure of the debate between Rawls and his critics it becomes clear that the success of part of Sandel's challenge does not depend upon the soundness of his arguments against individualism and in favour of communitarianism or collectivism. Correspondingly, however, while Rawls, therefore, need not refute these arguments his task is in an important respect made harder, for he needs to show not that liberal individualism is reasonable but rather that his political conception of justice is entirely free of metaphysical foundations. If it is not, then, by the conditions for success which he himself sets, the project of formulating such a conception fails. In the remaining sections I shall mainly be concerned to argue by stages towards the conclusion that Rawls' account of justice does violate the prohibition on controversial philosophical doctrines imposed by the principle of toleration; but I shall also suggest (and here not argue) that this conclusion is not bad news for political *philosophy*, since it is only by reference to broadly metaphysical doctrines drawn from moral psychology that any *normative* content can be given to the idea of justice.[12]

---

[11] 'Justice as Fairness', p. 239. The corresponding passage in *Political Liberalism* is on p. 29.

[12] For some discussion of this point in connection with Rawls's later work see the *Symposium on Rawlsian Theory of Justice: Recent Developments*, a special issue of *Ethics*, 99 (1989) in particular William Galston, 'Pluralism and Social Unity', Kurt Baier, 'Justice and the Aims of political Philosophy' and Jean Hampton, 'Should Political Philosophy be done without Metaphysics ?'.

The Principle of Toleration and the Original Position

Sandel and like-minded critics claim that Rawls' theory presupposes a distinctive notion of the political subject which is in fact incoherent. Contained in this challenge are two objections which are best treated separately:

(1)   That contrary to Rawls' contention, justice as fairness does rest upon a substantial philosophical view of persons.

(2)   That this view is at best false and at worst simply incoherent.

In his response, Rawls ignores the second objection given its presupposition of the first which he believes to be mistaken. By his own account of the liberal theory, no appeal *need* be made to any particular notion of persons and none *should* be — otherwise it would be impossible to fashion a concept of justice adequate to govern the conduct of social affairs and secure the allegiance of citizens in a pluralist society:

> … the public conception of justice should be, so far as possible, (*sic*) independent of controversial philosophical and religious doctrines.
>   Thus, to formulate [it], we apply the principle of toleration to philosophy itself: the public conception of justice is to be political not metaphysical.[13]

> … a conception of the person in a political view, for example, the conception of citizens as free and equal persons, need not involve, so I believe, questions of philosophical psychology or a metaphysical doctrine of the nature of the self. No political view that depends on these deep and unresolved matters can serve as a public conception of justice in a constitutional democratic state.[14]

There is some tension between these two statements and Rawls' claim to have formulated a coherent liberal theory. For while the first suggests it may not be possible to free the notion of justice entirely from controversial philosophical

---

[13] 'Justice as Fairness', p. 223; see also 'Overlapping Consensus', pp. 6-8 and *Political Liberalism*, p. 10 ff.
[14] 'Justice as Fairness', pp. 230-231; see also 'Overlapping Consensus', p. 4. and *Political Liberalism*, p. 29.

assumptions, the second asserts that unless this can be done the concept cannot be employed in political liberalism. The question arises therefore: is Rawls successful in demonstrating the independence of the political conception from contentious metaphysical psychology?

In reply to Sandel's objection, that the description of the original position involves the idea of the parties in it as being non-empirical selves, constituted 'independently of and prior to their contingent attributes', Rawls argues that this miscontrues the function and character of the device. It is not a description of the metaphysical nature of (we) political subjects but is a representational instrument which models a set of reasonable constraints. Just as Adam Smith's *impartial spectator* is a means of characterising a way of thinking (from the moral point of view) which any person can come to adopt through imagination but which makes no assumptions about their ontological nature—and certainly does not require them to *be* independent of their interests, affections and prejudices, etc.; so the *original position* only characterises a perspective available to political subjects and makes no claims about the kinds of beings they are— beyond those implicit in the assumption that they are capable of imaginatively entering into it. For all that is presupposed in the device as Rawls conceives it, therefore, the essential nature of subjects could be as envisaged by Descartes, by Kant, or even by strict mental/physical type identity theorists. More importantly, however, whatever the truth about this aspect of persons, the device can continue to operate so as to yield the liberal concept of justice. What it relies upon is an ontologically neutral idea of them as *citizens*.

This account of the original position, as primarily an epistemological device and not a metaphysical description of the social world, is persuasive.[15] However, as Rawls acknowledges, disclaiming ontological implications does

[15] For further defence of this aspect of Rawls' argument against Sandel's challenge that it presupposes Kantian transcendentalism (in the form of absolutist, *a priori* deontology and a metaphysical view of the self as constituted independently of its empirical embodiment) see Amy Gutmann, 'Communitarian Critics of Liberalism', *Philosophy and Public Affairs*, 14, (1985) (hereafter, 'Communitarian

not establish the absence of all such doctrines from the theory. It is compatible with its being *intended* only to serve a political end that it involves metaphysical assumptions and hence, given the liberal principle of toleration, fails to achieve that goal. What still needs to be shown, therefore, is that the operative political conception of subjects is indeed free of such assumptions; that in the idea of *the person as citizen* neither the notions of *citizenship* nor of *personhood*, are controversial philosophical ones.

Citizens as Persons

The difficulty in accomplishing this latter task is that it is not sufficient for success to show that justice as fairness does not rest upon a view of persons as being (what Sandel terms) 'deontological selves'. This can, I think, be demonstrated. Rawls' interpretation of the original position as only modelling a point of view and not describing a class of (almost) bare particulars meets one specific challenge to its metaphysical neutrality. However, it has to be proven that *no* contentious doctrines are presupposed and it is implausible to claim that the notion of the social or political subject is entirely non-philosophical in the relevant sense.

This implausibility is increased when one considers the account of the political conception of the person offered in defence of his neutrality claim. Its salient features are as follows: that society is composed of free and equal persons co-operating with one another throughout their lives; that persons are the basic units of thought, deliberation and responsibility; that, following on from the latter fact, they possess capacities for a sense of justice and a conception of the good; and that their freedom has three aspects:

> (1)   ... as free persons, citizens claim the right to view their persons as independent from and as not identified with any particular conception of the good, or scheme of final ends ...

Critics') especially pp. 310–14. I differ from Gutmann, however, in thinking that the metaphysical presuppositions of Rawlsian liberalism present a major problem for it. Discussion of this issue follows below.

(2)   … they regard themselves as self-originating sources of valid claims …

(3)   … they are regarded as capable of taking responsibility for their ends.[16]

Together these elements compose a substantial account of citizens as irreducibly distinct continuants; embodied centres of consciousness, reason and agency. This is undeniably a metaphysical conception, a 'controversial philosophical doctrine'. Of course, Rawls need not endorse the account to draw the conclusions about the nature and priority of justice for a society of persons so conceived. Justice as fairness is a political notion formulated for citizens thought of as being of this type and (so far at least) he need not claim that as a matter of metaphysical fact all possible, or indeed any actual, political subjects are persons as the account articulates the notion.

There is, however, good reason to suppose that Rawls thinks we are beings of this sort. More importantly, whether or not he actually subscribes to the metaphysical view the Rawlsian concept of justice assumes it. Someone wishing to insist upon the truth or intelligibility of the liberal theory (so as to employ its normative force against other political doctrines) would be concerned both to refute the challenge that its assumptions are false or incoherent and to attack the metaphysical basis of opposing views — perhaps along the lines sketched above. For Rawls to do so, however, would be to concede the failure of liberalism as he conceives it — not because its controversial philosophical foundations are faulty but because they exist at all.

Metaphysical Methodology

Although the title and stated aim of his main response makes reference to 'Justice as Fairness [being] political [and] not metaphysical', Rawls concedes that it may be difficult to refute the charge that it presupposes contentious

---

[16]   'Justice as Fairness', pp. 241, 242 & 243. *Political Liberalism*, pp. 29–35.

doctrines.[17] One reason he suggests for this difficulty is that 'metaphysical' has no agreed definition. Another is that it might be thought that to formulate a political conception without employing particular metaphysical ideas is to presuppose a controversial philosophical thesis, *viz.*, that this task requires no metaphysical notions.

The first of these suggestions is easily set aside, though not in a way that benefits Rawls. If there were no understanding of the term 'metaphysical' or there were radical disagreement about its sense then it would not be possible to engage in debate about the status of the liberal theory in this regard. But the nature of the collectivist challenge and of Rawls' response show the antecedent to be false. The use of the term in both cases assumes a common content: a concept, doctrine, theory, etc., of *F*s is *metaphysical*, if it is concerned with *F*s as a theoretically-basic category of entities. For Sandel, persons are 'intersubjective' dependent beings, partly constituted by prior social relationships and communal ends.[18] Whereas for Rawls, they are 'basic units of thought, deliberation and responsibility' and thus are 'independent from and not identified with any particular conception of the good, or scheme of finals ends'. These are clearly distinct and conflicting philosophical views. Thus Rawls remains faced with the problem of refuting the charge that the theory of justice is metaphysical; not for the suggested reason that the latter concept gets application by being vague but because in the quite precise sense indicated above the political conception is metaphysical.

The suggestion that the claim of independence from metaphysical presuppositions is itself a metaphysical doctrine, is less clearly dealt with. There is no true general logical principle of the following sort:

(P):   To formulate the concept of *C* without presupposing a doctrine of kind *K* is already to presuppose a *K* type doctrine: *viz.*, that no *K* type doctrine is necessary for the task.

---

[17]   See especially section V of 'Justice as Fairness' for this and other points discussed below. *Political Liberalism*, pp. 29 ff.
[18]   Sandel, *Liberalism*, Ch 1.

This is easily proven by counterexample. Let the concept be *Cat* and the doctrine kind *Economic*. It is not, by any intelligible notion of the discipline, a doctrine of economics that the concept *Cat* can be explicated without reference to economic theory. Accordingly, such plausibility as the original suggestion possesses does not derive from the general principle to which it is related. Instead, its force originates in the special character of the concepts involved in the particular claim. More precisely, it derives from the idea of metaphysics.[19] Whatever substitution one considers, if kind *K* is *metaphysics* then the theoretical claim is true. To believe that one can formulate a conception of justice, persons or anything else, that is independent of any particular metaphysical doctrine or doctrines, is to make a (minimal) metaphysical assumption: namely, that no metaphysical doctrine need be implicated.

One reply to this argument might be to concede something to the claim but to insist that the implied assumption is of a special 'meta-metaphysical' sort and not on a par with familiar philosophical doctrines. However, as a point about classification this invokes a distinction without a difference: meta-metaphysics is metaphysics, just as a meta-theory is a theory. The prefix in both tasks is only an indicator of level. A second more pertinent reply would be to allow that a metaphysical thesis of this highly abstract sort is assumed but to insist that it is not a philosophically contentious claim about the nature of persons, since it is not a thesis about these things at all. It has no first order metaphysical content and thus is not in conflict with any particular theory at that level. In this sense, then, while the claims of justice as fairness are 'metaphysical' they are not such in the manner intended by those who levelled that charge against it and so escape the objection that any political conception which rests upon controversial philosophical notions cannot serve in a liberal theory of justice.

---

[19] That its plausibility is not connected with the concept in question being that of Justice, as such, is seen again by employing counterexamples. For kind *K*, substitute *economics*, *physics* or *homeopathy*.

Unfortunately, however, this second line of reply is also flawed. As regards the conclusion that neutrality is preserved because, although it is a higher order philosophical thesis, no controversial doctrine about persons is involved, this is easily met by the objector following the move upwards and reissuing his challenge at the second-level. That is to say, inasmuch as the point presently at issue is not the truth or falsity of any metaphysical assumption but the *existence* of one it is of no avail to the Rawlsian liberal to try to restrict his philosophical commitment to the higher level. For this, no less than if he insisted upon an avowedly Cartesian account of political subjects, offends against the principle of toleration, at least as Rawls presents it.[20]

A second flaw in the reply is more serious since it returns the discussion to the conception of persons and again shows it to involve first-order metaphysical assumptions. Granted that the repudiation of controversial foundations while being a 'metaphysical' thesis is not in conflict with the content of particular ethical or ontological claims, the question arises as to why Rawls make this methodological disavowal. That question is ambiguous. It can be read as asking either, why does he think he needs to repudiate such assumptions? or, why does he think he is entitled to deny making them? The answer to the first is familiar and presents no difficulty. The *motivation* is the wish to respect the principle of toleration as applied to philosophy itself, and whatever one may think about this principle it is independent of theories of the person. The *justification* of disavowal, however, is not unconnected with such notions. Rawls believes that no controversial claims are implicated in his formulation of justice because he thinks that the account of citizens which he offers is not metaphysically contentious.

Earlier I suggested that this latter belief is false and will return to the issue again shortly. The point of immediate concern, however, is that whether or not the higher-level general thesis is non-controversial its assertion in the present context is liable to dispute. For here it rests on the partic-

[20] See especially 'Justice as Fairness', pp. 230–1.

ular claim that the political conception of persons as distinct, morally responsible agents does not involve any contentious doctrines. Clearly if the latter is a matter of controversy, *and it is*, then so long as it remains such it can hardly serve to secure acceptance of the general thesis that the task requires no questionable philosophical notions — let alone serve to establish its truth.

Thus, considerations of the two special ways in which it was proposed that Rawls' account of the original position could be regarded as involving metaphysical doctrines, and of the replies that might be made to these suggestions, yields the following conclusions. First, there is a familiar and agreed sense of the term in which it is true that Sandel asserts and Rawls denies that justice as fairness relies upon 'metaphysical' notions. Second, the assumption that no concepts of this sort are required for the task is itself such a doctrine — be it a highly abstract one, as is its denial. Accordingly, the theory is not free of metaphysical connections.

It might be thought that Rawls can afford to concede the foregoing conclusion, and although he does not pursue the issue beyond noting the original proposal its introduction suggests that he may be prepared to grant it.[21] The thought that the concession is not fatal to the theory is again the idea that the relevant philosophical commitment is highly abstract and removed from debates about the nature of persons, agency, freedom, and so on. Whether or not it incurs damage, and if so how severe is the harm suffered by granting that such a commitment is presupposed, depend upon how strictly the principle of toleration is applied. As was noted, however, Rawls oscillates between prohibition and minimisation on this point:

> ... we apply the principle ... to philosophy itself: the public conception *is to be* political not metaphysical ... we try, *so far as we can*, to avoid disputed philosophical ... questions... No political view that depends on these deep unresolved matters *can serve* as a public conception of justice ... As I

[21] 'Justice as Fairness', p. 236, footnote 19.

have said, we must apply the principle of toleration to philosophy itself.[22] (*my italics*).

The less strict requirement, that contentious philosophical claims be kept to a minimum, is the more judicious. It is implausible to suppose that political philosophy, as contrasted with politics, could be conducted without any involvement with broadly metaphysical ideas. However, the question now arises as to whether the principle can be applied less strictly while still excluding more substantial views, e.g. about the nature of persons, the reality of value and so on. If it cannot then the project of formulating a liberal conception of justice as Rawls and Ronald Dworkin conceive it cannot be executed.[23]

The Substantial Metaphysical Assumption

Supposing then, as seems reasonable, that there is some regular, non *ad hoc* basis for applying the principle in such a way that the political conception cannot presuppose controversial doctrines of the person but may involve more abstract, quasi-formal, philosophical claims of the sort discussed above. The crucial question remains: does the theory of justice satisfy this principle? Earlier I connected Rawls' general repudiation of metaphysical assumptions with the particular thesis that the account given of persons is free of such doctrines and claimed then that the latter is false. On this much I am in agreement with Sandel. The description of political subjects around which the theory is articulated is a metaphysical description. Where I disagree is in the second part of the objection, ie., that its individualist presuppositions are incoherent.

Interestingly, although Rawls takes trouble to argue that the person as citizen is purely political notion, he also offers a way of conceding the counterclaim while yet preserving the theory under the constraint imposed by the principle of

---

[22] 'Justice as Fairness', pp. 223, 230 & 231. *Political Liberalism,* pp. 10 and 154.
[23] For Dworkin see *A Matter of Principle* (Oxford: Clarendon Press, 1986) Part III 'Liberalism and Justice'.

toleration. The argument is best stated in his own words (the emphasis is mine).

> One might ... say that our every day conception of persons as the basic units of deliberation and responsibility presupposes, or in some way involves, certain metaphysical theses about the nature of persons as moral or political agents. Following the method of avoidance, I should not want to deny these claims. What should be said is the following. If we look at the presentation of justice as fairness and note how it is set up, and note the ideas and conceptions it uses, *no particular metaphysical doctrine about the nature of persons, distinctive and opposed to other metaphysical doctrines appears among its premises, or seems required by its argument. If metaphysical presuppositions are involved perhaps they are so general that they would not distinguish between the distinctive metaphysical views – Cartesian, Leibnizian or Kantian; realist, idealist or materialist – with which philosophy traditionally has been concerned.* In this case, they would not appear to be relevant for the structure and content of a polititcal conception of justice one way or another.[24]

The passage begins as if to suggest that whatever may be true of our pre-reflective ways of thinking about persons the political conception remains entirely free of metaphysics. However, the argument proper is given in what follows. Justice as fairness involves no *distinctive*, and therefore potentially controversial, philosophical thesis. Hence, even if the description of citizens is metaphysical it is not such as to prevent the theory serving its liberal political purpose. Reading this back into the account of the principle of toleration as applied to philosophy it implies a weakening of it. The requirement now cannot be as previously stated, i.e., that no political view involving questions of philosophical psychology or a metaphysical doctrine of persons can function as a public conception of justice. Instead, it must be that no view that rests on *distinctive or disputable* assumptions of these sorts can serve. As before, this move raises general questions about the scope of tolerance but again my concern is with the issue of whether Rawls' theory succeeds in satisfying the less demanding requirement.

---

[24] 'Justice as Fairness', p. 240.

It may seem reasonable to suppose that any view whose metaphysical assumptions are compatible with such diverse philosophical theories of persons as those of Descartes, Leibniz and Kant, and again do not conflict with realism, idealism and materialism, cannot be philosophically controversial. This is a mistake, however, and one that is glaring in its context. For the argument is presented partly in response to the challenge of radical communitarianism which invokes an account of persons precisely at odds with those offered by the philosophers named above, *viz., collectivism*. Recall that for Sandel, as for Bradley and Hegel, persons are 'intersubjective beings'; 'parts of the moral organism'; and 'essentially related to other persons'.[25] It then becomes clear that the presuppositions of the Rawlsian theory are not so general as to fail to 'distinguish between the distinctive metaphysical views ... with which philosophy has traditionally been concerned'.

The list of theories disguises this point in two ways. Firstly, Descartes, Leibniz and Kant present obviously very different and probably incompatible philosophies of mind. Secondly and likewise, realism, idealism and materialism may be thought to exhaust the range of general metaphysical doctrines relevant to the issue of the nature of persons. But whatever the differences between them, the philosophers mentioned all refer psychological states and other personal properties to autonomous subjective unities: the *self*, the *rational soul*, and the *transcendental ego*, respectively. The list might be extended to include most other major figures and I take it to be implicit in the original claim that it could be added to. However, the only criterion of inclusion which will preserve the compatibility of the views gathered by it with the content of the political conception of persons is an *individualist* one — the now familiar thesis that persons are independent centres of consciousness, deliberation and agency. By the same token, any view of persons which denies this will fall on the far side of the distinction marked by the metaphysical presuppositions of the original posi-

---

[25] See *Hegel's Philosophy of Right*, III, (ii), Civil Society.

tion. The latter are not so general, for example, as to fail to be incompatible with the claim associated with Hume and more recently with Parfit, that where one might think to find enduring subjects there exist only causally related psychological contents. And again they are sufficiently specific to be distinguished from and opposed to the neo-Hegelian thesis reaffirmed by Sandel: that 'the relevant description of the self may embrace more than a single empirically-individuated human being'.[26] Similarly, the failure of a metaphysical doctrine to discriminate between realism, idealism and materialism does not show it to be philosophically uncontentious. In this case, the point is not that these share a common assumption about the nature of persons but that considered in themselves they have nothing to say about the dispute between individualism and collectivism. It would be a category mistake to suppose otherwise. For whereas the former concern the question: *Is there a mind-independent reality?* the latter bear upon the quite different question: *are persons, if they exist at all, independent or relational beings?*

Writing in defence of Rawls, Amy Gutmann pursues the suggestion that justice as fairness does not presuppose any distinctive, metaphysical psychology but allows that it is not compatible with all such views and concedes to Sandel that the conception of persons as free and equal subjects is at odds with an account of selves as 'radically situated' or as intersubjective beings whose identity is partly constituted by antecedent social relationships. She then concludes:

> Rawls must admit this much metaphysics — that we are not radically situated selves — if justification is to depend not on 'being true to an order antecedent to and given to us, but ... [on] congruence with our deeper understanding of ourselves and our aspirations.'
> ... [but] If this, rather than Kantian dualism, is the meta-

---

[26] Sandel, *Liberalism*, p. 80. He uses these words in connection with a view of political subjects as 'intersubjective selves', to which he argues Rawls is committed by the defence of the difference principle.

physics that liberal justice must admit, Sandel's critique collapses.[27]

This assessment is correct so far as concerns the objection that Rawls theory rests on a false or incoherent metaphysical foundation. However, it is the concession to the first part of Sandel's challenge that is of interest here. The original position may not presuppose Kantian dualism but it does assume a substantial, generic, philosophical view of which the theory of the transcendental ego is a specific instance, *viz*: the claim that persons are individuals and *not* clusters of psychological states annexed to bodies or emergent social phenomena supervening upon collections of non-personal entities. Justice as fairness functions by characterising a perspective from which the rules it proposes can be seen to be preferable to other principles of justice given the understanding of citizens as free and equal; as distinct subjects of consciousness, deliberation and agency. It is open to Rawls to allow that this conception may be mistaken and hence to claim that our metaphysical nature may be other than as distinct individuals. It remains, however, that the latter view is *presupposed*, that it is *philosophical* and that it is *contentious*. Thus, even on the weakest formulation of the requirement imposed by the principle of toleration the theory fails to provide an acceptable public conception of justice.

---

[27] Gutmann, 'Communitarian Critics' p. 314. Here she associates the notion of 'radically situated selves' with Sandel's idea of the subject as 'socially constituted'. As a point of interpretation this seems to be a mistake, for Sandel appears to distinguish between these views and to argue against the former while endorsing the latter. (*Liberalism*, pp.11–13, 20–21 & 149–53). However, the general style of Sandel's writing makes it difficult to be certain of his view; having an 'intersubjective constitution' could perhaps be one way of being a 'radically situated self'. The philosophical point is in any case independent of the interpretative one, for both of these accounts are at odds with the Rawlsian conception of persons as distinct centres of thought and agency. The internal quotation is from Rawls, 'Kantian Constructivism in Moral Theory', *Journal of Philosophy*, 77 (1980), p. 519, see *Political Liberalism*, pp. 99 ff.

Persons as Empirical

Before proceeding, it is appropriate to distinguish further
the claims with which the previous section ended from
those made by Sandel and rejected by Rawls and Gutmann
in their replies to communitarian criticism. Most importantly, while I maintain that the political conception presupposes metaphysical individualism I have not argued, and as
yet see no reason to believe, that it rests upon a view of
selves as essentially independent of their empirical realisation. Nothing in the complex notion of persons as the basic
subjects of consciousness, deliberation, agency, freedom
and social co-operation implies this conclusion. Indeed, for
reasons lightly touched upon earlier the latter conception
runs counter to the idea of non-empirical selves. Accordingly, this much of Rawls' and Gutmann's interpretation of
the original position seems correct: that the abstraction from
particular, contingent interests which it involves does not
imply a notion of the subject as constituted prior to natural
'personal possessions' such as values and goals, social
attachments and shared purposes. The necessary abstraction is only from the particular ownership of these properties. The principles of justice which result are thus not
transcendental (nor even trans-social and trans-historical)
and thereby binding on all rational subjects but reflect the
general empirical circumstances of those for whom they are
formulated.

Sandel regards Rawls' philosophical psychology as being
directly determined by his conception of the nature and status of justice. Thus he traces the (alleged) Rawlsian idea of
persons as Kantian selves to the espousal of deontological
political theory: the view that justice is prior and universal
'the first virtue of social institutions'.[28] However, supposing
that a logical link between the notions of *justice* and of *persons* were granted, the correct interpretation of the original

---

[28] For discussion of this interesting claim see Sandel, *Liberalism*, p. 15 ff.
      It focuses the debate on the point with which the present essay began,
      i.e., the challenge that liberalism and metaphysical individualism go
      hand in hand. It also echoes Bradley's charge against his liberal
      contemporaries.

position as abstracting only from particular contingent facts would then imply equally conditional conceptions of justice and of those subject to it, and the latter are precisely what Rawls claims to employ in his theory.

Philosophical Anthropology and the Natural Foundation of Justice

I have discussed two philosophical assumptions: one general — relating to the necessity or otherwise of invoking certain kinds of concepts in the formation of philosophical theories of justice; the other particular — concerning the idea of persons employed in one such theory, the main focus of interest is clearly the latter. Indeed, I argued that the former methodological assumption derives its source and interest from Rawls' claim not to have relied upon any distinctive metaphysical view of persons in constructing the original position. Correspondingly, the most significant of my conclusions in regard to these assumptions is that concerning the claim of independence from controversial philosophical doctrines. As I see it, the attempts to deny and then failing this to minimise, metaphysical commitments collapse. In consequence the principle of toleration is violated. Strictly, then, it has not been shown that such presuppositions are in principle ineliminable, though one reason for believing this to be so is the thought that a theory of justice is an account of certain *normative* relationships between moral subjects and that this latter notion cannot be given content without invoking some idea of the nature of persons *qua* persons.

For the present, however, the general claim need not be demonstrated. It is enough to have shown the failure of the attempts to discharge the metaphysical load carried by the particular theory of *justice as fairness*. It is worth adding, however, that the existence of such a load within Rawls' account is connected with his own concern to find a normatively-relevant common foundation to which reference can be made in the resolution of disputes between proponents of competing political views. Rawls insists that this foundation is nothing other than the conception which citizens have of themselves as free and equal members of a political community ('citizens'), but this insistence invites the following dilemma. Either membership of a political community is *just another fact* about an individual, in which case such membership has no special status with respect to membership of other groups, e.g. religious or common-interest ones, or else it is *a special fact* invocation of which serves to trump demands deriving from membership of other associations. If the former then no special normative significance attaches to one's political identity, if the latter then this special significance demands to be explained. It will not do to say in reply that while not everyone is a member of a church, or of another common-interest group, everyone is a citizen, for while this may be true it carries no normative force against demands generated from occupancy of these other roles. If citizenship has priority it must be because the fact it expresses is a prior or deeper one, presumably one about our very nature as 'free and equal persons'. Without some such foundation the claims of citizenship have no special weight—other than a socio-psychological one; and notwithstanding Rawls' recent emphasis on the importance of an 'overlapping consensus', he cannot mean to substitute sociology for political philosophy in the determination of principles of justice.

The question which now arises, then, is this: supposing that a metaphysical foundation cannot be dispensed with, what is to become of the liberal understanding of justice? The term most in need of analysis in the question is 'liberal'. Certainly as Rawls conceives its meaning the eliminability of controversial assumptions renders a theory unfit to serve in this role. However, one might seek to compromise by conceding the strict requirement of metaphysical independence, with the thought of then being able to formulate an account of justice that would at least be acceptable to (and therefore could serve to regulate the social relations between) citizens conceived of by themselves, and in the theory, as individuals—be they Platonists, Aristotelians, Cartesians, Leibnizians, Kantians or whatever else.

This suggestion is addressed to Rawls' insistence that a political conception should not make appeal to doctrines of moral psychology and philosophy of mind. I have not considered the way in which it might be argued that it is *only* by reference to these that any *normative* content can be given to the idea of justice. That is to say not merely that the concept cannot be articulated without taking some very general view of the nature of political subjects but that a theory of our nature as psychophysical substances of a complex but determinate sort provides the necessary and only available basis for an account of moral and political virtue.[29]

This line of thought, which has its origins in Plato's *Republic* (Book IV) and Aristotle's *Nichomacean Ethics*, is the inspiration for teleological theories of value and conduct and differs from Rawls and from recent philosophical liberalism generally, in denying that *Justice*, and more widely the *Right*, have their foundation independently of that of the *Good*. On the contrary, it claims that the theory of justice can only be an offshoot of the theory of value. Accordingly, principles of fair distribution and even individual rights themselves derive from the conception of values provided by a theory of human nature and of its flourishing. Assuming a teleological account of value such as I have argued for earlier, it will follow that there is a determinate range of ways of living which are worth pursuing. And inasmuch as the purpose of politics is to secure the good life for human beings existing in society there is accordingly an objective basis for deliberating about the form and content of their political institutions and the rights and duties these embody.

Of course, much work needs to be done to show that the various stages of this kind of derivation of justice can in fact be completed, and part of that work involves considering the extent to which a 'second nature' is acquired through socialization, about which I shall have more to say in relation to education. But even if this task were accomplished the resulting theory would seem to remain liable to the liberal objection that it must be intolerant of alternative metaphysical conceptions of persons and of rival systems of

[29] For the outlines of such a theory see again earlier chapters, especially one ('Practical Ethics') and four ('Ethics and the Human Body').

value. However, if this is to say that it will regard them as false the objection is trivial; and if it is to be understood as claiming that such a theory cannot provide a basis for respecting those who hold competing views it is question-begging. Indeed, one might consider that an important reason for favouring justice is precisely that it gives expression to one's understanding of oneself and of others as sharing a common nature and thereby having a common interest in the goods appropriate to that nature—including those arising from civil associations. I shall develop this idea further in chapter ten ('Public Reason, Truth and Human Fellowship') but before doing so I need to elaborate an account of the relationship between individuals, society and the state, and that will require further discussion of Rawls' position in its fully developed form.

9

The Individual, the State and the Common Good

Introduction

Let me begin with what should be a reassuring thought, and one that may serve as a corrective to presumptions that sometimes characterize political philosophy. The possibility of wise and virtuous political deliberation resulting in beneficial and stable civil order no more depends upon possession of a philosophical theory of the state and of the virtues proper to it, than does the possibility of making good paintings depend upon possession of an aesthetic theory of the nature and value of art.[1]

This is not to claim that theory is, or must be, irrelevant or unhelpful, let alone that philosophical understanding is gratuitous or inert. A superficial reading of conservative philosophers such as Michael Oakeshott and Roger Scruton is frequently taken to support an antitheoretical interpretation of their outlook, but, in addition to neglecting these authors' own understanding of their own work, this interpretation begs the question of the nature and role of political

---

[1]   Indeed, as I will argue in chapter fifteen ('Philosophy and the Restoration of Art') the importation of a philosophical theory of art as an intellectual guide to the practice of art-making can wreak havoc and seriously undermine the very practice, causing artists and critics to lose sight of its properly aesthetic purposes.

theory.[2] Regarding the value of philosophy in relation to practice more generally, I agree with G.K. Chesterton when he writes that 'philosophy is merely thought that has been thought out … [M]an has no alternative, except between being influenced by thought that has been thought out and being influenced by thought that has not been thought out.'[3] But to say that reflective understanding is worth having, and even that unless one has it one's practice will be confused and misdirected, is not to day that the possibility of a reasonable political order awaits the articulation and reception of an adequate general theory.

This much may seem obvious, but the scale and style of contemporary political philosophy assumes an importance for the subject which, viewed from the side of political and social life, it simply may not have. More germane to what follows, it is important to bring forward the idea that the fate of political order need not, indeed should not, depend upon the development of a general and generally acceptable theory of the state, the source of its authority, and the scope of its operations. I place that positive thought at the outset, because shortly I shall be suggesting that what John Rawls and many others involved in philosophical debates about liberalism have been trying to do cannot be done. In the circumstances in which we find ourselves there cannot be a full legitimation of the liberal or communitarian state as the arbiter of social justice.

---

[2]   See Michael Oakeshott, 'The Concept of a Philosophy of Politics' in Oakeshott, *Religion, Politics, and the Moral Life,* ed. Timothy Fuller (New Haven: Yale University Press, 1991); and Roger Scruton, *The Meaning of Conservatism* (Harmondsworth: Penguin, 1980) 3rd rev. ed. 2002. Scruton writes 'Conservatism may rarely announce itself in maxims, formulae or aims. Its essence is inarticulate, and its expression, when compelled, sceptical. But it is capable of expressions', *The Meaning of Conservatism* (1980) p. 11.

[3]   G.K. Chesterton, 'The Revival of Philosophy — Why?' in Chesterton, *The Common Man* (London: Sheed and Ward, 1950), p. 176. Regrettably, Chesterton's writings have hardly been appreciated by social philosophers. See, for example, Chesterton, *What's Wrong with the World* (London: Cassell, 1910; San Francisco: Ignatius Press, 1994). An exception to this want of appreciation is Stephen R.L. Clark, *G.K. Chesterton: Thinking Backward, Looking Forward* (West Conshohocken, PA: Templeton Foundation Press, 2006).

This sort of thing is sometimes said by cultural relativists and by anti-realist pragmatists such as Richard Rorty;[4] but the broadly Aristotelian-cum-Thomistic standpoint I favour is certainly opposed to both of these. Indeed, it is because I believe in an objective moral order and in its relevance for the conduct of political life, that I find trouble with what many contemporary liberals have to say on such issues as abortion, marriage and the family, education, and the place of substantive moral positions and religion in public life. Yet just as the morally neutral state seems an illusion, so the extensively morally committed state seems an impossibility. Communitarians are correct, I shall argue, in some of the criticisms they make of philosophical liberalism. They are wrong, however, to the extent that they think that moral community — in the precise sense that Augustine, for example, has in mind when he speaks of 'a gathering of rational beings united in fellowship by their agreement about the objects of their love'[5] (and one might add, of their aversion) — can be a general model for the legitimation of the modern nation-state. Here, indeed, I find myself in *qualified* sympathy with Rawls when he writes that 'the hope of political community must indeed be abandoned, if by such a community we mean a political society united in affirming the same comprehensive doctrine'[6] (the nature of the qualification will become apparent).

In the remaining sections, then, I shall be arguing for the following claims. First, the project of liberal political theory, of the neutralist and individualist sort pursued by Rawls, fails and does so for foundational and structural reasons. Second, an important but still neglected notion in social philosophy is that of the common good — Aquinas's *'bonum commune'*. Third, while communitarian conceptions of social life may include a nonreducible common good, it is

---

[4]   See, for example, Richard Rorty, 'The Contingency of Community' in Rorty, *Contingency, Irony, and Solidarity* (Cambridge: Cambridge University Press, 1989); and Rorty, 'The Priority of Democracy to Philosophy' in *Reading Rorty* ed. Alan Malachowski (Oxford: Blackwell, 1990).

[5]   Augustine, *De civitate dei* (London: Loeb, 1960), Book XIX, ch. 26.

[6]   John Rawls, *Political Liberalism* (1993), p. 146.

certainly questionable whether the conditions necessary for the establishment of communitarian states generally exist. In these circumstances we should be grateful for the possibilities for moral development offered by various other forms of community — for which, following Augustine, I propose the term 'fellowship'. The acknowledgement that acceptance of a transcendent justification of the political order and its essential operations is not likely to come about (not that such a justification is altogether impossible) suggests that the appropriate attitude toward the state is a blend of long-term moral aspiration, and short- to middle-term practical participation in limited political goals. Contrary to the position of Rawls, this latter element involves a defence of a form of political arrangement that probably is a *modus vivendi*. However, the proportions of this blend, as indeed the need of it, are matters of sociohistorical contingency. It is not inconceivable, therefore, that they may change over time, or differ geopolitically, as between the United States and the United Kingdom, for example (or internally between England and Wales, Scotland, and N. Ireland should the Union dissolve). Indeed, I end with the thought that English-language political philosophy suffers from a condition related to that noted by Oscar Wilde when he wrote of 'two nations separated by a common language.'

Rawls and the Unavoidability of Comprehensive Doctrines

1993 saw the publication of two long-awaited, and since much-discussed, works on issues of values and prescriptions, namely, John Rawls's *Political Liberalism* and Pope John Paul IIs *Veritatis Splendor*.[7] I have not seen these examined in tandem, though there is certainly scope for comparing and contrasting them. That is not my aim on this occasion, but I shall discuss a difficulty for Rawls' position arising from the existence of a work such as this encyclical addressed to the Roman Catholic Bishops, directing them in

[7] John Paul II, *Veritatis Splendor* (London: Catholic Truth Society, 1993); to which may be added the *Catechism of the Catholic Church* (London: Chapman, 1994) published in the following year.

their teaching of the billion faithful to uphold the unconditional and unlimited character of fundamental moral
requirements.

First, however, recall from the previous chapter the basic
enterprise pursued in Rawls' later work. His concern was to
give an account of how political institutions governed by
principles of justice can be warranted in circumstances in
which they are required to regulate the lives of people who
may, indeed do, pursue different conceptions of their own
good. Early on, Rawls presents this issue as a question:
'[H]ow is it possible for there to exist over time a just and
stable society of free and equal citizens, who remain profoundly divided by reasonable religious, philosophical,
and moral doctrines?'[8] Although this form suggests a
Kantian enquiry into the *a priori* conditions of the possibility
of justice, the content of the question looks to be socio-
empirical and as we have seen, Rawls repeatedly emphasized the non-metaphysical character of his investigation
and of its conclusions.

Already, however, that suggests a problem. To the extent
that principles of justice carry normative force, they must
appeal to considerations that can serve as justifying reasons
and not mere psychological motives for those to whom they
are addressed; but in order to do that they must have, if not *a
priori* universal validity, at least some element of necessity
or rational inescapability. Otherwise it will be too easy for
the claims of justice to be evaded by those who fail to
acquire, or choose to divest themselves of the relevant
desires. One possibility here would be to follow Aquinas (at
least as I read him) and Aristotle (as he is traditionally read)[9]
and argue that while prescriptions generated by practical

[8] Rawls, *Political Liberalism*, p. 4.
[9] For a recent and influential departure from this tradition, see John
     McDowell, 'Are Moral Requirements Hypothetical Imperatives?'
     Proceedings of the Aristotelian Society, supplementary volume 52
     (1978); and McDowell, 'The Role of Eudaimonia in Aristotle's Ethics'
     in Amélie O. Rorty ed. *Essays on Aristotle's Ethics*, ed. (Berkeley:
     University of California Press, 1980) both collected in McDowell,
     Mind, Value and Reality (Cambridge, MA: Harvard University Press,
     1998).

reason are not categorical in Kant's sense, nonetheless in appealing to an agent's strivings they need not be void on account of the contingency of desire.[10] For, as I suggested in chapter one 'Practical Ethics' the strivings in question may be ones the agent cannot fail to have inasmuch as they are partly constitutive of a normal (i.e., normative) human nature.

Such 'assertoric hypotheticals' (to stay with Kantian terminology)[11] rooted in an animate essence *may* be available to those who reject the pure practical reason of the categorical imperative, but they remain too deeply stained in the hue of metaphysics for Rawls' purpose. His opposition is not to the possibility of a philosophical justification of practical reason. Though this disclaimer sometimes seems unconvincing,[12] he insists that his objection is not an expression of scepticism, but rather an implication of the concern to provide principles which can be drawn upon to regulate the lives of those who hold competing philosophical doctrines: 'the conception of justice should be, as far as possible, independent of the opposing and conflicting philosophical and religious doctrines that citizens affirm.'[13] The avoidance of metaphysical theory is a consequence of the application of the principle of toleration to philosophy itself. However, and setting aside the doubt about an underlying moral scepticism on Rawls' part, the question remains of how, having disavowed philosophical justifications, what

---

[10]   For Aquinas, see *Summa Theologiae* Ia, IIae, q.i, a.6.

[11]   See *The Moral Law: Kant's Groundwork of the metaphysics of Morals,* ed. and trans. H.J. Paton (London: Hutchinson, 1976), ch 2, p .78; and my discussion of these as giving the correct logical form of moral imperatives.

[12]   See, for example, Rawls, *Political Liberalism:* '[T]his reasonable plurality of conflicting and incommensurable doctrines is seen as the *characteristic* work of practical reason over time under enduring free institutions'; we also view the diversity of reasonable religious, philosophical, and moral doctrines found in democratic societies as a *permanent* feature of their public culture'; and '[a]s always, we assume that the diversity of reasonable religious, philosophical and moral doctrines found in democratic societies if a *permanent* feature of the public culture and not a mere historical condition soon to pass away' (pp. 135, 136, 216–17; my emphases). Why 'characteristic' and 'permanent' unless for sceptical reasons?

[13]   *Ibid.,* p. 9.

results can be anything other than an appeal to contingent preferences.

A Rawlsian response to such an objection is likely to draw upon discussions offered in *Political Liberalism* under the headings 'The Idea of an Overlapping Consensus' and 'The Idea of Public Reason' (Lectures IV and VI respectively). To begin with, however, we are required to grant a distinction between two branches or spheres of practical reasoning, that associated with *ethical* and that concerned with *political* deliberation. The latter is the site of Rawls's contractualist construction 'the political conception of justice' while the former is the arena within which are to be found 'general and comprehensive doctrines'. In these terms 'generality' is a matter of range of application – to few, many, most, or all subjects (i.e., agents) – and 'comprehensiveness' concerns aspects or departments of life. Thus, a 'fully comprehensive and entirely general moral conception' would identify values and prescribe directives for all persons in all aspects of their lives. *Ex hypothesi,* and assuming an organized social context, such a conception will include an account of justice and other political virtues – as do the general and comprehensive views drawn upon in *Veritatis Splendor* and the *Catechism of the Catholic Church.*

In contrast to comprehensive doctrines which present political values as instances of more general principles, Rawls offers the idea of a 'free-standing' political conception:

> [One that] is neither presented as, nor [is] derived from, such a doctrine applied to the basic structure of society, as if this structure were simply another subject to which that doctrine applied. ... I assume all citizens to affirm a comprehensive doctrine to which the political conception they accept is in some way related. But a distinguishing feature of a political conception is that it is presented as freestanding and expounded apart from, or without reference to, any such wider background. ... [I]t tries to elaborate a reasonable conception for the basic structure [of political society] alone and involves, so far as possible, no wider commitments to any other doctrine.[14]

---

[14] See *ibid.,* pp. 12–13; see also *ibid.,* Lecture V, 'The Priority of the Right over the Good.'

Additionally, we are to consider a threefold distinction among a *comprehensive doctrine*, a p*olitical conception* of justice, and a *modus vivendi*. For these purposes, the last is to be thought of as an agreement or treaty adhered to because the participants regard it as being to their individual benefit. Such a convergence of interest is contingent, and therefore any appearance of political unity among the parties is illusory; all that exists is a precarious arrangement sustained by self-interest. It is against the background of this tripartite division that the claims of political liberalism are elaborated in answer to the question of how, given a pluralism of comprehensive doctrines, there can nevertheless be a just and stable society consensus on a political conception of justice—that is, a principled agreement on values and norms whose content and justification are independent of any distinctive comprehensive doctrine, but are compatible with many, most, or all such doctrines. Unlike a *modus vivendi*, such a condition does express and sustain genuine social unity, but compatible with Rawls's requirement that liberalism be neutral between competing conceptions of the good, it is not the expression of one, as against another, comprehensive doctrine.

Such is the claim, but the problems seem resistant to this form of solution. First, the initial separation of practical reasoning into ethical and political spheres is not innocuous. If it were, it would hardly serve Rawls's argument, which requires a degree of independence of the political from the moral. There are several traditions, including the Aristotelian–Thomistic and the Kantian ones, which would deny that a political conception can be 'freestanding', precisely because they assert the unity and continuity of practical reasoning. Put in terms of Thomism, for example, the counterassertion would be that there can be no account of a political 'right' that does not derive from a theory of the good, and that this latter is the general presupposition of all individual and social action. A related claim is expressed by

John Paul II in a section of *Veritatis Splendor* where he is considering objections to traditional natural-law moral philosophy:

> The separation which some have posited between the freedom of individuals and the nature which all have in common, as it emerges from certain philosophical theories which are highly influential in present-day culture, obscures the perception of the universality of the moral law on the part of reason. But inasmuch as the natural law expresses the dignity of the human person and lays the foundation for his fundamental rights and duties, it is universal in its precepts and its authority extends to all mankind.[15]

It is important to see that concerning the issue of the duality of practical reason and the further critical points that follow, Rawls may be in some difficulty even if Thomist, Kantian, and other theories are themselves defective, since, to pick up a theme from the preceding chapter, it is central to Rawls's approach that it not rely on contentious philosophical doctrines. Thus, if it is controversial whether the moral and the political stand in the required relation, this fact alone undermines the possibility of advancing the political conception as the object of an overlapping consensus. Certainly one might argue directly for it, but to do so would be to violate the requirement of political autonomy.

Perhaps, however, that requirement is not absolute but admits of degree. Certainly Rawls sometimes suggest this. Earlier I quoted him writing that 'the conception of justice should be, *as far as possible,* independent of the opposing and conflicting philosophical and religious doctrines that citizens affirm' (my emphasis), and at one point he considers directly the possibility of opposition to his political conception from an advocate of a comprehensive religious doctrine. What he says is very revealing and it faces, I believe, a serious objection. In order to show both points I need to quote at some length:

---

[15]   John Paul II, *Veritatis Splendor,* section 51, p. 80.

[B]y avoiding comprehensive doctrines we try to bypass religion and philosophy's profoundest controversies so as to have some hope of uncovering a basis of a stable overlapping consensus.

... Nevertheless, in affirming a political conception of justice we may eventually have to assert at least certain aspects of our own comprehensive religious or philosophical doctrine (by no means necessarily fully comprehensive). This will happen whenever someone insists, for example, that certain questions are so fundamental that to insure their being rightly settled justifies civil strife .... At this point we may have no alternative but to deny this, or to imply its denial and hence to maintain the kind of thing we had hoped to avoid.

To consider this, imagine rationalist believers who contend that these beliefs are open to and can be fully established by reason (uncommon though this view might be). In this case the believers simply deny what we have called 'the fact of reasonable pluralism.' so we say of the rationalist believers that they are mistaken in denying that fact; but we need not say that their religious beliefs are not true, since to deny that religious beliefs can be publicly and fully established by reason is not to say that they are not true ... [W]e do not put forward more of our comprehensive view than we think needed or useful for the political aim of consensus.[16]

First, then, it is conceded that the method of avoidance may fail and that when it does so it may be necessary, and is permissible, to defend the political conception against challenges from a comprehensive conception by invoking a rival (one's own) religious or philosophical doctrine. Second, however, it is supposed that in the imagined example of believers who deny the (purported) fact of 'reasonable pluralism', one's doctrinal counter only challenges their epistemological claim and not the content of their own comprehensive conception. The point of this second observation is to emphasise the limited character of the departure from universal toleration. Against this, however, one should observe that any lapse from strict neutrality undermines the claim that a political conception can be founded on an overlapping consensus only and need not rest upon a distinctive comprehensive doctrine. Further still, the depar-

[16]   See Rawls, *Political Liberalism,* pp. 152–53.

ture may not be as limited as Rawls supposes, since it might be part of the rationalist believers' doctrinal commitment that pluralism with regard to fundamental claims is *not* reasonable. In short, epistemological claims may fall within essential doctrine. Consider, for example, another papal document – Pope Pius XII's encyclical *Humani Generis (False Trends in Modern Teaching)*:

> Notoriously, the Church makes much of human reason, in the following connexions: when we establish beyond doubt the existence of one God, who is a personal Being; when we establish irrefutably, by proofs divinely granted to us, the basic facts on which the Christian faith itself rests; when we give just expression to the natural law which the Creator has implanted in men's hearts.[17]

Here Pius is reiterating long-standing Catholic doctrines, the first of which is the provability of the existence of God: it being contrary to faith (not merely theological tradition) to deny that there can be such a proof. Earlier, having made similar claims, Pius asks why there should be disagreement over such matters and in response cites 'the impact of the senses and the imagination, [and] disordered appetites which are the consequences of the fall.'[18] The interpretation of papal encyclicals is an art that philosophers now rarely practice,[19] but it is difficult to escape the idea that so far as Pius is concerned pluralism with regard to the primary precepts of natural law (for example), though explicable, is not reasonable. In asserting otherwise, therefore, Rawls would be saying that the rationalist believers' religious beliefs are false.

---

[17] *False Trends in Modern Teaching: Encyclical Letter (Humani Generis) of Pius XII Concerning Certain False Opinions,* trans. Ronald A. Knox (London: Catholic Truth Society, 1950), Part II, 'The Field of Philosophy' para. 29, section 1, p. 16.

[18] *Ibid.,* p. 3.

[19] For a distinguished exception, however, see Alasdair MacIntyre, 'How Can We Learn What *Veritatis Splendor* Has to Teach?' *Thomist,* 58 (1994). I discuss philosophical aspects of *Veritatis Splendor* in 'From Law to Virtue and Back Again: On *Veritatis Splendor*' in M. Davis ed. *The Use of the Bible in Ethics* (Sheffield: University if Sheffield Press, 1995).

Here my point is not that there can be no argument on behalf of a political conception against the claims of those who would pursue their creed to the point of unsettling civil peace.[20] On the contrary, I believe that one can and should fashion robust defences of law and social order against, for example, Christian anti-abortionists who would murder clinic staff, Muslim jihadists who would assassinate blasphemers, Jewish Haredi (ultra-orthodox) zealots who would kill Palestinians, and so on across the range of religious extremists. As Rawls reluctantly concedes, however, the possibility of doing so depends upon bringing into the political domain a distinctive comprehensive moral doctrine. The tone in which he writes of this need suggests a socially regrettable necessity akin to the use of force to expel a drunk and boorish guest from a party, but the problem reveals faults in the very structure of political liberalism. By Rawls's own account, even though the political conception may not be the object of an overlapping consensus, it should nonetheless be affirmed (and upheld) because it is implied by a favoured philosophical perspective.

In connection with this objection, consider what Rawls has to say about public reason. He asks: 'How can it be either reasonable or rational, when basic matters are at stake, for citizens to appeal only to a public conception of justice and not to the whole truth as they see it?'[21] The answer elaborates interpretations of ideas that are supposed to be available and acceptable to all, and concludes with the demand that we live together politically on the basis of claims and justifications that everyone can reasonably be expected to endorse. As before, however, these formulations fail to withstand the test of real examples. Clearly almost everything turns on the interpretation of 'reasonableness'. Rawls writes:

> The only comprehensive doctrines that run afoul of public reason are those that cannot support a reasonable balance

---

[20] I offer such an argument in 'Religious Toleration', *Synthesis Philosophica*, Special Issue on Toleration, 9 (1994), also in Haldane, *Faithful Reason* (2004).

[21] Rawls, *Political Liberalism*, p. 216.

of political values. [And he continues, in a footnote whose importance it would be hard to exaggerate:]

As an illustration consider the troubled question of abortion. Suppose first that the society in question is well-ordered and that we are dealing with the normal case of mature adult women. ... Suppose further that we consider the question in terms of these three important political values: the due respect for human life, the ordered reproduction of political society over time, including the family in some form, and finally the equality of women as equal citizens ... Now I believe any reasonable balance of these three values will give a woman a duly qualified right to end her pregnancy during the first trimester. The reason for this is that at this early stage of pregnancy the political value of the equality of women is overriding and this right is required to give it substance and force ... [A]ny comprehensive doctrine that leads to a balance of political values excluding that duly qualified right in the first trimester is to that extent unreasonable.[22]

Without entering again into the abortion debate, it should be clear that any notion of reasonableness that renders an opinion contrary to that presented by Rawls 'unreasonable' is almost certain to be (reasonably) contentious and thus not fitted to occupy a central role in a conception of justice that purports to apply the principle of toleration to philosophy itself thereby 'to bypass religion and philosophy's profoundest problems'. In this connection consider again a view presented by an authoritative Roman document, this time an 'Instruction' on abortion *(Donum Vitae)* issued by the Congregation for the Doctrine of the Faith:

The inalienable rights of the person must be recognised and respected by civil society and the political authority. These human rights depend neither on single individuals nor on parents; nor do they represent a concession made by society and the state ... Among such fundamental rights one should mention in this regard every human being's right to life and physical integrity from the moment of conception. ... As a consequence of the respect and protection which must be ensured for the unborn child from the moment of conception, the law must provide appropriate

[22] *Ibid.,* pp. 243–44.

legal sanctions for every deliberate violation of the child's rights.[23]

In the face of a clear conflict of views of the sort which this example makes vivid, Rawls's true position reveals itself to be far from neutral: try for an overlapping consensus, but where it is not available and where important issues are at stake, affirm your own comprehensive doctrine. The whole raison d'être of *Political Liberalism*, however, was to offer a way forward that possesses the principles lacked by a mere *modus vivendi* while yet not relying upon any appeal to distinctive doctrines. It is apparent from the foregoing, therefore, that whatever its other merits this defence of liberalism fails in its own declared aim.

The Common Good

One way of presenting some of the problems that Rawls runs into is by saying, as above, that he tries, unsuccessfully, to secure a political *right* — that of justice — without deriving it from any distinctive account of the *good*. This is a criticism that is increasingly voiced, in one form or another, particularly by advocates of 'perfectionist' liberalism.[24] It might also be noted, though it rarely is, that although the notion of the right which Rawls seeks is a commonly shared one, he conspicuously eschews any theory of the common good. So far as I am aware, Rawls only mentions the idea once in *Political Liberalism* and that is in a passage characterizing views that contrast with his own account of justice as fairness:

> [W]hatever these religious and philosophical doctrines may be, I assume they all contain a conception of the right and the good that includes a conception of justice that can

---

[23] *Donum Vitae* (1987), as quoted in the *Catechism of the Catholic Church* (*supra* note 8), Part 3, section 2, paragraph 2273, p. 490.

[24] Here I am thinking especially of writings by Joseph Raz: *The Morality of Freedom* (Oxford: Clarendon, 1986), and *Ethics in the Public Domain* (Oxford: Clarendon, 1994).

be understood as in some way advancing the common good.[25]

This, then, brings me to the issue of the role within political and social philosophy of the idea of the common good. The body of anti-Rawlsian criticism generally dubbed 'communitarian' has several targets, but these can be gathered together under the general charge of 'erroneous individualism'. Thus, as was seen in the previous chapter, it has been alleged that Rawls' use of the notion of an *original position* implies a view of the identity of persons as constituted independently of their social attachments and inherited values. This claim is usually made in an effort to show that he has an incoherent metaphysical anthropology, but as with the criticisms of the previous section it is important to see how political liberalism may be undermined by the mere fact that it draws upon substantive philosophical assumptions. One need not engage the question of whether those assumptions are coherent, let alone true. So, for example, while I agree with Rawls in his defence of the original position, holding it to be an epistemological device and not a metaphysical description of the social world, I think he is mistaken in arguing that the idea of citizens as free and equal persons is without controversial assumptions.[26] Ask yourself why citizenship should have special normative significance ahead of some other aspect of a person's identity, such as his or her religious affiliation, to the extent that it can be appealed to as a trumping factor. The answer has to

[25] Rawls, *Political Liberalism*, p.109. In the later work *The Law of Peoples* (Cambridge, MA: Harvard University Press, 1999) the expression 'common good' appears but in the form the 'common good idea of justice' which Rawls uses to characterise the political organization of 'non-liberal but decent, well-ordered, hierarchical societies'. Rawls writes that 'the meaning of such an idea is not yet clear' (p. 71) and goes on to explain it in terms of three features: the assignment of human rights to all members of the society, the inclusion of a decent consultation hierarchy, and the sincere and not unreasonable belief that the law is guided by a common good idea of justice. Whether this serves to clarify the notion as Rawls intends it is moot, but it has little to do with the idea of the common good as that is understood in the traditon that coined the expression '*bonum commune*'.

[26] See chapter 8 above and John Haldane 'Identity, Community, and the Limits of Multiculture', *Public Affairs Quarterly*, 7 (1993).

be that for Rawls these other identities are in some important sense secondary to that of our nature as free and equal persons. The exact sense in which the latter identity is prior and deeper may be held to be normative and not meta-physical, but in either event its assertion is philosophically controversial.

Having noted this distinction between kinds of criticism, it is unsurprising that those who complain of individualist assumptions are concerned to provide a communitarian alternative to liberalism. It is an interesting question what features are essential to such an option. One dominant strand in recent thinking has been the thesis of social consti-tution: the claim that persons are made to be such—advanced from the status of mere human animals—by being worked into a network of social relations. An analogy here might be with the process of sculptural assembly, whereby various items, each possessed of a pre-sculptural nature, have a new compositional identity bestowed upon them; for example, what was (and in one respect remains) a piece of windshield wiper is then a grinning mouth. I believe that there is something in this idea and that it shows itself in the fact that most action descriptions presuppose socially constituted patterns of behaviour. Here, however, I am more interested in the claim that liberalism fails inas-much as it neglects, and cannot accommodate, the fact that some or all of the goods we pursue (and which a system of rights is concerned to protect) are goods possessed in common.

By contrast with *Political Liberalism,* the expression 'com-mon good' occurs frequently in recent Roman Catholic documents, including *Veritatis Splendor.* The history of the term's present prominence in Catholic social teaching goes back to the writings of Jacques Maritain and Yves Simon,[27] which in turn look to the moral theology of Thomas Aqui-nas. In the *Prima Secundae* of the *Summa Theologiae,* eight

[27] See, for example, Jacques Maritain, *The Person and the Common Good,* trans. John Fitzgerald (New York: Scribner, 1941); and Yves Simon, *The Tradition of Natural Law* (New York: Fordham University Press, 1965).

questions (qq. 90–97) are devoted to aspects of law (indeed, this group is often referred to as 'The Treatise on Law'). In question 90, article 2, Aquinas writes as follows:

> [S]ince every part is ordered to the whole as the imperfect to the perfect and one man is part of the perfect society, it is necessary that the law properly regard the order to the happiness of the society ... Hence, since law is most of all ordered to the Common Good, it is necessary that any other precept concerning a particular matter must needs lack the nature of law except insofar as it is ordered to the Common Good. And therefore every law is ordered to the Common Good.[28]

It is important to understand what Aquinas means by the common good, since present-day writers sometimes speak of general or collective goods in ways which superficially resemble the Thomist notion but which are in fact quite different from it.[29] Notice two elements in the quoted passage: (1) man stands in relation to society as a part to a whole; and (2) every law is directed toward the establishment, maintenance, and improvement of the common good. The first is a familiar thesis of communitarianism: the irreducibility of society as a unified substance that bestows a form of moral identity on its members. As a corrective to a radical corporatist reading, it is relevant to add that Aquinas also regards individual persons as complete substances. By implication, then, he rejects a dichotomy that bedevils current debates, that which regards persons as either *parts* of a greater whole—society—or else as *pre-existing individuals*

---

[28] See Aquinas, *The Treatise on Law*, trans. R.J. Henle (Notre Dame: University of Notre Dame Press, 1993), q. 90, a. 2, pp. 132 and 134.

[29] For recent accounts of the common good as it features in Aquinas and in modern Thomistic writings, see Louis Dupré, 'The Common Good and the Open Society' in D. Hollenbach & B. Douglass eds. *Catholicism and Liberalism*, ed. (Cambridge: Cambridge University Press, 1993); Gregory Froelich, 'Ultimate End and Common Good', *The Thomist*, 58 (1994), pp. 609–19; Kibujjo Kalumba, 'Maritain on 'The Common Good': Reflections on the Concept', *Laval Théologique et Philosophique*, 49 (1993); T. R. Rourke & C. E. Cochran, 'The Common Good and Economic Justice: Reflections on the Thought of Yves R. Simon', *Review of Politics*, 54 (1992); and Mary M. Keys, *Aquinas, Aristotle and the Promise of the Common Good* (Cambridge: Cambridge Universoty Press, 2006).

out of which society is formed. A way through lies in the direction of saying that persons are *both* wholes and parts — *wholes as selves, parts as social selves*.

This may seem evasive and invite the question: 'are selves made by society or is society made by selves?' Again, however, a way through the dilemma is offered by saying 'both'; that is to say, there is a process of mutual determination. Think again of an artistic analogy. Consider, for example, an artist working on a composition by moving around cut-out shapes of different colours within a rectangular background. The composition is made out of parts which can be described independently of it, but they also change their identities as aspects of a greater substantial whole as they move in relation to one another and the background. A more abstract account of the matter might be fashioned in terms of potentialities some of which are actualized in society, while at the same time the potentialities of a style of social arrangement are actualized through the exercise of natural intrinsic powers of individuals. To adapt a formula of Hilary Putnam's. coined to describe the relation between mind and world, 'the person and the society jointly make up the person and the society'.[30]

So far as concerns the common good, what is most striking is the idea that *every* law should have as its proper goal the well-being of society as a whole. This apparently radical anti-individualism is sometimes moderated by commentators who urge an interpretation of society as an aggregate, and thereby treat 'common good' as a distributive notion, equivalent to 'the good of each and every member'. At other times it is suggested that while some goods are indeed commonly possessed, they are social means to individual ends; in Aquinas' supernatural teleology, the beatific vision. On this account, law should promote civil order and public health, for example, because these are conditions that each may benefit from, since they and other public goods are objects of convergent interests.

---

[30] Hilary Putnam, *Reason, Truth and History* (Cambridge: Cambridge University Press, 1981) Preface, p. xi.

However, neither of these interpretations is plausible exegesis, for neither takes seriously enough the phrase *'bonum commune'* and Aquinas' claim that this is a *'bonum honestum'*, a genuine constituent of perfection. Consider first a modern attempt to interpret Aquinas's notion. I quote from Maritain's *The Person and the Common Good:*

> [T]hat which constitutes the common good of political society is not only: the collection of public commodities ... a sound fiscal condition of the state and its military power; the body of just laws, good customs and wise institutions, which provide the nation with its structure; the heritage of the great historical remembrances, its symbols and its glories, its living traditions and cultural treasures. The common good includes all these and something more besides ... the whole sum itself of these; a sum which is quite different from a simple collection of juxtaposed units ...
>
> It includes the sum or sociological integration of all the civic conscience, political virtues, and sense of right and liberty, of all the activity, hereditary wisdom, of moral rectitude, justice, friendship, happiness, virtue and heroism in the individual lives of its members. For these things are, in a certain measure, *communicable* and so revert to each member, helping him to perfect his life of liberty and person.[31]

The emphasis on the *communicability* of the integrated sum of social and personal elements contrasts with a notion of commonality as a mere function of convergent interests. The common good is essentially shared. It is a *good-for-many*, taken collectively, rather than *a good to many*, taken distributively. Aquinas' claim that this good is a *bonum honestum,* a perfecting end in itself, might be thought to be incompatible with a Christian view of human destiny which is usually treated individualistically. However, his trinitarian theology grants him the idea that, even eschatologically, the good of individuals resides in their participation in the life of a community of persons.

Theological possibilities aside, Aquinas' idea of the common good as a participatory end (for the sake of which civil society exists and must be regulated) has been insufficiently explored even by liberalism's 'communitarianism critics'.

---

[31]   Maritain, *The Person and the Common Good,* pp. 52–53.

Yet something of this sort seems to be presupposed in a wide range of moral-cum-social judgements. Concerns about the conduct of nations in going to war and in prosecuting wars are not easily represented in individualistic terms. To cite two examples from recent history, the agonies felt in the US about Vietnam present themselves as *collective* shame or guilt and not: a's guilt plus b's guilt plus c's guilt, etc., but 'ours'. Likewise the British experience of the Falklands war and subsequent reflection upon it are most perspicuously represented in terms of shared participation in honour and tragedy. It is too easy to respond to claims of communal good and evil with charges of romanticism, for there is unquestionably something that is recognized, particularly but not exclusively within older traditional societies, as 'our' well-being, or 'our' corruption, and it is a serious omission not to give an account of this.

Rawls' political liberalism cannot find a place for the common good because of its commitment to neutrality between life-shaping values. At most it can register and even celebrate convergence in evaluations, seeing in this happy coincidence possibilities for establishing and extending an overlapping consensus. However, the idea of citizens as free and equal persons remains individualistic: the good of citizens that results from participation in an order regulated by the political conception of justice is a private one. This is sometimes overlooked on account of the regulated order being a public good; but therein lies a lesson worth inscribing in departments of political science and economics: *public good does not equal common good.*

The argument in favour of the common good is not the defeater of Rawls' project. My objections to the latter principally concerned its inability to meet one of its own main criteria, namely, the need to establish a case for the form and content of the political conception without reliance upon controversial comprehensive doctrines. However, unless one is willing and able to argue the case for greater moral indifference in the political order, then the recognition that Rawls' neutrality lapses is likely to prompt the question of how the *good* should bear upon the *right* and what the nature of the right in question is. Having got that far, and recalling that the problem for resolution is the normative conditions of social life, one may then be better placed to see the possibilities offered by the idea of the common good, including, for example, the notion that what justifies the expenditure of society's resources upon universities wherein people are supported in their thinking about these very issues is the fact that the goods attained thereby are 'communicable', reverting to each member. Regrettably, it has become all too natural to ask how the intellectual endeavour of philosophers could possibly be of instrumental benefit to taxpayers, since it is assumed that this is the only value at issue. From the perspective of Aquinas the question betrays a kind of corruption, not merely because it overlooks the possibility of noninstrumental goods, but because it neglects the idea that within a community *we* are *all* better when some of us achieve understanding. Thus, discussing the communal division of virtue in connection with the contemplative life, Aquinas writes:

> There are things required of the community which one individual alone cannot meet; this community-duty is discharged when one does this and another that. ... [T]he command to be fruitful falls on the people as whole. They are bound not only to multiply in body but to grow in spirit. The human family is sufficiently provided for if some undertake the responsibility of bodily generation, while others devote themselves to the study of divine things, for the beauty and health of the whole human race.[32]

States, Nations and Communities

Not every state is a nation, nor every nation a state, as is indicated by the examples of the former Soviet Union and of Scotland respectively. Both sorts of social entities can be communities, but there is an internal connection between the ideas of nationhood and community that is absent between those of community and state. Let us say, then, that

---

[32]   Aquinas, *Summa theologiae* , IIa IIae q. 152, a. 2, ad. 1, p. 173.

a *state* involves the orgnization of a collection of people under a system of governance and within a given territory, and that a *nation* is a people united by common history, language, customs, traditions, and interests. Given these features it is unsurprising that nations aspire to be states, or indeed that they regard this condition as their final end.

In a weak sense, a community is any social group whose members cooperate in pursuit of common interests. So defined, it easy to see how many states will acquire the character of communities even if they do not originate as expressions of them. Thus, although a collection of previously unassociated individuals may be brought together within a jurisdiction, it will generally not be long before they begin to interact in ways and under descriptions that indicate membership in a self-identifying social group. Earlier, however, I quoted Augustine's definition of a people as 'a gathering of rational beings united in fellowship by a common agreement about the objects of its love'. This clearly specifies a narrower, moral notion of community, one which I termed 'fellowship'. Restricted as it is, Augustine arrives at this after having set aside an even more exclusive definition of a people and of a state as a gathering united under proclaimed obedience to divine law.

Rawls writes that the hope of political community must be abandoned 'if by such a community we mean a political society united in affirming the same comprehensive doctrine.'[33] Obviously this would be taken to exclude the possibility of fashioning the state along the lines specified in Augustine's more restrictive account. It is not that the latter requires as much as a theocracy, but that even the assumption of theism is no longer tenable as a basis for civil society. The current heir to the British crown, Prince Charles has reflected upon the fact that under the current constitutional arrangements were he to ascend to the throne he would become Supreme Head of the Church of England and *ipso facto* 'Defender of the faith', and said that he would prefer to be 'defender of faith'. From the position within which

---

[33]   Rawls, *Political Liberalism,* p. 146.

Rawls develops his political liberalism, however, even this concession to religious pluralism harbours an unacceptable attachment to the politics of commitment if it presumes that the institutions of the state should acknowledge and give priority to one attitude toward religion (belief) as against others (agnosticism and theism).

Even Augustine's modified account fails to meet the stated conditions for an adequate political conception of justice, since it violates what Rawls calls the 'general facts of the political culture of a democratic society', namely: *the fact of reasonable pluralism* (that a diversity of comprehensive doctrines is a permanent feature); *the fact of oppression* (that common adherence to one comprehensive doctrine can only be maintained by state oppression); and *the fact of majority support* (that a secure regime requires the support of 'a substantial majority of its politically active citizens').[34] Earlier I suggested that Rawls' insistence on the permanence of reasonably pluralism is difficult to make sense of save as an expression of scepticism. Equally, 'the fact of oppression' is presented not so much as a historical datum but as a claim to the effect that things could not be otherwise, the implied explanation for this being the inevitability of pluralism as a characteristic result of the exercise of reason. These are controversial claims and the rationalist believer may want to oppose them, but even so it is hard to make plausible the idea that modern Western societies might come to exhibit the unity of Augustinian fellowships, let alone that they already are so beneath their visibly variegated surfaces.

My purpose in observing this is not to reject the coherence of a communitarian polity, nor to distance myself from the implications of the earlier discussion of the common good, namely, that we are in some respects social beings, a genuine aspect of whose *telos* is participation in shared ends. Yet some acknowledgement of the claims of pluralism is certainly necessary, and in consequence a moderation of communitarian aspirations is called for. However, given

[34] *Ibid.*, pp. 37–38.

the earlier criticisms of Rawls' attempts at neutrality, and the briefer charge that his account of citizens gives (unwarranted) priority to liberal identities over those deriving from membership in other communities (including ones defined in relation to comprehensive doctrines) there remains a need to consider just where one should stand between the poles of Augustinian and Rawlsian citizenship.

One's political nature is not independent of that 'second nature' which results from being born and raised within particular social groups sharing aesthetic, moral, philosophical, and religious inclinations communicated to successive generations in part through the cultivation of a complex sensibility. Real-world political personae rest upon these cultural identities (which they rarely obscure). Accordingly, if the mask is to fit, it must be shaped to the contours of the face, which tells against the attempt to fashion it out of a universal mold. In consequence, the order of construction in practical political philosophy should be to define the characteristic values of given communities and reflect upon how these might be expressed in the political order of a state. Among other things this approach limits the scope for a prior reasoning about the conditions of justice and political stability and directs attention toward the historical facts of community. In a way, of course, this is what Rawls himself claims to be doing, but in order to maximize the acceptability of the political conception, he then tries, unsuccessfully, to detach the account from distinctive conceptions of the good.

Elsewhere I have developed these reflections in support of the ideal of nationhood and tried to respond to the familiar concerns that this notion is anachronistic, ontologically problematic, and politically coercive.[35] I shall not turn to these matters now save to emphasize that, as I understand it, the idea of a nation is a cultural and not a racial one, conjoining history, tradition, and language, not colour and blood-group; and to acknowledge that its deployment involves the sometimes uncomfortable notion that the state

[35] See John Haldane, 'Identity, Community, and the Limits of Multiculture', section IV.

may legitimately concern itself with social formation.[36] In the present circumstance, however, I want to suggest that while national identity may be an appropriate reference point for political reflection in some contexts, it may not be so in others. And where it is weakened or absent there may be no other unifying cultural form that can serve as a naturally eligible, pre-political foundation for civil society. Attempting to establish political divisions along ethnic lines is always possible, but if this is the true condition of things then it may be better to acknowledge that in these circumstances politics is a solution to a problem of disunity rather than the expression of prior community. For some, this picture of the political order as no more than a procedural arrangement for regulating the interactions between 'strangers' will be dispiriting, especially if they are attracted by the many-layered richness of a cultural-cum-nation-state such as Great Britain; but it is often, if not always possible to combine political thinness with a rich community life, and in circumstances of radical pluralism wisdom may caution against granting a greater role to the state than the maintenance of civil peace.

A *Modus Vivendi* and Political Philosophy in Context

By now the thought is emerging that in certain circumstances, which some might argue are coming to be general within Western societies, the hope of political community having had to be abandoned and the prospect of political liberalism having proved illusory, the way forward may lie in the development of political order as a *modus vivendi*. For Rawls, this is an unsatisfactory condition that must be sharply distinguished from an overlapping consensus on a political conception of justice. The difference is marked by three features: (1) an overlapping consensus focuses on a moral conception of justice; (2) it is affirmed on moral grounds; and (3) because of these facts it enjoys a kind and

---

[36] For an example of what this might validate, see John Haldane, 'Religious Education in a Pluralist Society: A Philosophical Perspective', *British Journal of Educational Studies*, vol. 34 (1986).

degree of stability different from that of a mere *modus vivendi,* which can only depend on 'happenstance and a balance of relative forces'.[37]

I shall not begin to consider whether Rawls is entitled to, or justified in his claims on behalf of the moral superiority of an overlapping consensus. All I am concerned with is the suggestion that it possesses a greater stability than a *modus vivendi.* For this possibility may seem to force a less critical reassessment of political liberalism. In fact, Rawls allows that an overlapping consensus may not be necessary for social unity and stability, and he goes on to address the concern that it is utopian to believe that it is sufficient for it. However, the idea remains unquestioned that while stability may be achieved by other means it then will be a very precarious condition.

Why should this be thought to be so? I suspect that part of the reason is that although he refers back to the religious wars of Europe, Rawls is thinking in terms of American society and political life, which may sometimes bear the appearance of an arrangement that could easily come apart as the balance of forces changes, and with it the distribution of power. This prospect seems less likely in a political culture such as that of Great Britain. Yet it is doubtful that the stability of British society is due to an overlapping consensus on a political conception in Rawls' sense. If any perspective or noble principle is entitled to claim credit for this civil order, it is a communitarian one.

But that is too quick and too simple. From the point of articulated theory, British political society is an enigma shrouded in a mystery. On the one hand, the intellectual demeanour of its public institutions owes much to the civil and eudaimonistic liberalisms of John Locke and John Stuart Mill, both of which are respectful of individual conscience. On the other hand, and notwithstanding its lack of a formulated constitution, it is ruled by a constitutional monarch who is the head of an established church and whose government is still conducted in part by an unelected

---

[37] Rawls, *Political Liberalism,* pp. 147–48.

nobility which is most effective when rallying to such causes as the preservation of rural bus services and the maintenance of Christian education in state schools. That education derives nominally from the Church of England (and from the Presbyterian Church in Scotland – of which the sovereign is also a protector), yet the largest worshipping denomination is Roman Catholic, whose members are debarred by the act of succession from ascending to the throne or marrying the sovereign.

It is difficult to discern a principled justification for this general pattern of arrangements; I also believe it is a mistake to seek one: both insofar as there is no coherent set of organizing principles and, more importantly because the whole set-up has no obvious political purpose independent of its own continuation. Piece by piece, the elements may have been fashioned to serve particular purposes, some internal, some external; but over time they have become part of a system that remains stable because it is an embodiment of a social order that is found congenial to a civilized life.

I realize this may sound self-satisfied; however, the point I want to end on is not the supposed superiority of the British political order but the fact that for good or ill this order exists and, to the extent that it offers any justification, justifies itself independently of a theory of the *right*. Even if it originates in and is maintained by a series of pragmatic resolutions these quickly come to be the object of civic allegiance, particularly as they are given the protection of law. If this is a *modus vivendi* writ large then it certainly seems no less stable than an overlapping consensus, and it is a way of going on socially that is compatible with active participation in a range of subordinate moral communities, and with the periodic accomplishment of principled political goals.

It would be presumptuous to speculate at any length on the extent to which a similar account might be given of the United States and other polities. However, if there are real differences, as the emphasis on individual rights and the recurrent preoccupation with the meaning of the founding constitution suggest, then it would be as well for political philosophers on both sides of the Atlantic to consider the possibility that these cultural and political differences may have found their way into the reflective understanding of such concepts as *community*, *individual*, and *state*, and that most of the foundational work done during the renaissance of English-speaking political philosophy initiated by Rawls has really concerned the political foundation of North American society—an issue formulated not inappropriately, but not altogether accurately either, as 'the problem of liberalism'. Of course, it may be that even if this diagnosis were once true, the influence of US culture in Europe and elsewhere has been such that we are all now in the same moral and political situation. I doubt that this is so, however, and I certainly hope that current uncertainties about the direction of political philosophy may lead to some cultural differentiation of issues, methods, and doctrines, and to a more extensive investigation of what is available from 'old' and 'new world' figures of the past, such as Aquinas and, for example, James Madison who in the 1788 *Debate on the Federal Constitution* spoke wisely as follows:

> If there be not [virtue among us] we are in a wretched situation. No theoretical checks, no form of government, can render us secure. To suppose any form of government will secure liberty or happiness without any virtue in the people, is a chimerical idea. If there be sufficient virtue and intelligence in the community, it will be exercised in the selection of these men [of virtue and wisdom].[38]

Conclusion

In challenging the project of liberal political theory I have been concerned principally with Rawls' neutralist and individualist version of it. Directed criticism of this sort raises both a general question of the adequacy of other forms of liberalism, and, given the perspective developed in later sections, a more specific question concerning the compatibility of Roman Catholic social teaching with *any* kind of liberalism. In an essay addressed to the question of

---

[38] See *The Debates in the Several State Conventions on the Adoption of the Federal Constitution*, ed. Jonathan Elliot (Philadelphia, PA: Lippincott, 1907).

whether a Roman Catholic can be a liberal, I described the opposition between liberal theory and Catholicism in terms of fundamental disagreements about the place of morality in politics, and the status of the community and the common good.[39] There as here, the liberalism in question was principally that associated with authors such as Rawls and Ronald Dworkin, rather than Locke and Mill. While the implied distinction between 'old' and 'new' liberalisms may not be as great as some like to suppose, there is certainly a question as to whether ideas of political liberty other than those associated with contemporary contractualism, better accommodate the value of community and the claims of morality in the public sphere. In a loose and popular sense, we are all 'liberals' now or should be, and the acknowledgement of this presents a challenge to advocates of general and comprehensive doctrines to show how they can endorse commonly held liberal values. Secular perfectionists such as Joseph Raz do so by arguing that personal political freedom is an aspect of the good life (deriving from the value of autonomy and from value pluralism),[40] and something similar has been proposed by American Catholic writers influenced by the likes of Maritain and John Courtenay Murray.[41] However, while I would certainly hope for success in these ventures, the arguments generally presented seem either to beg the important questions or to fall short of their conclusions. For now, and perhaps forever, the best hope of liberty lies not in a securely determined set of liberal principles but in a humanely shaped liberal sensibility.

At the close of the previous chapter I proposed one might consider that an important reason for favouring justice, and I may now add liberty, is that these values give expression to one's understanding of oneself and others as sharing a common nature, and thereby as having a common interest in the goods appropriate to that nature. Among these is the

---

[39] See John Haldane, 'Can a Catholic Be a Liberal?' *Melita Theologica*, vol. 43 (1992) also in Haldane *Faithful Reason* (2004).

[40] See Raz, *The Morality of Freedom*, esp. chs. 14 and 15.

[41] See, for example, the essays in Hollenbach and Douglass, eds., *Catholicism and Liberalism*.

good of fellowship and I now turn to explore this idea and its potential to resolve contested issues in the spheres of political thought and practice.

10

Public Reason, Truth and Human Fellowship

Introduction

In this chapter I am interested in whether it may be useful in thinking about the issue of *public reason*, to deploy philosophical categories and styles of argumentation that antedate the kind of thinking associated with Rawls, or else to advance to some new mode of reasoning about the sorts of questions that concerned him. At this stage, I also want to move the discussion outside the Rawlsian sphere of influence. This latter interest is connected with the question of the extent to which the issues and debates about public reason arise universally within liberal societies, or whether they are particular, if not unique, to the circumstances of North America, particularly the United States.

I shall consider, therefore, different theoretical grounds on which one might discuss these issues, and different forms of political life, public institutions and public culture to which one might look to see how liberalism can be implemented outside of the context of the kind of rational construction that Rawls provided in *Political Liberalism*.

It is relevant to note that in his later study *The Law of Peoples* (1999) Rawls himself moves some way beyond the terms of his earlier discussions, for as well as considering his own democratic liberal polity he has to contemplate different kinds of regimes or domestic societies. He classifies these according to a five-fold grouping:

(1) reasonable, liberal peoples, of which the US is, or aspires to be, a clear representation;

(2) non-liberal decent peoples;

(3) outlaw states;

(4) societies burdened by unfavorable conditions;

(5) benevolent absolutisms.

It is interesting to observe the way, and the extent, to which Rawls is forced to think on other grounds about the legitimation these various forms of social institutions and political societies might enjoy. He does this in part to determine their justification (or lack of it), but also to consider the relations that well-ordered liberal polities might have with other societies, considering what might be fair grounds of cooperation with them.

This chapter's title contains a reference to an essay by Jacques Maritain, 'Truth and Human Fellowship',[1] which is notable in part for its anticipation of Rawls' later concerns, but also for observing an interesting oscillation between a liberty-destroying zeal *for* truth, and a form of sceptical and intolerant detachment *from* truth. Maritain believes that scepticism and relativism ultimately lead to a kind of intolerance, and may themselves be expressions of it. His response to this oscillation is captured in an idea that initially may seem unpromising, for it sounds rather thin and pietistic. Maritain maintains that the oscillation between liberty-destroying zeal, and sceptical and intolerant detachment — the fanaticisms of absolutism and of doubt — may be arrested and transcended by "humility, together with faith in truth'. I quote:

---

[1] Jacques Maritain, 'Truth and Human Fellowship' in *On the Uses of Philosophy: Three Essays* (Princeton: Princeton University Press, 1961). Another of Maritain's writings on social philosophy that is both very interesting in itself and remarkably prescient when one explores the terms of the debate about liberalism as Rawls has conducted it is *Man and the State* (Chicago: University of Chicago Press, 1951).

[T]he error of the absolutists ... comes from the fact that they shift their right feelings about the object [truth and falsity] to the subject; and they think that just as error has no rights of its own ... so man when he is in error has no rights of his own ... [T]he error of the theorists who make relativism, ignorance and doubt a necessary condition for mutual tolerance comes from the fact that they shift their right feelings about the human subject ... to the object; and thus they deprive man and the human intellect of the very act—adherence to the truth—in which consists both man's dignity and reason for living.

[But] it is truth, not ignorance, which makes us humble, and gives us the sense of what remains unknown in our very knowledge. ... There is a real and genuine tolerance only when a man is firmly and absolutely convinced of a truth, or what he holds to be a truth, and when he at the same time recognizes the right of those who deny this truth to exist and to contradict him ... not because they are free from truth but because they seek truth in their own way, and because he respects in them human nature and human dignity and those very resources and living springs of the intellect and of conscience which make them potentially capable of attaining the truth he loves.[2]

Prominent among the resources he has in mind is a kind of knowledge relevant to the guidance of conduct which (following Aquinas) he elsewhere identifies as 'knowledge through connaturality' or 'knowledge through inclination'.[3] Maritain contrasts this with rational knowledge

---

[2]   Maritain, 'Truth and Human Fellowship' p. 24.

[3]   See in particular 'On Knowledge through Connaturality' *Review of Metaphysics*, 4 (1951) Ch. 3 of *The Range of Reason* (New York: Scribner's 1952). Anscombe uses the term 'connatural knowledge' in connection with ethics to refer to the knowledge possessed by the virtuous agent but writes 'I haven't been able to find St Thomas giving the term the application I have been describing. Indeed I don't know the source of that application', 'Knowledge and Reverence for Life' in *Human Life, Action and Ethics* (2005). I doubt she picked it up from reading Maritain (to whom, I believe, she nowhere refers in her writings); more likely she heard someone use the term who had got it from Maritain. As regards Aquinas, see *Summa Theologiae* II. II, q.45, a2. *responsio*, where he writes: 'Now rectitude of judgment is twofold: first, on account of perfect use of reason, secondly, on account of a certain connaturality with the matter about which one has to judge. Thus, about matters of chastity, a man after inquiring with his reason forms a right judgment, if he has learnt the science of morals, while he

which consists in conceptually-structured judgments and discursive reasoning, suggesting that while connatural knowledge may be obscure and unsystematic, it is nonetheless vital to morality and politics. The idea of connatural cognition needs some unpacking which I will provide later. Of immediate relevance, however, is the fact that Maritain is concerned with knowledge through the agent's or knower's inclinations, and the associated idea that this knowledge presupposes a philosophy of nature. That is to say, an account both of the nature of the knower and of that of the things known which reveals them to be part of the same structured reality; the upshot being a natural law account of value and conduct.

A moral or political theory is distinctively and fully a case of natural law only if it has something to say both about the way in which the *knowledge* it involves is natural, and about the *subject-matter* itself being part of nature; in short, only if it is naturalistic in form and in content.[4] In contrast to the so-called 'new natural law' theorists, who came to prominence in the period following his death (in 1973) Maritain does not think that natural law ethics or political philosophy is a matter of intuiting self-evident truths.[5] There is, for him, only one principle that admits of *a priori* resolution, and it is an axiom that is not itself part of the natural law, but is in some way regulative of it. He writes:

> The only practical knowledge all men have naturally and infallibly in common is as a self-evident principle, [the

who has the habit of chastity judges of such matters by a kind of connaturality'.

[4]   By 'naturalistic' in this context I do not, of course, mean only that which is recognized by natural science.

[5]   See Germain Grisez, 'The First Principle of Practical Reason: A Commentary on the *Summa Theologiae*, 1-2, Question 94, Article 2', *Natural Law Forum* 10 (1965); John Finnis, *Natural Law and Natural Rights* (Oxford: Clarendon Press, 1980); Germain Grisez, Joseph Boyle, and John Finnis, 'Practical Principles, Moral Truth, and Ultimate Ends', *American Journal of Jurisprudence* 32 (1987); and Robert P. George *In Defence of Natural Law* (Oxford: Clarendon Press, 1999). For criticism see Russell Hittinger, *A Critique of the New Natural Law Theory* (Southbend, IN: University of Notre Dame Press, 1994). In this connection also see John Haldane, 'Thomistic Ethics in America', *Logos*, 3 (2000).

synderesis rule] intellectually perceived by virtue of the concepts involved, is that we must do good and avoid evil. This is the preamble and the principle of natural law; it is not the law itself.[6]

This reveals what I described in chapter one ('Practical Ethics') as the 'internal' or conceptual relationship between action and the concept of the good. This is relevant to solving a problem with which moral philosophers are familiar, one which has given rise to the debate between internalists and externalists about the issue of motivation. Suppose reality contained fully objective non-relational values positioned above and beyond the nature, needs and interests (though not necessarily the interest) of human beings. One might then ask what claim they make on us. John Mackie sought to make difficulty for moral objectivism by saying that it was inconceivable that there should be intrinsically motivating features of mind-independent reality, and posited instead internal psychological forces.[7] The issue is not an empty one, but it is best dealt with by trying to understand the notion of practical rather than speculative truth, and the *synderesis* rule explained earlier and cited by Maritain is central to that understanding. I shall return to this.

Rawlsian Political Philosophy and its Assumptions

The tremendous influence of Rawls, not just in terms of ideas that he was concerned to communicate and argue for but in re-animating the entire subject of political philosophy within Anglo-American thought, derives in part from the fact that his work possesses an imaginative power that was extremely rare in the subject when he took it up. As a result of his example people were persuaded that serious analytical and normative thinking could get to work on the resolution of topics that many had hitherto supposed could only

---

[6]   J. Maritain, 'The Ontological and Epistemological Elements of Natural Law', Chapter 2 of *Natural Law: Reflections on Theory and Practice*, edited by W. Sweet (South Bend, IN: St Augustine's Press, 2001) p. 32.

[7]   J. L. Mackie, *Ethics: Inventing Right and Wrong* (Harmondsworth: Penguin Books, 1977) Part One, Ch. 1, sec. 9.

be the subject-matter of historical investigation. One only needs to know something of the state of political thought in the English-speaking world in the mid-twentieth century to see what a transformation Rawls effected. Writing in 1956 in the introduction to the first series of *Philosophy, Politics and Society*, Peter Laslett famously wrote that 'The tradition [of political philosophy] has been broken ... For the moment, anyway, political philosophy is dead'.[8] By 1979, however, the introduction to the fifth series records a dramatic change:

> 'No commanding work of political theory has appeared in the 20th century.' So said Isaiah Berlin, writing in 1962 in the second volume of *Philosophy, Politics and Society*, in answer to the question 'Does political theory still exist?' He was taking up [the] point made in the introduction to the first volume. The outstanding difference now, in 1978, is that Berlin's assertion is no longer true. It ceased to be so in 1971, when *A Theory of Justice* by John Rawls of Harvard was published in Cambridge, Mass.[9]

Conjoined with his imaginative power was an intense concern with the issue of fairness, particularly in the period of *A Theory of Justice* with fairness in the distribution of goods.[10] Again, Rawls demonstrated a seriousness of motivation that has not always characterized political philosophy. In addition there was the patent sincerity of his own discussions. All of that said, however, there may be some naiveté in his later work, in the aspiration to bring people on board by showing them that they are already more than halfway to the Rawlsian position.

This shows itself in part in his discussions of natural law and of Catholic teaching on the principles of the just war, as he describes them both. In *The Law of Peoples* Rawls notes the extent to which his views about just war are coincident with Catholic teaching, but then observes one point of diver-

---

[8]   *Philosophy, Politics and Society*, ed. P. Laslett (Oxford: Blackwell, 1956) p. 1.

[9]   *Philosophy, Politics and Society*, Fifth Series, eds. P. Laslett & J. Fishkin (Oxford: Blackwell, 1979) p. 1.

[10]   John Rawls, *A Theory of Justice* (Oxford: Oxford University Press, 1972).

gence: that in the circumstances of supreme emergency, it is (on his view) permissible to kill civilians. This point of difference is in fact so great that one should wonder whether there can have been much in the way of commonality to begin with. Rawls recognizes that doubt yet emphasizes and repeats that he and those in the Catholic natural law and just war traditions share values and understandings.[11]

In his discussion of the idea of public reason there are dubious assumptions about the nature of political disagreement itself and about the proper and necessary forms of agreement. In addition, there are difficulties in his treatment of the very idea of public reason. These flawed assumptions and difficulties involve a series of false oppositions.

One such assumption is that the only normatively warranted political scheme must either be a case of a universally-shared philosophy, where the participants in political discourse and political life share a comprehensive doctrine (an option that Rawls thinks is no longer viable); or else a restricted political conception of the sort he articulates. Again, he tends to assume that the only relevant attitudes towards governmental institutions and their exercise of power, are either that of agreeing with the normative grounds that are given for them; or disagreeing with those philosophical foundations. Further, he is inclined to think that the sole grounds of fair cooperation are either liberal, and largely formal; or else are substantive and generally illiberal. Finally, he assumes that institutions stand justified either by articulable reasons to which participants have access (at least ideally), or else they remain unjustified.

Each of those oppositions seems to be flawed: (1) that we can only have a normatively warranted scheme if we are talking about either a universally shared comprehensive doctrine, or a narrow political conception; (2) that we only have the options of agreeing or disagreeing with the grounds on which something is advocated; (3) that we have to be either liberal and formal, or substantive and illiberal;

[11]   For some discussion of this point see John Haldane, 'Ethics, Religion, and Relativism', *Review of Metaphysics*, 60 (2006).

and (4) that we need to have an articulated justification, or else institutions stand unjustified.

To some extent, these assumptions reflect a broader pattern in American political thought, and they look rather different when viewed from within European traditions, particularly if one considers those informed by certain strands of conservatism, especially that associated with Burke, in which there is a kind of imminent justification that is not articulated through reason but is expressed through the forms and conduct of institutions. This can be understood by looking at the problem of political legitimacy under conditions of pluralism. At the outset of *Political Liberalism*, Rawls asks 'how is it possible for there to exist over time a just and stable society of free and equal citizens, who remain profoundly divided by reasonable religious, philosophical, and moral doctrines?'[12]

If one thinks about political disagreement in modern societies this is a curious choice as the central problem of political philosophy. For a good deal of the time the issues that have concerned both political philosophers and political agents have not been the question of political agreement in the face of conflicting philosophical outlooks, but rather issues of political agreement and disagreement arising from the competition over material goods and social position. Aside from security, the most prominent issues in general elections in the United Kingdom (and in the United States, including Presidential elections) concern the ownership and distribution of society's resources, fair employment, the minimum wage, the extent to which socialized health care and public welfare is appropriate, and so on. There is extensive disagreement but the disagreement is around questions of the propriety of taxation and suchlike: in other words the familiar range of political issues debated within modern liberal polities. Accordingly, one might expect that the main focus of a discussion on political disagreement in the modern world would be over the principles and foundations of social justice, not justice in the respect in which

---

[12] *Political Liberalism*, p. 4.

that is contemplated by Rawls in *Political Liberalism*. Certainly his earlier concerns were precisely with justice as distributive fairness, but those were replaced in later work with concerns for what one might term 'participatory fairness'. For Rawls, and this should seem curiously abstract and rationalistic, the main challenge for contemporary political theory arises from philosophical disagreement, which he assumes yields political disagreement.

This invites two questions. First, is philosophical disagreement as widespread and as extensive as a reading of Rawls would suggest? are philosophical issues present in the very midst of political life? Second, even to the extent that they may be present in the background, do they actually yield political disagreement?

If one thinks about the circumstances of political dispute as those pose challenges for political regimes, there is certainly a good range of grounds of disagreement. One such involves issues of cultural diversity. This need not be about competing comprehensive doctrines; rather it may relate to behavioural and life-style differences arising from the mixing of cultures. So, for example, youths and young adult members of one group may spend much time on the street socializing. Members of another group may have very strong networks of family who tend to be mercantile in their dispositions and to be busy indoors. Examples easily multiply in number and in respect of contrasting features. Here there is cultural diversity with contests and disagreement and questions about political resolutions with regard to issues, for example, styles of policing. But these are not best represented as contests of competing comprehensive doctrines.

Again, think about the kind of positional competition that goes on over issues about social status. Even a society such as that of the US, that prides itself on having overcome traditional forms of class division, still behaves in ways analogous to those of older socially stratified societies. To take one familiar and topical example: colleges and universities have to make decisions about admitting students, and in the case of the most prestigious institutions there will be many more well-qualified applicants than can be admitted. These institutions are then faced with the challenge of distributing the educational goods they have to offer, while recognizing that there are other goods attendant upon being admitted to such places, to which applicants perhaps attach considerable value, but which admissions officers would not themselves necessarily value highly, if at all. In these circumstances students are competing for a positional good, having attended a socially well-regarded college, which the institution would not necessarily endorse, but nevertheless it has to make admission decisions among applicants all or most of whom are motivated by the idea of attaining that positional good. This is a further example of contested political values that has nothing to do with competition between comprehensive doctrines.

There are a number of grounds of disagreement that may or may not make one optimistic about the possibility of securing political good order. But they should give one reason to wonder whether we should strive for agreement about a substantive political conception, or instead rest content with a political *modus vivendi*

Why exactly for Rawls does political disagreement about a political conception seem to be so problematic? There are two connected reasons. First, there is the belief that the exercise of political power will only be legitimate where it is exercised through constitutional arrangements that all could reasonably be expected reasonably to endorse. This links in with the principle of reciprocity and related ideas. Second, there is the assumption, already considered that an order will only be stable if it is legitimate as previously (partly) specified. So in reply to the question as to why exactly political disagreement about a political conception is so problematic we get the answer: because in order to be stable a political order has to be legitimate; and it will only be legitimate when power is exercised in accord with constitutional arrangements and institutions that all could reasonably be expected reasonably to endorse.

It is clearly contentious, however, to suppose, as Rawls does, that legitimacy only obtains under those conditions.

Moreover, the argument he gives in support of this supposition moves between two kinds of endorsement in which one might be interested. One sort would involve simply *accepting an arrangement*; another would involve *accepting the reasons* that might be given for it: the foundational, substantive reasons afforded in support of it. But the first of these endorsements, agreeing to the arrangement, permits one to dispute the foundations on which that arrangement might have been based.[13]

This is illustrated by two examples from the United Kingdom touched on earlier. First, there is the existence of an externally unelected legislative assembly, including some element of the hereditary principle. The upper chamber of the UK Parliament, the House of Lords, is just such an unelected body. Second, there is the establishment of religion: not religion in general, but a specific denomination of a particular faith: the Church of England. These come together in the Lords in the form of the Lords Spiritual where the senior Anglican Bishops are in the House as unelected members representing the established church.

It is possible for an individual to have no objection to the unelected upper house, and to have no objection to the establishment of the Church of England, and even to want to uphold those two arrangements. But that is not to say that such a person agrees with the foundational reasons that might be given for them, such as the principles expressed in the 1534 Act of Supremacy, the 1563 Thirty-Nine Articles, the 1660 Lords Restoration Act, the 1689 Bill of Rights, the various Acts of Settlement, and so on. If somebody were laying out foundations and principles from which religious establishment and constitutional religious monarchism might be argued for in a principled way, and on the basis of comprehensive doctrines, a person who accepted the fact and operation of these elements of the state might nevertheless dispute those reasons as grounds. In that sense he is not endorsing the arrangement on the basis of agreeing with the

---

[13] By the same token, endorsing an arrangement as being justified by the reasons given for it, does not commit one to accepting that arrangement as being a reasonable one.

foundation provided for it, but nonetheless is happy to agree *to* the arrangement inasmuch as he sees it as having a certain kind of value.

So much for *legitimacy*. With regard to *stability* the claim that an order is stable only if it is legitimate is even more contentious. Setting aside a question-begging definition of stability in terms of Rawlsian legitimacy, the thesis will not bear much scrutiny. Rawls suggests that if you look at polities that do not enjoy the kind of political legitimacy that would be required by Rawlsian argumentation these can be seen to be liable to factionalism, division, and so on. But this is contestable. Once again the United Kingdom suggests itself as an obvious example of a state that enjoys enormous stability but does not meet the conditions of Rawlsian political legitimacy, at least in respect of several of its main institutions.

A further aspect of Rawls' approach worth identifying and to some extent worrying about, is the ambition to remove issues from the domain of political contest and to embed and protect them as constitutional rights. This can leave people frustrated, feeling that with regard to seriously contested issues it ought to be possible to make the argument, and to go on making the argument even if you lose it, in the hope that one day you may be successful. The Rawlsian aspiration is to remove as much as possible that is contentious out of the sphere of ongoing political contention. In the United Kingdom, unlike the USA, there is still no written state constitution and Parliament is sovereign; hence any law that has been made can in turn be unmade by subsequent legislation. One might worry that this would induce anxiety and instability, as against the assurance of constitutional protection, but history shows it to be otherwise.

Indeed, constitutional entrenchment may undermine more extensively citizens' sense of participation in the life of the state. Opponents of bills of rights and of codified constitutions argue the danger that certain things will be put beyond the sphere of political contest; where instead society should facilitate argument about contested issues, and not seek to see them removed from the forum of debate. If that means that one side loses the battle at some time, it can still hope to return and argue it successfully another day. Members of society who hold clear and definite views, articulate them and are a part of the public debate are more committed and happier citizens — and recalling Maritain's observations, they may also be more tolerant ones. By contrast, in circumstances in which there is a continuous effort to try and remove contentious issues from the sphere of political oppositions, such persons are at risk of having their active citizenship diminished because they are no longer able to articulate their views with intent of affecting these matters.

Rawlsian Public Reason and its Restrictions

Rawls identifies three respects in which reason may be said to be 'public'.[14] First, it is the reason *of* the public, the reason of free and equal citizens. Second, it is public inasmuch as it has as its subject the public good, and not individual goods. Third, it is public in its nature and in its content. Indeed, a good deal of his essay 'The Idea of Public Reason Revisited' (hereafter 'Public Reason') is concerned with articulating the sense in which it is public in this last respect.

In advance of the particular interpretation that Rawls attached to some of these terms, the general three-part characterisation is one with which many could agree. Public reason is the reason of the public, concerning the public good, and is public in nature and content. The problem, however, comes with the interpretation of the idea that public reason is public in character (and again in substance). Rawls constrains the sense of this via an interlocking system of concepts. Thus *citizen, liberty, equality,* and *reasonable public persons' political values* exist in a kind of inter-defining network of relationships. This gives the system one kind of strength, but it also opens it to the risk of being rejected in total, or much more likely of simply being bypassed.

Rawls progressively closes the discussion by insisting on certain interpretations of these central terms. So you may

---

[14] See p. 133 of 'The Idea of Public Reason Revisited' in *The Law of Peoples* (Cambridge, MA: Harvard University Press, 1999).

begin by saying, 'I agree that public reason is public in the following three respects', but then it turns out that the notion of 'free and equal citizens' gets a particular interpretation, as does the notion of 'public good', and also the idea of it being 'public in nature and content'. The fact that those terms receive special renderings is not in itself reason to object to them, but it is extremely important to be aware that they are further defined, often in unobvious ways.

To illustrate this it is worth looking at three or four places in 'The Idea of Public Reason Revisited' where this interpretative demand is placed on these terms, or is introduced in the explication of them. Early on we get the criterion of reciprocity, which again seems unexceptionable antecedent to any interpretation. But reciprocity is given Rawls' own particular interpretation, as when he writes that 'those proposing terms as being the most reasonable of fair cooperation must think it at least reasonable for others to accept them as free and equal citizens and not as dominated or manipulated or under pressure caused by an inferior political or social position.'[15] The problem here is that this mixes the commonplace with an implicitly defined theoretical expression 'free and equal citizens'. Shortly thereafter, he writes:

> Those who reject public reason, who seek to resolve fundamental political questions by best reasons as these derive from their idea of the whole truth—including their religious or secular comprehensive doctrines—and not by reasons that might be shared by all citizens as free and equal, will of course reject the idea of public reason. Political liberalism views this insistence on the whole truth as incompatible with democratic citizenship and the idea of legitimate law.[16]

Here the danger is of equivocation on the notion of *insistence on the whole truth*. A person might insist on the whole truth in terms of this argumentation, but not insist on the implementation of the whole truth as that argument yields it. So such a person might well want to say 'the whole comprehensive doctrine has to be advanced here, but it does not

[15] 'Public Reason', p. 136-7.
[16] 'Public Reason', p. 138.

have all to be implemented'. He might be willing to compromise over how much of the whole truth gets into the political order. So the idea that critics of public reason inappropriately and improperly 'insist on the whole truth' seems to derive some of its plausibility from the suggestion that those who want to argue in a certain way are insisting on the implementation of the whole truth. Whereas one might want to insist upon reliance upon the whole truth but then negotiate how much of it goes into the political regime.

Again Rawls says, 'a citizen engages in public reason when he or she deliberates within a framework of what he or she regards as the most reasonable political conception of justice. One would express his political values that others as free and equal citizens might also reasonably be expected reasonably to endorse.'[17] This is heavily loaded with Rawlsian interpretations. The claim that 'a citizen engages in public reason when he or she deliberates within a framework of what he or she regards as the most reasonable political conception' sounds like something we might all want to sign up to. It is the unpacking that follows, however, that makes it clear that it expresses political values specified in Rawlsian respects. Just as 'free and equal citizens' is defined in terms of political liberalism; so 'reasonable political conception', and 'reasonably be expected reasonably to endorse' are given particular interpretations within Rawls's theory. Again, now under the heading of 'The Content of Public Reason' he writes:

> Political liberalism, then, does not try to fix public reason once and for all in the form of one favoured political conception of justice. That would not be a sensible approach. For instance, political liberalism also admits Habermas's discourse conception of legitimacy (sometimes said to be radically democratic rather than liberal), as well as Catholic views of common good and solidarity *when they are expressed in terms of political values*.[18] [*my emphasis*]

But once more 'political values' gets a Rawlsian reading. At one point he describes the proviso, the circumstance

---

[17] 'Public Reason', p. 140.
[18] 'Public Reason', p. 142.

under which we can rely upon the expression of comprehensive doctrines (particularly religious ones) so long as we are willing at some future point to substitute public reason discourse. Describing this Rawls appears concessive, saying that there should be 'no restriction as to how doctrines may be expressed.' Indeed, this apparent licence might well dismay an avowedly secular liberal. Yet the concession is only temporary for the believer is required in due course, and before too long, to move to public discourse constrained by the requirement to eschew comprehensive doctrines.

As I argued in the preceding chapter the weakness of Rawls' attempt to make space for religion in the public square, and to bring its adherents on board in the journey to political liberalism, shows itself in his treatment of abortion. This was the subject of a controversial footnote in *Political Liberalism* and what he offers in 'The Idea of Public Reason Revisited' is no less problematic. Matters are not to be resolved on the basis of truth or moral rationality, but by reference to reasonability. It is worth quoting the passage; and to sharpen attention by adding the expression 'and infanticide' following occurrences of 'abortion'.[19] This, of course, does *not* occur in the original and Rawls nowhere discusses infanticide.

> In particular, when hotly disputed questions, such as that of abortion [and infanticide] arise, which may lead to a stand-off between different political conceptions, citizens must vote on the question according to their complete ordering of political values. Indeed, this is a normal case: unanimity of views is not to be expected. Reasonable political conceptions of justice do not always lead to the same conclusion; nor do citizens holding the same conception also agree on particular issues. Yet the outcome of the vote, as I said before, is to be seen as legitimate provided all government officials supported by other reasonable citizens of a reasonably just constitutional regime sincerely vote in accordance with the idea of public reason. [Note: not the idea of individual conscience, but the idea of public rea-

[19] This is not to make a claim about the nature of abortion. Instead, it serves to highlight the terms under which we might find ourselves contesting the question of the legitimacy of a polity of infanticide.

son.] This doesn't mean the outcome is true or correct, but that it is reasonable and legitimate law, binding on citizens by the majority principle.

Some may, of course, reject a legitimate decision, as Roman Catholics may reject a decision to grant a right to abortion [and infanticide]. They may present an argument in public reason for denying it and fail to win a majority, But they need not themselves exercise the right to abortion [and infanticide].[20]

Then he goes on to say:

I do not discuss the question of abortion [and infanticide] in itself since my concern is not with that question but rather to stress that political liberalism does not hold that the idea of public reason should always lead to a general agreement of views, nor is it a fault if it does not. ...

However, as I said at the beginning, in public reason, ideas of truth or right based on comprehensive doctrines are replaced by my idea of the politically reasonable addressed to citizens as citizens.[21]

Here Rawls positions himself centrally within contemporary political philosophy in seeking to remove moral issues from the content of politics; interpreting the proper subject of the latter as being *not* substantial moral questions, but instead the circumstances and character of the kind of reasoning and settlement that might be arrived at concerning the legitimation of law and observance of it. This outlook is distinctly modern and might be viewed as a case of a more general limitation of the ambition of philosophy to address substantive questions about the character of reality, the structure of nature, and the ends and activities proper to humanity — each in turn having been largely deemed to be either illusory topics or else the province of empirical sciences.

Thomistic Natural Law

Maritain's approach to political philosophy stands in marked contrast, as does that of Aquinas whom he follows. For the Thomistic-Aristotelian, the notions of practical

---

[20] 'Public Reason', pp. 170–1.
[21] 'Public Reason', p. 171.

truth, and of objective value and requirement are keyed to an account of the nature of agents as persons, conceived not in narrowly political terms but as rational, animate substances. All of which contribute to a general and comprehensive moral doctrine.[22] Imagining a diagram dividing Thomistic and Rawlsian approaches to political philosophy, the foregoing elements would be listed on one side and then on the Rawlsian half would be the politically reasonable (set opposite truth and objective value), based on the contractualist demand of reciprocity (rather than on objective requirement), and then accounts of the nature of agents as citizens, and of the nature of society as political (set against a philosophy of human nature). Rawls himself implicitly recognizes something of this contrast in his discussions.[23]

Thomistic natural law proceeds to the political via the more broadly moral; that being drawn from a normative philosophical anthropology, which is itself situated within a teleological philosophy of nature; the whole being located inside a general metaphysics. Consider Aquinas writing on the precepts of the natural law in the *Summa Theologiae*:

> Now as 'being' is the first thing grasped simply [in cognition], so 'good' is the first thing grasped by the practical reason [*primum quod cadit in apprehensione simpliciter, ita bonum est primum quod cadit in apprehensione practicae rationis*], which is oriented to action: for every agent acts for an end conceived of as good. Consequently the first principle of practical reason is one founded on the notion of the good. ... Hence this is the first precept of law, that 'good is to be done and pursued, and evil is to be avoided.' All other natural law precepts are based upon this: so that whatever practical reason naturally apprehends as man's good (or evil) belongs to the precepts of the natural law as something to be done or to be avoided.
>
> Since, however, good has the nature of an end, and evil, the nature of a contrary, so those things to which man has a natural inclination, are naturally apprehended by reason as being good, and consequently as objects of pursuit, and their contraries as evil, and objects of avoidance. Thus, the

[22] For Rawls' definitions of general, comprehensive and fully comprehensive moral doctrines see *Political Liberalism*, p. 13.

[23] See 'Public Reason', pp. 103–5.

order of natural law precepts corresponds to the order of natural inclinations.

(i) There is first of all an inclination to good in accordance with the nature which human beings share with all substances: inasmuch as every substance seeks the preservation of its own being, according to its nature: and by reason of this inclination, whatever is a means of preserving human life, and of warding off its obstacles, belongs to the natural law.

(ii) Second, man has an inclination to things that relate to him more specifically, according to that nature which he shares with other animals: and in virtue of this inclination, those things are said to belong to the natural law, 'which nature has taught to all animals'[24] such as sexual intercourse, education of offspring and so forth.

(iii) Third, man is inclined to good, according to the nature of his reason, which is proper to him: thus human beings have a natural inclination to know the truth about God, and to live in society: and in this respect, whatever belongs to this inclination belongs also to the natural law; for example, to shun ignorance, to avoid offending those among whom one has to live, and other similar things.[25]

This is an important passage exhibiting the link between *nature, reason, action* and the *good*, and introducing the idea of a dependent correspondence between right rule and natural inclination, or between precepts and purposes. The philosophy of natural law has three fundamental aspects or components:

(1)   an account of knowledge of the law;

(2)   an account of the grounds of the law (and of their deeper ontological roots);

(3)   an account of the content of the law.

In respect of its epistemology, the Thomistic version recognises a via media between pure rational *a priorism*, and scientific *a posteriorism*. The former is represented by those who think that ethical knowledge is a matter of intuition of a synthetic *a priori* sort. The latter by those who look to a narrowly empirical anthropology, but then struggle with the

[24]   Quote from *Digesta seu Pandectae* part of the body of civil law *Corpus Juris Civilis*, issued under Justinian I. from Pandect. I, i.

[25]   *Summa Theologiae*, q. 94, a. 2 *responsio*.

question of how facts about human beings could give rise to any normative properties — the familiar challenge to ethical naturalism.

According to Aquinas and Maritain the answer comes through a mode of practical knowledge whose object is practical truth. This is not a form of speculative or scientific knowledge focused upon an array of facts that stand independent of engaged and committed animate agency. Rather, it is a way of understanding what it is you are already doing, not by observing it from the spectator perspective but by doing it as an expression or exercise of first person practical knowledge. Herein also lies the importance of the *synderesis* rule, for it shows that the first principle of practical reason is one that expresses the essential orientation to action of the practical recognition of the good. As we saw in chapter one, given this practical orientation the 'is-ought' problem cannot be formulated as one of an unbridgeable gap, since 'good' and 'ought to be done' are already inter-defined.

It is a principle of Aristotelian methodology that acts are specified by their objects, powers are specified by their acts, and agents are specified by their powers. In other words, if you want to know what a thing is, identify its capacities, and to know what capacities it has, look at what it does, and to see what it does, observe how it interacts with its environment. An understanding of the nature of the thing is arrived at by studying its characteristic operations. In many cases this will be a form of speculative or theoretical knowledge. When you observe chemistry experiments you see how substances interact. You work out whether some have corrosive powers with respect to others. On the basis of those, you then define the agents as acids, say. But in the case of the practical mode, where you are yourself the acting substance, finding out what you are about is not generally a matter of observing yourself in that way. It is found out in and through *doing*. This is part of what Maritain has in mind when he talks about co-naturality: a nature expresses both itself and its orientation to the good through its activities.

In the case of non-rational agents, animate or otherwise their operations are just that, non-rational. But where an agent is rational so too are many of its activities which are directed by its cognitive powers and appetites. And here there is the possibility of knowing the nature of the agent reflexively, by coming to understand what one is doing through doing it. Human beings have, individually and socially, an immanent orientation towards the good. Their nature, powers, and acts, in the case of practical rationality, are directed towards value. Intellectual powers are those fitted for and aimed at attaining truth; active powers are fitted for and oriented towards obtaining the good.

Truth, Disagreement and Fellowship

Returning to the political mode, human beings discover the object of their collective agency, the social good, through the pursuit of it. This reflexive practice of the good is also embodied in institutions. Save, however, under conditions of considerable intellectual refinement it is not expressible independently of the social forms and structures to which it has given rise. An institution such as an established church, or the hereditary principle in politics, are instances of immanent social rationality, and of the collective pursuit of the good.

What then of moral and political disagreement? Rawls is inclined to see this as involving clashes of outlooks each of which is assured of its own credentials and correctness and thereby discounts the corresponding claims of the others. Instead, however, one may view the matter in terms of a common human project limited by shared human fallibility. When considering social policy one has to bring into into play a variety of factors: experience, evaluative sensibilities, historical knowledge, philosophical clarification, and so on. Inevitably there will be disagreements, but these are more easily accepted when there is a shared aspiration to discover a common normative grounding in objective truth. While working towards that end in faith, hope and charity (not necessarily conceived of theologically) we should in the meantime, and for as long as it takes, settle for a *modus vivendi*, recognizing it to be a respectable and responsible arrangement given our common fallibility in discerning practical truth.

When Maritain wrote of the problem of truth and human fellowship being important for democratic societies because their members hold to a diversity of religious or philosophical creeds, he made the point that fanaticism and intolerance are primarily features of people, not of ideas. Those who believe that truth is one and indivisible must remember that (by their account) these are features of the *object* of judgement; and not transfer their attitudes of resolve, conviction and commitment from the goal of attaining truth towards their fellow citizens, transforming them in the process so that the latter's presumed errors become grounds for excluding them from fellowship. Maritain's message to those who see truth as warranting tyranny is not to affirm or to deny both jointly but to hold fast to truth while giving up on tyranny. Yet that itself is a moral undertaking. There is no direct route to it other than through habituation, which is why ultimately liberalism is a sensibility, and not a set of principles. The only way of avoiding tyranny is by cultivating the virtue of liberal toleration,

Let the comprehensive doctrines come to the table, the forum or the assembly. Let them present themselves in their own terms, but also in a manner whose animating principles include toleration. Rawls insists that it is not part of his position that the burdens of judgment under which political deliberation operates constitute scepticism.[26] But if we are not to be sceptical about practical rationality (concerning ends as well as means), then there is no reason to fear the advancement of comprehensive doctrines in a context in which we settle for a *modus vivendi* sustained by a shared humane liberality. Indeed, there is reason to regard this as a desirable goal, and one more ennobling in its account of humankind than is the conception of political society as sustained by the systematic curtailment of substantive philoso-

[26] *Political Liberalism*, II, 2.

phies of human nature and conduct. Finally then, whereas for Rawls, 'in public reason ideas of truth or rights based on comprehensive doctrines are replaced by [the] idea of the politically reasonable addressed to citizens as citizens'; for Maritain, by contrast, the idea of practical truth is the basis of practical reason, including political reasonability as addressed to others in human fellowship.

Conclusion

In this chapter the idea of common human fellowship has emerged as a pre-political relational condition available to those who recognize a common nature directed towards certain families of natural goods. It has been focused on from the point of view of the pursuit of truth and thus primarily as cognitively oriented. Yet fellow enquirers are also associates of other kinds and in the contexts that exercised Rawls, namely ones of conflict within particular political societies, fellow enquirers would also be fellow citizens. Seen in this light one might now consider what their wider moral relationships to one another might be. That is evidently a very large question but in the following chapter I seek to deal with one quite specific part or region of it concerning an aspect of social solidarity and its implications for government policy and public law.

11

Crime, Compensation and Social Solidarity

Introduction[1]

At the close of chapter seven in which I discussed the nature and value of family life I suggested that the best advice that philosophers and social theorists might offer to policy makers is to allow, and to some degree to enable families to flourish in the ways that families themselves recognise are best. In that connection it would be no bad thing if critics of parental autonomy who seek to strengthen 'the government's role in the parent-child-State axis' were to reflect upon the following sets of words of Edmund Burke:

(a) I set out with a perfect distrust of my own abilities, a total renunciation of every speculation of my own, and with a profound reverence for the wisdom of our ancestors.

(b) The mutual desires of the sexes uniting their bodies and affections, and the children, which were the results of these intercourses, introduced first the notion of society, and taught its conveniences. This society, founded in natural appetites and instincts, and not in any positive institution, I shall call *natural society*

(c) To be attached to the subdivision, to love the little platoon we belong to in society [the family], is the first principle (the germ as it were) of public affections. It is the first link in the series by which we proceed to a love to our coun-

---

[1] This chapter incorporates (as sections 2–6) an essay co-authored with Anthony Harvey first published in the *Journal of Applied Philosophy*, 12 (1995) and later anthologized in Hugh LaFollette, *Ethics in Practice* (1997). That essay originated in a longer co-authored text which appears as *Appendix A* to *Compensating the Victim of Crime*, Report of an Independent Working Party (London: Victim Support 1993).

try and to mankind. The interests of that portion of social arrangement is a trust in the hands of all those who compose it and none but bad men would justify it in abuse.[2]

As I also argued, however, in exceptional circumstances it may be necessary for the state, operating at one or more levels, to intervene to protect children from their families. This is a case of the exercise of political authority and coercive power applied in the interest of the good of members of society. While it is natural to think of that good as attaching to the immediate beneficiaries of state intervention there is also the common good to be considered. In chapter nine 'The Individual, the State and the Common Good' I explored something of this idea as it was introduced by Aquinas and developed by later Thomists. For Aquinas himself *'bonum commune'* and the need to provide for it both justifies and constrains the existence and operations of what he terms 'a principle of government' i.e. a political authority. Earlier I quoted him saying that 'since law is most of all ordered to the common good, it is necessary that any other precept concerning a particular matter must needs lack the nature of law except insofar as it is ordered to the common good'[3] and elsewhere he writes:

> The fellowship of society being natural and necessary to man, it follows with equal necessity that there must be some principle of government within the society. For if a great number of people were to live, each intent only upon his own interests, such a community would surely disintegrate unless there were one of its number to have a care for the common good.[4]

Although the idea of the common good is generally neglected in recent Anglo-American philosophy (and where the term is used the meanings are often confused and confusing, as with Rawls) there is a long tradition in politi-

---

[2]   Edmund Burke, (a) 'Speech on Conciliation with the Colonies', 22 March 1775); (b) 'A Vindication of Natural Society' 1757; and (c) 'Reflections on the Revolution in France' 1790, see P.J. Stanlis ed. *Edmund Burke: Selected Writings and Speeches* (New Brunswick, NJ: Transaction, 2009).

[3]   Aquinas, *Summa Theologiae,* Ia IIae, q. 90, a. 2, pp. 132 and 134.

[4]   Aquinas, *De regimine principum,* I, see *Aquinas Selected Political Writings,* ed. A.P. D'Entreves, trans. J.G. Dawson (Oxford: Blackwell, 1959), p.3.

cal philosophy which argues that all laws and state actions must be directed to the good of society as a whole. Against this background, and given the power, resources and ambitions of modern states it is perhaps surprising, therefore, that it is only recently that governments have come to accept the idea that the State has a responsibility for the victims of crime.

The first comprehensive compensation scheme was enacted in New Zealand in 1964; and a few months later a scheme was instituted in the United Kingdom. During the following decade similar schemes were adopted in the United States, Canada, Australia and some member states of the European Community. In 1983 a European Convention on the Compensation of Victims of Violent Crime was formulated, drawing attention to the 'need' to compensate victims and declaring it 'necessary' for governments to make provision to do so.

The Development of Social Conscience

Given the rapid development of victim compensation laws one may wonder what happened to bring the needs of victims, which appear for so long to have been almost totally ignored by governments, into recent prominence. If society has a duty to provide compensation to the victims of violent crime, this duty might be thought to rest on fundamental principles of equity and social responsibility which were surely as valid in earlier times as they are today. This may be so; but state compensation for the victims of crime requires significant expenditure of public money, and in earlier times a sense of responsibility for the plight of such victims was not felt sufficiently strongly among the public at large to warrant any government to address the matter.

In the years after the Second World War, however, the moral conscience of the West became increasingly preoccupied with the needs and legitimate claims of the socially disadvantaged. The UN Declaration of Human Rights of 1948, which was motivated principally by the concern to prevent any repetition of the atrocities committed by the Nazi regime, was subsequently adopted as a charter for protection against discrimination and oppression of all kinds, and for the firmer establishment of democratic rights and freedoms. A number of universal and regional Human Rights Conventions achieved recognition and ratification by many countries, and the ever-widening categories of those deemed to be in need of such protection were bound to arouse interest in the sufferings of innocent people who had been the victims of violent crime.

At the same time, society in the developed world was becoming rapidly richer, and welfare arrangements were being steadily extended to victims of various forms of disability and disadvantage. In this climate some provision for the victims of crime could hardly be far behind. In addition, there was strong political pressure in Western societies to make more generous provision for the poor and to ensure a fairer distribution of society's resources. With ever-growing public expenditure on the enforcement of law and the punishment of criminals, the public was increasingly likely to be moved by an appeal to the apparent unfairness involved in devoting no comparable resources to relieve the plight of innocent victims of crime.

The Want of a Rationale

If it was this degree of moral consensus that impelled some governments in the 1960s to make provision for compensation, then the theoretical justification for doing so remained obscure. In 1961, for example, the UK government could find 'no constitutional or social principle on which state compensation could be justified', and the British Home office vigorously resisted any suggestion that the victim has a legal 'right' to compensation. This did not prevent the same government from making arrangements to award such compensation and from setting up a quasijudicial agency to administer them; but the same fear that to acknowledge a 'right' to compensation would commit the government to meeting an unlimited number of claims in full, and thereby create an uncontrollable channel of public expenditure, lay behind its reluctance to bring into force the statutory criminal injuries compensation scheme established by the Criminal Justice Act, 1988. A similar lack of clarity characterises the wording of the European Convention. In the preamble the reasons given for the 'necessity' of providing at least minimum provisions for compensation are 'equity' and 'social solidarity', but these reasons are not further elucidated. In the Explanatory Report (1984) a number of other arguments are listed, without comment; it is also stated that recent victim studies 'have thrown light on victims' psychological and physical distress after a crime', which 'points to the need to compensate the victim' (para 6 & 7). Thus, even if there is now public consensus on the need to provide compensation, the justification for doing so remains both obscure and controversial.

The Concept of Compensation

Part of the difficulty resides in the notion of *compensation* itself. In Hebrew law (*Torah*) the guiding principle for the assessment of criminal damages was the *lex talionis*, an eye for an eye and a tooth for a tooth.[5] This was echoed in an early judgement of the US Supreme Court (*Monongahela Navigation Co* v *US*, 1893) which described compensation as the provision of a 'full and perfect equivalent'. The difficulty, of course, is that in the majority of cases perfect equivalence is unattainable. If you take my car and in using it damage it, then it *may* be sufficient compensation if you make good the damage and provide for the inconvenience. The relative ease of calculating adequate compensation in such a case is due to the fact that cars are not generally regarded as *ends* in themselves but as *means* of transport. If, however, you assault me in the process, then it is likely that

---

[5]　*Exodus* 21.23–27: 'If any harm follows, then you shall give life for life, eye for eye, tooth for tooth, hand for hand, foot for foot, burn for burn, wound for wound, stripe for stripe. When a slave-owner strikes the eye of a male or female slave, destroying it, the owner shall let the slave go, a free person, to compensate for the eye. If the owner knocks out a tooth of a male or female slave, the slave shall be let go, a free person, to compensate for the tooth'.

the loss I suffer constitutes damage to things which I regard as intimately connected with the very sense of my life's having the qualitative value it does have, things such as bodily and psychological integrity. People desire good health in order to pursue their chosen ends; but equally the point of some activities is that they produce and help to maintain health. The same is true in respect of psychological wellbeing. Thus, in taking someone's property against their will — either by theft or, for that matter, by legally sanctioned confiscation — there may be losses in respect of mental and physical health which are not wholly compensated for by providing alternative instruments for the attainment of those goals for which mental and bodily health were the agent's means.

Similarly, physical damage or shock may render someone unfit for employment which is likely to be their sole or main source of income. If one compensates them for loss of earnings one has provided equivalent means in the sense of restoring financial powers. But this may fall short of adequate compensation if it neglects the fact that someone's employment may be a constituent feature of their life, not merely a means but an end in itself. To the extent that this has been denied them they have suffered a special kind of loss; one that is often deeper than the loss of income, for it affects their very sense of purpose and thereby their idea of what makes their life a liveable one.

But the fact that it is seldom possible to compensate a victim of crime by providing an exact equivalent of the loss sustained does not mean that compensation is either useless or arbitrary. It is true that any provision of alternative goods may be inadequate or inappropriate, and that there may always remain what one may call an 'ineliminable residue of loss'. It is also true that the damage a person sustains may be mitigated by care and treatment and may eventually be healed. Nevertheless the very fact that compensation is provided may of itself be a source of help and satisfaction to the victim. At the very least, it represents an acknowledgement by society of undeserved loss or damage. Ideally, both the acknowledgement and the material reparation should be

provided by the offender. But in practice this is seldom possible, and one of the strongest arguments for the state taking
responsibility for compensation is that victims may thereby
receive something of that which they have a right to expect
but which in the normal way cannot be obtained from the
offender.

Compensation and the Law

Mention of the offender at this point makes it necessary to
distinguish between different consequences of liability for
injury to another person. Civil law has traditionally provided for compensation in cases where the agents of injury
to the interest of others are deemed to be at fault. An award
of damages is the most familiar form of compensation,
though for reasons explored later civil actions for personal
injuries arising from the commission of crimes of violence
are rare. In criminal law, on the other hand, the principal
consequence is the sanctioning of the offender. The primary
justification for judicial punishment has nothing to do with
the individual victim; it is that the offender has broken the
laws of society, and it is the responsibility of the state to
punish the transgression, to deter further such offences and
(where possible) to rehabilitate the offender. It is therefore
not surprising that justifications for judicial penalties are
concerned mainly with the offender and with the need to
protect society from such offences: the rights or interests of
the immediate victims play no part in the reasoning.

So far as the criminal law is concerned, a victim is viewed
simply as a citizen in whose person civil society itself has
been offended against. But this does not necessarily mean
that the state has no further responsibilities towards the
victim. It is of the essence of any criminal justice system that
the individual citizen ceases to have a right to personal
revenge. A political society, it is often said (following
Weber) is one in which the state has a monopoly of coercive
force. The individual may be imagined to have ceded to the
state the duty of exacting retribution for unlawful injury,
and once this is done the victim has no further claim on the

offender. However, even if a victim has handed over to the state the responsibility for punishment, this does not altogether settle the matter of reparation. Where the offender is in a position to make restitution or offer compensation this should be enforced by the courts. Where the offender is not apprehended, or has no means to pay, it is for the state to provide compensation.

But to bring the question within the scope of a general theory of punishment is to enter a famously difficult field. Traditional justifications for judicial punishment are of three broad sorts *non-consequentialist, consequentialist,* and *contractualist;* arguing, respectively, that punishment is right

(1)   in and of itself;

(2)   on account of its beneficial effects
        (for society and/or the criminal);

(3)   because it is implied by a social consensus.

In practice penal policy is usually based on a combination of these; but it is important to distinguish them, and in fact they correspond to three main lines of traditional philosophical theory discussed previously. Allowing for simplification, one may group the various social and political theories that we have already encountered under three headings:

(1)   *natural law theories* which hold that the nature of human beings implies certain universal values for them;

(2)   *consequentialist theories* which argue that an action or policy is justified to the extent that it maximises the level and, perhaps, the distribution of some given value within a defined community;

(3)   *contractualist theories* (including Rawls' theory of justice) which argue that the rightness or wrongness of policies depends upon whether they, and/or the institutions which establish and enforce them, have the uncoerced support of the members of society.

This is not the place to discuss the merits of these competing theories, though they have been at issue in other chapters. The important point to notice is that, so far as the judicial process is concerned, more than one of them is customarily invoked to support a particular sentencing policy (e.g. a deterrent element is consequentialist, a retributive element is non-consequentialist); and that different moral theories can be appealed to in support of similar moral claims or policies, e.g. a more severe regime of punishment may be justified both because it is deterrent (consequentialist) and because it is deserved (non-consequentialist). Thus it may not be necessary to agree on the philosophical basis of all moral actions in order to be able to commend a particular policy on moral grounds. If it can be shown that more than one philosophical theory supports the proposal, there is a reasonable presumption that the proposed policy has moral justification.

Understanding Victims

These considerations have all arisen from the notion of *compensation*, and they provide some basis for an argument that the State has an obligation to provide it. But before going further it is necessary to say something about the notion of *victims*. It is arguable that those who suffer grievous harm through accident or natural disaster are entitled to at least as much support as victims of crime. That this is the public perception seems to be shown by the huge response to appeals on behalf of the victims of any particularly sensational natural disaster. On this equity of treatment view, victims of violent crime would simply be a particular category of those requiring public assistance, and there would be no question of *compensation* at all. It could be said, for instance, that the state might provide assistance to victims through an expanded national insurance scheme. Building on existing arrangements such a scheme could, but need not, make special provision for victims of crime as opposed to subjects of other misfortunes for which redress through the civil courts is, for whatever legitimate reason, unavailable. One reason for according special treatment for crime victims would be the presumption of a distinctive harm suffered by those

who have been wronged. But equally a reason for not singling out this group might be the thought that it is a socially
and historically relative matter what constitutes crime, and
so to attach special significance to this gives inappropiate
emphasis to these misfortunes and stigmatises their victims. Furthermore to treat crime-victims differently is, in
effect, to compensate them for a loss additional to those
shared with victims of accident or disease.

A second non-compensatory option would be for the
state to provide the victim with the means of taking civil
action against the offender, suing him or her for damages in
respect of a tort. The rationale for this approach would be
that when a criminal damage is inflicted two distinct interests are affected: those of the society or the state, for which
the remedy is punishment, and those of the immediate victim, for which the remedy is damages. On this view the residue calls for state treatment, not through compensation but
by way of state provision of legal services, or of the means to
secure them. In this regard the role of the state would be an
enabling one again related to that which it already occupies
with respect to the provision of education, health and social
services.

Interesting as it may be, this second way of proceeding is
inadequate in circumstances in which the offender is not
apprehended, or disappears before civil action can proceed,
or in which he or she lacks the means to provide damages.
One could of course take the view that these possibilities are
part of life's lottery and that the state has no further duty
beyond that of punishing and providing the means for civil
actions. But the application of such a policy would certainly
be perceived as unfair to a large number of the victims of
violent crime; and the claim that the government has no
duty to compensate would be in defiance of the view, now
commonly embodied in the practice of courts, that every
punishment administered by the state should, where
appropriate, include an element of reparation.

Yet even if victims of violent crime cannot be simply sub-
sumed into the general category of victims of misfortune —
even if they are 'special' — there are certain respects in

which the obligation which the state has towards them is similar to that which it has towards those who are disadvantaged in other ways. Various kinds of aid may be required and are available. The most urgent needs of the victim may be counselling, help from the police, legal advice or protection from the media.

None of this need be controversial: it is part of what government is now expected to do for any who suffer disadvantage through no fault of their own. Indeed some would argue that, if properly administered, this form of provision for victims is more beneficial than any monetary compensation. As we have seen, compensation in any particular case is not likely to be objectively quantifiable or in any real sense equivalent to the loss or damage sustained. Monetary values bear little relation to the personal impact of violence. On the other hand moral, psychological and financial support can be provided through the health and social services, and there is a strong case for saying that generous provision of these services for victims is a better use of public money than a system of monetary compensation that will seldom have any real equivalence with the hurt actually suffered. At present, partly perhaps for historical reasons, monetary compensation is still given a far higher priority in public expenditure than the provision of social and psychological aid for victims. Simply on grounds of value for money, a strong case could be made out for reversing these priorities.

Yet, once it is granted that some compensation must be given to the victim, money remains the one practical means by which the state can provide it in any systematic way; further, as was noted earlier, the fact of compensation may be more significant to the victim than the amount, even though the amount must be perceived to be equitable in relation to other awards made to victims in similar circumstances. It remains to consider in more detail the arguments that are used to justify such awards.

Philosophical Justifications of State Compensation

We have seen that different kinds of philosophical reasoning may be invoked to justify particular policies, and that this does not weaken the case for them; indeed, where arguments based on different premises support the same conclusion, the force of the argument as it is directed towards the shaping of practice may be strengthened. Interestingly, and perhaps because of the general lateness in the development of the idea of state compensation, the philosophical literature on the subject remains very limited.[6] The present discussion, though brief, may therefore be of some use in stimulating, and providing a conceptual structure for further discussion of the issues.

It will be convenient to list the arguments for a state obligation according to the broad philosophical categories of 'consequentialist' (or forward-looking) and 'non-consequentialist' (or backward-looking) and to note those which draw their strength from both (i.e. mixed theories).

1. Consequentailist

An element of reparation in the criminal system is necessary if individuals are to retain respect for the administration of justice and not take the law into their own hands, seek to recover their property by force, or commit acts of personal revenge. Also victims may be more ready to report offences and co-operate with the police and the courts if the successful outcome of a prosecution will strengthen their claim to

---

[6] The following is a brief list of writings relevant to the principles and policies of state compensation: A. Ashworth, 'Punishment and Compensation: Victims, Offenders and the State', *Oxford Journal of Legal Studies*, 6 (1986); P. Cane, *Atiyah's Accidents, Compensation and the Law*, 5th edition (London: Widenfeld & Nicolson, 1993); J.W. Chapman ed. *Compensatory Justice, Nomos, xxxiii* (New York: New York University Press, 1991); R. Goodin, 'Theories of Compensation', *Oxford Journal of Legal Studies*, 9 (1989); N. MacCormick, 'The Obligation of Reparation', *Proceedings of the Aristotelian Society*, 78 (1978); reprinted in MacCormick *Legal Right and Social Democracy* (Oxford: Clarendon, 1982); D. Miers, 'The Responsibilities and the Rights of Victims of Crime', *Modern Law Review*, 55 (1992); and P. Montague, P. 'Rights and Duties of Compensation', *Philosophy & Public Affairs*, 13 (1984).

compensation. This is presumably the sense of the *Explanatory Report on the European Convention*, when it speaks (para 7) of the need 'to quell the social conflict caused by the offence and make it easier to apply rational, effective crime policy'.[7]

2. Non-Consequentialist

The European Convention includes 'equity' among its arguments for the necessity of compensation. This can be understood in at least two ways. It may mean that it is unfair that victims should receive nothing from the state when substantial public expenditure is devoted to the apprehension, conviction and punishment of criminals; and also that it is unfair if help and relief is not given to victims of crime on a scale comparable with that given to sufferers from other forms of disadvantage or disability. If such a disposition of public funds is felt to be inequitable, it is arguably wrong in itself and ought to be rectified. It can also be argued (though not perhaps so plausibly) that every offence marks a failure by the State in its obligation to protect its citizens from unlawful attack, and therefore that it owes something to the victim as compensation for this failure. Moreover, since human life and dignity are overriding social priorities, since compensation in various forms (from simple recognition to monetary reparation) can contribute to the continuance of quality of life and the restoration of dignity, and since only the state has the resources to provide such compensation, the damaging consequences of violent crime for the life and dignity of the victim lay a positive duty on government to respond with such means as are available.

Yet if it is recognised that government has a duty or an obligation, it may follow that the victim has a right to be compensated. This consequence has evidently alarmed politicians, who appear to have inferred that the exercise of such a right would make victims legally entitled to what-

---

[7] *European Convention on the Compensation of Victims of Violent Crime: An Explanatory Report* (Strasbourg: Council of Europe, 1984).

ever level of compensation a court or official agency might determine, and that this would result in public expenditure outside political control. But this is to misunderstand the meaning of 'rights'. It is widely agreed that every citizen of this country has a right to health care and education. But in order to claim this right applicants have to show that they meet the appropriate conditions (such as an illness that would benefit from treatment or the standard of educational achievement qualifying for a particular course). Moreover, the right is to no more than a fair share of that which the state may reasonably be expected to provide within the limits of its economic circumstances. Similarly with a right to compensation. This is a right to an equitable share in such provision for compensation as the government can reasonably afford. It is not a blank cheque to be filled in by a Compensation Board.

3. Mixed Theories

The second reason adopted in the European Convention for the necessity to compensate victims of violent crime is 'social solidarity'. Here the focus of concern is upon the common good and the idea that in the person of the victim a harm is done to society which he or she has no duty to bear alone. Accordingly compensation is a means by which the loss is distributed across society as a whole, so recognising the reality of social existence and deepening a sense of community. To promote such social solidarity is widely seen as a proper objective of government and is an aim shared by many organisations and agencies in the community. It may also be viewed both as something which is good as a means to the greater happiness and well-being of the citizens and also as something good in itself and a laudable aim of public policy.

A further argument under this heading, which has already been spelt out, derives from the theory of punishment. Judicial punishment should include some element of reparation to the victim. If this cannot be recovered from the offender, it becomes the duty of the government to supply it. This argument presupposes that the provision of reparation is good in itself; but it may also take into account the beneficial consequences for the victim of acknowledgement and compensation.

Finally, a government may be said to have assumed an obligation to maintain arrangements for compensation by ratifying the European Convention in 1990. This again may be justified by the beneficial consequences it is likely to have for citizens of European countries who suffer criminal injuries when abroad. It may also be regarded as good in itself in so far as a government has an absolute duty to honour treaties into which it has entered in the name of its people. The philosophical theories on which these arguments are based may now be set out schematically (see Table on opposite page).

The diagram shows that these arguments depend for their theoretical justification on more than one philosophical theory. But, as was argued above, this does not weaken their cumulative force. As in other issues in practical philosophy, similar moral claims may be supported by different moral theories; and the resulting moral consensus is often more significant than the different routes by which it is reached. And where (as in the central column) the same conclusion is reached by both consequentialist and non-consequentialist reasoning, the force of the argument as it is directed towards the fashioning of public policy may be regarded as particularly strong.

Not all the theories advanced, of course, are of equal weight. In particular, that of social maintenance and enhancement (i.e. that compensation increases social cohesion around respect for the law) is open to question on empirical grounds, and that of social damages (i.e. that the government has failed to provide protection) seems to presuppose the impossible condition that government should be able to protect all citizens from all criminal assaults. But taken together they amount to a formidable case, and any government which sought as a matter of general policy to evade or reduce its responsibility for compensation would properly incur severe moral censure.

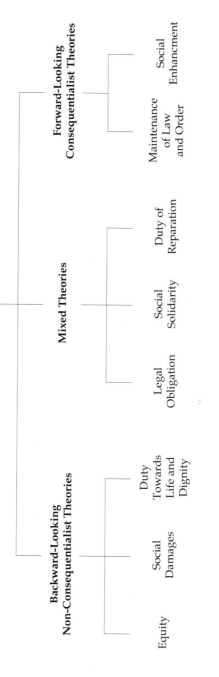

THEORIES OF STATE COMPENSATION

Backward-Looking
Non-Consequentialist Theories

Equity

Social
Damages

Duty
Towards
Life and
Dignity

Mixed Theories

Legal
Obligation

Social
Solidarity

Duty of
Reparation

Forward-Looking
Consequentialist Theories

Maintenance
of Law
and Order

Social
Enhancment

A Better Foundation

In some respects the foregoing represents a form of pragmatic argumentation, marshalling different styles of reasoning, deploying different starting points, methods and rationales to arrive at a common conclusion. From a practical point of view there need be no harm in that, but intellectually there is a danger of regressing to the mean, or less generously 'reversion to mediocrity'. From the fact that a range of viewpoints can be oriented towards a common object it does not follow that that the consensus is as well placed as its best perspective. It is worth considering, therefore, whether there is a viewpoint that might accommodate the claim that victims of crime within one's society ought to be compensated within a broader vision of the relations of fellow community members one to another.

The aim of the philosophical exploration of political liberalism by its advocates is to find a normatively relevant common foundation to which reference can be made in the resolution of disputes between proponents of competing views and interests. Rawls insists that this foundation is nothing other than the reflexive idea that citizens have of themselves as free and equal members of a political community, i.e. as *citizens*. But this insistence suggests the following dilemma. Either membership of a political community is just another fact about an individual, in which case such membership has no special status in relation to membership of other groups, e.g. religious or common interest ones; or else it is a special fact appeal to which serves to trump demands deriving from membership of other associations.

If it is the former then no special significance attaches to one's political identity, if the latter then this special significance calls for an explanation. It will not be relevant to reply that while not everyone is a member of a church, or a trade union, or a professional association, for example, everyone is a citizen, for while this may be true it carries no normative force against demands arising from occupancy of these other roles. If, for Rawls, citizenship has priority it must be because the fact is a prior or deeper one, presumably that attaching to our very identity as 'free and equal persons'. For how else can it be a trumping suit?

The special identity or 'transcendental' (as in beyond other social categories) reading of Rawlsian liberalism seems inescapable; but it is also deeply problematic given the dependency of self-consciousness upon social environment. Social influence is not a contingent fact about our actual identities, additional to a necessary truth about the essences individuals possess as persons. Rather, the original social context of a human life shapes it making it to be the kind of thing it is. The very idea that we can conceive of ourselves as agents entering into a scheme of political association independently of knowing ourselves (however inarticulately) to have a particular, socially-constituted nature is incoherent. As incoherent, indeed, as supposing that one could think of oneself as entering into a commercial transaction as a banker independently of locating oneself within a pre-existing order of financial exchange. The very acts of lending money, of being a *financier*, and of borrowing presuppose a system of social relationships in terms of which these particular roles, as of that of money itself, can be defined. The charge, then, is that liberalism rests on a theory of social agents as constituted independently of societies or as pre-social individuals.

To this extent it is hard to deny the communitarian thesis that *political* personhood, 'citizenhood' in Rawls's terms, is not independent of personhood generally, and this in turn is a function of one's induction into and continuing membership of communities that may well be committed to comprehensive doctrines of the good life. This leaves us with the idea that political values must find their place within a broader conception of the life of society in which the aim must be to harmonise the variety of goods insofar as this is possible. This is not the ambition to devise a scheme of life for all societies at all times. On the contrary, it suggests that one should work to define the characteristic values of a given community and then look to see how they can be publicly expressed in various ways including in the political order of the state. Here, then, we arrive at the important issue of *culture and institutions*.

Moving from the formal philosophy of liberal individualism to its political expression, it is open to the charge of being a cause of the disintegration of civil society into a set of interest groups and communities whose dealings with one another are often characterized by resentment and at best rarely rise above co-operation under the terms of a fragile *modus vivendi*. More positively, I want to urge reconsideration of the ideal of society as a community united, as Augustine puts it in fellowship by extensive agreement about the objects of their afftection.[8]

The idea of a political order rooted in general commitment to a common set of values is likely to face two objections: (1) does it not involve commitment to something over and above individual persons? (2) is it not bound to limit the possible variety of forms of life, or at least their public expression?

As regards the first question it is worth saying that a commitment to the reality of the community or of society need not involve belief in another agent alongside men and women; rather it can take the form of seeing fellow citizens in the light of a certain pattern of historically extended loyalties sustained through the agency of traditions and institutions (see again chapter nine).

As regards the second question, there is the concern that community or society based politics is bound to exclude those who do not share the relevant values or cannot feel any loyalty to it. The elements of social identity include some at least of the following: a shared *history*, a common *language*, and a common *culture*, all of which are products of human action not deterministic genetics. Societies can be made, strengthened and weakened as more or fewer objects of greater and lesser importance are brought within the field of shared affection. The phenomenon is well-enough known from the experience of common hardship and the achievement of common endeavour, from the sense of a

[8]   Augustine, *De Civitate Dei*.

common cultural tradition and from the shared horror at attrocities and tragedies.

Conclusion

Human activities are directed towards ends conceived of as good. Where those activities are subject to, and pass the test of general criticism, a practice is established which can find its place in the fabric of social life. But that life itself is a proper object of evaluation and where it is judged to be good so its goodness deserves to be announced and needs public recognition if it is to persist over generations. The celebration of what is good and held in common requires public forms of expression apt to the nature of the values in question. These forms of expression then constitute a symbolic order in whose articulation the members of a society can recognize the meaning of this common social life. The scale, the manner and the pace of proceedings associated with public mourning or celebration incorporating historical and cultural references, give expression to the sense of a common present, inherited from a common past and foreseeing a common future. Common pieties, affections and revulsions can shape a form of social life imbued with meaning and transcendent of the sorts of alliances forced by commercial interest or fear of violence. They bestow a significance on the individual which he could not begin to secure by his own efforts and thereby they create the preconditions of a political order as the community realizes itself politically in the form of a polity.

Inevitably and legitimately this pattern of social relationships and civic membership is intolerant of ways of behaving that threaten its integrity. The lawlessness of certain groups, the self-serving commercial aggression of some, and moral-cum-aesthetic insensibility of others are all reasonable objects of public criticism. A society united by a common culture can contain sub-cultures, just as it can contain constituent societies. But there is a limit to what can be taken up into the life of a unified polity. There is no *a priori* specification of what may be excluded, but equally the corollary of social unity is limitation. What the limits of this may be is a matter for collective public debate but that is exactly what the line of reasoning developed in this section has established, *viz.* the necessity of a politics of culture and of public institutions existing to embody it. The case for the compensation of victims of crime is made in this perspective primarily through the idea of social solidarity among fellow citizens, but that is no longer a formal notion rather it is keyed to membership of real communities or societies.

With this conclusion in place I now turn to a set of reflections about certain aspects of our common political, social, intellectual and aesthetic culture.

12

Private Life and
Public Culture

Introduction

The character and quality of a society's culture matter far beyond the rarefied realms of high art and scholarship. Its culture is its way of expressing itself through language, customs, and modes of social interaction, as well as shared beliefs and practices. It is also often through culture that people find (or lose) a sense of meaning and value in their lives. In this respect culture is neither rare nor for the few; like the environment it is everywhere; and just as foul air and polluted waters affect our physical health, so a degraded culture damages our psychological and moral wellbeing. Again, like the physical environment, culture reaches into the past and out to the future. We cannot create it as individuals just for ourselves, or just for the present; but our attitudes and actions can damage it for all and for generations.

I ended the previous chapter by looking to shared cultural identity as providing a ground for social solidarity, as well as setting the formal and material preconditions for a political order. In the next three chapters I shall be considering, first, the nature and role of education as a central element in the transmission of culture; second, postmodern challenges to the idea that culture embodies any kind of objective knowledge or values; and third, the relation of philosophy to one area of high culture, namely art. Before that, however, I wish to explore an aspect of public culture that combines some of the themes of part I, 'Ethics', with

some of those of part II, 'Society' and which might therefore
be termed part of the morality of common and public life.

The Private and Personal Lives of Public Figures

In recent years it has become increasingly common in the
United States and in the United Kingdom for newspapers
and other media to expose problematic aspects of the private lives of political (and other public) figures; or, since the
facts may already be in the public domain, to draw wider
attention to them and to make them the subject of commentary. These 'problematic aspects' may include past or continuing physical or psychological illness, eating disorders,
drug and alcohol abuse or dependence, financial difficulties, family conflict, infidelity, or certain sexual proclivities
of both the political figures themselves and of their family
members or intimates.

In the United States, the most prominent cases are probably those of President Bill Clinton in relation to a series of
alleged extramarital affairs leading up to the scandal
involving White House intern Monica Lewinsky, and of
President John F. Kennedy, also in relation to marital infi-
delities. The latter exposure was, of course retrospective, as
were revelations of similar matters concerning other presi-
dents and holders of high office. Up until the mid-1960s,
while it was sometimes known to the press that politicians
had 'problems' in their private lives, it was rare for these to
be made public. Sometimes it might be reported, or more
likely hinted, that a figure had a 'complex' or 'difficult' personal life, and the public was left to infer whatever it might
from this (generally concluding that infidelity, alcoholism,
or both, were probably at issue). The recent culture of exposure results from a combination of factors, including
changed attitudes toward public discussion of sexual conduct, changed standards of sexual behaviour, recognition
of the scale of Cold War espionage and of its practice of
blackmail, a general decline in social deference, a threat to
the print media posed by the growth of television, and the
rise of satirical entertainment. All of these elements were

present in the case that marked the establishment of the culture of exposure in the UK: the 'Profumo scandal' of 1963. For those unaware of this episode, it may be sufficient to say that it involved the then Secretary of State for War, members of the British aristocracy, a Soviet naval attaché, and a number of 'society' call girls, and that it contributed to the resignation of Prime Minister Harold Macmillan and the subsequent fall from power of the Conservative Party.[1] In the United States, the culture of exposure developed somewhat later and took shape in the period of the Watergate scandal, which damaged the American public's perception of the governing classes just as the Profumo scandal had in Britain.

The reticence in reporting and commentary characteristic of the first half of the twentieth century was largely cultural; it was a matter of general discretion and of judgment as to what it was decent to say of someone, and of what information was fit matter for reception into family homes. No doubt, however, it also expressed a degree of solidarity among members of the political class, and of self-interest on the part of journalists who could not afford to lose access to sources. These considerations now apply far less extensively: the idea of restraining reportage on the ground of respect for the parties in question, or out of regard for readers' sensitivities, now seems remote and almost quaint. Memories of the Clinton scandal being securely fixed in public consciousness, I need not cite the sort of salacious details that are now commonly reported in newspapers or in other media. Suffice it to say that they presume on the part of audiences very different attitudes regarding what are tolerable, let alone welcome, subjects of public discussion. As for solidarity and mutual interest, the intensity of competition within and between the various media, which has been made all the more intense by the development of the Internet, is now such that no reporter is likely to forgo an

[1] For details of this and other scandals involving members of both houses of Parliament, see Matthew Parris, *Great Parliamentary Scandals: Four Centuries of Calumny, Smear, and Innuendo* (London: Robson Books, 1996).

opportunity to relay a scandal for fear of losing subsequent
access to sources. Everyone talks, everyone wants to talk,
and everyone wants to listen — or so it can seem.

As in the United States, so in the United Kingdom: as
memorable as Clinton's problem-strewn career is the troubled life of Princess Diana, which was also charted in ever
increasing detail. This coverage was the subject of some
complaint, and following her tragic death there was much
talk of curbing the trend to report and comment on the private lives of public figures. However, this talk was without
discernible serious intent and certainly without effect. The
year of the princess's death also saw the election of the New
Labour government; since then, several of its leading figures have seen aspects of their lives, and those of their families and intimates, become the subject of intensive reporting
and commentary. The press carried accounts of the former
Prime Minister Tony Blair's wife's property dealings with a
'confidence man' and the public intoxication of Blair's son;
of attempted drug dealing by the son of a Home Secretary;
of the Lord Chancellor's son's drug addiction and associated prosecution in the US; and of a Foreign Secretary's and
a Deputy Prime minister's extramarital affairs, as well as
reports of the personal peccadilloes of other lesser government officials. The press has also raised the issue of people's
sexual proclivities to the point where a shadow cabinet con-
tender for the leadership of the Conservative Party admitted to a homosexual past, and another front-bencher
confirmed his settled gay identity. Assuming that members
of the royal family also count as political figures in the context of a constitutional monarchy, the list of subjects of exposure, dissemination, and commentary must include the
marital difficulties of three of the queen's children, as well
as the behaviour of other royals.

Such are some of the facts concerning the presentation
and discussion of public figures' private lives. How should
one judge these facts? It is pretty clear that any reasonable
answer will have to take account of circumstances, form,
and content. That is to say, some methods of acquiring
information about public figures violate norms of justice by

being intentionally deceitful or otherwise dishonest, or by involving threats. Also, some forms of exposure or public presentation are so gross and gratuitous as to be beyond principled defence. Had, for example, explicit photographs of Ms. Lewinsky and President Clinton been taken during their intimacies, it would have been quite improper for these to be made public, for they would be shockingly offensive, and such obscenity would serve no clear public purpose not already achieved by general verbal reports of the sort of thing that took place (whatever that public purpose might have been).

Again, some matters are so far removed from a public figure's office, or from the exercise of his or her duties, that no case for revelation or publication can be made from the side of public interest (as against public prurience). It may be of relevance to know the state of the lining of the president's bowels, inasmuch as this bears upon his capacity to carry on the work of his office, but it is hard to conceive a likely circumstance in which it would be relevant to know of the size of his private parts. That said, however, it is reported that at least one postwar occupant of the Oval Office was keen to draw attention to this aspect of himself, and it might well be a matter of public interest to know about *that* behavioural fact.

Similarly, while some matters may be of sorts that are relevant to evaluating the conduct of public figures, revelation may still be ill advised. Even if the means of acquiring such information were not unjust and the proposed manner of presentation would not be gratuitously sensational, it may well be the case that other concerns outweigh the benefits of revelation. The interests of third parties might be such that publication would irreparably damage them. The cost of these unintended but foreseen secondary effects of otherwise legitimate exposure may simply be too high. Public humiliation is a terrible thing and it ought not to be occasioned lightly.

An Initial Dialectic

So much will readily be agreed, I think, even when it is accepted that there is a general liberty of public speech and a particular freedom of the press and media (whether derived from general liberty or independent of it) to report and comment upon what, in good conscience, they judge to be appropriate subject matter. But what of other cases in which the foregoing objections to revelation do not hold, or in which further considerations may defeat them? Among the most common grounds given in justification of exposing or making more widely known private problems are the following.[2]

First, that public figures are in a categorically different position from other members of society. They stand upon a stage, presenting one or other aspects of themselves to the populace or some constituency within it. Like musical or theatrical performers, or street or media evangelists, their occupancy of the public realm is not *per accidens* but *per se*, and as such their lives may legitimately be inspected and commented upon. In short, the right of privacy is implicitly relativized to a status or role, and it diminishes in scope as these features become more extensively public.

Second, that while all persons have a general interest in privacy, and perhaps, thereby have a right to keep personal information undisclosed or closely confined, this establishes a defeasible presumption of privacy, not an absolute entitlement to it. This presumption lapses when disclosure serves some relevant and pressing public interest. The state of health of the commander in chief evidently bears upon matters of public interest, as does the fact that a legislator's personal circumstances provide an immediate incentive to favour (or disfavour) relaxing prohibitions on activities in which he, his family, or his close associates are involved.

---

[2]   This initial taxonomy of justifications for public disclosure follows David Archard's discussion in David Archard, 'Privacy, the Public Interest, and a Prurient Public' in Matthew Keiran, ed., *Media Ethics* (London: Routledge, 1998). Archard suggests that public gossip about the private lives of individuals may serve a valuable social purpose.

Likewise, the fact that someone's reputation for honesty, reliability, and so on, is a fabrication sustained by publicists and is belied by a personal history of deceit, duplicity, and disloyalty, provides reason to disclose relevant aspects of this history in the service of disabusing the public of its illusions. (It is here allowed that this category of warrant for disclosure may not be conclusive, for other interests may prove countervailing.)

Third, it may be supposed that some general public good is realized by the disclosure of personal details where these provide entertainment or satisfaction. This justification can be developed in a variety of ways — some high, some low, some simple, some complex — but the basic idea is that people benefit from learning of the lives of others, and this benefit can only be common and extensive where the others in question are commonly known public figures.

Later I will consider a further kind of justification that is related to all three of those given above, but which is more complex and is linked to a particular philosophy of common public and political life that has receded in recent times, namely, traditional conservatism. In this kind of justification, four considerations are prominent. First, political morality supervenes upon a range of normative social relations that imply various mutual responsibilities. Second, there are different, reasonable expectations associated with different roles and stations. Third, the character of public agents is of legitimate interest because of their special normative relationship to others. Fourth, we learn about ourselves and develop apt responses by viewing the lives of others, and people with public roles provide salient and influential examples. In showing how these four considerations cohere as part of a single account, one needs to see how freedom and value, and individuals and society, stand in relations more or less opposite to those in which they are now commonly conceived. Thus, to illustrate the relation between individuals and society, for example, the family might be analogized to a complex organism, the parts of which function and enjoy life through their contribution to the life of the whole. While the limits of such a comparison should be evident even to those who favour it, the point that I wish to make is that for the traditional conservative a comparison such as this makes better sense of his experience and understanding of society than do discussions of individuals and their relationships in markets, contracts, and wholly voluntary associations. Before pursuing the kind of justification linked to traditional conservatism, however, let me acknowledge three rather obvious responses to the three grounds given above for exposing or making more widely known hitherto private aspects of the lives of public figures.

First, those who find themselves the objects of public interest may do so in virtue of public offices that they have chosen to pursue, but, equally, they may not. The occupant of the Oval Office arrived there by having placed himself before the American public and having sought and won electoral approval; this is not true of Britain's sovereign, nor of the immediate members of his or her family. However, while the resources of hereditary office may provide some protection from or compensation for the liability to probing investigation, there are likely to be no such mitigating factors available to those who find themselves unexpectedly drawn into the limelight in consequence of special circumstances or associations. The lover of someone who murders children, and who herself has been party to consensual torture at his hands, may have chosen her intimate unwisely, but she is not, on that account alone, fair game for exposure, any more than are countless others who find themselves in undesirable relationships. Even those who have sought the limelight might have done so on the implicit understanding that it was this or that aspect of themselves that was to be displayed for appreciation and criticism, and not other, 'reserved' features. The sportsman who seeks employment and reward on the basis of his physical prowess does not by this fact alone render himself a legitimate target of inquiries into his marital fidelity or financial competence. The principle 'if public then fair copy' has no credibility, save to the extent that it represents an elliptical reference to some other, more feasible but limited justification.

Such a justification may be forthcoming under the heading of the second category of warrant, namely, public interest. There are documented cases where the competence of public figures has been chronically impaired due to causes that, like the impairment itself, have been kept secret from the public. Likewise, there are known cases where public figures have sought to change laws for reasons of personal interest. There are also on record cases where the reality of a public figure's life gives the lie to each and every claim to merit or virtue that he had presented in his public declarations. All such cases provide some warrant for disclosure and commentary, but for every example like these there are twenty or thirty or a hundred specious defences along the following lines. 'The man is a drunk or has a chronic illness.' Well, we are all in some way or another and to some degree slaves to our appetites, and it is too easy to point to a single impediment or addiction, overlooking a spread of vulnerabilities or dependencies. Likewise we are all prone to sickness, to days off, and to impaired efficiency, and we may be less aware of the fact and the effects of these, and less diligent about managing and compensating for them, than is someone burdened with a significant and continuing health problem. 'She favours relaxation of the ban because her son is in violation of it'. Might not the experience of her son's situation have drawn her attention to a legislative situation that she had not previously considered, thus leading her to see its iniquity? 'He criticizes pornography but then spends time with it.' Is not the troubled transgressor well placed to recognize the vice and the character of his transgression? May not his verdict be more valuable than that of one abandoned to temptation, or of another impervious to it? The overall point is clear, I hope: here, we are in the field of particular cases, not of a general justification.

The third would-be warrant for disclosure, publicization, or commentary — that some public good is served by entertaining or otherwise satisfying people's curiosity — is liable to shock those who take themselves to be formed of finer material. The simple fact, however, is that humankind does delight in tales of fracture and dislocation, the more so when these involve abandonment to base appetites or expose inabilities to cope. This datum is not easily explained, but only the ignorant, the ideologically blinded, or the self-deceived would deny it. The relevant rejoinder is not that it isn't so, but that its being so provides no more warrant for disclosure than does the fact of our common baseness provide justification for gratifying it.

Individuals and Institutional Contexts

Thus far, then, I have considered how the circumstances, form, and content of the disclosure or broader dissemination of personal information might render the exposure unjustified and reprehensible. I have also considered grounds on which the presumption of privacy or confinement might be defeated. To carry the discussion forward, I shall next describe two examples (both real), and discuss the ambivalence some decent and conscientious souls might feel in contemplation of them.

First, it happened some while ago that someone stood for the leadership of a major political party in the UK who had been viewed with favour by a former leader of that party who was very widely admired within (and beyond) it. The candidate's personal life, however, at least in the past, was at odds with the values of the majority of the party and probably of the majority of its core supporters. In addition, there was reason to think that the candidate's moral opinions were likewise at odds with the party and its followers, though he was cautious about how he expressed himself and could not be quoted as publicly endorsing views considered to be anathema by those sharing the party's traditional outlook. The party being one that favoured discretion and decorum but also upheld traditional personal morality, its members felt themselves in something of a bind. Would it be permissible, let alone proper, to advert to facts about the candidate's personal life in public discussion of his suitability for the leadership of the party? (The matter was never fully resolved in the minds of the faithful. Later, a senior member of that same party revealed in her memoirs that she had had an affair with a previous [married] leader, who had subsequently become Prime Minister.)

In the second example, the generally well-liked leader of another British political party was the subject of an extended interview on the BBC's principal television news and current affairs program. The purpose of the interview was to review the progress of the party since the general election and to assess the interviewee's leadership. In the course of the program, the interviewer, who is known for his generally combative style, surprised his guest and viewers by commenting that when he and his researchers were preparing for the interview, they were advised that the leader might well be drunk, this being purportedly his common condition. Having announced this, the interviewer then asked the leader how much he was liable to drink in the course of an evening, and whether he thought that he drank too much. In reply, the guest managed about as well as any human being might in such unexpected circumstances, and in the following days there was much commentary to and fro on the matter. Initially the leader survived the controversy, but in time he confessed to his alcoholism and resigned, and no one can doubt that he suffered, both in public repute and in personal embarrassment. Setting aside the question of whether his drinking impaired his fitness for office, broader issues arise about the manner of this disclosure and its relation to the character and quality of British public culture. (One MP from the governing New Labour Party complained in Parliament that the questioning was 'highly personal and irrelevant to political debate'. In response, the Leader of the House of Commons acknowledged that '[many MPs were] taken aback and distressed at the degree of personal questioning'. The original interviewer was then moved to offer the following, less than fulsome apology: 'I am sorry if any offence has been caused. Maybe there was one question too many on drink'.)

Here, it is important to be aware that the BBC is a national public broadcasting service, free of commercial advertising and funded out of a compulsory UK licence fee. The BBC was established and is regulated under a series of royal charters dating from 1922; its governors are appointed by the Crown to ensure that, among other things, it 'maintains the high standards and values expected of the BBC as the nation's broadcaster'. The formal opening declaration of the current charter serves as a reminder of the constitutional context within which the BBC is located: it begins, 'Elizabeth the Second by the Grace of God of the United Kingdom of Great Britain and Northern Ireland and of Our other Realms and Territories Queen, Head of the Commonwealth, Defender of the Faith', and later continues

> [I]n view of the widespread interest which is taken by Our Peoples in broadcasting services and of the great value of such services as means of disseminating information, education and entertainment, We believe it to be in the interests of Our Peoples in Our United Kingdom and elsewhere within the Commonwealth that there should be an independent corporation which should continue to provide broadcasting services.

The historic and continuing main home of the BBC is Broadcasting House in London. In the marble entrance hall stands an untranslated Latin inscription:

> *Templum hoc artium et musarum Anno Domini mcmxxxi rectore Johanni Reith primi dedicant gubernatores precantes ut messem bonam bona proferat sementis ut immunda omnia et inimica paci expellantur ut quaecunque pulchra sunt et sincera quaecunque binae famae ad haec avrem inclinans populaus virtutis et sapientiae semitam insistat.*

> (This temple of the arts and muses is dedicated [to Almighty God] by the first governors in the year of Our Lord 1931, John Reith being the Director General, and they pray that good seed sown may bring forth good harvest [and] that all things foul or hostile to peace may be banished hence, and that the people inclining their ear to whatsoever things that are lovely and honest [and] whatsoever things are of good report may tread the path of virtue and of wisdom).

It is likely that a far greater percentage of the early generations of BBC studio and management staff would have been able to construe all or part of the meaning of this inscription than could their counterparts in Broadcasting House today. More importantly, it is very probable that whether or not they could read the Latin original, those earlier generations would have recognized, if only in general terms, the New Testament origins of the metaphor and of the message, drawn respectively from Christ's parable of the sower (*Matthew* 13) and from Paul's instruction to the Philippians. 'brethren, whatsoever things are honest, whatsoever things are pure, whatsoever things are lovely, whatsoever things are of good report; if there be any virtue, and if there be any praise, think on these things' (*Philippians* 4.8). Finally, it is likely that most of the early BBC staff members agreed with the message, and aspired to embrace and implement its ideals. From the outset, and under Lord Reith's strong direction, the BBC cultivated a high-minded public service ethos, which saw broadcasting as contributing to the common good of the nation by enlightening and improving the minds and morals of its listeners.[3] In this connection the BBC was involved with the Adult Education Movement and began the practice of broadcasting a daily Christian religious service. Certainly the type of ennobling programming that the BBC was long associated with conformed to the ideal of contributing to the common good.

Current BBC output indicates how far the corporation and the culture have come from Lord Reith's lofty conception of public broadcasting. Even those in the BBC who certainly would not share his Calvinist puritanism and opposition to unalloyed entertainment are increasingly given to worrying about whether the corporation retains any significant public service vocation. All of this noted, however, the example of the party leader challenged over his drinking, like the preceding example of the would-be leader with a 'problematic' personal past, is a case where a figure who is already in the political sphere seeks further popular support and in this context is subjected to public inspection. Is it unreasonable that in such circumstances the

---

[3]   For an account of the aims and values of the BBC as Reith himself conceived them, see John C. W. Reith, *Broadcast over Britain* (London: Hodder & Stoughton, 1924). For a more impartial and rounded account, see Asa Briggs, *The BBC: The First Fifty Years* (Oxford: Oxford University Press, 1985).

issue of sexual ethics should be introduced or the matter of intemperance raised?

Contexts Ideas and Values

Anyone who studies the history of philosophy, or of ideas more generally, from a period when people held presuppositions very different from his own—say, the period of classical antiquity, or of the patristics, or the high Middle Ages—is likely at some point to be struck by the inadequacy of his own contemporaries' understanding of the past. He may come to regard their flawed understanding as due in part and perhaps overwhelmingly to their failure to understand the premises commonly deployed by thinkers of that other time. These premises may, but need not have been entertained as self-evident; they may have been regarded as hard-won insights. Examples of the latter are the idea that nature exhibits teleological structures and hence is implicitly normative; the idea that existence is analogical, such that individuals, families, principalities, and cultures all *really* exist, be it in a different way in each case; and the idea that knowledge may be acquired by conaturality as well as by empirical discovery or theoretical inference. These ideas are not always expressed in contexts in which they are relied upon, hence the liability of later thinkers, missing what may have been essential, to dismiss the ideas of earlier times as inadequate to the problems that still confront us, or even as inadequate *tout court*.

This reflection is brought to mind when thinking about the difficulties that now confront moral and political conservatives of a certain traditional type or family of types. In Britain and America, the second half of the twentieth century saw a long war between Right and Left in which, by the 1980s, the Left was defeated. The victory was in the field of political economy but so convincing was it that conservatives could easily have thought that it was only a matter of time before other ground would be retaken. Those who did think so were wrong. What became apparent as the smoke cleared and the generals gathered their troops was that the forces of the Right were massed in two camps, pitched at quite some distance from one another. In one camp stood economic/social liberals, in the other social conservatives. Alternatively, if both are to be termed 'conservatives' (because of their common suspicion of generalized claims of social justice and their wish to conserve older modes of material acquisition, use, and retention in the face of radical redistributivists), then we should follow the American practice and distinguish them as 'economic' and 'traditional' conservatives, respectively.[4]

The fact and the extent of their differences were to some degree obscured by their history of shared opposition to domestic state socialism and by their structural relationship within political parties (in Britain the Conservatives and in the US the Republicans). These parties were committed to protecting 'traditional ways of life' from the announced threat posed by international Communism. Once this threat receded, however, it became clear that the Right was divided between those who thought that the defeat of the Left should bring a restoration of the social forms that had been celebrated in popular imagery, literature, and broadcasting during and after World War II, and those who thought that liberty, not virtue, was the business of politics. Many in the latter group had little interest in the social modes of the past. Examples of this division include attitudes toward sexual and family issues, reproduction, abortion, euthanasia, drug control, arts funding, public support and censorship of broadcasting and publications, separation of church and state, public support for religious schools and other faith-based services, and so on. While the division is twofold — first, concerning the issues themselves, and second, concerning the proper role of government in relation to them — it is the prevailing views on the issues themselves that most concerns traditional conservatives.

---

[4] For a taxonomy and description of the different styles of contemporary conservatism in the United States, see Charles W. Dunn and J. David Woodward, *The Conservative Tradition in America* (Lanham, MD: Rowman & Littlefield, 1996).

The general drift in political discourse in the English-speaking world has moved through four phases. The first phase consisted of judging that government (be it state and local, or national) had a responsibility to promote personal rectitude. In the second, people thought that while something might be morally right, it was not the business of government to promote or inhibit individual virtue (other than that pertaining to regard for the rights of others and for the rule of law). The third phase was one of uncertainty in which people were unsure about what might be right in this or that regard. Hence, they concluded that these were matters for individual conscience and not public policy. In the fourth phase, people reasoned that there simply were no moral-cum-political issues of the sort hitherto supposed, or that if there were such issues, then they would fall within the realm of individual autonomy and personal choice; hence, they would fall either outside the scope of law or within it as matters to be protected as liberty rights. Any attempt to identify phases in this drift of political thought and culture is liable to be imprecise, given that the four phases described above have not always been made explicit and they remain in contest. Nonetheless, lines can be traced, both socially and intellectually, as, for example, in the history of the American Right, with the four phases exemplified by the writings of Alexander Hamilton [1757–1804], Andrew Jackson [1767–1845], H. L Mencken [1880–1956], and Murray Rothbard [1926–95], respectively.)[5]

So, by stages, values and practices once nourished and tended to by the state have been left to flower or fade by themselves, and others that the state once sought to suppress and even to uproot have been tolerated and supported to the extent of being allowed public expression and validation. Evidently, from the perspective of traditional conservatives this is an unhappy and unexpected move-

---

[5]   For an account of these developments, see again Dunn and Woodward, *The Conservative Tradition in America,* and the classic presentation of a form of Burkean conservatism by Russell Kirk, *The Conservative Mind* (London: Faber & Faber, 1954). See also Bruce Frohnen, *Virtue and the Promise of Conservatism: The Legacy of Burke and Tocqueville* (Lawrence: University Press of Kansas, 1993).

ment away from their vision of society and understanding of politics. Ironically, they may even find that when it comes to particular policy issues, they now share common ground with some on the old Left. This should not be surprising to anyone familiar with the history of 'Christian Socialism' in Britain and in some European countries (and even in one narrow strand in the United States represented, for example, by Dorothy Day and Peter Maurin, the founders in 1933 of the Catholic Worker Movement).[6]

Christian Socialism is of older vintage than the now more familiar form of anticapitalist socialism, which held that traditional social values were instruments of oppression fashioned and deployed by the forces of capital. In contrast, Christian Socialism took these values to reflect genuine human goods of common life, and its demand for political change was directed at the fact that economic and social circumstances made it impossible for the mass of men and women to realize these traditional values. To put it oversimply, the only changes that Christian Socialists wanted were ones that would make it possible for the many to flourish as did the few, allowing the many to enjoy the benefits of a traditional home, a traditional education, and a traditional lifestyle. Not for these people the politics of cultural revolution, the hermeneutics of suspicion, the praxis

---

[6]   The Christian Socialist movement, which unlike Marxist socialism believed in private property and was opposed to revolution, originated in the middle of the nineteenth century and drew its inspiration from a surprising variety of sources, including the Chartist movement, the cooperative communitarianism of Robert Owen, and the counter-Enlightenment romanticism of Thomas Carlyle and Samuel Coleridge. The founding figures of British Christian Socialism are Frederick D. Maurice and Charles Kingsley, who with others authored a series of pamphlets under the general title *Tracts on Christian Socialism*. Members of the movement later founded and led the Independent Labour Party (formed in 1893), from which Labour and New Labour derive. The Society of Christian Socialists was formed in the United States in 1889. Given some knowledge of this history, it is perhaps more intelligible that traditional conservatives may find points of agreement with this strand of socialism. It also serves to explain why figures such as G. K. Chesterton and other distributivists are claimed by both the Left and the Right.

of subversion, the rhetoric of redefinition, and so on, some of which will be under discussion in chapter fourteen.

Thus a new kind of opposition has emerged within the conservative fold, primarily over social values. By contrast, disputes between traditional conservatives and economic/ social liberals over political economy seem largely instrumental. Traditional conservatives have no objection to the idea that the resources and power of political society may be used to uphold traditional moral values, and that some redistribution of wealth and some provision of public services might be legitimate means, though they are likely to enter a series of reservations. First, that just as property is the bulwark of responsible liberty, so the family is the primary locus of moral formation and of the goods of common life. Second, that initiatives implemented and administered by permanent bureaucracies should be viewed with some suspicion, in part because bureaucrats tend to favour uniform policies without regard to particularities of time and place, in part because they tend to become removed from the moral realities of everyday life, and in part because bureaucratic power tends to corrupt in the measure to which it is possessed. Such considerations also lie behind the traditional conservative's opposition to 'professional politicians', an opposition often misrepresented by critics as a self-serving defence by those who wish to reserve ample time for making money — which is not to say, of course, that the critics' charge is never justified.

Even so, the problem for traditional conservatives is not the state *per se*, but the existence of what they regard as false and harmful conceptions of it. One such conception was that associated with Communism, but that was a problem of the past. The problem of the present and of the foreseeable future is that the state is now widely conceived in terms that are no less damaging to human virtues and values as traditional conservatives understand them. These include various forms of contractualism, such as the rights-based, egalitarian liberalism of Ronald Dworkin, and to a lesser but still significant degree the political liberalism of Rawls, as well as the market liberalism associated with certain kinds of individualism.

The division of the Right that I have adumbrated may also be cast in terms of 'conservatives' versus 'neoliberals', a distinction that has been a commonplace of American political commentary for the past twenty five years, if not longer. More recently, this distinction became prominent in British commentary as the Conservative Party under David Cameron tried to determine its broad orientation in the post-Thatcher era and in the wake of two devastating general election defeats. To understand the challenge faced by the Conservatives one needs to appreciate the extent to which the traditional scheme of opposition between Britain's parties is no longer applicable or even intelligible. The rightward move toward the political center that began under Tony Blair's predecessor as leader of the Labour opposition was carried further by Blair to the point where New Labour even under his successor Gordon Brown, ceased to use the term 'socialism'. At the same time, New Labour repositioned itself as the party willing to tackle crime at home and oppose tyranny abroad. These changes removed the party from the main line of right-wing criticism and left Conservatives in a state of enduring uncertainty as they tried to work out what they stood for, beyond opposition to socialism.

In nineteenth-century Britain, industrialization brought men and women from the countryside into towns and cities, changing the modes of their labour and introducing them first to new kinds of property (factories, machinery, manufactured goods, and shops) and then to a new concept of property. This new concept was not the familiar idea of the personal ownership of visible, tangible things, but the ownership of stocks and shares. These changes in the circumstances of the population resulted in a new kind of insecurity, not resulting directly from the vicissitudes of nature (as had been their situation on the land), but arising from financial speculation and short-term capital investment. By the end of the century, conservatives and socialists alike agreed that the gathering of the populace into centres of seasonless manufacture had changed the environment of politics by giving rise to general national problems calling for collectivized solutions. It was this belief that resulted in such social legislation as the creation of national insurance, the establishment of labour exchanges, and the introduction of old-age pensions. Moreover, it was this collaboration that gave meaning and warrant to the claim of Sir William Harcourt, made during the passage through Parliament of the 1894 budget, that 'We are all socialists now'.[7]

Consensus on the idea of collectivized solutions to national needs continued up to the period of the Thatcher revolution which began in 1979 with the election of the Conservatives and continued until Margaret Thatcher's resignation as leader in 1990. What went somewhat unnoticed, at least by traditional conservatives, was the fact that in the years following World War II a second social transformation had supervened upon the material base established by nineteenth-century industrialization, urbanization, and the later shifts from heavy manufacture to light industry, to assembly work, to retailing, and then to service industries.

This postwar transformation involved the contraction of the family through declining birth rates (as discussed in chapter seven) and relocation for housing and employment opportunities. The transformation also entailed changing conceptions of production, further removing goods from traditional notions of labor. A relatively affluent urban populace, freed from the material necessity of mutual dependence within the family and neighborhood, and increasingly detached from and unfamiliar with the historic narratives of God, of ordered nature, of paternal governance, and of nation and family as nonvoluntary forms of association, gave rise to the need for a new style of politics, no longer responsive to persons as members of collectivities but to individuals directly. This resulted in a raft of liberalizing social legislation in the areas of personal relations, sexual

---

[7]   Harcourt was Professor of International Law at Cambridge (appointed in 1869), Solicitor-General (appointed in 1873), Home Secretary (1880–85), and then Chancellor of the Exchequer (1886, 1892–95) in William E. Gladstone's last two administrations.

practice, conception, leisure, and culture. So far as political consciousness is concerned, it is in respect to such matters as these, and the conditions from which they arose, that someone might recall Harcourt's words and say (as I did in chapter nine) 'We are all liberals now'.

But if this really is the state of affairs, and if it endures, then traditional conservatism has no future, at least at the level of the state. Someone of the generation of those who established the BBC as a public corporation and composed its inscription, when confronted with the issue of how to deal with a public figure whose personal life was problematic, might well have returned for guidance to Matthew's gospel. There he or she would have read the following:

> Moreover, if your brother sins against you, go and tell him his fault between you and him alone. If he hears you, you have gained your brother. But if he will not hear, take with you one or two more, that by the mouth of two or three witnesses every word may be established. But if he refuses even to hear the church, let him be to you like a pagan and a tax collector (*Matthew* 18.15–20).

This is the principal site in the New Testament for the idea of what later came to be termed 'fraternal correction': the charitable criticism by one community member of the behaviour of another. Following Augustine's *Treatise Concerning the Correction of the Donatists*, and Aquinas's discussion in *Summa Theologiae* (IIa, IIae, q.33, a.1), Catholic moral theologians traditionally distinguished 'fraternal' from 'judicial correction' (the latter being the responsibility of a duly constituted authority to those within its jurisdiction), and distinguished both from 'paternal correction', which is the prerogative (and duty) of a superior with regard to those in his charge. In addition, theologians developed (in the style of just war theory) a set of conditions specifying the circumstances under which the obligation to offer fraternal correction becomes grave. The two sets of conditions listed below, which have no single source but are a gloss based on my consideration of various casuistical discussions, refer respectively to (A) private and (B) public correction. In the case of the former, the reproof is to be addressed directly to the wrongdoer; the latter arises where the former is for some reason infeasible or proves ineffective, or where the common good is directly threatened.

(A) Private Fraternal Correction

1. The matter at issue is itself grave.

2. There is little prospect of self-amendment.

3. There is no one else in a position to offer the correction.

4. There is a likelihood that the correction will bear fruit.

5. There is no prospect of harm arising from making the correction (such harm being unmerited or dispropor-tionate to the good of correction).

(B) Public Fraternal Correction

1. The matter at issue is itself public.

2. The matter bears on the standing of a third party or on the common good of the whole community.

3. A public correction is required in order to prevent scandal.

4. The wrongdoer has relinquished or forfeited the right not to be subject to detraction.

There is much that might be said about these and other aspects of the notion of fraternal correction. In this context, however, I am not concerned with the details but with the general idea. Of course, its original circumstance is that of a community of like-minded believers, and this might be thought to exclude its application outside such a context. I can see no reason, however, to think that its religious origin occasions such a general restriction. Nevertheless, I believe that this notion of fraternal correction needs to be applied to our era with some caution, for the reasons that I mentioned above when speaking of ideas drawn from a period when people held presuppositions very different from our own. For presupposed by this notion of fraternal correction are inter-personal relations akin to those of a family rather than of a voluntary association. Likewise, there are presumptions of objectivity in moral judgment, of morality's application to human beings as such, and of moral knowledge being naturally available to all. There are also presumptions of the continuity of moral action through the unifying structure of a person's character, and of a relationship between the 'personal' and the 'social', which is different from that of the 'private' and the 'public' as these terms are now conceived in liberal theories.

Someone might balk at this last claim, recalling a passage in the writings of Mill, who is, after all, nothing if not a liberal. Having insisted in *On Liberty* that 'the only purpose for which power can be rightfully exercised over any member of a civilized community, against his will, is to prevent harm to others', [8] Mill later goes on to say the following:

> There is a degree of folly, and a degree of what may be called (though the phrase is not unobjectionable) lowness or deprivation of taste, which though it cannot justify doing harm to the person who manifests it, renders him necessarily and properly a subject of distaste, or, in extreme cases, even of contempt: a person could not have the opposite qualities in due strength without entertaining these feelings. Though doing no wrong to anyone, a person may so act as to compel us to judge him, and feel to him, as a fool or as a being of an inferior order; and since this judgement and feeling are a fact which he would prefer to avoid, it is doing him a service to warn him of it beforehand, as of any other disagreeable consequence to which he exposes himself. It would be well, indeed, if this good office were much more freely rendered than the common notions of politeness at present permit, and if one person could honestly point out to another that he thinks him in fault, without being considered unmannerly or presuming. We have a right, also, in various ways, to act upon our unfavourable opinion of anyone, not in the oppression of his individuality, but in the exercise of ours. We are not bound, for example, to seek his society; we have a right to avoid it (though not to parade the avoidance), for we have a right to choose the society most acceptable to us. We have a right, and it may be our duty, to caution others against him, if we think his example or conversation likely to have a pernicious effect on those with whom he associates. We may give oth-

[8]   John Stuart Mill, *On Liberty* (1859), ed. Gertrude Himmelfarb (London: Penguin Books, 1974), chap. 1, para. 4, p. 68.

ers a preference over him in optional good offices, except
those which tend to his improvement.[9]

This comes in a section of chapter 4 entitled 'Of the Limits to
the Authority of Society over the Individual', and there are
those who will judge that in this passage Mill himself far
exceeds those limits. Some may say that this is a passing
aberration and not evidence of the inadequacy of a criterion
of public policy limited to the prevention of harm. What
then might they make of another apparent lapse, as when in
the following chapter of the same work Mill contends that
'there are many acts which, being directly injurious only to
the agents themselves, ought not to be legally interdicted,
but which, if done publicly, are a violation of good manners,
and, coming thus within the category of offences against
others, may rightly be prohibited'?[10] Here the point concerns prohibition rather than correction, but if the greater
interference with liberty is held to be permitted then it is
hard to see how the lesser should not be. I leave it to others
to worry whether the policies that Mill appears not only to
countenance but also to recommend sit ill with contemporary liberalism. To the extent that they may be felt to do so
this should remind us of the proximity of Mill's thought to
that of older 'perfectionist' ideas reaching back to Aristotle,
and the natural law theories associated with traditional conservatism. These ideas provide a distinctive basis on which
to address the examples of public disclosure that I gave
earlier, but they also entail presuppositions of a communitarian and teleological sort that may be rejected. If this
should be so, then what is the Aristotelian, or the
Augustinian, or the Thomist, or the Burkean to do?

Earlier, I opposed traditional conservatism to neoliberalism, but perhaps there is a basis for re-alliance. Each has
strong reservations about the modern state: the latter
because of doubts about the very idea of political community; the former because, while they fully believe in community they also believe that the modern state does not and
probably cannot realize it. In this situation, advocates of

[9]   *Ibid.*, chap. 4, para. 5, pp. 143–44.
[10] *Ibid.*, chap. 5, para. 7, p. 168.

these two camps might do well to set aside their differences and collaborate in the effort to devolve political power downward. If this devolution were to occur, then certain questions about the extent and separability of the public and the private would seem less pressing, because for one or another reason they would indeed be so. Devolution to the constituent nations has already begun in the UK, and in the US there is an increasing trend to emphasize the constitutional fact that state governments, and not the federal government, are governments of general jurisdiction. What may be said of the role of quasi-political institutions, such as the BBC and the Public Broadcasting Service in the United States, is less clear, but needs more serious philosophical reflection than it has received hitherto.

Conclusion

I have not been concerned to provide a general answer to the question of when it is right to advert to problematic aspects of the private life of a public figure, or to draw wider attention to the person's misdeeds and to make them the subject of commentary. Evidently, cases have to be considered in relation to general principles and values, as well as in regard to their circumstances, form, and content. It is easy enough to observe that some methods of acquiring information are unjust, that some styles of exposure are beyond principled defence, that some matters are so remote from a public figure's office as to fail any reasonable test of public interest, and that the anticipated consequences of exposure may be so grave that what would otherwise constitute legitimate revelation should be avoided or at least postponed until relevant circumstances have changed.

Important as these considerations are, however, they are supplementary to general issues concerning presumptions of privacy, entitlements to free speech and commentary, and responsibilities of correction and caution. It is unsurprising that the issues of privacy, on the one hand, and of public commentary, on the other, have been subjects of considerable interest to liberal social and political philosophers, since both sets of issues seem to flow from the idea of liberty, especially the liberty of individuals. Within this framework, the matters to be resolved are how best to conceive of the relevant freedoms and how to relate them one to another so as to avoid, limit, or arbitrate conflicts among them.

There are, though, further matters to be considered arising from the interests of the community and the responsibilities of social membership. In essence, these are neither liberties nor rights (though they may entail both); rather, they belong within the sphere of personal and social values. What is at issue is the good of individuals and of societies. Mill wrote of how degrees of folly and lowness render persons 'necessarily and properly' subjects of distaste, and of how corresponding actions 'though doing no wrong to anyone' compel us to judge the agent. As the rest of the passage and the context of the work make clear, however, Mill is not concerned simply with warrants for private judgments and discretionary policies. He also has in mind our responsibilities to such persons as fellow citizens and to others whom they might influence, perhaps especially through their occupancy of public offices.

In deliberating about when and how to exercise these responsibilities one should begin to see the merit of the criteria that I set out above under the headings of private and public fraternal correction: *grave matter*, the *standing of others*, the *common good*, the *avoidance of scandal*, and so on. How strongly one feels the draw of these, and how far one is disposed to see public and private correction as interconnected and nondetachable, provide measures of the extent to which one's conception of social life is akin to that of the traditional conservative. Traditional conservatism is not the only political outlook that can accommodate the idea of mutual responsibilities set within a framework of common life and the common good, but it can lay claim to have been the tacit philosophy of the communities that constituted most of Europe and America until quite recently. To the extent that many people still regard this conception of social life as having genuine appeal, traditional conservatism remains a viable alternative to both liberalism and neoliberalism as a basis on which to found a social and political morality. That said, I return to my earlier observation that traditional conservatism cannot serve as a political philosophy for the modern state. Whether this tells against traditional conservatism or against the modern state is as much a matter for history as for philosophy to judge.

13

Understanding Education

Introduction

In the previous chapter I quoted Mill in terms that may discomfort some contemporary liberals, and by the same token commend him to social conservatives of right and left. What these passages indicate is that as a political philosopher he in certain respects more in the natural law tradition of Aristotle and Aquinas than he is in the contractualist one of Rawls and Dworkin. Mill also finds an important, but often overlooked place in his moral psychology for acquired and settled habits of character, i.e. for virtue and vice. In *On Liberty* he writes as follows:

> It *really* is of *importance*, not only what men do, but also what manner of men they are that do it. Among the works of man, which human life is rightly employed in perfecting and beautifying, the first in *importance* surely is man himself. … Human nature is not a machine to be built after a model, and set to do exactly the work prescribed for it, but a tree, which requires to grow and develop itself on all sides, according to the tendency of the inward forces which make it a living thing.[1]

Then in 1867 less than ten years after the publication of *On Liberty*, Mill delivered his Inaugural Address as Rector of the University of St Andrews on the subject of education. In it he offers the following:

> If we wish men to practice virtue, it is worth while trying to make them love virtue, and feel it an object in itself, and not

---

[1]   J.S. Mill, *On Liberty* (1859), Ch. III, para 4.

a tax paid for leave to pursue other objects. It is worth training them to feel, not only actual wrong or actual meanness, but the absence of noble aims and endeavours, as not merely blamable but also degrading.[2]

For Mill, as for Aristotle and Aquinas, virtue is necessary to the attainment of a good human life, and education is necessary for the attainment of virtue. At the outset of his 'Address' Mill explains that he is not concerned with education in the broad sense of 'whatever helps to shape the human being' but intends to confine himself 'to education in the narrower sense; the culture which each generation purposely gives to those who are to be its successors'[3] and it is in connection with this that he discusses the need to inculcate virtue as a matter of judgement and feeling. Mill takes all of this for granted, as would his audience, but this may seem to beg large and important questions about the aims of education, the authority of the teacher, and the legitimacy of 'training in virtue'. In this chapter I shall be concerned with these matters and with the course of recent philosophical thinking with regard to them.

Let me begin, however, with a figure born in the year following Mill's death in 1873, from whom I have already quoted in advocacy of the value of practical philosophy, *viz.* G.K. Chesterton. In 1910 Chesterton published *What's Wrong with the World* containing a section on education within which there is a chapter headed 'Authority the Unavoidable'. What this suggests, and what Chesterton like Mill clearly saw is that education involves a process of authoritative transmission of beliefs, attitudes and abilities from those who possess them to those who lack them. He makes this point with characteristic style:

> Education is only truth in a state of transmission; and how can we pass on truth if it has never come into our hand ... I know that certain crazy pedants have attempted to counter this difficulty by maintaining that education is not instruction at all. They present the process as coming not from outside, from the teacher, but entirely from inside the boy.

[2]   J.S. Mill, *Inaugural Address* delivered to the University of St Andrews (London: Longmans, Green, Reader and Dyer, 1867), p. 44.

[3]   Mill, *ibid.* p. 4.

> Education, they say, is the Latin for leading out or drawing
> out the dormant faculties of each person [*educare*]. ... There
> is, indeed, in each living creature a collection of forces and
> functions; but education means producing these in particu-
> lar shapes and training them to particular purposes, or it
> means nothing at all. Speaking is the most practical
> instance of the whole situation. You may indeed 'draw out'
> squeals and grunts from the child by simply poking him
> and pulling him about ... But you will wait and watch very
> patiently indeed before you draw the English language out
> of him. That you have got to put into him; and there's an
> end on the matter.[4]

It is tempting to leave the issue there, confident that anyone reading Mill's and Chesterton's words will be convinced of their truth; but a philosophical discussion calls for
a more elaborate articulation and defence of a thesis than
these quotations provide. In the following sections, therefore, I shall say something about the philosophy of education as an area of systematic thought, and then embark
upon the task of giving an account of education itself as a
norm-bearing and norm-constrained social practice.

As will become clear, I believe that in some sense education is conservative, indeed that it *must* be so. But this necessity indicates that the conservatism in question is not that of
a particular political or cultural outlook. Of its nature education involves a commitment to the transmission from one
generation to the next of a set of cognitive and social values;
otherwise expressed, it involves inculcating in its recipients
understanding of and respect for certain traditions. That
does not imply, however, a commitment to educational
practices designed to instill an unquestioning respect for
the established political order, or for political authority
more generally, or for market liberalism. Arguments for
and against these views rest on moral, social, historical and
economic premises additional to those that I claim establish
the case for a tradition-conserving idea of education. For
those with a Chestertonian appetite for paradox, the main
point could be put by saying that reason makes conserva-

---

[4]   G.K. Chesterton, *What's Wrong with the World* (London: Cassell,
        1910), pp. 200–1.

tive traditionalists of us all even those of us who are, for example, radical anti-schoolers.

Philosophy of Education

As a branch of academic study the philosophy of education is a quite new subject, going back perhaps to the second world war but not much before then and not taking its present form until the 1960s.[5] Of course some major philosophers occasionally thought and wrote about education in earlier periods, most famously Plato in the *Republic*, St Augustine in *De Magistro*, Aquinas in *De Veritate*, Descartes in his *Discourse on Method*, Rousseau in *Emile*, and Dewey in *Democracy and Education*. Other figures such as Comenius, Pestalozzi, Herbart, Froebel and Montessori set out systematic theories of educational aims and methods. Nonetheless, it is only in the second half of the twentieth century that philosophy of education established itself as an area of organised philosophical speculation.

This establishment and the future prospects for the subject are keyed to a number of social and academic factors of which I shall only comment on two, both of which are related to more general developments in philosophy. First, is the post-war development in Anglo-phone academic philosophy of an understanding of its own competence and proper methods of enquiry as constituting a second order activity concerned with the task of clarifying confusions in various areas of thought, such as the natural and social sciences, religion, and morality. Given this conception of philosophy as 'thought about thought' and about the practices that thought informs, it was not long before some philosophers began to examine the central ideas and assumptions

[5]   For an interesting account of its history as an academic subject related to mainstream Anglo-American philosophy see R. F. Dearden, 'Philosophy of Education, 1952-82', *British Journal of Educational Studies*, 30 (1982); and Randall Curren, Emily Robertson and Paul Hager, 'The Analytical Movement' in Randall Curren ed. *A Companion to the Philosophy of Education* (Oxford: Balckwell, 2003). See also Randall Curren, 'History of Philosophy of Education' in Edward Craig ed. *The Routledge Encyclopedia of Philosophy* (London: Routledge, 1999).

of education. So was born and grew *analytical philosophy of education*, the leading proponents of which included Israel Scheffler, Richard Peters and Paul Hirst at Harvard, London and Cambridge, respectively.[6]

True to its self-conception this approach saw its aim as being that of understanding the nature of education in its most general structure; not studying the particularities of this or that teaching method, or proposing specific educational goals, but discerning the overall form of educational activity and distinguishing within this the supporting framework of concepts and values. Typically this involved analysing the notions of *teaching* and of *learning*, of *education*, *socialisation* and *indoctrination*, of knowledge and commitment, and so on. Although such a study was primarily reflective, aiming at understanding practice rather than at supporting or changing it, there were several points where theory touched upon policy.

First, analysis sometimes reveals confusions in pre-reflective and theoretical ways of thinking. For example, although he was not concerned with educational issues Peter Geach's arguments against so called 'abstractionist' accounts of concept formation were taken up by philosophers of education and used in criticism of certain educational theories and methods.[7] Second, and relatedly, a familiar conclusion of philosophical analysis is the demonstration of inconsistency and fallacious reasoning. One area

---

[6]   See I. Scheffler, *The Language of Education* (New York: Thomas, 1962). Peters' important early contributions include *Authority, Responsibility and Education* (London: George Allen and Unwin, 1959), and *Ethics and Education* (London: George Allen and Unwin, 1966). Characteristic samplings of the interests and methods adopted by philosophers considering educational issues in the 'golden age' of analytical philosophy of education are to be found in two anthologies edited by Peters: *The Concept of Education* (London: Routledge & Kegan Paul, 1967) and *Philosophy of Education* (Oxford: OUP, 1973). For a later set of essays some of which reflect back upon Peters' work see D. Cooper ed. *Education, Values and Mind: Essays for R.S. Peters* (London: Routledge & Kegan Paul, 1986).

[7]   See P. Geach, *Mental Acts* (London: Routledge & Kegan Paul, 1958) and for the deployment of related considerations in connection with educational theory see D.W. Hamlyn, *Experience and the Growth of Understanding* (London: Routledge & Kegan Paul, 1978).

of education in which this sort of result has important implications is that of moral and religious instruction where
issues of rationality and justification are to the fore. The
question of whether the inculcation of virtue and of religious commitment is consistent with educational goals, as
contrasted with the aim of indoctrination, is clearly an
important one the answer to which should bear upon actual
practice.

This leads to the third point of contact. The analysis of
educational concepts often showed them to be evaluatively
or normatively laden inasmuch as the processes and outcomes they describe are implicitly held to be desirable. This
has sometimes been put in terms of a contrast between
internal and external features and relations. For example,
the fact that the injection into a human body of certain
chemicals leads to the destruction of particular kinds of tis-
sue leaves unanswered the question whether to do so is
good, bad or indifferent. By contrast, it is not an open question whether medical treatment is a desirable practice;
hence if administering the chemical is part of such a treatment we can assume, other things being equal, that what is
going on is good. This is because the description 'providing
medical treatment' is internally related to the idea of bringing about or restoring health. This aim is a non-contingent
feature of medicine. Similarly, it is a non-contingent goal of
education to bring about understanding, and it is a conceptual truth that, other things being equal, understanding is
worth attaining, not merely as an instrument to some
further end but for its own sake.

This sort of analytical reasoning was deployed to good
effect in writings by Peters and others revealing the extent
to which education expresses a commitment to the value of
human development. In his book *Ethics and Education*, for
example, Peters argued that education involves processes
leading to the development of a desirable state of mind in
which one achieves some understanding and cares about
what is held to be of value. This is not to say that education is
necessarily successful, or that it cannot be perverted to bad
ends. Just as medical skills can prove inadequate to the res-

toration of health, or even be used to inflict injury, so education can fail or be abused; but these constitute failures or perversions precisely because of the defining goals of medicine and of education: health and virtue, respectively.

Critics of analytical philosophy of education as it was developed in its short 'golden age' from the 1960s to the early 80s often seem to forget that it had these practical and normative connections. They write as if it simply constructed conceptual maps while remaining studiously neutral on issues of policy. This is not so. It is true, however, that philosophy of education in this style had a detached, impersonal quality as contrasted with writings influenced by phenomenology, existentialism, and genealogical hermeneutics[8] and that it lacked the political commitments of left- and right-wing theories and critiques.[9] As economic, demographic and political developments brought about changes in the organisation and funding of schools, colleges and institutes of education an attitude of reflective detachment was criticized as a serious failing in educational theorising. Thus it was argued that analytical philosophy was no longer able to provide the inspiration and methodology for serious thinking about education.[10] Additionally, and ironically, the very changes in government educational policies to which its critics accused it of failing to respond, themselves resulted in reductions in the number of academic posts available to philosophers of education. So the subject began to go into something of a decline within departments and institutes of education; and in the new circumstances of financial recession and cut-backs in higher

[8]   See, for example, Van Cleve Morris, *Existentialism in Education* (New York: Harper and Row, 1966); Bernard Curtis and Wolfe Mays eds, *Phenomenology and Education: Self-Consciousness and its Development* (London: Methuen, 1978) and David Cooper, *Authenticity and Learning: Nietzsche's Educational Philosophy* (London: Routledge & Kegan Paul, 1983).

[9]   See K. Harris, *Education and Knowledge* (London: Routledge and Kegan Paul, 1979); Harold Entwistle, *Class, Culture and Education* (London: Routledge and Kegan Paul, 1979); David Cooper, *Illusions of Equality* (London: Routledge & Kegan Paul, 1980).

[10] See, for example, John Harris' review 'Recent Work in the Philosophy of Education', *Philosophical Quarterly*, 33 (1983).

education expenditure it is unlikely to see any reversal of its institutional position.

Education as a Theme Within Social and Political Philosophy

This would suggest a bleak future for philosophy of education had it not had a new lease of life in another guise. To explain this I need to turn to the second factor bearing upon the position of the subject and to show how developments within Anglo-American philosophy have led to a resurgence of philosophical thinking about education, be it largely outside the context of the professional sub-discipline. This trend, however, is not back towards the analysis of educational concepts. For one thing the results achieved by Peters and others remain available, though we may need to be reminded of them. Rather it is towards the development of philosophy of education as an aspect of practical philosophy.

I remarked that some critics of the analytical approach accused it of having neglected the ethics and politics of education, and suggested that this may overlook the extent to which analysis may bear upon practice. Nevertheless there is justice in the charge, though it is somewhat ironic as it reveals a failure of philosophy of education to keep pace with trends in the parent discipline rather than a slavish attachment to its orthodoxies. For, during the period that Peters and his followers were applying the methods of conceptual analysis, moral and political philosophers were re-examining and frequently rejecting an assumption associated with those methods, namely, that philosophy can only describe the structure of thought and action and not judge it to be good, bad, right or wrong.

As we have already seen, from the early 1970s a new sense had emerged of the potential of philosophical enquiry in areas of individual conduct and social policy. The decade that began with the publication of Rawls's *A Theory of Justice* (1971) then saw other major works such as Robert Nozick's *Anarchy, State and Utopia* (1974) and Michael Walzer's *Spheres of Justice* (1980). In moral philosophy several authors attempted to derive substantial moral claims and even entire ethical systems from the logic of practical reason. Important contributions of this sort include Thomas Nagel's *The Possibility of Altruism* (1970), Alan Donagan's *Theory of Morality* (1977) and Alan Gewirth's *Reason and Morality* (1978). In the 1980s these were joined by studies which argued that values cannot be understood or justified save in their historical context, the most important contributions in this genre being MacIntyre's *After Virtue* (1981), *Whose Justice? Which Rationality?* (1988) and *Three Rival Versions of Moral Enquiry* (1990).

There is no single preferred method employed by these philosophers but they share a belief in the possibility of diagnostic and practical reasoning and a conviction that this is something that it is important for philosophers to do. While such reasoning takes different forms a recurrent tendency, in keeping with its analytical heritage, is to demonstrate the conceptual and normative structure of a way of thinking and to exhibit its relation to other notions and practices. Rawls, for example, tries to show how our thinking about justice is shaped by an ideal common in Western societies of citizens as free and equal persons. I have discussed Rawls' ideas in some detail in previous chapters and all that needs to be added here is that for Rawls we do not begin political philosophy in a moral vacuum but instead start with certain shared commitments and concerns and try to work out acceptable forms of justification in the light of these, or of critically refined versions of them. As the process proceeds further, values come into view and lines of arguments begin to take definite form. Meanwhile, MacIntyre and Charles Taylor[11] who both stress the historical and cultural contexts of moral and political thought use their explorations of the past to locate the sources of our normative assumptions and to relate them to our evolved

---

[11] See, for example, Taylor's major studies *Sources of the Self* (Cambridge: CUP, 1990) and *A Secular Age* (Cambridge, MA: Harvard University Press, 2007).

sense of ourselves and of our many and various relations with others.[12]

Reflection upon education now needs to draw more extensively from recent philosophy adopting the full range of concepts and methods developed in the last twenty or so years. There is no shortage of issues requiring attention but I offer a few to indicate something of the relevant range:

1.   How do the claims of universal liberal education stand when challenged by the particular values and limitations associated with national and other cultural identities?

2.   What is to be made of the idea that education is a form of personal development when some philosophers of mind are attacking the central notions of common-sense psychology, including that of persons as unified moral subjects, and others arguing that personhood is a projected construct?

3.   Are there universal educational values or is the best we can arrive at a set of socially relative norms?

4.   How are we to conceive language-learning in the face of philosophical critiques of the very idea of objective meaning and relatedly of correct and incorrect usage?

5.   How can the state justify funding public education out of taxes levied from childless individuals?

6.   How, if at all, can the allocation of resources for the provision of art and sport education be justified in societies whose industrial economies are in need of scientists and engineers, and in a world where millions live out their short lives in ignorance and pain?

7.   How should educators respond to the cognitive and moral values of popular culture, particularly as this is influenced through the various news and entertainment media?

---

[12]   See also MacIntyre, *The Tasks of Philosophy: Selected Essays, Volume 1*, and *Ethics and Politics: Selected Essays, Volume 2* (Cambridge: Cambridge University Press, 2006).

8.   In what sense, if any, are clever and educated people better and more admirable than unintelligent and ignorant ones?

I shall not attempt to resolve these questions but only stress their practical importance and philosophical character. We need answers to them, however qualified and provisional these might be, and philosophers of education who have nothing to say about them cannot expect to command the interest let alone the respect of other practical philosophers, or more importantly of those who feel the need of understanding and resolution but who recognise their own inability to achieve them. To date, educational theorists have not shown sufficient interest in the challenges and opportunities presented by the best of recent work in moral and social philosophy and in the philosophies of mind, action and language. But as writers in these latter fields find themselves engaging with aspects of educational principles and policies, and as some philosophers of education have acquired a command of the more general philosophical literature, the situation has been improving.[13] In saying that, however, it does not follow that what is drawn from general philosophy is sound as I will illustrate in the following section.

Aristotelian philosophy of Education

Several academic writers on educational theory have begun to use the phrase 'post-analytic philosophy of education' to characterize recent work produced by Anglophone philos-

---

[13]   For relevant contributions from the side of moral and social philosophy see Thomas Nagel, *Equality and Partiality* (New York: OUP, 1991); Charles Taylor, *Multiculturalism and the Politics of Recognition* (Princeton, NJ: Princeton University Press, 1992) and Bernard Williams, *Truth and Truthfulness* (Princeton, NJ: Princeton University Press, 2002); and for educational studies informed by contemporary ethical and political theory see Eamonn Callan, *Autonomy and Schooling* (McGill-Queen's University Press, 1988) and *Creating Citizens: Political Education and Liberal Democracy* (Oxford: Oxford University Press, 1997); and David Carr, *Educating the Virtues* (London: Routledge, 1991).

ophers.[14] Like the term 'postmodernism' which I shall be
exploring in the next chapter this expression is sometimes
employed to denote particular ideas (not always the same
ones) but more often it serves simply to indicate a range of
work united principally by its contemporaneity and by its
rejection of the methods and preoccupations of post-war
conceptual analysts. One familiar element in this recent
movement is normative or first-order ethics. Another distinctive component is the trend towards the development of
philosophies of education derived from general metaphysical theories.

This is a return to an older tradition, but the main form of
recent development is very different to familiar philosophies inasmuch as it aims to give a theory of education
(often with prescriptions for practice) derived from a
reductive physicalist ontology. Two writers in this area *viz.*
J.C. Walker and C.W. Evers describe their approach as 'Materialist Pragmatism'.[15] In one respect I have considerable
sympathy with this development. In an introduction to
their materialist educational philosophy Walker and Evers
write as follows:

> Without doubt one of the most serious gaps in analytical
> philosophy of education has been its failure even to
> acknowledge major developments in philosophical logic,
> epistemology, ontology and philosophy of language stem-
> ming from the work of such philosophers as Davidson,
> Donellan, Putnam, Rorty, Sellars and, most importantly,
> Quine. ... We hope that the way might now be clearer for an
> explicit, tough-minded yet open-minded resumption of
> theory-competition in philosophy of education, and that
> this will serve to enhance the development of educational
> theory and practice.[16]

[14] See essays in 'Post-Analytic Philosophy of Education', special issue
of *Educational Philosophy and Theory*, 19 (1987).
[15] James Walker & Colin Evers, 'Towards a Materialist Pragmatist
Philosophy of Education', *Education Research and Perspectives*, 11
(1984).
[16] See Walker & Evers, *op.cit.*, pp. 25 & 31. Compare the remarks about
the 'serious gaps' in analytical philosophy of education with
Cooper's observations in *Education, Values and Mind, op.cit.*, p. 6.

Certainly philosophy of education has been conducted largely in isolation from the main body of the subject. Likewise the aspiration to return to substantial theorizing about education merits endorsement. Where I part company with the Materialist Pragmatists is over the issue of what general metaphysical and related views commend themselves. For while I also am drawn to a version of philosophical naturalism the two underlying conceptions of nature are mutually opposed.

Earlier I argued that in considering the purposes of education one must focus attention on the character of its products. Education is a process of formation involving the realization of certain potentialities. Whatever the particularities of the case, education is part of a general movement towards the full actualization of the subject's nature. To formulate the goals of human education, therefore, and to determine how best these might be achieved one needs to have an account of the kind of thing a human being is. That is to say one needs an organized set of descriptions of the various capacities characteristic of human beings *per se*: the pattern of their development and inter-relations and of the states and activities in which a developed human being most fully realizes his or her nature. Such an organized body of knowledge answers to the interests of both theoretical and practical reason. It serves to answer questions both as to what is the case and as to what ought to be done — achieving the latter indirectly by determining what ought to be the case. This position has been sketched from different perspectives in earlier chapters and identified as a form of Aristotelian naturalism.

Education is aimed at developing our nature by systematically cultivating various capacities in accordance with their inbuilt structure and teleology. On this account education may be both instrumentally and intrinsically valuable. As regards the first, it is of worth inasmuch as it satisfies a pre-requisite of human flourishing. It is needed because it is the means of developing those practical and intellectual skills whose exercise is required to achieve a good human life. It is also intrinsically valuable because some of the activities it involves are themselves realizations of capacities the exercise of which is partly constitutive of human flourishing. Again various activities spring to mind such as art-making, interpretative enquiries, sport and intellectual problem solving.

The central philosophical concepts in a theory of education of this sort are those of a *human person* and of *human virtues*. The role of the former is obvious enough. A teleological theory requires an account of the agents involved. The role of the idea of appropriate virtues, meanwhile, is most easily grasped if one thinks of virtue not in a restrictedly moral sense but rather as an enduring excellence of character with respect to any given human activity. One of the best and most sensitive thinkers on the subject of the philosophy of virtue is Aquinas who forges the connection between human nature, teleology and virtue in the first section of his 'Treatise on Habits'. He writes:

> Habit implies a disposition in relation to a thing's nature and to its operation or end, by reason of which disposition a thing is well or ill disposed thereto ... By the form the nature of a thing is perfected: yet the subject needs to be disposed in regard to the form by some disposition ... But if the form be such that it can operate in diverse ways [as is the case with man who can choose how to act] it needs to be disposed to its operation by means of habits.[17]

and later he writes:

> Virtue denotes a certain perfection of a power. Now a thing's perfection is considered chiefly in regard to its end. But the end of power is act. Wherefore power is said to be perfect, according as it is determinate to its act ... But the rational powers, which are proper to man, are not determinate to one particular action, but are inclined indifferently to many: and they are determinate to acts by means of habits ... Therefore human virtues are habits.[18]

According to this view, then, the purpose of education is to promote good human lives by cultivating virtue. Remember that the terms 'good' and 'virtue' are not being used here in a narrowly moral sense. Indeed, their primary meanings

---

[17] *Summa Theologiae* Ia, IIae, q.49, a 4.
[18] *Summa Theologiae*, Ia, IIae, q. 55, a 1.

are in fact non-moral ones. This form of ethical naturalism gives an account of the proper application of moral notions in terms of the promotion and achievement of certain kinds of life, the description of which employs only value concepts appropriate to the various aspects of human nature. The idea of virtue is likewise to be explicated by reference to whatever capacities and dispositions are required as means to the achievement of a good life or are partly constitutive of it.[19]

Writing in answer to the question 'Must an Educator Have an Aim?' R.S. Peters observed that: 'Many in recent times have blamed philosophers for neglecting their traditional task in relation to education. For, in the old days, it is argued, philosophers explained what the good life and the good society were; and this provided aims for educationalists'.[20] In the following discussion he elaborates the theme that a feature of traditional philosophies of education is that they have implications for curriculum planning regarded as a matter of determining particular methods for the achievement of the good kind of life. However, he claims that this model of how to proceed, as involving the adoption of means to premeditated ends, 'misleads us in the sphere of education'. Part of his reason for objecting to it is precisely that the model presupposes a view of education as having a generally accepted purpose and this is something which he, and many others, wishes to deny.

I shall consider and offer responses to two ways in which this objection might be understood. But before moving on to the general task of defence it will be as well to note that Peters is right in thinking that views which propose an aim of education may serve as sources for the derivation of curriculum policy. So far as concerns the virtue-centred teleo-

---

[19] In speaking of the 'proper application' of moral notions I am deliberately avoiding the issue of whether ethical naturalism of the sort proposed should claim to be giving a full account of the intensions or senses of moral concepts or restrict itself to the claim that it is delineating their extensions or referents or doing something in between. The issue is an important one but cannot be addressed here.

[20] R.S. Peters, *Authority, Responsibility and Education* (London: Allen & Unwin, 1963) pp. 83 ff.

logical approach which I have advocated, this derivation may proceed in appropriately Aristotelian fashion by way of the construction of series of practical syllogisms leading from one or more characterizations of the desired end down divergent strings of prescriptions to actual policies.[21] So far as concerns the content of these it will be sufficient to say that the appropriate curriculum would be one structured around the task of enabling children to realize and to understand their nature as rational and social animals, and to comprehend the structure of their environment as an object of theoretical knowledge, practical activity and aesthetic contemplation. In short, a rather traditional blend of sciences, humanities and arts and one at odds with the socially contingent, utilitarian life-skills approach still favoured among many educationalists.

Recent Challenges

At this point let me turn from advocacy to defence against three kinds of objection to the approach outlined above. These can be strung together in the following tripartite challenge. First, my view assumes an account of persons as bearers of 'folk-psychological' attributes and this has been shown to be flawed and perhaps even incoherent. Second, even if human persons are as everyday psychology represents them as being, the attempt to derive normative conclusions from facts about human kind relies upon a long-discredited teleology and in any event commits the naturalistic fallacy. Third, even if an appropriate view of persons and of the good life for them could be established it would be illegitimate to invoke it in the context of determining educational policy since the latter may not invoke substantial metaphysical and ethical outlooks.

As I noted earlier, the distinctive feature of Materialist Pragmatism is its presumption of an unqualified physicalist

---

[21]   For some discussion of this see Gregory Mellema, 'An Aristotelian Approach to Thinking about Educational Aims', *New Scholasticism*, 198 (1983).

ontology. Something of the character of this is apparent in the following sample of quotations.

> If the cultivation of rationality is to be an important educational aim then some account of rationality needs to be given. Strong realism and strong physicalism imply that a plausible theory of rationality needs to take account of what thinkers are as physical systems ...
>
> ... Worries about the truth of folk platitudes can be allayed if we view commonsense thinking as a beginning of science and expect revision and refinement as science progresses. Central to [these] worries is the idea that psychological concepts and physical concepts cross-classify one another in such a way as to preclude the identification of properties across psycho-physical reduction. ... I propose we can [overcome this problem] by making use of functionalist frameworks.[22]
>
> Of course, not all explanation as yet admits of reduction to physics or elimination in favour of physical explanation, and many deny that the job can be done even in principle. For M[aterialist] P[ragmatism], however, the general direction is clear. The tests for social and educational theory are whether it can be systematised in the required fashion and whether it is physicalist.[23]
>
> The strategy behind this demand for coherence with physical theory is not just the elimination of substance dualism ... and attendant methodological bifurcations. Rather the aim is to press for the elimination of property dualism, either through the provision of type-type reductions for mental elimination, of mental types by other non-equivalent types, drawn from the developing theoretical taxonomies of scientific theory. This approach might be regarded as a form of what Paul Churchland calls 'eliminative materialism'.[24]

These authors are drawing upon arguments that originate in the writings of Quine and Wilfred Sellars. For brevity I shall sketch an outline of the latter's ideas only. These are also of partiular interest inasmuch as they have again

---

[22] Valina Raimer, 'Physicalism, Realism and Education: A Functionalist Approach' *Educational Philosophy and Theory*, 19, *op.cit.*, pp. 47, 49 & 50.

[23] Walker & Evers, 'Towards a Materialist Pragmatist Philosophy of Education', *op.cit.*, p. 30.

[24] Walker, 'Naturalism and Philosophy of Education', *op.cit.*, p. 18.

become influential through the work of Sellars' former student Paul Churchland.

Everyone agrees that we have an idea of ourselves and of others as centres of consciousness and agency. We explain our fellow human beings' behaviour by interpreting it as engaged in on the basis of certain beliefs and in pursuit of certain purposes. We regard beliefs as logically structured attitudes which, if all is in order, represent objects and features of our common environment. We suppose that in discourse and through the manipulation of other media we are able to communicate with one another: conveying information, expressing feelings, inducing responses and so on. In brief, we have an idea of ourselves as bearers of psychological states and subjects of intentional activity.

The question is whether this idea is correct. Sellars invites us to consider how one might come by such a view.[25] Imagine a group of creatures apparently like ourselves who engage in various primitive forms of group behaviour. Suppose they develop some sign system which in due course acquires the complexity of language. They use this to co-ordinate their efforts and to assess its progress. Imagine now that they extend its application to characterize each other's verbal and non-verbal behaviour. One member of the group, say, announces that he wants to bring something about and so is going to proceed in a certain way. He then goes on to carry this out. Others might now comment: 'He said he wanted to do such and such and then he did it'. This might become a regular pattern: utterance followed by non-verbal performance followed by commentary. Suppose, however, that at a later stage the same member embarks upon the task in the usual manner and circumstances but with the difference that in the period preceding his activity he is silent. His companions wanting to explain his behaviour as due to prior conditions might now say: 'He acted in the way he usually does consequent upon saying what he wants to achieve and how he is going to achieve it.

[25] Wilfred Sellars, 'Empiricism in the Philosophy of Mind' sections XII-XV in Sellars, *Science Perception and Reality* (London: Routledge & Kegan Paul, 1963).

So there must have been something unobservable happening which is like what occurs in the usual circumstance and produces the familiar behaviour'. That, in short, is an account of how we might have constructed the concept of thought as 'inner-saying' which sometimes gives rise to overt bodily behaviour.

The central idea which drives Churchland's eliminative aspirations is that psychological concepts are theoretical notions introduced via hypotheses created to explain observable events and processes by positing internal (and unobserved) causes. More generally the concept of *persons*, as centres of consciousness and agency, is a large scale theoretical construct composed out of these various explanatory notions. But whereas the creatures in the myth, and ourselves until quite recently, could do little better by way of explanation than this, we are now in a position to delve deep into the internal causes of systematic bodily movement. In doing so what we find are peripheral sense organs, afferent nerves, synaptic networks, efferent nerves, motor organs and the such like. What we have not found, however, are beliefs, desires, intentions, motives and other instances of folk-pyschological categories. What we ought to do, therefore (if only as theorists) is to abandon 'person psychology' in favour of a theoretically respectable physicalist alternative: that being cognitive science and/or neuroscience. At any rate we must reject any philosophical position that involves a concept of persons as thinking agents. And this, of course, puts paid to the account of education and its purposes proposed above.

I have discussed eliminative materialism in connection with Churchland's views elsewhere and at some length I shall not dwell on these issues here.[26] Let me simply offer some observations by way of response to the general objection to personal psychology. First, one should be suspicious

---

[26] John Haldane, 'Folk Psychology and the Explanation of Human Behaviour', *Proceedings of the Aristotelian Society* Supplementary 62 (1988). This is a contribution to a symposium with Paul Churchland. Our exchange continued in *Proceedings of the Aristotelian Society*, Vol. 93 (1993).

of the claim that concepts of thought and action are theoretical notions purporting to designate unobserved entities postulated in causal-explanatory laws. Against this, consider the possibility (faithful to the phenomenology of much psychological description) that many of these concepts are observational. We, quite literally, see human beings speak, laugh, cry, lose their nerve, fall into confusion, comprehend a point, provoke one another, offer comfort and so on. And since these are all person-involving features in seeing them we see persons. Second, on the theoretical view the meaning of such concepts must be given by their roles in closed universal generalizations which relate their instances as cause and effect. But there are no such psycho-behavioural causal laws.[27] Third, the effort to eliminate psychological descriptions in favour of physicalist ones by identifying the relevant bodily events, otherwise characterized in the language of action, fails because the only coherent principles of identity and individuation are those provided by concepts of intentional behaviour.

This last point is best made by example. Suppose I want to check on the source of an essay I have discussed. I reach over to a pile of papers on an adjacent desk. Consider various descriptions couched in the terms of folk-psychology which might be given of this behaviour. I am producing an essay, checking a reference, finding a piece of paper, reaching across a space and so on. It is a familiar thought that no type-type identity theory is possible correlating actions and bodily movements. There are, for example, many ways of checking a reference and not all extensions of arms are reachings. What should be added, however, is that it is equally impossible to provide token-token identities. That is to say the claim that actions can be wholly accounted for within a physicalist ontology, as movements of quantities of matter, is false. The nature of the problem for physicalism emerges as soon as one asks what is the candidate (token) physical event with which my act of checking on the reference is to be identified? Presumably some bodily move-

---

[27] Haldane, 'Folk Psychology and the Explanation of Human Behaviour', *op.cit.*, section III.

ment, but which? One might proceed to individuate one by specifying spatio-temporal boundaries—a movement within a certain space occurring during a given period of time. But think of all the movements involving my body that might have occurred in the relevant spatio-temporal location: heartbeats, blinks, limb-trembles, contractions of foot muscles and so on. Of course, some of these will have been parts of the action but two points should be noted. First, there is no prospect of individuating relevant movements of matter save via some applicable action concept. Second, the relationship between the movements so individuated and the action itself is not one of identity but one of constitution. Actions are in this sense more than bodily movements and in the same sense and for the same reason (the invovlement of psychological properties) persons are more than bodies. The prospect of physicalist reduction or elimination is thus illusory.

I began this section mentioning two further objections to an Aristotelian-Thomistic approach to educational theory and practice. First, that the attempt to derive normative conclusions from facts about human kind relies upon a long-discredited teleology and commits the fallacy of attempting to derive *ought* from *is*. Second, even if the relevant view of persons and of their good could be established it would be illegitimate to invoke it in the context of determining educational policy since the latter may not invoke substantial metaphysical and ethical outlooks. Having addressed both of these issues more than once in the preceding chapters I shall not discuss them further, save to say that by this point I hope that having considered my responses on these various matters readers may feel that the position that has been developed cannot easily or unquestion-beggingly be set aside.

Conclusion

So much then for the general question of philosophy of education and its relation to practical philosophy. In conclusion I want to return to the specific issue introduced at the outset,

that of the nature of education as a social practice concerned
with the transmission of certain traditional values. To
describe education in these terms may seem to beg the question against other possible accounts, or if it fails to do this
that may suggest that the description is so accommodating
as to be vacuous. Earlier I concluded, somewhat provoca-
tively, that reason must make 'conservative traditionalists'
of us all; now I need to explain and substantiate that claim
while ensuring that it does not in the process reduce to
triviality.

I claimed that it is a non-contingent goal of education to
aim at bringing about understanding. There are important
and difficult philosophical and empirical questions concerning the relative contribution to this process of teacher
and pupil. I cannot explore these now but it is clear enough
that no activities on the part of the teacher could produce
understanding, as contracted say with a behavioural
response, unless the pupil had the potentiality to acquire
and exercise concepts and practical skills. This in turn raises
questions about the nature and extent of human intellectual
predispositions. Whatever these, however, it is also obvious
that if left to his or her own devices a child will not self-
generate understanding. Put in terms of the ancient and
medieval vocabularies in which these issues were once
debated, the growth of knowledge depends upon innate
structures but these are 'potentialities' not 'actualities'. And
in order for these potentialities to be realised and given
determinate content there need to be external sources of
formation and instruction. As Chesterton well expressed it
in the passage quoted earlier:

> There is indeed, in each living creature a collection of forces
> and functions; but education means producing these in
> particular shapes and training them to particular purposes
> or it means nothing at all. Speaking is the most practical
> instance of the whole situation. ... You will wait and watch
> very patiently indeed before you draw the English lan-
> guage out of [a child]. That you have got to put into him.

The example of language is particular apposite. Along with
co-ordinated movement, speech is the first thing we try to

teach a child. That is because we regard it as the primary mode of expression and communication for rational, social animals. We try to establish contact with an infant as a potential participant in ongoing social and personal practices that are largely mediated by language. But it is very important to see that the child's acquisition of its first language is not a matter of coming to possess a medium *externally* related to the various activities, traditions and institutions that shape the infants social environment; rather the language is itself part of the social fabric and is shaped by, and in turn influences, the development of these various ways of thinking and acting. To acquire a language is to acquire a culture. It is to become part of a socially and historically extended tradition.

Moreover, what is true of socially embedded natural languages is also true of other symbolic forms. When a child learns to use numerals or to draw pictures it is not acquiring a medium of representation that is neutral with respect to its primary exercises. A child simply has not mastered the use of the numeral '2', or of a basic pictorial element unless it can deploy these in ways that make sense to those who instructed him or her in them. To learn English, or arithmetic or drawing or basic morality is to be inducted into a complete set of rule- or norm-governed practices. It simply makes no sense at this stage to regard instructor and pupil as equals with respect to the content that might be expressed through the system of representations. It is not just that the art teacher can draw better than the child what lies on the table before them, but that through acquiring and gaining some mastery of the tradition of draughtsmanship the teacher sees the objects in ways as yet unavailable to the child. Learning to draw is a way of learning to see and understand; learning to read and write is a way of coming to organize experience and imagine possibilities; learning moral values is a way of developing a respect for others.

Since learning, as I am concerned with it here, is the correlative of being taught what one learns is to a greater or lesser degree ways of seeing, understanding, valuing, imagining and behaving that are antecedently possessed by the teacher who is thereby authoritatively qualified with respect to them. Of course this is not to say that education is or should be a process of social cloning. Differences in experience, ability, temperament, and imagination will lead to both extensions of existing practices and to criticisms of them. But in the first instance is a matter of conserving bodies of knowledge, sentiment and conduct as these are incarnate in traditional practices. Even if it were not welcome, authority is unavoidable.

14

Cultural Theory and the Study of Human Affairs

Introduction

In the previous chapter we met with one kind of radical cultural critique, that of Materialist Pragmatism, which challenged the assumptions of traditional philosophical humanism from a standpoint influenced by neuro-psychology and science more generally. In this chapter I wish to consider and respond to another radical critique that again would sweep away traditional understandings of human nature, values and purposes. In doing so it would also undermine moral objectivity, normative political theory, and the practice of education conceived of as an introduction to settled facts about human nature and what pertains to its good. It is somewhat ironic, therefore, that the standpoint from which this second critique emerges is a 'humanist' one, associated with modern literary and cultural studies. As we shall see, however, the self-conception of this form of radical postmodernism is as remote from the kind of 'pre-modern' philosophical naturalism I have been exploring as is materialist reductionism.

Reading some of the remarkably varied literature which features in its titles, or otherwise makes great play with the words 'postmodernism' and 'postmodernity' (and indeed of 'post-postmodernity') it is difficult to resist the conclusion that these are terms in desperate, and unpromising, search of a unified theory. Of course, it might easily be conceded that much of this material is flotsam, fragments of ideas gathered together only by the currents that underlie the tide of fashion, but then observed that beneath this debris there is a more serious and better integrated body of critical literature which characterises itself (or is characterised by others) as 'postmodernist'. Even among this, however, the virtues of clarity, precision and self-discipline are often conspicuously lacking, and the resulting confusions vitiate the attempts of the authors to say something true, significant and useful about the general character of western thought and culture in the contemporary period and in the centuries preceding this. Greater scholarship and improved critical skills, including those involved in self-criticism, would do much to assist the chroniclers of 'modernism' and the prophets of 'postmodernity' in their efforts. Beyond these points, however, there are difficulties of other kinds that may not be surmountable, and the intractability of which would help to explain the often poor standard of literature of these sorts. This chapter is concerned to identify and articulate these philosophical difficulties.

Postmodern Analysis and Cultural Historicism

The problems in question concern the presuppositions of postmodernism (or, more accurately, of some postmodernisms, remembering the ambiguity and vagueness of the term). One such assumption is that of philosophical anti-realism in respect of knowledge, ontology and value. That is to say, the rejection of any view of reality as constituted independently of our conception of it—as being 'there' to be discovered by the exercise of reliable cognitive powers of conception and detection—and of values as forming part of this belief-independent reality. I shall return to this assumption later. A second common but problematic presupposition is that of a broad and theory-driven historicism. This regards the history of thought and culture as dividing into distinct periods, each unified by a set of dominant ideas and social forces and related one to another in significant ways, thereby composing a pattern of development into which the histories of philosophy, art, economics, science, psychology, religion and so on can be fitted. Inasmuch as this sort of cultural historicism is associated with the idea of laws of development, it belongs to a philosophy of history which some postmodernists reject as part and parcel of modernism, but which others embrace as being the only enduring insight of modernist theory. What therefore distinguishes these latter theorists from their modernist predecessors are their views about the current stage of historical development and about the future course of events.

The idea, familiar from Hegel and Marx and indeed from Judaeo-Christian sacred history, that the course of human affairs is in some sense intrinsically intelligible, or is rationally ordered, or exhibits a narrative structure, is a controversial one and not just, or even for the most part, because of the difficulty of providing empirical evidence in support of it. The deepest difficulty is posed by the philosophical question: how is this possible? But setting that metaphysical puzzle to one side, large-scale historical claims about the development of thought and culture *are* challenged by the empirical facts. I do not want to say that the historical assumptions of much postmodernist literature are false. They may be true; I simply do not know. But I do want to insist that they are unwarranted *assumptions*, and to suggest that as our knowledge of the history and internal structure of the various branches of thought and culture grows there is more reason to doubt than to accept the now familiar historicist theses.

I say this notwithstanding that in Anglophone philosophy, for example, there has been a growing fashion among practitioners for the sort of synoptic vision offered by writers such as Alasdair MacIntyre, Richard Rorty, Charles Taylor and Bernard Williams.[1] Indeed, my doubts are not so

---

[1] See the writings of MacIntyre referred to in chapter 1, but in particular *After Virtue* (1981); also Richard Rorty, *Philosophy and the Mirror of Nature* (Oxford: Blackwell, 1980) and *Consequences of*

much allayed by these authors as stirred by them. This said, however, I also believe that students of philosophy, art, religion, politics, economics and so on, can learn something from the attempt to set phases and aspects of these subjects into historical and logical relationships, and that part of what may be learnt in doing so is that the direction of progress need not be co-incident with that of time. To this extent, therefore, I am not altogether unsympathetic to wide-ranging cultural characterisations undertaken in the service of illuminating specific patterns and trends, though to be of value these require to be tethered to secure vantage points, and to be clear and accurate.

What this cautions, then, is great care and attention to detail in the development of cultural analyses and of theories in the history of ideas, especially where these are employed in the service of philosophical arguments, be they in epistemology, metaphysics, aesthetics or social theory. Indeed, my first thesis arises from what has been said so far: it is that the general and unrestricted vocabulary of 'modernism' and of 'postmodernism' is of little worthwhile service to serious enquiries and would be better resorted to rarely, if at all.[2] It encourages reckless generalisation and limits the possibilities of genuine understanding by discouraging independent enquiry in accord with heterodox intuitions: in short in induces hot heads and cold feet. In due course I shall discuss something of what has come to be described as 'postmodernist epistemology' versions of which are associated with Nelson Goodman, Hilary Putnam and other neo-pragmatistsas as well as with Rorty, but at this point it will be apt to turn to the latter's much-celebrated and oft-cited book *Philosophy and the Mirror of Nature* by way of illustrating the dangers of historicising philosophy.

Rorty and the History of the Philosophy of Mind

Rorty's central and highly influential theses are that philosophy, as traditionally conceived of and practised, is in a state of terminal crisis and that the origins of its final phase lie in the modern invention of the mind by philosophers of the seventeenth century, most especially Descartes.[2] According to Rorty, the Cartesian philosophical creation was a conception of the mind as the locus of self-intimating states possessed by an enduring 'I', which is only contingently associated with the human figure it inhabits and through which it interacts with the empirical world; that is to say, a view of the mind as a distinct thing known directly to itself, a conscious subject resident within the frame of the physical body: in short, *mind-body dualism*. On Rorty's account, the idea of the self as the occupant of a logically private viewpoint and the associated epistemology of mental representations (ideas and images) concerning whose existence and character the subject is an incorrigible authority, provided the foundations for philosophy in the modern period. The various aspects of the 'philosophical project of modernity' are thus projected back to the invention of the Cartesian mind. It is essential to Rorty's historicist account of past thought, and to the argument for his 'postmodernist' sequel in which epistemology gives way to edification within the historically conditioned 'conversation of mankind', that there should be this point of origination of classical dualism. Without this history, the 'problematic of modernity' and the 'postmodernist critique' lose their significance and we are just back into largely ahistorical philosophical debate.

Consider, then, the following statements of dualist theory of mind and epistemology, and of their rejection:

> We ... have images that closely resemble [external] physical objects, but they are not material. They live in our minds where we use them in thinking ... But it is without any deceptive play of my imagination with its real or unreal visions that I am quite certain that I am, that I know that I am, and that I love this being and this knowing. Where these truths are concerned I need not quail when [it is said]: 'What if you should be mistaken?' If I am mistaken then I exist. For whoever does not exist can surely not be mistaken either, and if I am mistaken, therefore I exist. ... It fol-

---

[2]   See Rorty *Philosophy and the Mirror of Nature* especially Part One, ch. 1, and Part Two, chs 3 and 4.

lows also that in saying that I know that I know, I am not mistaken. For just as I know that I am, so it holds too that I know that I know. And when I love these two things, I add this same love as a third particular of no smaller value to these things that I know. Nor is my statement, that I love, a mistake, since I am not mistaken in the things that I love; [for] even if they were illusions, it would still be true that I love illusions.[3]

Some have held that our cognitive faculties know [directly] only what is experienced within them, for example, that the senses perceive only impressions. According to this opinion the intellect thinks only of what is experienced within it, i.e. ideas [*species*] ... The opinion, however, is obviously false ... we must say, therefore, that ideas stand in relation to the intellect not as that *of which* it thinks but as that *by which* it thinks [of things].[4]

Nobody knows that he is knowing save in knowing something else and consequently knowledge of an [external] object precedes intellectual self-consciousness.[5]

Each is conscious that it is he himself that thinks ... [but] one and the same man perceives himself both to think and to have sensations. Yet sensation involves the body, so that the body must be said to be part of man ... therefore the intellect whereby [one] thinks is a part of one in such a way that it is somehow united to the body.[6]

It was because [some] held that sensation belonged to the soul that [they] could speak of man [dualistically] as a soul using a body.[7]

The first passage, which offers a very clear statement of epistemological representationalism, of the *cogito ergo sum* argument and of the doctrine of first-person incorrigibility (each identified by Rorty as central components of the Cartesian theory of mind), comes from St Augustine's *De Civitate Dei* (*The City of God*) written about twelve hundred years before Descartes' *Meditations*. The subsequent

[3]   Augustine, *De Civitate Dei* trans. D.S. Weisen (Cambridge, MA: Harvard University Press, 1968) pp. 533-5.
[4]   Aquinas *Summa Theologiae* (London: Eyre and Spottiswoode, 1967-75) la, q. 85, art. 2.
[5]   Aquinas *Super Boethium de Trinitate* trans. and ed. R. Brennan (St Louis, MO: Herder, 1946) i, 3.
[6]   Aquinas, *Summa Theologiae*, la, q. 75, art. 1.
[7]   Aquinas, *Summa Theologiae*, la, q. 75, art. 4.

passages, opposing representationalism and dualism with currently fashionable 'post-Cartesian' doctrines of direct realism and psychophysical monism, are from works written by Thomas Aquinas seven hundred years before Rorty's *Mirror of Nature* and the emergence of 'post-analytic philosophy'.

Clearly something is amiss in the intellectual narrative. I have chosen for criticism just one example of an influential thesis flourished by a fashionable writer. Another suitable case for inspection is the set of claims made by Alasdair MacIntyre about the history of moral thought from the Greeks to the Enlightenment and beyond into the supposed crisis of modernity.[8] MacIntyre is a much better informed writer than Rorty but as one examines the evidence, the general claims, in this case about the development of moral and political thought, again become increasingly problematic and this undermines the characterisation of the contemporary period and *ipso facto* the philosophical theses to which the historicism is related. Let me say again that I am not denying the possibility of insight arising from thinking in an historical mode, from doing philosophy or social theory historically. But I am questioning the notion that there is a general tale to be told about the passage of western thought and culture through certain stages identifiable by period-specific sets of ideas and doctrines.

In part my resistance to this way of thinking is methodological: it encourages prejudgements of uniformity and inattention to differences. But I am also resistant to the attempt to have historicism do the work of argument. For there is a liability to commit two fallacies. The first is that of supposing that if sets of ideas or attitudes have come to be dominant in succession to others then the former are more likely to be true or appropriate. The second is related but runs deeper: it is the thought that the *actual* is somehow an indicator of the *necessary*; that is to say, that the current state

---

[8] MacIntyre, *After Justice* and *Whose Justice? Which Rationality?* For relevant commentary on the former see Charles Larmore *Patterns of Moral Complexity* (Cambridge: Cambridge University Press, 1987) , ch. 2.

of things, being part of an historical movement, points in the direction of what must be, of true reality (notwithstanding that this may be a condition of Heraclitean flux). I characterised this as a fallacy; but, of course, there is a tradition of thought in which it is an axiom: Hegelianism. It is not difficult to read some of the literature in which talk of the 'failure of the project of modernity' and the 'emergency of postmodernity' feature prominently in neo-Hegelian terms; nor is it implausible to do so given the influences on much of this sort of writing.

Cultural History in the Approved Style

One might observe in response to the foregoing that while it might be a suitable warning against prejudgement and perhaps an effective illustration, in connection with Rorty, of the dangers of historicising philosophical and other forms of thought, it does nothing to show that the content of any major claims associated with postmodernist writers is mistaken. Furthermore, I have not yet said anything, save by way of abstract generality, of relevance to social scientific study of human affairs. Let me address these points by first rehearsing the sort of historico-philosophical analysis about which I have been expressing reservations.

The senses of 'postmodernism' are many, disparate and possibly incompatible. None the less, some are predominant. These can be classified roughly as either (a) *analytic-cum-descriptive* or (b) *critical-cum-prescriptive* (or, in some uses, as a blend of the two). That is to say, the term 'postmodernism' is most often used either (a) to characterise a historical period, a cultural condition or a set of attitudes and practices; or (b) to abbreviate a form of criticism of widely held assumptions, and a class of proposals as to how matters should be conceived of and dealt with. By and large these different senses of the word are related to a common use of the term 'modernism', and it may be useful, therefore, to give a rough account of this (admittedly vague) common usage before proceeding to assess certain 'postmodernist' theses and to consider their bearing on the social sciences.

Here, then, is a quick guide to western culture presented in the approved style.

Pre-modernism

The ancient world was the site of the birth of two great forces: monotheism and philosophical rationalism. For a variety of reasons, in part to do with historical contingencies and in part due to the intrinsic character of these forces, there was a union of them in Christianity; most significantly, for what follows, in its western branch. Following well-known difficulties during the fourth, fifth and sixth centuries, the Holy Roman Empire came into its own and by the eleventh century the Papacy gained supremacy over the Emperor. The succeeding few hundred years saw the rise and domination of scholasticism as the intellectual elaboration of the theological, philosophical and political structure of Western Latin Christendom.[9] But then things began to change.

Modernism – Phase 1

In religion, the idea of *Church* as a mystical union bestowing spiritual identity upon persons as a body bestows organic identity upon its parts, of *sacraments* as media by which divine graces are bestowed upon human individuals, and of *liturgy* as a mode of communication between God and creature, came to be replaced by an individualist theology in which each person has access to God via *Scripture*, 'His' directly revealed word, without the mediation of church, mass or priesthood. In philosophy, the presumption of knowledge of reality, and confidence in the general reliability of the cognitive powers, came to be questioned and means were sought to establish the possession and security of knowledge by locating it in a certain and permanent foundation: either self-evident principles (as in *rationalism*) or imme-

---

[9]   For a sketch of the development of moral theology and ethics during this and the following period, see John Haldane, 'Medieval and Renaissance Ethics' in P. Singer ed. *A Companion to Ethics* (Oxford: Blackwell, 1990).

diate experience (as in *empiricism*). In politics, the religious wars unsettled the doctrine of a social magisterium and the version of natural law which supported it, giving rise to new attempts to provide generally compelling reasons to regulate one's behaviour in accord with principles of civil society. In art, meanwhile, the mediaeval conception of painting, sculpture and architecture as practical activities directed towards broadly utilitarian ends, and of artists as craftsmen co-operating with others in the production of works useful to man and glorifying God, came to be replaced by the renaissance idea of the artist as an original and autonomous creator of objects of contemplation.

Modernism – Phase 2

The transition in religion from Church to individual, from sacramental liturgy to private prayer and from scholastic theology to self-authenticating religious experience, proceeded towards greater fragmentation of Christendom, with each new denomination establishing itself through a preferred interpretation of scripture and in associated lifestyles. In connection with this, the eighteenth century attacks on natural theology led to a preference for historically-warranted practices over transcendentally derived doctrine. In philosophy, the efforts to provide a secure foundation for knowledge in either *a prioristically* determinable metaphysical necessities or in indubitable immediate experience both came to be abandoned, and with them went epistemological and metaphysical realism. In place of these came Kant's 'Copernican Revolution', re-establishing the conformity of mind and world by treating the latter as, in some sense, 'made by' the former. In this way philosophical enquiry could again regard itself as discovering the structure of reality and the terms of the moral law – but now the investigation was conducted within the domain of thought itself. The implication of this for politics was to restore optimism about the possibility of justifying principles of social organisation by appeal to a perspective beyond the contingent viewpoints of individuals but immanent within human reason itself and hence, in principle, attainable by each. In art, the ancient tradition of *mimesis* or representation grew steadily weaker as the idea of the artist as a creator of self-contained worlds developed into a full-blown theory, *romanticism*, and the corresponding aesthetics of disengaged contemplation came to dominate the culture.

Relative to this three-stage history, some of the overlapping features of the various uses of the term 'postmodernism' can now be brought into focus. None the less, it will be a point of contention whether what I mention next belongs to a late stage of 'modernism' or to an early phase of its successor. The prospect of such contention is more or less guaranteed by the uncritical methodology characteristic of the sort of historico-cultural analysis which favours this vocabulary.[10] To the extent that I consider there to be some value in thinking in these terms, I incline to the former view.

Modernism – Phase 3 / Postmodernism – Phase 1

Following upon the rise and continuing success of the physical sciences as explanatory and predictive theories (and the accompanying development of technology), earlier preoccupations with *justifying* the content of beliefs and the principles of conduct gave way to the attempt to explain them *non-rationalistically* by reference to the causal efficacy of underlying forces. Religion, art and human relationships came to be accounted for in terms analogous to those employed in the physical sciences: to which witness the writings of Mill, Marx, Durkheim and Freud. In short, human thought and action were taken to be more amenable

---

[10] For an example of this sort of contention, see Scott Lash, 'Post-Modernism or Modernism?: Social Theory Revisited' in J. Doherty, E. Graham and M. Malek eds., *Postmodernism and the Social Sciences* (London: MacMillan, 1992). In a manner that has become common Lash is concerned to argue that '[M]uch of what is usually regarded as postmodern culture is in fact really part and parcel of modernism ... what is characteristically understood in terms of a cultural paradigm (postmodernism) becoming pervasive in the past one or two decades is in fact much more characteristic of the set of modernist movements of the last century.'

to empirical investigation and explanation than to non-empirical rational justification.

Postmodernism – Phase 1 / Postmodernism – Phase 2

The previous departure from the ambitions of modernism, in its first and second phases, to provide reassurance about the ability of the mind to attain metaphysical and moral knowledge, be it through philosophy or art, did not go so far as to question its own reliance upon realist and rationalist assumptions. The emergent social sciences presumed the legitimacy of their methods of enquiry, the independence of their objects of study and the fixity of meaning and truth so far at least as these are required for a conception of human studies as genuinely scientific, that is, as apt to yield objective knowledge. But once reflexivity is added to scepticism the result is the corrosion of the residual elements of rationalism. Social observation can no longer be informed by presumptions of objectivity, universality and rationality. The naive acceptance of the world and of thought as secure *givens* (which characterised the pre-modern world) and the belief in at least the possibility of re-establishing them by means of *reflection* (which was the conviction of modernism) are no longer available in the postmodern condition. All that remains, therefore, is to celebrate, lament or be indifferent to, the plurality of incommensurable, uncodifiable and radically contingent social worlds.

One could, of course, elaborate upon the features depicted in this representation of the 'postmodern (western) world' as these take shape in the various areas of life: self-reference in visual imagery, the promotion of paradox and reflexivity in writing, the attempt (be it self-refuting) to employ *reductio ad absurdum* on the assumptions of realism and rationalism in philosophy, the attack upon the transcendental aspirations of neo-Kantian moral and political theory, the eclectic combination of culturally diverse elements, and so on. The pattern is familiar, notwithstanding that, as I argued previously, the method of design may be suspect.

The Philosophy of Postmodernism

I shall not be concerned further with the weaker versions of postmodern cultural analysis; those which simply claim that something such as I have set out above describes the course of western intellectual and social history. I have already observed that such analysis is liable to heady generalisation and of its nature encourages rhapsodies of association.[11] My interest now is in those other much more ambitious accounts in which this pattern of development, particularly in its latest elements, is treated as disclosing the ultimate facts of the human condition: what might be described as the 'philosophy of postmodernity'. Before turning to evaluate it, however, it will be as well to consider further the content of this philosophy.

There are, I think, three main routes into this: the *aesthetic*, the *socio-political* and the *epistemological*. Earlier I remarked upon the romanticist idea that the artist can be said to imitate nature not by mimetically reproducing its forms but rather by paralleling its world-making activity. This favours a conception of *art* as expressive rather than as representational, and of *content* as non-referential but self-contained. Works of art are then conceived of as symbols constituting their own significance. This is clearly a move away from the kind of aesthetic realism which regards the *world* as the source of meaning and *art* as a method of selectively representing this and thereby communicating it to an audience; that is, a view which regards art as only derivatively significant. None the less, the romanticism so far described is objectivist inasmuch as it implies standards of

---

[11] As witness to which, consider the following passage from Richard Kearney 'The crisis of the post-modern image' in A. Phillips Griffiths ed., *Contemporary French Philosophy* (Cambridge: Cambridge University Press, 1988): 'Meanings multiply themselves indefinitely. There is no identifiable origin or end to the Postal network of communications: "In the beginning was the Post" [Derrida. *La Carte postal* (Paris: Flammarion, 1980) pp. 154-5]. The "post" of postmodernity would thus seem to suggest that the human imagination has now become a postman disseminating images and signs which he himself has not created and over which he has no real control', pp. 115–16.

correct and incorrect interpretation fixed by reference to the independently constituted content of a given work. There is, on this view, a *fact* of the matter about what a work *means* which it is the task of interpretation to *discover* and to which a *true* account will *correspond*.

In 'postmodernist' aesthetics, however, realism about art is abandoned in favour of a kind of subjectivism which focuses upon the interpretative activity of the spectator. In the official view this is part of a rejection of Romanticist theory,[12] though in fact it remains close to romanticism in treating the creative exercise of the imagination as the essence of art. None the less, it is anti-realist in spirit and in formulation. There is no interpretation-independent *fact* of the matter about the content of an image or the meaning of a text; which is to say there are no visual or literary meanings to be *discovered* as opposed to constructed, there is neither *truth* nor *correspondence*. Talk of the artist's 'creative imagination' is, in some versions of this account, a deceptive figment of bourgeois humanism, an illusion sustained by the impersonal language of the ruling art criticism. On the other hand, the interpretative activity of the spectator is unconstrained save by the social force of competing interpretations, and hence can claim no special status. As one commentator, drawing upon Derrida for style and substance, expresses it:

> Disseminated into the absolute immanence of sign-play, the imagination ceases to function as a creative centre of meaning. It becomes instead a floating signifier without reference or reason …
>
> … Post-modern culture jibes at all talk of original creations. It exclaims the omnipresence of self-destructing images which mime each other in a labyrinth of inter-reflecting mirrors.[13]

---

[12] See J. Culler, *On Deconstruction: Theory and Criticism after Structuralism* 2nd edition (London: Routledge, 2008) and T. Eagleton, *Literary Theory* (Oxford: Blackwell, 2008).

[13] Kearney op. cit., pp. 115 and 118. See also J-F. Lyotard *The Postmodern Condition: A Report on Knowledge* (Minneapolis, MN: University of Minnesota Press, 1984). The latter is a highly regarded and widely cited source of commentary on contemporary thought and culture.

The idea that where it was previously supposed that reason shapes thought, the true occupant of that role is in fact social force or power, is a familiar feature of continuing debates in social and political theory. Setting aside classical Marxist analysis (as retaining presumptions of a supposedly discredited rationalism) postmodern social theory treats the terms of political discourse as elements in a rhetorical fiction: 'truth', 'meaning', 'reason', 'knowledge' and so on are all represented as instruments of oppression (or of some other power relationship) operating under, in Foucault's phrase, the 'illusion of autonomous discourse'. Thus, political and social thought are themselves subjected to a sociological analysis which must either deny itself the resources of rationalistic theorising, or else use the traditional terminology with ironic disingenuity. (I shall return to this dilemma shortly.)

For Saussure, rational thought is possible, be it that it is not taken (as in Cartesian or Kantian theories) as prior to and more secure than language: 'Without language, thought is a vague uncharted nebula. There are no pre-existing ideas, and nothing is distinct before the appearance of language'.[14] Likewise for Lévi-Strauss language constitutes an objective rationally structured phenomenon which (somehow) influences human conduct and thereby makes it intelligible.[15] But for Foucault the idea that there is such a thing as human nature which expresses itself in intrinsically intelligible, and hence rationally explicable activity is part of the fiction of modernist universalism. The reality, such as it is, is a plurality of distinct (and competing) historically determined 'discursive practices' involving the exercise of power not reason. What this implies, then, is the final rejection of a theory of human nature and *ipso facto* of the human

---

From it comes the phrase, now much quoted: 'eclecticism is the degree zero of contemporary general culture'.

[14] F de Saussure, *Course in General Linguistics* (London: Fontana,1974), p. 112.

[15] C. Lévi-Strauss, *The Savage Mind* (London: Weidenfeld & Nicolson, 1966).

sciences—an implication captured by the hyperbolical phrase 'the end of man'.[16]

The role of reflections on the nature of language in shaping the development of European social theory is obvious enough, as is the route by which such reflections have led to the radical relativism of Foucault and Derrida. A similar concern, leading to only slightly less extravagantly stated conclusions, has been a characteristic of recent analytic philosophy of language and epistemology. Here the argument runs roughly as follows. Pre-Cartesian philosophy was unreflective about the nature of knowledge itself. It presumed man was the measure of reality, *not* by constituting it but by being a reliable indicator of its condition; a fact explicable in terms of the mind as an undistorting receiver. Descartes put paid to this naive realism and instituted a conception of the mind according to which knowledge could only be accounted for as involving adequate mental representations: the imagery *within* accurately depicting the world *without*. In Kant, the representational character of thought is formulated non-imagistically in terms of concepts, that is, rules of interpretation, which organise sensory input. These differences apart, the implication is the same: traditional realism is an unwarranted or, worse, an unintelligible assumption. The notion of an adequate representation involves the idea of fit or correspondence between one set of (mental) items and another set of (non-mental) items. But to make sense of this we need to have an account of the non-mental side of things—that is, an account of the world. However any attempt to formulate that (even to give content to the idea of 'the world') must, on the given epistemological assumptions, involve the formation and deployment of representations. In short, all we do, or can, have are our ways of thinking.

---

[16] M. Foucault, 'The Subject and Power' in H. Dreyfus & P. Rainbow eds., *Michel Foucault: Beyond Structuralism and Hermeneutics* (Chicago, IL: Chicago University Press, 1983).

What emerges, then, is as before a form of relativism which cannot even speak its name.[17] For the realist, thought and language take their content from the world. For the contemporary anti-realists, however, content, meaning, truth and knowledge are determined from within the human realm and cannot be held constant as measures by which to assess thought and action wherever, whenever and by whomsoever they are engaged in. The attack by Quine on analyticity and necessity is taken to have undermined the possibility of providing secure foundations for knowledge by *a priori* reflection, in the style favoured by the rationalists. The parallel challenge presented by Wilfred Sellars to the idea of experiential 'givens' is presumed to have had the same effect on the empiricist effort at foundationalism. And, to repeat, the quite general considerations concerning the nature of concepts as representations or mental rules is taken to demonstrate the general incoherence of realism in anything other than an internal (that is, roughly coherentist) sort.

The Self-Refuting Character of 'Postmodern Social Science'

So much, then, for the considered verdict of postmodern and contemporary analytic philosophy on realism and reason. The foregoing sketch has been rough and ready, but it includes all the elements that I need to proceed to my conclusions. These can be stated as follows. First, if what I earlier titled 'the philosophy of postmodernism' is true, then,

---

[17] This, I think, is all that the famous argument given by Davidson in 'On the Very Idea of a Conceptual Scheme' actually establishes; see Donald Davidson, *Inquiries into Truth and Interpretation: Philosophical Essays Volume 2* (Oxford: Oxford University Press, 2001). Later writings, however, suggest a more ambitious line of reasoning in opposition to relativism. See, in particular, Davidson 'A Coherence Theory of Truth and Knowledge' in Davidson, *Subjective, Intersubjective, Objective: Philosophical Essays Volume 3* (Oxford: Oxford University Press, 2001). See also M. Root, 'Davidson and Social Science' and Rorty 'Pragmatism, Davidson and Truth' both in E. LePore ed., *Truth and Interpretation: Perspectives on the Philosophy of Donald Davidson* (Oxford: Blackwell, 1986) and Rorty (1986).

along with traditional humanities, social science in general, in the sense of the systematic study of human affairs within and across cultures and over time, and cultural theory in particular, are impossible. Likewise if analytical anti-realism, in the style advocated by Rorty is the case. But second, it is premature to suppose that the conditions necessary for the possibility of humanities and social science do not obtain. That is to say, it is not obvious that realism is excluded. On the contrary, there is reason to presume it to be true and to try to show how it can be and that it is so.

The considerations gathered together in the first conclusion can be articulated around the following briefer conditional proposition: *if relativism is true then social science is impossible*. Setting aside indifference or bemusement, there are two attitudes one can take to this conditional: to reject it or to accept it. Since acceptance is formally compatible with each of two further conflicting attitudes, let me first indicate why it should be accepted.

Relativism of the extensive (indeed global) sort under discussion holds that the idea of an object or of a state of affairs or, at the highest level, of the world, or again such ideas as those of truth, knowledge, reason and meaning, lack the fixity given them by the realist. Rather, they are defined within and restricted to particular cultures, 'language games', 'discourses' or 'conversations'. But if that were so, then there are no objective criteria by which to assign meaning to the activities of those outside one's own 'conversation', or to assess their rationality, truth or value. It is obvious enough how this implication bears upon anthropology and history. Without the possibility of deciding between rival interpretative claims made in respect of culturally distant peoples there can be no such studies. But the erosion of social science runs further. Human geography, economic theory, social psychology, linguistics and so on, all presuppose the objectivity of the phenomena under investigation, the rationality of the methods of enquiry, the determinacy of assignments of meaning and of explanations by reference to agents' reasons, and the culture-indifferent existence of non-human objects and states of affairs implicated in such explanations. But these presuppositions are just what the postmodern and analytical relativists are concerned to reject. Hence, if that rejection is warranted then social science and cultural theory are indeed impossibilities.

Suppose one takes these considerations to establish the conditional — *if relativism is true then social science is impossible* — how should one respond? There are two options: accept that relativism is true and therefore that social science is impossible; or contrapose, affirming that social science is possible and concluding that relativism is not true. I said there are two options, but immediately a difficulty suggests itself. In the minds of some authors, and of many readers, postmodernism of the sort described is a social scientific cultural theory standing in opposition to, say, varieties of rationalist, empiricist and realist conceptions of the social sciences. But this precludes anyone who takes this view from moving in either direction through the conditional. He or she cannot affirm that postmodernist social science is true and that social science is impossible; or that social science is possible and hence that the philosophy of postmodernism is false. In short, I am claiming that the idea of *postmodernist* (in the sense described) *social science* (in the sense described) is incoherent and that the attempt to articulate it is self- refuting.

Conclusion

What now? One could try to reconceive that which cannot, on its own terms, be a set of social scientific theories or methods of enquiry, as a 'culture-theoretic discourse', and hold, consistent with this, that social science is indeed impossible. But the first part of this is either a polite or a self-deceiving way of failing to observe that it is *just* talk; an aspect of the ungrounded, non-truth-bearing, group-specific conversation of some very small sub-set of mankind. As regards the second part, it is contrary to abundant evidence that there are operative and effective social sciences and also far less plausible than the claims of postmodern philosophy. Indeed, it is not difficult to see how the argument might be extended (along familiar anti-relativist lines) to show that these claims are incoherent.

What this suggests, then, is that the earlier conditional should be contraposed and that the central tenets of postmodern and analytical anti-realism must be rejected. It is not a requirement of doing this that one give a positive alternative account of truth, knowledge, reason and so on, for jumping out of the frying pan isn't always jumping into the fire. This said, however, I think it is a proper challenge to show what the presuppositions of social science are and how they can coherently be conceived to obtain. In analytical philosophy this challenge is too rarely pressed, and by and large the responses to it seem to be quite inadequate. Those who believe that history, psychology, economics and other studies of human affairs are forms of objective enquiry, with the potential to disclose important truths about people and their relation to the social and natural environment, ought not to lack the courage of their convictions and should push against current orthodoxies in cultural theory. In doing so, and in seeking an account of how things must be in order to satisfy such an apparent truism as that there are embodied rational agents with the power to discover facts about the world and their place in it enquirers may well see merit in the kind of Aristotelianism advanced in the account of practical philosophy presented in these pages.

15

Philosophy and the Restoration of Art

Introduction

The previous chapters in this section have been concerned with two pervasive features of social life: the moral environment of public culture and the practice of general education; and then with challenges to a tradition of reflective understanding of human nature posed by theories inspired by scientific reductionism and by forms of radical relativism.

In this final chapter I turn to high culture as represented by art and consider the impact upon it of certain ideas generated from within philosophy itself. This serves to illustrate the claim of the opening chapter 'Practical Ethics' that philosophical ideas make a difference, but that flawed ideas can lead practice into confusion. I concluded that 'if philosophy has a vocation to help people think their way to truth about fundamental matters part of its task may not be to provide an education in new philosophical ideas so much as a re-education out of old ones, or out of the versions of these that have taken shape as ideas have trickled down through the culture' (p. 32 above). The following is an instance of carrying through that vocation but it also serves to show how practical philosophy can be pursued in a department of life other than the ethical and the political.

It is widely believed that much contemporary art is shallow, willfully obscurantist and unrewarding of attention. In consequence it is also felt to be a misuse of public funds for government to act as a patron in its support. Of course, some charges brought against current art-making are misplaced, and it is not inappropriate for the state to sustain cultural traditions. There is however, a tendency for those involved in the institutions of art: practioners, college teachers, gallery directors, critics and journalists, etc., to be contemptuous of external criticism and to dismiss it without serious consideration. This is itself a subject for complaint, for the wide-spread rejection of the professional art of the period by the population whose taxes do much to sustain it is a proper matter for concern and requires examination of its causes. Principal among these is the belief that as art developed through the twentieth century it offered less and less in the way of interest, virtuosity and delight. Yet the view from within the art institutions is of a progression leading to forms more economical of expression and more complex and varied in content than those of the nineteenth century to which popular taste is apparently irremovably attached.

One aspect of the problem is that there is fundamental disagreement as to what art, and *ipso facto*, good art is. The first step towards a possible reconciliation therefore, is to identify something of the nature and scope of this difference. As will become clear, the tasks of characterising the opposition between the two views and of assessing the positions thereby delineated, are largely philosophical ones.

The Reductionist Impulse

The modern movement started with Post-Impressionism, accelerated after Cubism and continued to gather pace until beginning to disintegrate in the 1960s. Its driving force had been one of the central concepts of late nineteenth century theorising *viz., reductionism*: the view that plurality belies unity; that phenomena within a particular area manifest a single element or force and accordingly that the appearance of diversity is illusory. This powerful idea derives from the relentless pursuit of explanations. In order to understand some range of events it seems necessary to discover a principle that represents their diversity as compatible with unity among them. There is something in this thought, not least the logical fact that descriptions are implicitly general and philosophical understanding proceeds to the highest level of generality in its explanation of the common features of apparently different things.

The adoption of reductionism in modern artistic theory is due, however, not solely to considerations of conceptual methodology but also to the dominance of the technique in the major cognitive disciplines particularly the physical sciences. For those wishing to secure for art the status of a branch of knowledge the application of the respected methodology of enquiry was an obvious course. The idea that beneath the varied surface lies an essential nature informed the development of chemistry and physics, and in turn was adopted in the human sciences in order to reduce the complexity of personal and social phenomena to the expression of fundamental forces. Just as various events in nature were explained by reference to the system of elements and their reactive dispositions, so events in human history were viewed as the result of a systematic interplay of basic forces.[1]

Following the pattern of the sciences, modern aesthetic theories have sought to identify the essence of art by looking for features common to all forms and instances, and recognizing that none are to be found at the level of appearances have moved to a further level in the hope of abstracting a generic essence. In this respect art theory is less like science and more like philosophy. While it shares with both the method of eliminating differences it does not, like science, drop below the level of ordinary experience to

[1]   See, for example, Mill whose reductionist methodology is aptly illustrated by the following passages: 'Human beings in society have no properties but those which are derived from and may be resolved into the laws of the nature of individual man. In social phenomena the Composition of Causes is the Universal Law', Mill, *A System of Logic* (London: Longmans, 1949), p. 573. Then, 'The theory of life on which this theory of morality is grounded (is that) pleasure and freedom from pain are the only things desirable as ends; and that all desirable things ... are desirable either for the pleasure inherent in themselves, or as means to the promotion of pleasure and the prevention of pain.' (*my emphasis*), *Utilitarianism* (London: Dent, 1931) p. 6.

one at which familiar distinguishing descriptions are replaced by others which, though of the same logical type as those they replace, characterize physical objects as essentially similar. Rather it transcends experience and unites the phenomena by descriptions of a different logical sort. Consider, for example, the different directions of movement away from the language of perception indicated by a scientific description of distinct objects, a table and a chair, say, as alike in having the same fibrous or molecular constitution, and a philosophical account of them as qualitatively identical in being spatio-temporal particulars or primary substances. Art theory, itself in part a philosophical enquiry, is in this sense a 'transcendental' enterprise.

Notwithstanding a shared methodology modernist theoreticians have arrived at different conclusions as to the essential nature of the subject. Here I am less concerned with the content of the various accounts than with their common reductionist character, but it is appropriate to identify three broad categories of theory, *viz. communicative, formalist,* and *institutional.* Each maintains, that all artworks are manifestations of a single, determinate constitution: either (1) the communication of information: about the artist's psychological state, as in *expressionism*; or about the world, as in *realism* and *symbolism*, or (2) the presentation of sensible properties structured so as to afford spectators various kinds of experience; or (3) the realization of a certain functional role defined either socially or historically.

The exclusivity of Modernist accounts is only partly motivated and made plausible by the reductionist model of explanation. In order to gain acceptance and inspire art-making certain other ideas are required. Earlier I linked the reduction of plurality to unity with a shift from the level of *experience* to that of *abstract thought*. There are two further components: the distinction between *concept* and *artefact*, and that between *form* and *content*. It is the conjunction in a single methodology of these several notions that encouraged writers of the nineteenth and early twentieth centuries to move towards monistic accounts of the nature and value of art. It is essentially the same methodology that has been employed more recently to support the elimination of figurative content and, in turn, of material artworks, and from a different direction, the abandonment of compositional form in favour of unstructured expression.

Early stages of this development appear in the dispute between those like Walter Pater, and subsequently Clive Bell, who apply a *form/content* distinction and then identify art with the first of these, and others such as Tolstoy and later Collingwood who argue that art is essentially communication of content not provision of sensory delight.[2] The character of this dispute is familiar and effectively illustrated by brief quotations from Walter Pater, Clive Bell, Leo Tolstoy, and R.G. Collingwood, respectively:

> Art, then, is thus always striving to be independent of the mere intelligence, to become a matter of pure perception, to get rid of its responsibilities to its subject or material.[3]

> To appreciate a work of art we need bring with us nothing but a sense of form and colour and a knowledge of three-dimensional space.[4]

> Art, like speech, is a means of communication, and therefore of progress, i.e. of the movement of humanity forward towards perfection.[5]

> [The business of] an artist is to speak out, to make a clean breast. But what he has to utter is not, as the individualist theory of art would have us think, his own secrets. As spokesman of his community, the secrets he must utter are theirs.[6]

It is important to observe that the contrast between the views of the first and second pair of authors relies upon their common agreement on the composition of artworks. For, it is only if one conceives of works as constituted out of

---

[2] Also at issue in these debates is the argument between 'aestheticists' and 'moralists' advocating, respectively, art for art's sake and art for life's sake. For discussion of these issues see R.W. Beardsmore, *Art and Morality* (London: MacMillan, 1971) and Berys Gaut, *Art, Emotion and Ethics* (Oxford: Oxford University Press, 2007).

[3] Walter Pater, *The Renaissance*, (New York: Mentor, 1959) p. 97.

[4] Leo Tostoy, *Art* (London: Chatto and Windus, 1947) p. 27.

[5] Clive Bell, *What is Art?* (London: Brotherhood, 1898) p. 156.

[6] R.G. Collingwood, *The Principles of Art* (Oxford: Oxford University Press, 1974) p. 336.

two distinct, elements that it makes sense to dispute the relative importance of form and content.

Theoretical Art

The art of the post-war period is distinguished from what went on before in two important respects. First, it carries forward lines of development initially explored in earlier painting and sculpture. Second, it is highly theoretical, both in the sense of being informed by art theory and in that of seeking to contribute to it. The clearest recent example of these tendencies is afforded by Conceptual Art, in which pictorial or sculptural imagery is eschewed in favour of printed texts or abstractly specified procedures. An additional interest of this movement is that it applies and extends the reductionist methodology in conjunction with *concept/artefact* and *form/content* distinctions. Indeed, in a sense it is the conclusion reached by modernism when this is pursued in the direction of the elimination of sensible form. A commentary-cum-text-piece by one such artist. Ian Wilson, illustrates these themes very clearly.

> Nonvisual abstraction is more difficult to grasp than visual abstraction …

> Nonvisual abstraction is difficult to grasp because we continue to look for something. This tendency of looking for visual meaning, of trying to use the visual faculty, causes meaningless-ness to occur …

> Nonvisual abstraction is at the heart of conceptual art.

> Nonvisual abstraction is formless.

> There is still content in visual abstraction, but nonvisual abstraction has no content.

> A concept without content is formless.

> True conceptual art does not compromise itself by re-entering the traditional context of the visual arts …

> Conceptual art is concerned with the internal, intellectual nature of a concept. The more removed from external references, the stronger the concept.

The nature of concepts is antithetical to sensual reality. Conceptual art, when it is taken seriously, separates consciousness from the exterior world.[7]

This follows both the style and substance of an earlier text widely regarded as one of the founding works of a new artform. Sol Lewitt's 'Sentences on Conceptual Art' (1969) consists of a set of thirty-five numbered statements arranged sequentially, three of which (8 -10) run as follows:

8. When words such as painting and sculpture are used, they connote a whole tradition and imply a consequent acceptance of this tradition, thus placing limitations on the artist who would be reluctant to make art that goes beyond the limitations.

9. The concept and idea are different. The former implies a general direction while the latter is the component. Ideas implement the concept.

10. Ideas can be works of art; they are in a chain of development that may eventually find some form. All ideas need not be made physical.[8]

In his piece Wilson speaks of the elimination of *both* form and content: 'Nonvisual abstraction is formless … [and] has no content', but one can save his claims from incoherence by a charitable interpretation which distinguishes between different kinds of content and takes him to be saying that nonvisual abstraction eschews pictorial themes, subject matter and media in favour of the contemplation of ideas. This interpretation is supported by the concluding section of the work which also illustrates a relentless reductionism. What is presented as reasoning in support of conceptual art, in the form of a justifying description, also serves as an outline of the history of part of the modern movement itself.

---

[7] Ian Wilson, 'Conceptual Art', *Artforum*, 22 (1983). I describe this as a 'commentary-cum-text-piece' for as is characteristic of work in this genre there is some uncertainty as to whether the text is to be regarded as a critical account of conceptual art or an instance of it. Such examples provide evidence of the tendency towards the coincidence of art and art theory.

[8] Sol Lewitt, 'Sentences on Conceptual Art' (New York: 0-9, 1969; and Leamington Spa: Art-Language, 1969). He had previously published 'Paragraphs on Conceptual Art', *Artforum*, 1967.

This is no accident but derives from the increasing intimacy between theory and practice mentioned above. Wilson writes:

> Passing toward the center of conceptual art, idea orientated figurative writing, photography and printing are on the remote periphery. Passing the visual realm of colour and natural form we pass closer to the center. We have already passed idea-orientated performance and social and political writing. We have passed abstract colour painting. We pass black and white abstract painting. Approaching the limit of visual abstraction we pass from three into two dimensions and into language description of abstract physical objects and events. Passing beyond metaphor, beyond criticism, beyond art, beyond space and time, we come upon the formless abstractions of language. Infinite and formless what is presented is neither known nor unknown. This is the center. This is the heart of conceptual art.[9]

It is easy to pick at the incoherence of such notions as those of 'abstract, physical objects', and of that which is 'neither known or unknown'. As before however, suitable reformulations suggest themselves which better express the artist's claims. The question remains, however, as to whether having understood his thesis we should accept it. I have hinted at a modernist fallacy but while I have discussed various aspects of modernism I have not yet indicated a general failure of reasoning. I believe there is such and that much Conceptual Art embodies its blatant commission, but it is important that in attending to a conspicuous case one does not fail to discern it elsewhere, particularly when the former has been arrived at by a series of movements each one of which commits the same error. The fallacy is one pictured by Wittgenstein when he comments: 'In order to find the real artichoke, we divested it of its leaves'.[10]

Modernism inherits from general philosophy the notion that understanding involves grasping the essences of

[9]   Wilson, *op. cit.*, p. 61.
[10]   Wittgenstein, *Philosophical Investigations* (Oxford: Blackwell, 1976), p. 23.

things. To adopt this assumption as a universal principle may already involve error but setting that worry aside there remains the thesis that the essence of a thing is distinct from and simpler than its phenomenal character. Accordingly the process that leads to understanding is conceived of as requiring an ascent from sense experience to abstract speculation. This idea is encouraged by two considerations. First, that explanations are general and unificatory. Second, that no informative, general, unifying descriptions are available at the level of common experience. The fallacy then, consists in the supposition that all explanations must be of the monistic, essentialist sort and that anything attempted at the phenomenal level is simply a rediscription of that to be explained. Conjoined with this error is the related one involved in applying a pattern of explanation in a context in which it may be inappropriate. In the imagery aptly invoked by Wittgenstein these two points can be expressed by saying that not all understanding is achieved by the removal of surface layers and this is certainly not the form of investigation suitable in cases where the essential nature is located in what is given to experience.

Common-Sense Aesthetics

Earlier I set out to characterise the disagreement between the understanding and expectations of an intelligent but untutored public, and the view(s) of the nature and value of art presupposed in contemporary art-making. Underlying the latter is a movement towards monism resulting from the adoption of a general model of explanation on the assumption that it is the only route to understanding.[11]

---

[11] Here I have only considered the conclusion reached by pursuing the reductionist strategy in the direction that favours conceptual content. One could trace corresponding lines of reasoning, again realized in the history of art itself, leading to pure formalism (consider, for example, minimalist sculpture and colour-field painting); or to the view that the essence of art is to be located in the position occupied by an activity and its products in the life of a society. For an example of the adoption of this last philosophical idea as subject matter of practice see Victor Burgin 'Margin Note' in *The New Art* (London:

Given this account the popular rejection of contemporary art reveals the ignorance of a public who are like those of whom Heraclitus comments: 'Evil witnesses are eyes and ears for men if they have souls that do not understand the language ... Of the Logos which is as I describe it men always prove to be uncomprehending'.[12] They remain attached to conflicting appearances failing to discern the truth disclosed to thought alone. The analogy is apt since while common opinion offers no detailed, rival theory its expectations nonetheless imply a general view at odds with the central claims of modernism, in particular its monistic tendency. In outline this view regards artworks as products of intentional processes involving skill in the use of a medium and the exercise of a range of refined sensitivities and sensibilities. It further regards them as intended to have value as objects of experience and interpretation and as expressions of the imaginative and inventive powers of their authors.

This sketch of common opinion emphasizes its central assumptions but is not offered in the spirit of a philosophical definition, something to which pre-analytic thought does not aspire.[13] More importantly it suggests that no such definition is available since the subject does not admit of precise specification. Part of the reason for this is that artists exercise imagination and invention, which implies the impossibility of stating in advance where exactly the boundaries of art lie. Certainly it is no part of the view to

Arts Council, 1972) where he writes: 'What counts as art varies through history and between societies, as does does art's function. A de-reified notion of art places it ... as socio-culturally contingent, implying we should seek formation rules for art within the complex of synchronous social practices contemporary with the given work' p. 23.

[12] Fragments 107 and 1; see Kirk and Raven, *The Presocratic Philosophers* (Cambridge: CUP, 1975) pp. 187–9.

[13] For a modest attempt to identify the core notion of an *art form* (something less than a reductive analysis) which is compatible with the character I attribute to the informal conception of art see: E.J. Bond, 'The Essential Nature of Art', *American Philosophical Quarterly*, Vol.12, No.2, 1975. In somewhat similar spirit see also Monroe Beardsley, *The Aesthetic Point of View* (Ithaca, NY: Cornell University Press, 1982) and Gary Iseminger, *The Aesthetic Function of Art* (Ithaca, NY: Cornell University Press, 2004).

permit anything, and one of the main complaints against some contemporary work is that it fails to respect appropriate constraints.

But the appearance of tension between these expectations of novelty and conformity is misleading. Both are accommodated within the conception of art as a traditional activity bringing to bear human capacities and interests with the aim of producing objects apt for visual contemplation. Such a conception links personal discovery and general intelligibility through the idea of the embodiment of thought in sensible form which, if it is to be intelligible, must employ conventional devices having public significance. Common opinion also has it that the appeal to the senses is not simply as channels through which information passes. There is the appetite for sensory delight to be satisfied. And again, while this involves turning to the artist as a provider of fresh and unimagined pleasures the movement brings with it a set of constraints upon what could count as appropriate offerings. Not every arrangement of sensible properties is relevant to the aesthetic interest. And implicit in the thought that the artist should extend the spectators sensibilities is the idea that he must also respect them.

Earlier I noted a widespread belief that lines of development in recent art have resulted in a loss of interest, virtuosity and delight. I do not endorse the philistine rejection of all new forms. There is much in the work of the twentieth and twety-first centuries which is confusing or opaque to the uneducated but which exhibits mastery of its media and illuminates the nature of art-making, as well as feeding both sense and intellect. Nonetheless the earlier complaint deserves to be taken seriously. Deriving from the set of assumptions articulated above it embodies an informed response to the art of the past as part of our common culture. Furthermore, given the philosophical commitments of modernism it should now be apparent that the disparity between common opinion and much contemporary artistic activity manifest at the level of critical response is paralleled by a general disagreement about the very nature of art and of the values appropriate to it. The attempt to discount all public criticism as no more than uninformed prejudice is therefore itself guilty of begging the question.

Set against the efforts of theorists to abstract some single, underlying essence from the multitude of media, styles, forms, themes, concerns and interests is the view that these differences must be respected both in critical judgement and in one's reflective thought about what art is. It is not that they are as important as the similarities between works but that from the points of view of philosophical understanding and aesthetic appreciation they actually have greater significance. As regards the former, they imply the falsity of any kind of monism; while their implication for the latter is that art criticism cannot be adequate to the task of understanding and evaluating particular works if its primary concern is to give account of them as instances of something general.

The pluralistic character of common-sense is clear enough. It permits artistic concern with the communication of thoughts and feelings, or with the articulation of compositional elements but does not assert the primacy of one or other. Moreover, while it views certain sorts of values, e.g. sensuous quality (of colour, tone and texture) as essential to the worth of art it does not restrict it to them and countenances the suitability of a multitude of non-aesthetic values for inclusion within an artist's creative concerns.

So much then for the character of common opinion and its affirmation of pluralism. It will be clear where my own sympathies lie in this dispute but it has yet to be shown that truth rests with ordinary judgement, and there are two objections open to the modernist in defence of his position.

First, acknowledging the reductionist character of his theory and conceding that if there are different kinds of explanations then his assumption, that to understand the nature of art one must depart from the level of experience, is fallacious (since some other form of understanding may be available), he may argue that it has not yet been demonstrated either that an account of art can be obtained by attending to the phenomenal level, or that it ought to be. Second, he may refer back to my comments about the essentially sensible character and appeal of art and propose that the commitments of common opinion are not after all opposed to reductionism and amount to one kind of monist theory, *viz*: *Formalism* — be it of a not very precise sort.

The second point might simply be an *ad hominem* objection to the claims made on behalf of conventional opinion. Alternatively it could be thought to contribute to the case in favour of reductionism by showing that the attempt to understand art leads inevitably to a monistic account of it — since only this could provide the required explanations. In either event the appropriate response must be to show that common opinion is not implicitly reductionist and that its preference for interpretation of a broadly phenomenological sort yields a better understanding of artworks than does the methodology of modernism.

It is important to recognize that this task has a different standard of success from that of the alternative enterprise. Unlike the latter it does not aspire to a detailed, essentialist specification of art which can then be superimposed upon descriptions of particular works to reveal which aspects are necessary to them *qua* art, and which are accidental. This warning is called for as there is a risk of conceding everything to the modernist by allowing his question-begging criterion of adequate explanation.

As regards the challenge that the common conception is implicitly *formalist* because of its insistence that works present an engaging and sensuously satisfying appearance, it is possible to show both the invalidity of this inference and its dependence upon the assumption that there is a sharp distinction to be drawn *in rebus* between form and content. Assuming this division the advocacy of aesthetically significant appearance as necessary to art does indeed suggest a kind of *formalism*. But part of my aim is to show how, when correctly understood, the idea that art is properly concerned with the manufacture of perceptually engaging objects apt for interpretation, undermines the form/content distinction.

Aesthetic Phenomenology

Consider an occasion of looking at a painting. An object is sensuously given and various concepts are exercised in association with sensory presentations transforming them into the unified awareness of a particular thing possessed of various characteristics. Suppose then that this phenomenal object is found pleasing. The delight is taken not in one's state of mind but in the object. This is important because certain familiar varieties of subjectivism gain plausibility by likening aesthetic experience to the having of sensations, like a tingling feeling in the head or a warm glow in the stomach. If its nature were of this kind then certainly there could be no logical space for critical judgement resting as it does on the operation of reason and yielding the idea of correctness. It is not like this however. The aesthetic transcends the merely sensory through the involvement of thought, and the resultant intentionality of this form of experience implies that its various aspects are referred to the intended object. In seeing the painting and taking pleasure in its blend of colour and varied surface my enjoyment is not of my sensations but of the colour and texture of the painting. The pleasure, its character and its quality are determined by and are referred to its object.

The intentionality of aesthetic experience is important also in showing the inadequacy of Formalism and the falsity of the assumption that the common understanding of art is a version of it. In its self-consciously theoretical guise Formalism excludes the concerns of life by claiming that the sole purpose of art is the manufacture of satisfying arrangements of sensible properties. Presupposed in such theories is the assumption of *empiricism*: that the contents of the mind are constructed out of sensory elements. On this view (whose implications for the understanding of nature and of value were discussed in chapter one) theoretical and practical thought involve a continuing process of structuring complex sense-presentations, and alongside this the working out of logical relationships between derived ideas. In shifting to the aesthetic mode the intellect rests and impressions are enjoyed for their qualitative feel, or for the pleasing relationship that is perceived to obtain between them. This latter perception is conceptualised but only to the extent of referring patterns to a sensory surface. Thought simply relates sensible elements but does not 'penetrate beneath' this formal structure.

The only aesthetic values recognised by such views therefore, are sensuous quality and form. Concerns about theme, subject matter, expression and representation are set aside as lying beyond the properly aesthetic in the realms of the practical and the theoretical. This division is misconceived however, and threatens even the availability of formal values. For these relate to modes of perception in which the concepts implicated are only rarely those of protogeometry. The discernment of structure presupposes a network of concepts that extends beyond the purely formal. Accordingly, even were we to accept the sensory surface account of the objects of experience it would still be necessary to make reference to the human conception of the world in order to account for the intentional content of these perceptual thoughts.

Such reference is not to be understood as a genetic or causal explanation but rather as part of the analysis of what is contained in the experiences. It is an extended phenomenological description. But, of course, we do not need to accept the empiricist view and have reason to reject it. The concerns of life enter in directly to aesthetic experience. The recognition that perception is thoughtful undermines attempts to mark a strict division between attention to form and discernment of content and to force a choice of one or other as the object of concern. What philosophy shows to be a possibility experience reveals to be a fact. For it is clear that the discernment of form is usually related to an explicit conception of that of which it is the form. Indeed the relation is often one of constitution i.e., the form is only available via an understanding of its bearer as a thing of a certain kind.[14]

---

[14] For an application of this idea in opposition to certain varieties of physicalism see John Haldane, 'Folk Psychology and the Explanation of Human Behaviour' (1988).

Philosophy looks to Art

It may be useful to illustrate the foregoing by reference to experience of a particular painting. An appropriate choice for the purpose is Raphael's Vatican fresco popularly known as *The School of Athens*.[15] Two formal features of this work are immediately apparent: its very considerable compositional power, and the refined draughtsmanship and use of delicate colouring. In articulating the content of any thoughtful experience of the painting, however, it is necessary to draw upon non-formal concepts. This is so even in the characterisation of the compositional structure, since the latter is created in part by narrative elements. Indeed, without the capacity to understand something of the general representational content one could barely see the formal structure, notwithstanding that once it has been seen one may, to some extent, abstract the formal pattern from the depicted scene. The point is that in doing so one is attending to something that is not available save via perception of the narrative. Also what is abstracted is only a formal scheme and not the structural essence of the work.

The painting depicts a crowd of figures from classical antiquity; natural and speculative philosophers engaged in instruction and debate. Compositionally it is set within a semi-circle and arranged in three horizontal sections the topmost of which comprises about half the height of the frescoe and displays the architectural grandeur of the setting. A series of archways lead the eye into the distance and between them the ceiling gives way to the open sky. From there light penetrates downwards into the hall below, fanning out upon the heads of the figures but descending especially upon the central characters of Plato and Aristotle. They are also framed by the most distant archway which stands behind and above them like a halo, an acknowledgment of their intellectual blessedness. From these figures the eye is led to either side across the groups of other specu-

---

[15] See illustration on next page. For a high-resolution colour image of the fresco see: http://academic.shu.edu/honors/Raphael_School_of_Athens.jpg

lative philosophers that together form the middle of the horizontal sections of the composition. Below this (literally and in terms of depicted height – four steps lead down from the higher platform to the hall floor) are gathered two groups of figures to left and right. This is the third of the compositional bands and is comprised of various natural philosophers: cosmologists, astronomers and geometers.

It is apparent in even this limited description that form and narrative stand as mutually dependent aspects and not as discrete, or even blended but possibly separable, elements. This unity in the phenomenal object, and *ipso facto* in experience, is seen to be more extensive as one continues to explore it in perceptual thought. The horizontal sectioning of the painting corresponds to theoretical and depicted ascents. At the first level are gathered the scientists of the natural order (*physis*): Pythagoras, Ptolemy, Euclid and various students. These figures are largely seated, crouching or bending. On the right is a group gathered around Euclid whose outstretched arm leads downwards to where he is measuring a geometrical figure. This is a point of compositional and narrative focus. Some truth is being demonstrated and the students' heads are located at different distances from this locus corresponding to the degree of their understanding. Those farthest from his hand belong to figures most nearly upright, elevated to the status of knowers. The effect of this complex grouping (the structural geometry apt to the depicted field of study) is like that of a flower bud opening into full bloom as first one and then another petal expands outwards.

This movement is further developed at the next level where the characters almost all stand upright. The ascent from the study of nature to abstract philosophical speculation is continued beyond these figures who, gathered in their different groups, suggest the fluctuating, fragmentary and divided state of human understanding. The architectural structure above them is both regular and stable and serves as a pointer to the heavens above, the realm of timeless essences and beatific visions. From the highermost opening the downpouring light leads back again to the central figures of Plato and Aristotle and to their gesturing right hands. That of the former points upwards towards the transcendental realm of forms (*universalia ante rem*); that of his student is outstretched, facing downwards indicating that the true objects of intellectual enquiry are intelligible natures embodied in the empirical world (*universalia in re*).

This focus of thematic opposition is marked by figurative gesture and at the same time marks the centre of the composition, the mid-point of the painting and the meeting place of two triangular elements. The first is formed by the fan of light and has as its base the heads of the middle band of figures (illumination from on high). The second has its apex at Aristotle's hand and again rests upon the heads of philosophers, this time those of the scientists (blessing and approval from above). Thus the characters of Plato and Aristotle form the core of an animated composition entering into both physical and intellectual structures.

Such a description of aesthetically relevant features indicates the ways in which the sensuous, formal and narrative aspects of a work constitute a *single object* of perception and interpretation. This is not to deny that the refined colour and graphic sensibilities of such as Raphael might not have found expression in non-figurative painting, or even that they can be considered in abstraction from the creation of paintings in which they are used in the service of formal and narrative composition. Likewise, such structural ingenuity as this work exhibits might equally have been exercised and appreciated in the context of abstract formalism. Yet, the point remains that the actual relation between sensuous, formal and narrative elements in the particular case is not contingent. To perceive the painting as the work it is, both requires and deepens perceptual understanding of the human world. As phenomenological description makes clear, the dependence between formal features and representational content is mutual. Although one may concentrate on some aspect of a work in partial abstraction from others it is not possible to give account of the full significance of this in isolation. *A fortiori* it is absurd to attempt to locate the nature of the particular piece, and of art in general, in something essentially incomplete.

The Philosophical Understanding of Art

Reviewing my argument it might be thought that reductionism has been rejected at too high a cost. If explanation requires simplification through reduction to a common nature and the latter misrepresents the experience of particular works, then one faces an unhappy dilemma. Either pursue theoretical understanding along the lines discussed earlier and accept the implications, or else reject these but at the price of foregoing a general account of art. Given my advocacy of experience against theory, it appears that the loss to be borne is that of ever achieving a philosophical understanding of the phenomena.

It is not open to me to reject the opposition between the phenomenological interpretation of works and the abstract accounts of them given by reductionist theories. Accordingly, if the only form of philosophical understanding were of the latter sort I should be committed to the position that art cannot be understood philosophically. It is evident that such a Procrustean conception of philosophy is untenable in other areas and has been regularly attacked, if not wholly defeated, under the guise of the rejection of foundationalism; but it would be a less than adequate response simply to appeal to these other disputes for support in the present case. I have claimed that the modernist fallacy involves the inappropriate application of a model of explanation and have accepted the corollary of this challenge, *viz.* to indicate some other form of enquiry better suited to the task. Previous discussion was concerned with the character and suitability of the available alternative: the provision of detailed accounts of the intentional content of particular works as these are experienced. There only remains to be considered the question whether such descriptions may be regarded as philosophically illuminating.

What is at issue is the nature of our understanding of ourselves. In these terms the present dispute is between those who seek the underlying essence of the human in abstraction from cultural and personal variations, and others who suppose that if human kind is to be understood at all this must be at the level of intentional experience. It would be wrong to think of this opposition as being between absolutism and relativism. No doubt it serves the cause of reductionism to present the matter in this way, and it is true that some who have rejected the trio: foundationalism, essentialism and monism have substituted varieties of relativism in their place.[16] It is no part of my concern, however, to deny that there are universal truths about human kind. Nor do I have reason to restrict these to biological facts having only indirect, if any, connections with questions of agency and value. I claim however, that the only route towards understanding the meaning and worth of intentional human activities is through reflection upon them. This reveals that human life is neither structurally nor qualitatively simple, and that the sensible embodiment of experience in art (as in other areas) exhibits the full variety of concerns, interests, sensibilities and sensitivities characteristic of it. Metatheoretical resistance to the claim that there can be no general, unifying account of art, but that nonetheless an understanding of particular works is still possible, has several supports chief among which are impersonal conceptions of reason and of practical and evaluative knowledge. It is appropriate therefore, to conclude by indicating something of the inadequacy of these.

Conditions of Common Appreciation.

Action is distinguished from movement by the presence of guiding thought, and perception differs from sensation by the involvement of structuring concepts. These truths are embodied in an influential (and perhaps dominant) account of rational activity as issuing from deliberation in which information is conjoined with practical maxims to yield pre-

[16] An example of this tendency in the ethical sphere is provided by Bernard Williams, *Ethics and the Limits of Philosophy* (London: Fontana, 1985) especially Ch.9.

scriptions which are then realised; and in a view of the prior activities of identifying and evaluating features as involving the application of general principles of various sorts. Given these notions of motivational and cognitive psychology the task of understanding some area of human interest and activity presents itself as that of developing a theory of the basic principles underlying it. Philosophical accounts of social institutions, of linguistic meaning, of morality and of art all must aim to identify sets of axioms and rules to which particular complex phenomena can be reduced. And it is these conceptions which support the claims: first, that explanation necessarily involves simplification through reduction; and second, that attention to the distinctive features of individual judgements, actions and artefacts can do no more than describe the phenomena to be explained.

I am not concerned to argue that this view of understanding is never appropriate but reject it now in the case of artistic activity. It is unsurprising that in the modern world the first applications of this doctrine to art are coincident with the rise of a philosophical psychology which sees action as rule guided. In this connection consider the following passage from an influential, early eighteenth century guide to painting by Antonio Palomino who, in writing of working 'according to exact rules', provides a clear example of this doctrine of rule-guidedness:[17]

> Science is essentially concerned with speculative processes, and does not depend on practical or manual operations. Art does not exclude speculative processes and includes those practical and manual actions which are wrought upon external and perceptible matter in order to construct a definite work according to exact rules and infallible teachings.[18]

---

[17] It is a matter for further debate whether these rules are prescriptions of our invention for the production of satisfying forms, or whether they embody relations of fittingness. Like the rational intuitionists in ethics, Palomino takes the latter view and in allowing that 'Art does not exclude speculative processes' also resists the draw towards Formalism discussed above.

[18] Antonio Palomino, *El Museo pictorico y escala optica* (Madrid, 1715). This translation from *Pictorial Museum and Optical Scale* is that of M.S.

Some aspects of the manufacture and experience of artworks may admit of codification, just as some features of moral thought may be represented in terms of rules governing conduct. But there is more to morality than is addressed by axiomatic theories of right action, and even less of what we find significant in art can be exhibited in this systematic fashion.

In the moral realm there is a need to give account of the interests and affections that motivate action, i.e., of virtuous character. In this we make the nature of the moral agent rather than that of abstractly specified action-types the focus of enquiry. Again however, the resistance to abstraction presents itself in that the question: is this a good person? is not answerable by consulting some independent specifications derived from a set of 'principles of virtuous life'. There are 'for-the-most-part' generalisations rooted in experience and passed from one generation to another. Yet while these may be epistemologically prior to particular judgements of virtue they are logically posterior to them. In evidence of this note that where such rules for the application of virtue-predicates are available they are liable to be abandoned in the face of exceptions. The resulting modified generalisations are thus not to be viewed as nearer approximations to universal first principles since they stand in just the same logical relation to individual evaluations of character. Given the greater implausibility of codification in art there is stronger reason to affirm the primacy of particular assessments of an agent's sensibilities and artistic concerns as these are given by the pattern of actions and reactions discernible in his or her work.

In denying that critical judgements presuppose principles it is not being suggested that the former are unsupported by reasons, only that the rule-guided conception of rational belief and behaviour is inadequate and that the appropriate form of justification is that implicit in the phenomenological method sketched earlier. In making the case for an interpretation and evaluation one adverts to rel-

Soria collected in E.G. Holt (ed) *A Documentary History of Art* (New York: Anchor, 1958) Vol. II, pp. 225–41.

evant features of the case inviting others to see things in one way rather than another and, having discerned this pattern, to see its point and worth.

The pull of reductionism is the resultant of several perennial attractions in philosophy: (1) the unification of seemingly diverse phenomena; (2) the achievement of simplicity and economy of explanation and, consequent upon these, (3) the provision of a simple decision procedure based on a single dimension of assessment thereby avoiding problems of incommensurability and eliminating irresoluble conflict. Additional to all of which is (4) the concern that without theories of this sort we can neither render wholly intelligible nor rationally assess and discuss the content of experience. Two thoughts have emerged as correctives to reductionism. First, its application to art and other important human institutions involves the radical misrepresentation of the actual character of experience and the impoverishment of related activities. Second, fear of blind irrationality in the absence of such rules is unwarranted. Art has a rational foundation in human intelligence, in our natural capacities for discerning values of various sorts and in our affective attitudes towards them.

In recent philosophy it has been customary to associate with Wittgenstein the rejection of an exclusively rule-guided conception of rationality and the substitution of a view which sees various aspects of human nature, including its affective and social dimensions, as entering into the constitution of our reason. It is with irony therefore, that I end with the repetition from earlier chapters of a quotation from St. Augustine, whom Wittgenstein elsewhere famously criticises,[19] in which the Augustine gives voice to a similarly naturalistic conception of rational life as against the Stoic legalism of Cicero. He writes:

---

[19] In *Philosophical Investigations* I, 1–3. This discussion of language learning is not unrelated to the present issue and the coincidence of their views about reason suggests the question: Is Wittgenstein's account of Augustine on meaning faithful to the latter's actual opinions? For the suggestion that it is not see: Anthony Kenny 'The Ghost of the Tractatus' In G. Vesey ed. *Understanding Wittgenstein* (London: Macmillan, 1974) pp. 1–2.

> A people is a large gathering of rational beings united in fel-
> lowship by their agreement about the objects of their love.[20]

The purpose of this final chapter has been to show how the
alienation of society at large from the professional art of
recent and contemporary periods is due in no small part to
the insinuation of philosophical ideas into the practice of art
making. In this way a philosophy may be held responsible
for art's undoing. This at any rate confounds the sceptics who
speak of the 'impotency of ideas'. More positively however, I
also hope to have shown how philosophy might be invoked
to restore a conception of art, and so renew confidence in
traditional art forms which again may secure the allegiance
of both practioners and spectators — a possibility of reunion
based in common affections engaged by the human world.

Practical philosophy as I have been concerned to describe
and practise it does not descend upon its subjects from out
of the pure world of *a priori* ideas and principles. Rather it
grows out of the experience and reflection of rational
animals whose concepts are already products of practical
thought and purposeful agency. As regards the case for
practical philosophy, not only as an intelligible form of
enquiry but as a necessary one, there is in addition the need
of reflective animals to understand themselves and their
activities, their need to act well, in accord with practical
reason, if they are to live good and happy lives. With that in
mind I am happy to leave the last word on practical philosophy to G.K. Chesterton:

> The idea of being 'practical', standing all by itself, is all that
> remains of a Pragmatism that cannot stand at all. It is
> impossible to be practical without a Pragma. ... Philosophy
> is merely thought that has been thought out. It is often a
> great bore. But man has no alternative, except between
> being influenced by thought that has been thought out and
> being influenced by thought that has not been thought
> out.[21]

---

[20] *De Civitate Dei*, (London: Loeb Classical Library, 1960) Bk.XIX,
      C.XXIV, pp. 231–33.
[21] G.K. Chesterton, 'The Revival of Philosophy — Why?' in Chesterton,
      The Common Man (London: Sheed and Ward, 1950), pp. 173–4.

Acknowledgements

The foregoing chapters draw upon a number of previously published essays, though all have been adapted and revised to a greater or lesser extent for the purposes of the present volume. As well as avoiding repetition as far as possible, I have also excised, revised or expanded material to take account of developments in my own thinking and for the sake of composing an integrated whole. I am grateful to the various publishers for permission to re-use this material. In the order in which they appear in the present volume, the original sources are as follows:

Introduction.
    'Some Metaphysical Presuppositions of Agency', *Heythrop Journal*, 35, 3 (1994) pp. 296-303.

1.   'The Foundations of Professonal Ethics', in G. De Stexhe and J. Verstraeten eds *Matters of Breath: Foundations for Professional Ethics* (Louvain: Peeters, 2000) pp. 89-106.

2.   'Persons and Values', *Journal of Medical Ethics*, 14, 1 (1988) pp. 39-41'; and 'Intuitions and the Value of a Person', *Journal of Applied Philosophy*, 14, 1 (1997) pp. 83-6.

3.   'Recognising Humanity', *Journal of Applied Philosophy*, 25, 4 (2008) pp. 301-13.

4.   'Bioethics and the Philosophy of the Human Body', in L. Gormally ed. . *Issues for a Catholic Bioethic* (London: Linacre Centre, 1999) pp. 77-89.

5. 'Being Human: Science, Knowledge and Virtue', in J. Haldane ed. *Philosophy and Public Affairs* (Cambridge: Cambridge University Press, 2000) pp. 189-202.

6. 'Defence, Deterrence and the Taking of Life', in R. Bauckham and J. Elford eds. *Theological and Ethical Issues in the Nuclear Weapons Debate* (London: SCM, 1989) pp. 131-45.

7. 'Family Matters', *Philosophy*, 81 (2006) pp. 577-89.

8. 'Political Theory and the Nature of Persons: An Ineliminable Metaphysical Presupposition', *Philosophical Papers*, 20, 2 (1991) pp. 77-95.

9. 'The Individual, the State and the Common Good', *Social Philosophy & Policy*, 13, 1 (1996) pp. 59-79.

10. 'Public Reason, Truth, and Human Fellowship', *Journal of Law, Philosophy and Culture*, 1, 1 (2007) pp. 101-16.

11. 'The Philosophy of State Compensation', with A. Harvey, *Journal of Applied Philosophy*, 12, 3 (1995) pp. 162-78.

12. 'A Subject of Distaste: An Object of Judgment', *Social Philosophy and Policy*, 21, 1 (2004) pp. 202-20.

13. 'Metaphysics in the Philosophy of Education', *Journal of Philosophy of Education*, 23, 2 (1989) pp. 171-183; and 'Education: Conserving Tradition', in B. Almond ed. *An Introduction to Applied Ethics* (Oxford: Blackwell, 1995) pp. 73-88.

14. 'Cultural Theory, Philosophy and the Study of Human Affairs', in J. Doherty, E. Graham and M. Malek eds, *Postmodernism in the Social Sciences* (London: Macmillan, 1991) pp. 179-95.

15. 'The Modernist Fallacy: Philosophy as Art's Undoing', *Journal of Applied Philosophy*, 5, 2 (1988) pp. 227-37.

List of References

Historical writings

Aquinas, *Summa Theologiae. The 'Summa Theologica' of St Thomas Aquinas* literally translated by Fathers of the English Dominican Province, second and revised edition (London: R. & T. Washbourne, 1920); or *Summa Theologiae* (London: Eyre & Spottiswode, 1964-1981).

Aquinas, *The Treatise on Law,* trans. R.J. Henle (Southbend, IN: University of Notre Dame Press, 1993).

Aquinas, *De regimine,* in *Aquinas Selected Political Writings,* ed. A.P. D'Entreves, trans. J.G. Dawson (Oxford: Blackwell, 1959).

Aquinas, *de Anima. The Soul: St Thomas Aquinas' De Anima* trans. P. Rowan (London: Herder, 1949).

Aquinas, *Sententia libri de anima. Aristotle's De Anima in the version of William of Moerbeke and the Commentary of St Thomas Aquinas* trans. K. Foster and S. Humphries (London: Routledge and Kegan Paul, 1951).

Aquinas, *Sententia libri Politicorum,* trans, P.H. Conway and R.F. Larcher in Mary T. Clark ed. *An Aquinas Reader* (New York: Fordham University Press, 2000).

Aquinas, *Super Epistolam Pauli Apostoli ad Corinthios.* 'On the Epistle of Paul to the Corinthians' extract in T. McDermott ed. & trans. *Thomas Aquinas: Selected Philosophical Writings* (Oxford: Oxford University Press, 1993).

Aquinas *Super Boethium de Trinitate* On Boethius's *On the Trinity,* trans. and ed. R. Brennan (St Louis, MO: Herder, 1946).

Aristotle, *Metaphysics* trans Hugh Lawson-Tancred (London: Penguin, 2004).

Aristotle, *Nicomachean Ethic* trans. C. Rowe, and commentary by S. Broadie (Oxford: Oxford University Press, 2002).

Augustine, *Confessions,* trans. H. Chadwick (Oxford: Oxford University Press, 1998).

Augustine, *De Civitate Dei* trans. D.S. Weisen (Cambridge, MA: Harvard University Press, 1968).

Augustine, *De Quantitate Animae,* 'On the size of the soul', trans. J.J. McMahon, *Fathers of the Church,* Vol. 4 (Washington: Catholic University of America Press, 1947).

Bentham, J. *Introduction to the Principles of Morals and Legislation* (1789) eds. J.H. Burns & H.L.A. Hart (Oxford: Clarendon Press, 1996).

Berkeley, G. *Principles of Human Knowledge* in *A New Theory of Vision and Other Writings* (London: Dent & Co., 1960).

Boethius, *Contra Eutychen* in H.F. Stewart, E.K. Rand and S.J. Tester eds. & trans. *Theological Tractates* (Cambridge, MA: Harvard University Press, 1973).

Burke, E. 'A Vindication of Natural Society' (1757) in P.J. Stanlis ed. *Edmund Burke: Selected Writings and Speeches* (New Brunswick, NJ: Transaction, 2009).

Burke, E. 'Speech on Conciliation with the Colonies', (1775) in *Burke Selected Writings*.

Burke, E. 'Reflections on the Revolution in France' (1790) in *Burke Selected Writings*.

Cicero, *De re publica, The Republic and The Laws* trans. N. Rudd (Oxford: Oxford University Press, 2008).

Justinian, *Digesta seu Pandectae* (533) *Annotated Justinian Code* 2nd edition trans. H. H. Blume ed. T Kearley (

Descartes, R. *Descartes Philosophical Letters* ed. A. Kenny (Oxford: Clarendon Press, 1970).

The Debates in the Several State Conventions on the Adoption of the Federal Constitution (1787-89) ed. J. Elliot (Philadelphia, PA: Lippincott, 1907).

Hegel, G.W.F. *Philosophy of Right* (1822) trans. T.M. Knox (Oxford: Clarendon Press, 1977)

Hume, D. *Enquiry Concerning Human Understanding* (1748) ed. L. A. Selby-Bigge (Oxford: Clarendon Press, 1978) and other editions.

Hume, D. *A Treatise of Human Nature* (1739-40) ed. L. A. Selby-Bigge (Oxford: Clarendon Press, 1978) and other editions.

Kant, I, *Groundwork of the Metaphysic of Moral* (1797) trans. H.J. Paton as *The Moral Law* (London: Hutchinson, 1976).

Mill, J.S. System of Logic (1843) *The Collected Works of John Stuart Mill: System of Logic, Ratiocinative and Inductive* vols 7 & 8 (Indianapolis: Liberty Fund, 2006).

Mill, J.S. *On Liberty* (1859 ed S. Collini (Cambridge: Cambridge University Press, 1989)

Mill, J.S. *Inaugural Address* delivered to the University of St Andrews (London: Longmans, Green, Reader and Dyer, 1867).

Mill, J.S. *Utilitarianism* (1863) ed. R. Crisp (Oxford: Oxford University Press, 1998).

Palomino, A. *El Museo pictorico y escala optica* (1715) *Pictorial Museum and Optical Scale* trans. M.S. Soria in E.G. Holt (ed) *A Documentary History of Art*, (New York: Anchor, 1958) Vol. 2.

Plato, *Euthyphro* trans. B. Jowett (Oxford: Clarendon Press, 1903).

Plato, *Phaedo* trans. B. Jowett (Oxford: Clarendon Press, 1903).

Plato, *The Republic of Plato* trans. F.M. Cornford (Oxford: Oxford University Press, 1945).

Pythagoras, *Fragments* see Kirk and Raven, *The Presocratic Philosophers* (Cambridge: CUP, 1975).

Sidgwick, H. *The Methods of Ethics, 7th edition* (1907) (Indianapolis, IN: Hackett, 1981).

Thoreau, H.D. *Walden* (1854) (London: Dent, 1974).

Wolff, C. *Logic, or Rational Thoughts on the Powers of the Human Understanding with their Use and Application in the Knowledge and Search of Truth* (London: L. Hawes, W. Clarke, and R. Collins, 1770

Recent and contemporary writings

Almond, B. ed. *An Introduction to Applied Ethics* (Oxford: Blackwell, 1995).

Amato, P. & Booth, A. *A Generation at Risk: Growing Up in an Era of Family Upheaval* (Cambridge, MA: Harvard University Press, 1997).

Anscombe, E. *Intention* (Oxford: Blackwell, 1957).

Anscombe, E. *Human Life, Action and Ethics: Essays by G.E.M. Anscombe* eds. M. Geach & L. Gormally (Exeter: Imprint Academic, 2005).

Anscombe, E. *Faith in a Hard Ground: Essays on Religion, Philosophy and Ethics by G.E.M. Anscombe* eds. M. Geach & L. Gormally (Exeter: ImprintAcademic, 2008).

Anscombe, E. 'Modern moral philosophy', *Philosophy*, 53 (1958); in *Human Life, Action and Ethics* (2005).

Anscombe, E. 'Does Oxford Moral Philosophy Corrupt Youth?' *Listener* 57 (1957) in *Human Life, Action and Ethics* (2005).

Anscombe, E. 'The Dignity of the Human Being' in *Human Life, Action and Ethics* (2005).

Anscombe, E. 'Knowledge and Reverence for Life' in R. Hittinger ed. *Linking the Human Life Issues* (Chicago: Regnery, 1986) in *Human Life, Action and Ethics* (2005).

Anscombe, E. 'Were you a Zygote?' in A. Phillips Griffiths ed. *Philosophy and Practice* (Cambridge: Cambridge University Press, 1985) in *Human Life, Action and Ethics* (2005)

Anscombe, E. 'Authority in Morals' in J.M. Todd ed. *Problems of Authority* (London: Drton, Longman & Todd, 1962) in *Faith in a Hard Ground* (2008).

Anscombe, E. 'The Early Embryo: Theoretical Doubts and Practical Certainties' (1990) in *Faith in a Hard Ground* (2008).

Anscombe, E. 'Why Have Children?' in L. P. Schrenk, ed. *The Ethics of Having Children* (Washington, D.C: ACPA, 1990).

Archard, D. 'Privacy, the Public Interest, and a Prurient Public' in Matthew Keiran, ed. *Media Ethics* (London: Routledge, 1998).

Ashworth, A. 'Punishment and Compensation: Victims, Offenders and the State", *Oxford Journal of Legal Studies,* 6 (1986).

Baier, K. 'Justice and the Aims of political Philosophy' in *Symposium on Rawlsian Theory of Justice: Recent Developments*, special issue of *Ethics*, 99 (1989).

Beach, H. 'What if the Deterrent Fails?' in R. Bauckham & J. Elford eds. *The Nuclear Weapons Debate: Theological and Ethical Issues* (London: SCM, 1989).

Beardsley, M. *The Aesthetic Point of View* (Ithaca, NY: Cornell University Press, 1982).

Beardsmore, R.W. *Art and Morality* (London: MacMillan, 1971).

Bell, C. *What is Art?* (London: Brotherhood, 1898).

Bergström, L. 'Utilitarianism and Alternative Actions' *Nous* 5 (1971).

Bond, E.J. 'The Essential Nature of Art', *American Philosophical Quarterly*, 12 (1975).

Bradley, F.H. 'My Station and its Duties', in Bradley *Ethical Studies* (2nd Edition) (Oxford: Clarendon, 1927).

Briggs, A. *The BBC: The First Fifty Years* (Oxford: Oxford University Press, 1985).

Broome, J. 'The Value of a Person', *Proceedings of the Aristotelian Society*, Supplementary Volume, 68 (1994).

Broome, J. *Weighing Lives* (Oxford: Oxford University Press, 2004).

Bundy, M., Kennan, G., McNamara, R. & Smith, G. 'Nuclear Weapons and the Atlantic Alliance', *Foreign Affairs*, 60 (1982).

Burgin, V. 'Margin Note' in *The New Art* (London: Arts Council, 1972).

Callan, E. *Autonomy and Schooling* (McGill-Queen's University Press, 1988).

Callan, E. *Creating Citizens: Political Education and Liberal Democracy* (Oxford: Oxford University Press, 1997).

Cane, P. *Atiyah's Accidents, Compensation and the Law*, 5th edition (London: Widenfeld & Nicolson, 1993).

Carr, D. *Educating the Virtues* (London: Routledge, 1991).

Cavanaugh, T.A. *Double-Effect Reasoning: Doing Good and Avoiding Evil* (Oxford: Oxford University Press, 2006).

Chapman, J.W. ed. *Compensatory Justice, Nomos, xxxiii*, (New York: New York University Press, 1991).

Chesterton, G.K. *What's Wrong with the World* (London: Cassell, 1910; San Francisco: Ignatius Press, 1994).

Chesterton, G.K. 'The Revival of Philosophy – Why?' in Chesterton, *The Common Man* (London: Sheed and Ward, 1950).

Child, J. *Nuclear War: The Moral Dimension* (London: Transaction Books & Social Philosophy and Policy Center, 1986).

Clark, S.R.L. *G.K. Chesterton: Thinking Backward, Looking Forward* (West Conshohocken, PA: Templeton Foundation Press, 2006).

Collingwood, R.G. *The Principles of Art* (Oxford: Oxford University Press, 1974).

Cooper, D. *Illusions of Equality* (London: Routledge & Kegan Paul, 1980).

Cooper, D. *Authenticity and Learning: Nietzsche's Educational Philosophy* (London: Routledge & Kegan Paul, 1983).

Cooper, D. ed. *Education, Values and Mind: Essays for R.S. Peters* (London: Routledge & Kegan Paul, 1986).

Culler, J. *On Deconstruction: Theory and Criticism after Structuralism* 2nd edition (London: Routledge, 2008).

Curren, R. 'History of Philosophy of Education' in E. Craig ed. *The Routledge Encyclopedia of Philosophy* (London: Routledge, 1999).

Curren, R. Emily Robertson and Paul Hager, 'The Analytical Movement' in Curren ed. *A Companion to the Philosophy of Education* (Oxford: Blackwell, 2003).

Curtis, B. and Mays, W. eds, *Phenomenology and Education: Self-Consciousness and its Development* (London: Methuen, 1978).

D'Andrea, T. *Tradition, Rationality and Virtue: The Thought of Alasdair MacIntyre* (London Ashgate, 2006).

Daniel, N. *Islam and the West: The Making of an Image* revised edition (Oxford: Oneworld, 1993).

Davidson, D. 'Actions, Reasons and Causes' in *Davidson, Essays on Actions and Events* (Oxford: Oxford University Press, 2001).

Davidson, D. 'Mental Events' in *Davidson, Essays on Actions and Events* (Oxford: Oxford University Press, 2001).

Davidson, D. 'On the Very Idea of a Conceptual Scheme' in Davidson, *Inquiries into Truth and Interpretation: Philosophical Essays Volume 2* (Oxford: Oxford University Press, 2001).

Davidson, D. 'A Coherence Theory of Truth and Knowledge' in Davidson, *Subjective, Intersubjective, Objective: Philosophical Essays Volume 3* (Oxford: Oxford University Press, 2001).

Davidson, H. *Alfarabi, Avicenna, and Averroes, on Intellect* (Oxford: Oxford University Press, 1992).

Dearden, R. F. 'Philosophy of Education, 1952-82', *British Journal of Educational Studies*, 30 (1982).

DeMarco, J. & Fox, R. eds. *New Directions in Ethics: The Challenge of Applied Ethics* (London: Routledge & Kegan Paul, 1986).

Derrida, J. *La Carte postal* (Paris: Flammarion, 1980).

Doherty, W. J. et al *Why Marriage Matters: Twenty-One Conclusions from the Social Sciences* (New York: Institute for American Values, 2002).

Dunn, C.W. & Woodward, J.D. *The Conservative Tradition in America* (Lanham, MD: Rowman & Littlefield, 1996).

Dupré, L. 'The Common Good and the Open Society' in D. Hollenbach & B. Douglass eds. *Catholicism and Liberalism,* ed. (Cambridge: Cambridge University Press, 1993).

Dworkin, R. *A Matter of Principle* (Oxford: Clarendon Press, 1986).

Eagleton, T. *Literary Theory* (Oxford: Blackwell, 2008).

Entwistle, H. *Class, Culture and Education* (London: Routledge and Kegan Paul, 1979).

Fink, P. and A. Tasmai, eds. *Stigma and Mental Illness* (Arlington, VA: American Psychiatric Press, 1992).

Finnis, . *Natural Law and Natural Rights* (Oxford: Clarendon Press, 1980).

Finnis, J., Boyle, Jr. J.M., & Grisez, G. *Nuclear Deterrence, Morality and Realism* (Oxford: Clarendon Press, 1987).

Fletcher, J. *Situation Ethics: The New Morality* (London : S.C.M. Press, 1966).

Fodor, J. 'Special Sciences and the Disunity of Science' in Fodor, *Representations: Philosophical Essays on the Foundations of Cognitive Science* (Brighton: Harvester, 1981).

Foot, P. 'Morality, Action and Outcome' in Honderich, T. ed., *Morality and Objectivity* (London: Routledge, 1985).

Freedman, L. 'British Nuclear Targetting', *Defense Analysis*, 1 (1985).

Froelich, G. 'Ultimate End and Common Good', *The Thomist,* 58 (1994).

Frohnen, B. *Virtue and the Promise of Conservatism: The Legacy of Burke and Tocqueville* (Lawrence: University Press of Kansas, 1993).

Foucault, M. 'The Subject and Power' in H. Dreyfus & P. Rainbow eds., *Michel Foucault: Beyond Structuralism and Hermeneutics* (Chicago, IL: Chicago University Press, 1983).

Galston, W. 'Pluralism and Social Unity' in *Symposium on Rawlsian Theory of Justice: Recent Developments*, special issue of *Ethics*, 99 (1989).

Gaut, B. *Art, Emotion and Ethics* (Oxford: Oxford University Press, 2007).

Geach, P. *Mental Acts* (London: Routledge & Kegan Paul, 1958).

Geach, P. *The Virtues* (Cambridge: Cambridge University Press, 1977).

George, R. P. *In Defence of Natural Law* (Oxford: Clarendon Press, 1999).

Goffman, E. *Stigma: Notes on the Management of Spoiled Identity* (Englewood Cliffs, NJ: Prentice-Hall, 1963).

Goodin, R. 'Theories of Compensation'', *Oxford Journal of Legal Studies*, 9 (1989).

Grisez, G. 'The First Principle of Practical Reason: A Commentary on the *Summa Theologiae*, 1-2, Question 94, Article 2', Natural Law Forum 10 (1965).

Grisez, G, Boyle, J. & Finnis, J. 'Practical Principles, Moral Truth, and Ultimate Ends', *American Journal of Jurisprudence* 32 (1987).

Gutmann, A. 'Communitarian Critics of Liberalism', *Philosophy and Public Affairs*, 14 (1985).

Haldane, J. 'Individuals and the Theory of Justice', *Ratio*, 27 (1985).

Haldane, J. 'The Morality of Deterrence', *Heythrop Journal* 26 (1985).

Haldane, J. 'Religious Education in a Pluralist Society: A Philosophical Examination', *British Journal of Educational Studies*, 34 (1986).

Haldane, J. 'Ethics and Biological Warfare', *Arms Control*, 8 (1987).

Haldane, J. 'Folk Psychology and the Explanation of Human Behaviour', *Aristotelian Society* Supplementary 62 (1988).

Haldane, J. 'Persons and Values' *Journal of Medical Ethics*, 14 (1988).

Haldane, J. 'Voluntarism and Realism in Medieval Ethics' *Journal of Medical Ethics*, 15 (1989).

Haldane, J. 'Medieval and Renaissance Ethics' in P. Singer ed. *A Companion to Ethics* (Oxford: Blackwell, 1990).

Haldane, J. 'Can a Catholic Be a Liberal?' *Melita Theologica*, 43 (1992).

Haldane, J. 'Identity, Community, and the Limits of Multiculture', *Public Affairs Quarterly*, 7 (1993).

Haldane, J. 'Theories, Concepts and Common Sense' *Proceedings of the Aristotelian Society*, Vol. 93 (1993).

Haldane, J. 'MacIntyre's Thomist Revival: What Next?' with reply by MacIntyre in Horton & Mendus, *After MacIntyre* (1994).

Haldane, J. 'Medieval and Renaissance Philosophy of Mind' in S. Guttenplan ed. *A Companion to Philosophy of Mind* (Oxford: Blackwell, 1994).

Haldane, J. 'Religious Toleration', *Synthesis Philosophica,* special issue on *Toleration,* 9 (1994).

Haldane, J. 'From Law to Virtue and Back Again: On *Veritatis Splendor*' in M. Davis ed. *The Use of the Bible in Ethics,* (Sheffield: University of Sheffield Press, 1995).

Haldane, J. 'Rational Animals' in A. O'Hear ed. *Verstehen and Humane Understanding* (Cambridge: Cambridge University Press, 1996).

Haldane, J. 'A Return to Form in the Philosophy of Mind' in D. Oderberg ed. *Form and Matter* (Oxford: Blackwell, 1999).

Haldane, J. 'Thomistic Ethics in America' *Logos*, 3 (2000).

Haldane, J. 'Ethics, Religion, and Relativism', *Review of Metaphysics*, 60 (2006).

Haldane, J. 'Gravitas, Efficacy and Social Causes' *Analysis*, 68 (2008).

Haldane, J. 'Soul and Body' in R. Pasnau ed. *The Cambridge History of Medieval Philosophy* (Cambridge: Cambridge University Press, 2010)

Haldane, J. & Harvey, A. 'The Philosophy of State Compensation' *Journal of Applied Philosophy*, 12 (1995) and in H LaFollette, ed. *Ethics in Practice* (1997).

Haldane J. & Lee, P. 'Aquinas on Ensoulment, Abortion and the Value of Life' *Philosophy*, 78 (2003).

Hamlyn, D.W. *Experience and the Growth of Understanding* (London: Routledge & Kegan Paul, 1978).

Hampton, J. 'Should Political Philosophy be done without Metaphysics?' in *Symposium on Rawlsian Theory of Justice: Recent Developments*, special issue of *Ethics*, 99 (1989).

Harris, J. 'Recent Work in the Philosophy of Education', *Philosophical Quarterly*, 33 (1983).

Harris, K. *Education and Knowledge* (London: Routledge & Kegan Paul, 1979);

Hart, W. D. *Engines of the Soul* (Cambridge: Cambridge University Press., 1988)

Harwell, M.A. et al. *Environmental Consequences of Nuclear War* (New York: Wiley, 1989).

Hauerwas, S. *Against the Nations: War and Survival in a Liberal Society* (Southbend, IN: University of Notre Dame Press, 1992).

Heil, J & Mele, A. eds. *Mental Causation* (Oxford: Clarendon Press, 1993).

Henricson, C. & Bainham, A. *The Child and Family Policy Divide: Tensions, Convergence and Rights* (London: Joseph Rowntree Foundation, 2005).

Hittinger, R. *A Critique of the New Natural Law Theory* (Southbend, IN: University of Notre Dame Press, 1994).

Hollenbach, D. & Douglass, eds., *Catholicism and Liberalism* (Cambridge: Cambridge University Press, 2002).

Horton, J. & Mendus, S. eds. *After MacIntyre:* (Cambridge, Polity Press, 1994).

Hughes, G.J. 'The Intention to Deter', in F. Bridges ed. *The Cross and the Bomb* (London: Mowbrays, 1983).

Hughes, G.J. 'Philosophical Debate on Nuclear Disarmament', *Heythrop Journal*, 29 (1988).

Hursthouse, R. 'Virtue Theory and Abortion' *Philosophy and Public Affairs*, 20 (1991).

Husserl, E. *The Crisis of European Sciences and Transcendental Phenomenology*, trans. D. Carr (Evanston: Northwestern University Press, 1970).

Iseminger, G. *The Aesthetic Function of Art* (Ithaca, NY: Cornell University Press, 2004).

Jonsen, A.R. 'Casuistry' in J. Sugarman & D. Sulmasy eds. *Methods in Medical Ethics* (Washington, DC: Georgetown University Press, 2001).

Kalumba, K. 'Maritain on 'The Common Good': Reflections on the Concept', *Laval Théologique et Philosophique*, 49 (1993).

Kavka, G. 'The Paradoxes of Deterrence', *Journal of Philosophy* 75 (1978).

Kearney, R. 'The crisis of the post-modern image' in A. Phillips Griffiths ed., *Contemporary French Philosophy* (Cambridge: Cambridge University Press, 1988).

Kenny, A. 'The Ghost of the Tractatus' in G. Vesey ed. *Understanding Wittgenstein* (London: Macmillan, 1974).

Kenny, A. 'The Logic and Ethics of Nuclear Deterrence', in A. Ellis, ed. *Ethics and International Relations* (Manchester: Manchester University Press, 1986).

Kenny, A. *The Metaphysics of Mind* (Oxford: Clarendon Press, 1989).

Kenny, A. *What I Believe* (London: Continuum, 2006).

Kenny, A. 'The Beginning of Individual Human Life' in M. Baur ed., *Intelligence and the Philosophy of Mind*, Proceedings of the American Catholic Philosophical Association, 80 (2006).

Kim, J. *Supervenience and Mind* (Cambridge: Cambridge University Press, 1993).

Kirk, R. *The Conservative Mind* (London: Faber & Faber, 1954).

LaFollette, H. ed. *Ethics in Practice: An Anthology* (Oxford: Blackwell, 2006).

Larmore, C. *Patterns of Moral Complexity* (Cambridge: Cambridge University Press, 1987).

Lash, S. 'Post-Modernism or Modernism?: Social Theory Revisited' in J. Doherty, E. Graham and M. Malek eds., *Postmodernism and the Social Sciences* (London: MacMillan, 1992).

Laslett, P. *Philosophy, Politics and Society* (Oxford: Blackwell, 1956).

Laslett P. & Fishkin J. eds. *Philosophy, Politics and Society*, 5th Series, eds. (Oxford: Blackwell, 1979).

Lévi-Strauss, C. *The Savage Mind* (London: Weidenfeld & Nicolson, 1966).

Lewitt, S. 'Sentences on Conceptual Art' (New York: 0-9, 1969).

Lichtheim, M. *Ancient Egyptian Literature*, 3 volumes, (Berkeley, CA: University of California Press, 1975).

Lonsen, A. & Toulmin, S. *The Abuse of Casuistry: A History of Moral Reasoning* (Cambridge: Cambridge University Press, 1988).

Lutz, C. *Tradition in the Ethics of Alasdair MacIntyre* (Lanham, MD: Lexington Books, 2004).

Lyotard, J-F. *The Postmodern Condition: A Report on Knowledge* (Minneapolis, MN: University of Minnesota Press, 1984).

MacCormick, N. 'The Obligation of Reparation', *Proceedings of the Aristotelian Society*, 78 (1978) in MacCormick *Legal Right and Social Democracy* (Oxford: Clarendon, 1982).

McCormick, R. & Curran, eds. *Moral Norms and the Catholic Tradition* (New York: Paulist Press, 1979).

McDowell, J. 'Functionalism and Anomalous Monism' in E. LePore & B. McLaughlin, eds. *Actions and Events: Perspectives on the Philosophy of Donald Davidson* (Blackwell, Oxford, 1985) in McDowell, *Mind, Value and Reality* (Cambridge, MA: Harvard University Press, 1998).

McDowell, J. 'Are Moral Requirements Hypothetical Imperatives?' *Aristotelian Society* Supplementary 52 (1978) in McDowell, *Mind, Value and Reality* (1998).

McDowell, J. 'The Role of Eudaimonia in Aristotle's Ethics' in A. O. Rorty, ed., *Essays on Aristotle's Ethics* (University of California Press, Berkeley, Los Angeles, London, 1980) in McDowell, *Mind, Value and Reality* (1998).

MacIntyre, A. *After Virtue* , (London, Duckworth, 1985).

Mackie, J. L. *Ethics: Inventing Right and Wrong* (Harmondsworth: Penguin Books, 1977). MacIntyre, A. *A Short History of Ethics*, (London, Routledge & Kegan Paul, 1967, 2002).

MacIntyre, A. *First Principles, Final Ends and Contemporary Philosophical Issues*, Milwaukee, Marquette University Press, 1990).

MacIntyre, A. 'The Privatization of Good' *Review of Politics*, 52 (1990).

MacIntyre, A. 'Moral relativism, Truth and Justification', in L. Gormally ed. *Moral Truth and Moral Tradition:* (Dublin, Four Courts Press, 1994).

MacIntyre, A. 'How Can We Learn What *Veritatis Splendor* Has to Teach?' *Thomist*, 58 (1994).

MacIntyre, A. *Dependent Rational Animals: Why Human Beings need the Virtues* (London: Duckworth, 1999).

MacIntyre, A. *The Tasks of Philosophy: Selected Essays, Volume 1* (Cambridge: Cambridge University Press, 2006).

MacIntyre, A. *Ethics and Politics: Selected Essays, Volume 2* (Cambridge: Cambridge University Press, 2006).

McLanahan S. & Sandefur, G. *Growing up with a Single Parent: What Hurts, What Helps* (Cambridge, MA: Harvard University Press, 1994).

McMylor, P. *Alasdair MacIntyre: Critic of Modernity* (London: Routledge, 1993).

Maritain, J. *The Person and the Common Good,* trans. John Fitzgerald (New York: Scribner, 1941).

Maritain, J. *Man and the State* (Chicago: University of Chicago Press, 1951).

Maritain, J. 'On Knowledge through Connaturality' *Review of Metaphysics,* 4 (1951) Ch. 3 in Maritain *The Range of Reason* (New York: Scribner's 1952).

Maritain, J. 'Truth and Human Fellowship' in *On the Uses of Philosophy: Three Essays* (Princeton: Princeton University Press, 1961).

Maritain, J. 'The Ontological and Epistemological Elements of Natural Law', in W. Sweet, ed. *Natural Law: Reflections on Theory and Practice* (South Bend, IN: St Augustine's Press, 2001).

Mellema, G. 'An Aristotelian Approach to Thinking about Educational Aims' *New Scholasticism,* 98 (1983).

Miers, D. 'The Responsibilities and the Rights of Victims of Crime", *Modern Law Review,* 55 (1992).

Moore, K.A. et al, 'Marriage from a Child's Perspective: How Does Family Structure Affect Children and What Can we Do About it?' *Child Trends Research Brief* (Washington, DC: Child Trends, 2002).

Montague, P. 'Rights and Duties of Compensation', *Philosophy & Public Affairs,* 13 (1984).

Morris, V. C. *Existentialism in Education* (New York: Harper and Row, 1966).

Morton, A. 'The Value of a Person', *Aristotelian Society,* Supplementary 68 (1994).

Murphy, M. ed. *Alasdair MacIntyre* (Cambridge: Cambridge University Press, 2003).

Nagel, T. *Equality and Partiality* (New York: OUP, 1991).

Nagel, T. *The Last Word* (Oxford: Oxford University Press, 1997).

Narveson, J. 'Moral problems of Population', *Monist,* 57 (1973).

Narveson, J. *Moral Matters* (Peterborough, Ontario: Broadview Press, 1993).

Nussbaum, N. *Sex and Social Justice* (Oxford: Oxford University Press, 1999).

Nussbaum, N. *Women and Human Development* (Cambridge: Cambridge University Press, 2000).

Nussbaum, M. *Hiding From Humanity: Disgust, Shame, and the Law* (Princeton, NJ: Princeton University Press, 2004).

Nussbaum, M. *Frontiers of Justice: Disability, Nationality, Species Membership* (Cambridge, MA: Harvard University Press, 2006).

Oakeshott, M. 'The Concept of a Philosophy of Politics' in Oakeshott, *Religion, Politics, and the Moral Life,* ed. T. Fuller (New Haven: Yale University Press, 1991).

O'Donovan, O. The Just War Revisited. (Cambridge: Cambridge University Press, 2003). Parfit, D. *Reasons and Persons* (Oxford: Clarendon Press, 1984).

Parris, M. *Great Parliamentary Scandals: Four Centuries of Calumny, Smear, and Innuendo* (London: Robson Books, 1996).

Pater, W. *The Renaissance,* (New York: Mentor, 1959).

Peters, R.S. *Authority, Responsibility and Education* (London: Allen & Unwin, 1963).

Peters, R.S. *Ethics and Education* (London: George Allen and Unwin, 1966).

Peters, R.S. ed. *The Concept of Education* (London: Routledge & Kegan Paul, 1967).

Peters, R.S. ed. *Philosophy of Education* (Oxford; OUP, 1973).

Pettit, P. 'Social Holism and Moral Theory: A Defence of Bradley's Thesis', *Aristotelian Society*, 86 (1985).

Putnam, H. *The Collapse of the Fact/Value Dichotomy* (Cambridge, MA: Harvard University Press, 2002).

Quinlan, M. *Thinking about Nuclear Weapons: Principles, Problems, Prospects* (Oxford: Oxford University Press, 2009).

Raimer, V. 'Physicalism, Realism and Education: A Functionalist Approach' *Post-Analytic Philosophy of Education*, special issue of *Educational Philosophy and Theory*, 19 (1987).

Rawls, J. *A Theory of Justice* (Oxford: Oxford University Press, 1971).

Rawls, J. 'Kantian Constructivism in Moral Theory' *Journal of Philosophy*, 77 (1980).

Rawls, J. 'Justice as Fairness: Political not Metaphysical' *Philosophy and Public Affairs*, 14 (1985).

Rawls, J. 'The Idea of an Overlapping Consensus', *Oxford Journal of Legal Studies*, 7 (1987).

Rawls, J. *Political Liberalism* (New York: Columbia University Press, 1993).

Rawls, J. 'The Idea of Public Reason Revisited' in *The Law of Peoples* (Cambridge, MA: Harvard University Press, 1999).

Rawls, J. *A Brief Inquiry into the Meaning of Sin & Faith (with "On My Religion"),* ed. Thomas Nagel (Cambridge, MA: Harvard University Press, 2009).

Raz, J. *The Morality of Freedom* (Oxford: Clarendon, 1986).

Raz, J. *Ethics in the Public Domain* (Oxford: Clarendon, 1994).

Reith, J. C. W. Broadcast over Britain (London: Hodder & Stoughton, 1924).

Root, M. 'Davidson and Social Science' in E. LePore ed. *Truth and Interpretation: Perspectives on the Philosophy of Donald Davidson* (Oxford: Blackwell, 1986).

Rorty, R. *Philosophy and the Mirror of Nature* (Oxford: Blackwell, 1980).

Rorty, R. *Consequences of Pragmatism* (Hempel Hempstead: Harvester, 1982).

Rorty, R. 'Pragmatism, Davidson and Truth' both in E. LePore ed., *Truth and Interpretation: Perspectives on the Philosophy of Donald Davidson* (Oxford: Blackwell, 1986).

Rorty, R. 'The Contingency of Community' in Rorty, *Contingency, Irony, and Solidarity* (Cambridge: Cambridge University Press, 1989).

Rorty, R. 'The Priority of Democracy to Philosophy' in *Reading Rorty* ed. Alan Malachowski (Oxford: Blackwell, 1990).

Rourke, T. R. & C. E. Cochran, 'The Common Good and Economic Justice: Reflections on the Thought of Yves R. Simon', *Review of Politics,* 54 (1992).

Sagan, C. 'Nuclear War and Climate Catastrophe: Some Policy Implications', *Foreign Affairs,* 62 (1983).

Sandel, M. *Liberalism and the Limits of Justice* (Cambridge: Cambridge University Press, 1982).

Saussure, F de *Course in General Linguistics* (London: Fontana, 1974).

Scheffler, I. *The Language of Education* (New York: Thomas, 1962).

Scruton, R. *The Meaning of Conservatism* (Harmondsworth: Penguin, 1980) 3rd rev. ed. 2002.

Scruton, R. *Animal Rights and Wrongs* (London: Demos, 1996).

Sellars, W. 'Empiricism in the Philosophy of Mind' in Sellars, *Science Perception and Reality* (London: Routledge & Kegan Paul, 1963).

Shoemaker, S. *Identity, Cause and Mind* (Cambridge: Cambridge University Press, 1984).

Simon, Y. *The Tradition of Natural Law* (New York: Fordham University Press, 1965).

Solomon, D. 'Internal Objections to Virtue Ethics', *Midwest Studies in Philosophy* 13 (1988), in Statman, D. ed., *Virtue Ethics* (Edinburgh: Edinburgh University Press, 1997).

Stevenson, L. 'Applied Philosophy', *Metaphilosophy,* 1 (1970).

Taylor, C. 'The Diversity of Goods', in Sen, A. & Williams, B. eds. *Utilitarianism and Beyond* (Cambridge: Cambridge University Press, 1982).

Taylor, C. *Sources of the Self* (Cambridge; CUP, 1990).

Taylor, C. *Multiculturalism and the Politics of Recognition* (Princeton, NJ: Princeton University Press, 1992).

Taylor, C. *A Secular Age* (Cambridge, MA: Harvard University Press, 2007).

Teichman, J. *Pacifism and the Just War* (Oxford: Blackwell, 1986).

Thomas, J. 'A Comment on John J. Haldane's Article', *Heythrop Journal,* 26 (1985).

Thompson, J.J. 'A Defense of Abortion' *Philosophy and Public Affairs,* 1 (1971).

Thompson, R.A. 'The Development of the Person: Social Understanding, Relationships, Conscience, Self' in N. Eisenberg ed. *Handbook of Child Psychology*, Vol. 3, 6th edition *Social, Emotional and Personality Development* (Hoboken, NJ: John Wiley, 2006).

Tostoy, L. *Art* (London: Chatto and Windus, 1947).

Waite, L. & Gallagher, M. *The Case for Marriage: Why Married People are Happier, Healthier and Better-Off Financially* (New York: Doubleday, 2000).

Walker, J. & Evers, C. 'Towards a Materialist Pragmatist Philosophy of Education', *Education Research and Perspectives*, 11 (1984).

Walker, J. 'Naturalism and Philosophy of Education', in *Post-Analytic Philosophy of Education*, special issue of *Educational Philosophy and Theory*, 19 (1987).

Warner, R. Szubka, T. eds. *The Mind-Body Problem: A Guide to the Current Debate* (Oxford: Blackwell, 1994).

Weber, M. 'Politics as a Vocation' in Gerth, H.H. & Wright Mills, C trans. & ed. *From Max Weber: Essays in Sociology* (New York: Oxford University Press, 1946).

Weil, S. 'The Iliad, or the Poem of Force', trans. Mary McCarthy, *Pendle Hill Pamphlet* no 91 (Wallingford, PA: Pendle Hill Press, 1956).

Wiggins, D. *Ethics: Twelve Lectures on the Philosophy of Morality* (Cambridge, MA: Harvard University Press, 2006).

Williams, B. 'A Critique of Utilitarianism' in J. J. C. Smart and B. Williams, *Utilitarianism: For and Against* (Cambridge: Cambridge University Press, 1973).

Williams, B. *Ethics and the Limits of Philosophy* (London: Fontana, 1985).

Williams, B. *Truth and Truthfulness* (Princeton, NJ: Princeton University Press, 2002).

Wilson, I. 'Conceptual Art', *Artforum*, 22, (1983).

Winch, P. *Simone Weil: 'The Just Balance'* (Cambridge: Cambridge University Press, 1989).

Winch, P. 'How is Political Authority Possible?' *Philosophical Investigations*, 25 (2002).

Winkler, E. & Coombs, J. eds. *Applied Ethics: A Reader* (Oxford: Blackwell, 1993).

Wittgenstein, L. *Philosophical Investigations* trans. G.E.M. Anscombe (Oxford: Blackwell, 1953).

Woodward, P. ed. *The Doctrine of Double Effect: Philosophers debate a Controversial Principle* (Southbend, IN: University of Notre Dame Press, 2001).

Governmental and institutional documents

Catechism of the Catholic Church (London: Chapman, 1994).

Challenge of Peace: God's Promise and Our Response (London: CTS/SPCK, 1983).

Child and Family Policy Divide: Tensions, Convergence and Rights (London: Joseph Rowntree Foundation, 2005).

Church and the Bomb: Nuclear Weapons and Christian Conscience (London: Hodder & Stoughton, 1982)

CIA World Fact Book (Washington, DC: US Government, 2009).

Cloning Human Beings (Washington: National Bioethics Advisory Commission, 1997).

Compensating the Victim of Crime, Report of Independent Working Party (London: Victim Support 1993).

Donum Vitae On Respect for Human Life. (Vatican: CDF, 1987).

Effects of Nuclear War (Washington, DC:, Office of Technology Assessment, 1979).

European Convention on the Compensation of Victims of Violent Crime: Explanatory Report (Strasbourg: Council of Europe, 1984).

Facts on Induced Abortion Worldwide. (New York: Guttmacher Institute, 2008).

Humani Generis False Trends in Modern Teaching (London: CTS, 1950).

Peace and Disarmament: Documents of the World Council of Churches and the Roman Catholic Church (Geneva and Rome: 1982).

Report of the Director General of the UN (23 July 2004) regarding preparations for and observance of the 10th anniversary of the International year of the family in 2004, (New York: United Nations, 2004).

UK Local Government Act, (London: Her Majesty's Stationary Office, 1988).

Veritatis Splendor The Splendor of Truth (London: CTS, 1993).

Index